Business Strategies for Real Estate Management Companies

Editorial Consultants
Howard K. Lundeen, CPM®
John W. Magnuson, CPM®
Kathleen M. McKenna-Harmon, CPM®
Michael E. Packard, CPM®
David J. Wilson, CPM®

Joseph T. Lannon
Senior Manager
Publishing and Curriculum Development

Caroline Scoulas
Senior Editor

Business Strategies for Real Estate Management Companies

Richard F. Muhlebach, CPM®
Alan A. Alexander, CPM®

IREM Institute of Real Estate Management
CHICAGO

© 1998 by the Institute of Real Estate Management
of the NATIONAL ASSOCIATION OF REALTORS ®

All rights reserved. This book or any part thereof may not be reproduced, stored in a retrieval system, or transmitted, in any form or by any means, electronic, mechanical, photocopying, recording, or otherwise, without the prior written permission of the publisher. Inquiries should be directed to Publishing Department, Institute of Real Estate Management, 430 North Michigan Avenue, P.O. Box 109025, Chicago, IL 60610-9025.

This publication is designed to provide accurate and authoritative information in regard to the subject matter covered. Forms or other documents included in this book are intended as samples only. Because of changing and varying state and local laws, competent professional advice should be sought prior to the use of any document, form, exhibit, or the like.

This publication is sold with the understanding that the publisher is not engaged in rendering legal, accounting, or any other professional service. If legal advice or other expert assistance is required, the services of a competent professional should be sought.

The opinions expressed in this text are those of the authors and do not necessarily reflect the policies and positions of the Institute of Real Estate Management.

Library of Congress Cataloging-in-Publication Data

Muhlebach, Richard, 1943–
    Business strategies for real estate management companies / Richard F. Muhlebach, Alan A. Alexander.
       p.   cm.
    Includes bibliographical references and index.
    ISBN 1-57203-053-4 (hardcover)
    1. Real estate management.   I. Alexander, Alan A.   II. Title.
HD1394.M84   1997
333.33'068--dc21   97-15981
                                                                                             CIP

Printed in the United States of America

To my partner of thirty years, my loving wife Maria;
to my children, Katherine and Eric, who are embarking on
successful careers as commercial real estate brokers;
to a special daughter-in-law, Amy;
and to my new little friend, my grandson Joseph.

R.F.M.

To my loving wife, Jeanne, who is always there for me,
completely supportive in all that I do
and always my partner in all of my endeavors.

A.A.A.

Preface

Real estate management is a business of many rules and no rules. As soon as managers become comfortable with the notion that there may be some absolutes they can rely on, those facets of the business change.

We have witnessed many fundamental changes in our business in recent years that make management of a management company trying, challenging, and considerably more risky. As this book goes to press, we in the real estate management business have been through one of the most tumultuous periods our profession has experienced in decades. Reaffirming the cyclic nature of real estate were a variety of lows and highs. Along with the many challenges, we were also presented with many opportunities.

We saw apartment rents stagnating in most North American markets for close to ten years. At the same time, expenses continued to increase and governmental intervention also increased. Both of these factors contributed to a crunch on net operating income for most apartment properties. The only positive element was the fact that occupancy levels remained fairly high. On the other hand, new development and conversions of commercial properties have brought residential uses to the downtowns of many major cities and helped create a 24-hour environment there.

Office buildings went through a period of severe overbuilding that resulted in tremendous vacancy factors in most major markets in North America. It was not unusual to see double-digit vacancy rates and such low demand for office space that it would take many years to absorb the existing supply. Yet much of that excess space is being absorbed or converted to new uses, and some markets have already begun to see new development of office buildings.

With the exception of regional and super regional malls, shopping centers underwent a period of overbuilding accompanied by a no-growth position in retail sales, both of which resulted in substantial vacancies, lowering of retail rents, and the ultimate repossession of many properties. During this period, it was a struggle for both landlords and tenants to just survive until times improved. In spite of these challenges, outlet centers were expanded, and development of so-called power centers and lifestyle centers brought a new perspective to retailing.

During this prolonged period of adjustment, which included the collapse of the savings and loan industry and the take over of many properties by the Resolution Trust Corporation, many fairly sound properties were impacted because the depressed properties influenced the market for all shopping centers, office buildings, and apartment properties.

We also saw large numbers of income-producing properties entering portfolios of institutions and a concurrent reduction in the number of entrepreneurial owners. While this move had a stabilizing influence on the income-producing properties, it also triggered a major change in how we accounted for and reported on properties' progress. Reports became much more sophisticated, and accounting information was much more detailed. The computer became an essential tool for the orderly tracking of the properties we managed. It was no longer a case of, "Do you have a computer system?" but rather, "How will your system interface with that of the client?" Many fee managers had to work in several different software programs to properly service their clients, and many management companies were connected to clients' systems by modem so the client could draw information freely at any time. All of these factors were, by no means, negative; but they did require a major shift in the technological sophistication of the management office.

The last major factor to impact the industry was that, with major markets being oversupplied with product, many developers turned to property management activities. First, they would bring their properties in house for management; and second, they would offer their management services to third parties, many of whom were already clients for their development services. Owners were also taking management in house, especially institutions, real estate investment trusts (REITs), and syndicators. Many brokerage firms added fee management to their services, often offering very competitive rates in order to capture the clients' business, putting further stresses on the third-party fee management companies in their areas.

Trying to stay in business and, hopefully, make a profit during these difficult times has been, at best, a major challenge. We were able to draw some comfort in knowing other real estate managers were in the same position. We often met at professional and trade association meetings and commiserated about all the factors impacting our business, but we also helped each other: Many professionals were able to band together and discuss mutual problems, sharing solutions and drawing some comfort from being able to continue their operations.

This book is offered in the spirit of sharing—the more we share, the stronger we become as a profession. Between the authors and the editorial consultants who reviewed the manuscript, this book represents more than 150 years of combined experience in real estate management, with many years' involvement in managing real estate management companies. We have endeavored to suggest potential solutions to some of the challenges management companies face based on our years of experience discovering what works well or not at all. No one knows what lies ahead, but if we as real estate management professionals remain aware of where we have been and where we are now, and in the process become students of our business, we will likely be in position to meet the upcoming challenges and prosper.

The one thing we can be sure of is that there will continue to be changes in real estate management, and we need to anticipate those changes whenever we can and react as quickly as possible to remain competitive.

An important part of being aware of and ready for change is being fully informed. Books such as this one are a major step in that preparation, as are periodicals such as the *Journal of Property Management*. However, there is little that compares to being involved in professional associations such as the Institute of Real Estate Management and attending meetings and conventions on a regular basis as a means of keeping up with changes in the industry.

This book will not offer specific solutions to your problems. However, it can provide guidance and insights for many situations that, along with your personal experience and knowledge, should help you meet the challenges of the future.

Some Notes to the Reader

In writing this book, we have taken a big picture approach, addressing a wide range of topics and issues that impact the business of real estate management—exploring strategies and likely outcomes and weighing advantages and disadvantages.

To start, we set the scene with a discussion of how the industry has changed and continues to change. Within that context, we have outlined strategies for starting a real estate management business and operating it efficiently and profitably. We then looked at the accounting function, which is critical to the management of clients' real estate as well as the operation of the management company. Because real estate management is a people business, separate chapters have been devoted to personnel issues and client relations.

A large section on business development explores marketing and business acquisition strategies, preparation and submission of management proposals, negotiation of management agreements, and take-over of new accounts. Along with real estate management, there are often many other services that can be offered to established clients or developed into separate offerings to potential clients who do not need property management as such. These adjunct revenue sources are explored throughout the business development section.

Operating a business and managing real estate are potentially risky ventures. There are also numerous opportunities for problems to arise in the manager-client relationship. Strategies for minimizing risks are discussed in a section on special challenges to business. Separate chapters address risk management and insurance, legal issues, and ethical practices.

We began with a discussion of change and we conclude with a section on managing change. One chapter explores termination of management and a second looks at valuing a management business for sale or purchase. The last chapter discusses some of the technological and other changes that are impacting real estate management and the firms that provide this service, with suggested strategies for making change work for you.

In the real estate management industry, types of jobs and position titles are not uniform. Specific duties and responsibilities often depend on the way the company is organized. Since the focus of this book is the real estate management company, we believe the reader will be better served by consistent terminology. Unless it was important to differentiate a specific role such as property manager or site manager, we have used real estate manager (or, simply, manager) as a general term for the person responsible for managing a property. Similarly, we have used company executive to refer to the role of the executive property manager, company president, or other executive level personnel in the management company. Also within the industry, it has become preferred practice to refer to residential tenants as residents, and we have generally used the same approach in this text. Where it is important to differentiate between residential and commercial tenants, the distinction has been stated specifically or can be inferred from the general context. Otherwise, tenants is occasionally used as an inclusive term for building occupants regardless of property type.

In order to be consistent in our presentation, we have generally cited small-sized management companies as examples, in part because they are less complex, but also for ease of demonstrating a point. Few entrepreneurs start out with a large management portfolio and a large staff, although many companies that start small grow to substantial size over time. In fact, a large proportion of new management businesses are started by a single manager or a small group of managers (say two or three individuals). On the other hand, a large company is more likely to have been established for some time and to have the financial means and professional expertise available in house to handle many of the issues this book addresses. The concepts are similar regardless of company size, but the larger scale adds layers of complexity (e.g., multiple approvals, group decisions) that would not be considerations for a sole proprietor or a company with only a small staff comprising mostly property managers. This book is intended to be a primary reference for those who aspire to the entrepreneurial role and a resource of ideas and strategies for those company executives who are seeking ways to accommodate their established management businesses to the changing marketplace.

Finally, whole books have been written on business planning, financial and managerial accounting, and the employment cycle, so it is appropriate to consider in-depth discussions of such topics beyond the scope of this book. Likewise, the management of different types of properties is described in detail in numerous books on managing, marketing, and leasing apartments, office buildings, and shopping centers; we have discussed specific property types primarily from the perspective of management company operations. For those who wish to pursue further the subjects explored in this book, we have identified a wide range of books, periodicals, newsletters, and professional associations in Appendix C.

ACKNOWLEDGMENTS

This book would not have been possible without the experience, dedication, and insights of Caroline Scoulas, Senior Editor of the Institute of Real Estate Management. Caroline pulled together the experiences of these authors and the combined experiences of several reviewers using her editorial expertise and knowledge of property management gained from working for many years with real estate manager-authors.

Additionally, the authors would like to acknowledge the insights and experiences of the Editorial Consultants—Howard K. Lundeen, CPM®, RPA, Senior Managing Director of Landauer Associates, Inc., in Dallas, Texas; John W. Magnuson, CPM®, CRE, President of Magnuson Management, Inc., in Tacoma, Washington; Kathleen M. McKenna-Harmon, CPM®, President of McKenna Management Associates, Inc., AMO®, in Minnetonka, Minnesota; Michael E. Packard, CPM®, PCAM, Chief Executive Officer of Chaney, Brooks & Company, AMO®, in Honolulu, Hawaii; and David J. Wilson, CPM®, CSM, President of Brighton Pacific Realty Asset Management, AMO®, in Oakland, California—who took their valuable time to read, evaluate, and suggest changes to the manuscript, all of which make the final product more meaningful and all-encompassing for the target audience.

The authors also wish to acknowledge the contribution of the Institute of Real Estate Management Foundation for the collection, analysis, and publication of industry statistics and other information on management companies. Its reports were the basis for discussions of comparative operational data and valuation strategies in particular. The IREM position statement on licensing of property managers is reprinted by permission of the Institute of Real Estate Management.

Finally, the authors wish to acknowledge the contributions, although in an indirect way, of Joyce Travis Copess, Staff Vice President, Communications and Education, and Joseph T. Lannon, Senior Manager, Publishing and Curriculum Development at the Institute of Real Estate Management, for their support over the years, which was instrumental in bringing about this publication. Their positive influence is reflected throughout this book.

Richard F. Muhlebach, CPM®
Alan A. Alexander, CPM®

About the Authors

Richard F. Muhlebach, CPM®, SCSM, CRE, RPA, is President of TRF Management Corporation, AMO®, in Bellevue, Washington. TRF Management Corporation is responsible for the management and leasing of commercial properties in the Northwest and Alaska.

Mr. Muhlebach has more than 25 years' experience managing, leasing, and rehabbing commercial and residential buildings. Previously he served as Vice President for Tishman West Management Corporation and was Vice President and Director of Property Management of the Lusk Company, both in Orange County, California.

He developed a commercial property management and leasing company, headed a regional property management office for a national developer, and was the Director of Property Management for a major developer of residential and commercial properties.

Mr. Muhlebach is a Senior Instructor on the National Faculty of the Institute of Real Estate Management and, in particular, is a member of the faculty and board of the IREM course, "Managing the Management Company." He is also an instructor for the International Council of Shopping Centers (ICSC) and the Building Owners and Managers Association (BOMA), and he teaches real estate management and leasing at the University of Washington. He has lectured in Singapore, Canada, Mexico, and countries throughout Central and Eastern Europe.

As author of more than 70 articles on real estate subjects, he has been published in the *Journal of Property Management (JPM), Shopping Center World, National Mall Monitor, Journal of Real Estate Development, Real Estate Finance, Real Estate Today,* and *Buildings* magazine as well as journals published in Asia and Europe.

Mr. Muhlebach is the 1998 National President IREM and is a trustee of the Washington Center for Real Estate Research. He has also served on the board of directors for several community agencies.

In addition to holding the Certified Property Manager® (CPM®) designation from the Institute of Real Estate Management, Mr. Muhlebach is a Senior Certified Shopping Center Manager (awarded by the International Council of Shopping Centers), a Counselor of Real Estate (member of the Counselors of Real Estate—formerly the American Society of Real Estate Counselors), and a Real Property Administrator (awarded by the Building Owners and Managers Association). Mr. Muhlebach is a graduate of San Francisco State University.

Alan A. Alexander, CPM®, SCSM, is Senior Vice President of Woodmont Real Estate Services, Inc., AMO®, in Belmont, California, specializing in management, leasing, and consulting for income-producing properties in Northern California.

Prior to joining Woodmont, he was President of Alexander Consultants for more than twelve years, specializing in managing, leasing, and consulting for income-producing properties throughout the Western United States and South America.

Mr. Alexander is a former Senior Vice President of Fox and Carskadon Management Corporation with responsibility for a portfolio of commercial and residential properties in four Western states that was valued in excess of $300 million. As Director of Leasing for Fox and Carskadon Financial, he was responsible for leasing all shopping centers owned by the company throughout the United States, with a total portfolio in excess of $800 million.

Mr. Alexander is a Senior Instructor on the National Faculty of the Institute of Real Estate Management, and he is a past President of that organization's San Francisco Bay Area Chapter.

Mr. Alexander is a frequent speaker at International Council of Shopping Centers programs, including Idea Exchanges, the Annual Convention, Management Institutes, Maintenance Institutes, and the School for Professional Development. He has also taught in Singapore, Canada, Mexico, Malaysia, Taiwan, Hong Kong, the Philippines, Poland, and Jamaica.

Mr. Alexander has written numerous articles on commercial leasing and management published in the *Journal of Property Management (JPM)* as well as articles on other real estate subjects published in *Journal of Real Estate Development, Real Estate Business,* and elsewhere.

In addition to holding the Certified Property Manager® (CPM®) designation from the Institute of Real Estate Management, Mr. Alexander is a Senior Certified Shopping Center Manager (awarded by the International Council of Shopping Centers).

In addition to this work, Muhlebach and Alexander are coauthors of several books, including: *Shopping Center Management* published by the Institute of Real Estate Management; *Managing and Leasing Commercial Properties: Practice, Strategies and Forms* (second edition, two volumes), and *Managing and Leasing Commercial Properties: Complex Issues,* both published by John Wiley & Sons, Inc.; and *Shopping Center Tenant Relations: A Manager's Guide to Tenant Retention* and *Operating Small Shopping Centers,* both published by the International Council of Shopping Centers. Both are also members of the IREM Academy of Authors, and they have served as editorial consultants for numerous other IREM publications.

Contents

1   The Business of Real Estate Management 1
    Management Opportunities   2
    Internal Management Versus Fee Management   5
    Property Specialization   7
    Real Estate Management Positions   8
    Owners' Expectations and Requirements   10
    A Glimpse of Things to Come   12

OPERATIONAL ISSUES

2   Starting a Management Business 17
    Preliminary Considerations   17
    Management Specialization   19
    Business-Specific Considerations   25
    Developing a Business Plan   33
    Other Considerations   48
    A Sense of Personal Satisfaction   50

3   Strategizing Business Operations 51
    Focusing on Your Clients   52
    Focusing on the Management Company   64
    A Perspective on Operations   79

4   Strategizing the Accounting Function 81
    Accounting for the Management Business   82
    Real Estate Owners' Accounting Requirements   91

Operations of the Accounting Department 97
On-Site Accounting 117
The Cost of Accounting Functions 118
An Added Perspective on the Accounting Function 120

5   **Strategizing the Personnel Function** 123

General Staffing Considerations 123
Strategizing Employment Practices 132
The Work Environment 150
A Perspective on Personnel 151

6   **Strategizing Client Relations** 152

Understanding Clients' Concerns 152
Addressing Clients' "Hot Buttons" 155
Communicating with Owners 156
Dealing with Difficult Clients 164
A Perspective on Client Retention 164

BUSINESS DEVELOPMENT

7   **Strategizing Business Development** 169

Marketing Strategies 169
Developing Ancillary Sources of Income 186
A Perspective on Business Development 195

8   **Strategizing the Management Proposal** 196

Preliminary Considerations 197
The Contents of a Management Proposal 199
The Residential Proposal 209
The Commercial Proposal 213
Presenting the Management Proposal 216
Proposals in Perspective 220

9   **Strategizing the Management Agreement** 222

Management Agreement Considerations 223
The Issue of Fees 228
Whose Management Agreement Will be Used? 234
Contents of the Management Agreement 235
A Perspective on Management Agreements 249

10   **Strategizing Management Take-Over** 250

Planning the Take-Over 251
Creating a Take-Over Checklist 252

Information Acquisition Strategies 258
The Manager's Priorities 265
A Perspective on Management Take-Over 269

SPECIAL CHALLENGES TO BUSINESS

11 Strategies for Managing Risk 273

Insuring the Management Company 275
Management Agreement Considerations 279
A Perspective on Risk Management 290

12 Strategies for Avoiding Legal Problems 292

Laws Affecting the Real Estate Management Business 292
Laws Affecting the Management Company as Employer 295
Laws Affecting the Management of Real Property 306
Other Considerations 314
A Perspective on Legal Issues 316

13 Strategies for Maintaining Ethical Practices 318

The Certified Property Manager® (CPM®) Code of Ethics 318
The Accredited Management Organization® (AMO®) Code
  of Ethics 328
State Commissioner's Code of Ethics 331
A Perspective on Professional Ethics 337

MANAGING CHANGE

14 Management Termination Strategies 341

Management Agreement Considerations 341
Developing a Checklist for Terminating Management 344
Contents of a Termination Checklist Form 348
Facilitating the Transition 351
A Perspective on Management Termination 353

15 Strategies for Valuing a Management Company 355

Major Considerations in Valuation 356
The Basis for Valuing a Management Business 359
Structuring a Purchase 367
Strategizing a Hypothetical Sale 369
Employees as Potential Purchasers 375
A Perspective on Valuing the Management Company 378

16 Strategies for Adapting to Change 380
Changes Brought by Technology   381
Competition Is as Competition Does   387
Maintaining a Competitive Edge   388
Measuring Your Company's Performance   394
A Perspective on Adapting to Change   396

Appendix A: The Accredited Management Organization® Designation   399

Appendix B: Professional Organizations and Designations   401

Appendix C: Resources   407

Index   417

1

The Business of Real Estate Management

The business of real estate management is more than just managing different properties. The decision to move from employee to entrepreneur or business partner or corporate owner is a giant step and requires not only a major commitment of energy, time, and money but a leap of faith. It also requires a very different mind-set: The shift from employee to employer, from someone who earns a paycheck to the person responsible for funding the payroll, gives the entrepreneur a very different perspective on the business of real estate management.

Why would anyone want to start a business? What drives people to take that giant step forward? Most likely several things are involved—a chance to earn more income, the opportunity to act on one's own ideas and decisions without consulting others for approval, a desire to be self-sufficient. Perhaps most important in the realm of real estate management is the individual's belief that he or she can do a better job for an owner-client.

Many of the functions of the real estate manager as agent of the property owner are mirrored in the operation of a business: Generating income, controlling operating expenses, preparing annual and long-term budgets, managing employees, retaining current clients, and acquiring new business consistent with an established plan have direct parallels in real estate management. The skills employed in representing property owners and serving tenants are also applied in managing the management company.

The cyclical natures of business in general and real estate in particular challenge the real estate manager and the management company to identify, analyze, and adapt to changing circumstances. Change, more than anything else, will be a driving force into the twenty-first century. Those who accept and adapt to change—more to the point, those who proactively work with change and make it work for them—will have the competitive advantage in an industry that thrives on increasing competitiveness, and real estate management is just such an industry.

Management Opportunities

Real estate management as a profession offers unique and rewarding opportunities that are found in only a few industries. An individual—whether a property manager, an executive employed in the industry, or the owner of a management company—will find real estate management rewarding as a business if he or she can capitalize on its opportunities and manage its challenges. The opportunities are related in part to the size of the inventory of buildings available for management.

At the beginning of the 1990s, investment properties comprised nearly two-fifths (38%) of U.S. real estate holdings, and the bulk of these (79%) were commercial uses (retail, office, industrial). While most of the multifamily residential properties were held by partnerships, corporations owned most of the commercial properties and a small, but significant, percent of the latter were in portfolios of institutional owners. This represented a tremendous inventory of potential management opportunities. However, the ownership picture changed. By the mid-1990s, the holdings of institutional owners—e.g., pension funds, real estate investment trusts (REITs)—increased significantly. Institutional ownership of large real estate portfolios often meant a shift to self-management and a significant reduction in the number of properties available for third-party management. At the same time, relatively little new product was being added to the inventory of multifamily and commercial properties, and the excess space in overbuilt urban markets was being absorbed. These and other factors increased competition as more management entities were chasing fewer properties to be managed.

The Real Estate Management Industry. In the world at large, a few companies may dominate a product type or an entire industry (e.g., retailing, computers, automobile manufacturing), but the real estate management industry is fragmented, with no single company having a significant market share. Consequently, real estate management offers opportunities for companies of all sizes and for individuals who have dreamed of starting their own businesses. This fact also presents the challenge to established management companies of staying ahead of a steady stream of emerging competitors while they are also competing against existing local, regional, and national firms.

While a large amount of capital is needed to start a business in most industries, this is not the case in real estate management. A retailer must invest tens and even hundreds of thousands of dollars in inventory before

Investment Properties Distribution by Property Type	
Retail/shopping centers	33%
Office	30%
Multifamily residential	21%
Industrial	16%

Source: *Managing the Future: Real Estate in the 1990s* (Chicago: Institute of Real Estate Management Foundation, 1991).

the first sale is made. A manufacturer must purchase expensive equipment and stocks of raw materials before the first item can be manufactured and sold. A start-up real estate management company, on the other hand, does not need shelves lined with inventory or massive pieces of equipment. Its product is the knowledge and expertise of the firm's key personnel. On the other hand, increasing reliance on computers and communications technologies necessitates the purchase (or leasing) of appropriate equipment, increasing start-up costs and adding another expertise requirement to run the new company efficiently. In spite of this, an ambitious and enterprising individual can still start a management business in a small office and grow the company into a substantial operation.

Not every start-up business is an entrepreneurial endeavor. A real estate brokerage firm can add a property management division or department using its existing client base to build a management portfolio. A developer with an existing inventory of properties can use the management fees from the properties to fund a subsidiary property management company. Institutional investors (insurance companies, pension funds, lenders, REITs) often have a portfolio of sufficient size to justify developing an in-house property management organization, while corporations and governmental agencies will often self-manage the real estate they own. Each of these types of opportunities can be expanded from an in-house management operation to a third-party fee management business that operates as a profit center. Conversely, increased competition has encouraged real estate management professionals to consider other opportunities for generating income by expanding the services they offer to include consulting, expert witness testimony, tax appeals, leasing, and brokerage, among others.

Real estate management offers job opportunities at all levels—as front-line property managers, as mid-level managers (e.g., director of property management), and as company executives (e.g., president or chief executive officer), plus a variety of staff positions (e.g., accounting, maintenance, clerical administration)—as well as the opportunity to start a management business of one's own.

Real Estate Cycles. Real estate management is only one segment of the larger real estate industry. Historically, real estate has been one of the most cyclical businesses in America. The real estate industry is especially sensitive to changes in the national economy, demographic shifts, and new legislation. There are periods when other investment vehicles provide higher, more secure returns, when demographics of employment and household formation are unfavorable to new development, or when tax laws or environmental regulations diminish the possibility of a reasonable return on investment, not to mention the availability of financing at favorable terms. Real estate management is affected by the periods of expansion and contraction in the real estate industry at large. However, no two property types follow the same cycles or experience the same periods of expansion and contraction concurrently. As a consequence, management firms that specialize in one or two property types will not always be affected to the same degree during the periodic ups and downs.

Opportunities to acquire management accounts stem from development of new projects, changes of real estate ownership, and property owners' dissatisfaction with current management services. Real estate development has been punctuated by periods of excessive building and periods of under and over supply of product. When projects are not being developed, the inventory of buildings available for management is not growing. Conversely, development of new types of properties such as condominiums, industrial parks, and larger-scale shopping centers with more complex tenancies creates new property management opportunities.

High interest rates make it difficult for developers to finance proposed projects and for investors to purchase real estate. When lenders are unwilling to loan on real estate and investors are unwilling to provide capital in exchange for equity, the resulting credit crunch makes it almost impossible to obtain financing. On the other hand, low interest rates and "easy" access to capital can lead to overbuilding. When that happens, supply outstrips demand, resulting in high vacancy rates, low rents, and defaulted loans.

Because real estate competes with other investments for capital, investors seek alternatives that will provide a better return on their capital when real estate returns are low. When investors cannot pay back mortgage loans, their properties are foreclosed by the lenders, and they may become part of the lender's real estate owned (REO) portfolio or be placed in receivership pending foreclosure. However, even these types of transactions create potential opportunities—i.e., for managing lenders' REO properties or as court-appointed receivers.

External Factors. Technology is also changing real estate and its management. From fiber-optic communication cabling and just-in-time (JIT) deliveries aided by computers to the virtual office and on-line shopping projected for the future, technology is changing how companies do busi-

> **Characteristics of Real Estate**
> - Cycles of expansion and contraction make investment returns fluctuate.
> - Development drives other segments of the industry (brokerage, leasing, property management).
> - High interest rates discourage lending and impede investment financing.
> - Low interest rates that encourage borrowing can lead to overbuilding.
> - Real estate competes with other investments for capital; higher rates of return elsewhere discourage investment in real estate.
> - Economic downturns increase competition from inside the industry as other real estate interests turn to management to supplement or supplant their primary source of income.
> - Owners taking management "in house" reduces the number of properties available for third-party fee management.

ness, where they locate their businesses, and how much space they need. When the technological revolution provides additional options for locating a business, the demand for housing also changes. Real estate management company executives must anticipate how technology will change the ways businesses and individuals use real estate.

Property management is no longer a profession of people who just collect rents and maintain buildings. Real estate managers must provide sophisticated financial reports to owners; develop emergency procedures to protect people and property; comply with changing governmental regulations that affect leasing, marketing, and other requirements; and understand new lease provisions relating specifically to negotiated terms, as well as comply with state landlord-tenant laws and civil rights laws that are becoming ever more inclusive at the state and local levels. Real estate managers must understand how to market their services to clients—and the properties they manage to potential tenants—in an environment of change, where shifting demographics and psychographics are creating demand for new choices in housing as well as consumer goods, and where technology and economic pressures are forcing businesses to rethink their needs for personnel and work space. In a word, the profession is becoming more proactive.

Internal Management Versus Fee Management

Property management can be either an internal function (in house, for a company that owns or has ownership control of real estate) or an external one (third-party fee management). The skills and knowledge needed to manage residential and commercial properties are identical in either situation. The major differences depend on whether internal management is a profit center or strictly a service (cost center) and the differing requirements of managing for multiple property owners compared to managing for a single owner. (Start-up of an in-house management function is discussed in Chapter 2.)

Many companies prefer to manage their own properties, whether or not their primary business is real estate. In-house property management departments or subsidiary management companies (i.e., divisions) exist among financial institutions such as banks and insurance companies, large corporations such as Boeing or Microsoft, developers, family holdings, and real estate investment trusts (REITs), as well as individual investors. While firms with internal management may place greater emphasis on value enhancement of their properties and the service provided to the firm by its property management division or department, some do expect property management to be a profit center. This is often the case with a financial institution or when a developer's primary source of income and profits has declined. If the firm with internal management owns large buildings or numerous small- to medium-size buildings, the total management fees charged to the properties can exceed the cost to operate the management division or department (i.e., they can set fees at or above the top of the fee range in the market).

One of the primary differences between in-house management and third-party fee management is the number of property owners being served. An in-house function usually has the advantage of managing for only one owner whose business philosophy is the same for all properties, and there are uniform standards for monthly management reports, annual management plans, and financial reporting formats, as well as the potential for flexible deadlines for reporting and other activities. As a consequence, the services are generally less costly to provide. Third-party fee management firms, on the other hand, manage properties for several owners whose requirements are varied. In addition, while in-house personnel often manage only one property type—e.g., an apartment for a REIT or a mall for a developer—the fee management company is likely to be managing a diversity of property types which, at the very least, complicates the paper work. In addition, the computation of fees is more complicated, and it costs more to provide specific services.

Working for numerous owners presents unique challenges, the first being that different property owners have different goals and objectives for themselves and their real estate investments. One owner may prefer a long-term management plan that will enhance the value of the property while another may need all the cash flow from a property to support another investment or maintain the investor's lifestyle. Owners' financial resources also vary: An institutional owner usually has capital that can be invested in the property as necessary, while an individual investor who owns a troubled property may have problems paying the mortgage each month.

The attention each property owner gives his or her real estate investment will vary. Some owners consume an exorbitant amount of a manager's time reviewing and discussing every management and leasing activity, while an asset manager based hundreds or thousands of miles from the property may visit it only twice a year or every few months and need only a conversation with the manager once a month. Owners who are very knowledgeable about market conditions may provide a quick decision on rent adjustments or approval of a commercial lease, while one who is unfamiliar with the market may procrastinate or require the approval of several partners or a committee before making decisions.

One of the biggest challenges of managing for multiple owners is the different financial reporting required by each client: Most need their monthly reports during the same week, which creates an uneven work load for the accounting department. In addition, while an individual investor may accept the management firm's standard financial reporting format, an institutional owner will often require use of its chart of accounts and reporting format. Some also require the management firm to use their selected computer accounting software—a management firm serving a number of institutional clients may work in several different software programs.

Perhaps the most significant difference between the two situations is that the fee management company must develop a continual stream of new business in order to survive and be profitable. Business development is one of the most important responsibilities of the executives of a third-party fee management company, and this activity can consume a significant portion of their time. (Business development activities are discussed in Chapter 7.)

Property Specialization

Real estate management companies usually specialize in residential or commercial properties, although in areas where opportunities are limited companies will often manage both. Within these two general categories, there are several subspecialties. The residential subspecialties include rental apartments (government-subsidized as well as conventionally financed), single-family homes, and mobile homes or manufactured housing communities, as well as common interest realty associations—popularly called condominiums and cooperatives, these can be whole subdivisions. (Hotels, motels, and some types of student housing are managed by the hospitality industry.) The commercial subspecialties include office and medical buildings, shopping centers, industrial and warehouse properties, and self-storage facilities.

Though every property type requires application of the same basic management principles, each requires specialized skills and knowledge. For instance, apartment management requires specific knowledge of the state's landlord-tenant laws; shopping centers require a knowledge of merchandising and an understanding of tenant mix, while office and medical buildings require knowledge of space planning and construction of tenant improvements.

Real Estate Management Positions

Management companies offer many different kinds of job opportunities. Some are adjuncts to the real estate management function—e.g., marketing, leasing, and maintenance. Others serve two functions, providing support to the personnel who manage the real estate and handling many of the details of the management company's business operations—e.g., accounting, human resources, systems support, and administration.

The variety of real estate management-specific job opportunities can be classified as follows:

Site manager

Property manager

Portfolio supervisor or regional property manager

Director of property management (in-house function), or

President or chief executive of a real estate management firm

These are presented here in order of increasing responsibility and skill required, and the terms are descriptive rather than definitive. (Real estate management positions and job titles are not uniform; specific duties and responsibilities depend on the company or business entity and the way it is organized.) The primary difference between residential and commercial property management positions is the distinction between residential and commercial *site* managers.

Site Manager. Some states require a site manager for all apartment properties that have a certain number of units (e.g., 16 or more). At these small apartment complexes, the site manager typically is employed on a part-time basis. Medium to large apartment complexes (large numbers of units, either in a single high-rise building or spread among several low-rise buildings) will have full-time site managers who may reside at the complex or live off site. Qualifications for this position may include the Accredited Residential Manager® (ARM®) service award or the Certified Apartment Manager (CAM) designation. (Information about specific designations and the organizations that award them can be found in Appendix B.)

Depending on the size of the complex, the site staff may include rental agents, administrative staff, and maintenance personnel in addition to the manager. Another approach for apartment properties is the married-couple management team: The wife may be responsible for rental and administrative activities while the husband performs maintenance and janitorial duties. This was popular in the 1960s and 1970s and is still used today by many real estate management companies.

There are far more site managers of residential properties than of commercial properties because the vast majority of the latter do not require this type of manager. A small office or medical building (e.g., less than 100,000 square feet) is typical of this situation. Only a few large strip shopping centers need on-site management, while enclosed community and regional malls will have a substantial on-site staff. Industrial parks consisting of a few single-tenant buildings and small multitenant buildings do not have on-site management, while large multitenant industrial parks do.

The on-site staff for a mid-rise office or medical building or a large suburban office park will usually consist of a manager, an administrative person, and one or more maintenance personnel. High-rise office buildings will require these same staff positions plus an assistant manager, a tenant improvements coordinator, additional administrative personnel, and several building engineers. A community mall will have an on-site manager, a full-time or part-time marketing director, one administrative person, and several maintenance personnel. For a regional mall, it is typical to have more specific positions—an on-site manager, an operations manager, a security chief, a full-time marketing director, an assistant marketing director, administrative personnel, a bookkeeper, and a number of maintenance and security personnel. Actual numbers of personnel will depend on a variety of factors (geographic location, property age, complexity of facilities, etc.).

The on-site manager for a commercial property, often referred to as the *general manager* or *building manager,* usually is expected to hold one or more professional designations: Certified Property Manager® (CPM®), Real Property Administrator (RPA), Certified Shopping Center Manager (CSM).

Property Manager. The property manager's role is largely supervisory, with responsibility for several properties. One who manages apartments usually has a manager or management team on site at each complex to handle the day-to-day details, while those who manage condominiums or cooperatives work with the board of directors of the homeowners' association and, in many cases, with on-site management personnel. The commercial property manager, on the other hand, will typically be responsible for four to ten buildings—depending on their size, number of tenants, and location—each without an on-site manager; the day-to-day management duties are shared with the property manager's administrative assistants.

Portfolio Supervisor. Residential property managers and on-site commercial property managers are supervised by a portfolio supervisor or *regional property manager.* This person may also manage a small portfolio of properties directly. Many developers of regional malls or high-rise office buildings who have large portfolios of properties may assign to one of their senior on-site managers the responsibility of supervising two to three other office buildings or malls that also have on-site managers.

Executive Level. A firm whose primary function is not property management—a development or brokerage firm, for example—typically will appoint a *director of property management* to supervise the property managers. The *president* of a small- to medium-size management firm may assume this supervisory role. Responsibilities of these two positions are similar; the differences between them are usually related to whether the division under the particular director is a profit center or a service provided to the parent company and, therefore, a cost center (because it generates no separate income stream or profits).

Owners' Expectations and Requirements

A unique survey of real estate investors and owners was conducted by the Institute of Real Estate Management Foundation in 1990 (published as *Managing the Future: Real Estate in the 1990s*). To real estate management executives, the most valuable part of this study was the catalog of the chief concerns of property owners and what they expected from property managers and management firms. Owners rated integrity and reliability as the most important criteria they use when selecting management firms. Quality of the individuals assigned to manage the property, professional competence, and reputation also ranked in the top ten characteristics (out of 49 particulars queried). Among those least important were size of the firm and its proximity to the owner, although being near the owner's property was considered moderately to very important. (Exhibit 1.1 shows the characteristics in descending rank order as they were rated by property owners.) Even though professional designations, as such, received comparatively low ratings (2.87), they are among the means of validating many of the criteria that were given very high ratings—professional competence (4.55) and the quality of individuals to be assigned (4.58), in particular.

The survey also asked property owners which property management tasks were most important. Since the number one concern of property owners was vacancies, followed by operating expenses, it is not surprising that property owners rated retaining tenants as the most important property management task. In fact, five of the top six tasks were related to leasing and tenant relations (see Exhibit 1.2). Tasks that property owners expected to increase in importance included collections, capital budgeting, insurance

Exhibit 1.1
Relative Importance of 49 Property Management Firm Characteristics

Characteristic	Rating	Characteristic	Rating
Integrity	4.85	Networks and contacts	3.52
Reliability	4.83	Crisis management	3.46
Quality of individuals to be assigned	4.58	Asset management	3.30
Financial responsibility	4.56	Construction/remodeling	3.26
Professional competence	4.55	Length of time in business	3.21
Tenant relations	4.48	Sales	3.19
Reputation	4.47	Breadth of service lines	3.18
Timeliness of reports	4.38	Continuing education program	3.10
Local market information	4.29	In-house training	3.09
Maintenance	4.23	Other education	3.09
Accessibility	4.21	Environmental	3.02
Quality of administration	4.19	Human resources management	2.99
Budgeting	4.12	Formal educational requirements	2.96
Quality and scope of reports	4.06	Investment analysis	2.91
Accounting/bookkeeping	4.03	Ability to manage several different property types	2.89
Marketing	4.02		
Leasing	4.00	Market feasibility analysis	2.88
Specialization in property type	3.96	Professional designations	2.87
Continuity of staff	3.95	Government relations	2.87
Fees and costs	3.86	Workouts	2.86
Negotiating	3.86	Near you or your representative	2.69
Management contract terms	3.86	Size of firm	2.57
Information systems	3.83	Consulting	2.52
Near your property	3.73	Financing	2.40
Modern communications systems	3.63	Other specialized service	2.27

5 = Essential; 4 = Very Important; 3 = Moderately Important; 2 = Slightly Important; 1 = Not Important.

Reprinted with permission from *Managing the Future: Real Estate in the 1990s* (Chicago: Institute of Real Estate Management Foundation, 1991), p. 41.

procurement, governmental compliance, real estate tax monitoring, and environmental monitoring. The property manager of the future was described as professional, business-like, and sophisticated—a generalist rather than a specialist.

While the property management task ratings will change over time based on market conditions and the challenges facing property ownership, the relative importance of the criteria for selecting a management firm are not likely to change much in the future. The important considerations are solvency of the management company, appropriate insurance coverage (professional liability, employee theft), ethical conduct, and professionalism. The attributes that make a company attractive to clients also signal a healthy business. Coincidentally, these same characteristics are required of

Exhibit 1.2
Relative Importance of 36 Property Management Tasks

Management Task	Rating	Management Task	Rating
Retain tenants	4.59	Monitor property value	3.91
Negotiate leases	4.50	Approve rent schedule	3.90
Obtain tenants	4.50	Prepare rent schedule	3.90
Handle tenant relations	4.39	Establish/monitor/enforce operating	
Collections	4.30	policies and procedures	3.89
Review/approve leases	4.27	Analyze/implement financial	
Prepare financial reports	4.23	structures	3.86
Make decisions about		Real estate tax monitoring	3.85
acquisitions/dispositions	4.20	Establish/modify lease procedures	3.85
Prepare operating budgets	4.19	Construction/renovation supervision	3.81
Maintenance	4.19	Construction/renovation	3.78
Monitor property performance	4.16	Handle broker relations	3.75
Negotiate tenant improvements	4.12	Environmental monitoring	3.74
Prepare overall management plan	4.08	Insurance procurement and	
Prepare capital budgets	4.07	monitoring	3.74
Administration	4.07	Work with legal counsel	3.72
Make decisions about		Provide architectural and	
development/redevelopment	4.05	design control	3.63
Analyze project feasibility	4.05	Purchasing	3.57
Maintenance supervision	4.02	Government compliance	3.57
On-site inspections	4.02	Handle advertising/public relations	3.44

5 = Very Important; 4 = Important; 3 = Moderately Important; 2 = Slightly Important; 1 = Not Important.
Reprinted with permission from *Managing the Future: Real Estate in the 1990s* (Chicago: Institute of Real Estate Management Foundation, 1991), p. 46.

companies that are awarded the Accredited Management Organization® (AMO®) designation (see Appendix A).

A Glimpse of Things to Come

Studying past and current trends can help one understand the technological revolution society is experiencing, and asking questions—and finding answers to them—may provide some insights. However, it is difficult, if not impossible, to make predictions about the future. Some aspects of the business of real estate management are not likely to change. Building maintenance, marketing and leasing, accounting and reporting—all the traditional services are likely to continue, supplemented by new services as the field evolves and owners' requirements change. What has been changing and will continue to change are the ways these services are provided (e.g., paper reports being supplanted by electronic files).

Even more significant are the new skills needed by management company personnel. Most if not all positions require some degree of computer lit-

> **What Drives Real Estate Management?**
> - Change of property ownership
> - Residential and commercial space needs
> - Governmental regulations
> - Technological advances
> - Tax laws
> - Ownership demands
> - Competition within the industry
> - Corporate outsourcing of real estate services
> - Availability of development capital
> - Real estate development

eracy, and the general movement toward relationship marketing increases the emphasis on employees' attitudes and interpersonal skills. As technology creates ever more sophisticated computers and communications media become interlinked, management companies will need specialized expertise to service and maintain growing numbers of high-technology tools. Just as the accounting function supports the real estate management function, in-house experts will be needed to support the hardware and software applications used by accounting and other functions of the management business.

The externals that drive real estate management as a profession and as a business have also been experiencing changes. Demographics, economics, and technology are among the more frequently cited factors in what has been an ongoing process. Real estate has always been a cyclical industry, often with sharply defined peaks and valleys. Being driven by supply and demand, the real estate industry will always be cyclical, but in the future the peaks and valleys may not be so extreme. It will be a long time before lenders and equity investors forget the real estate debacle that occurred between the mid-1980s and the mid-1990s. Some of the causes of the recession experienced in the real estate industry throughout the United States during this period will not be repeated. Lenders will not provide 90–100 percent financing for the development of speculative commercial and residential buildings or the purchase of income-producing real estate. Equity investors will make decisions based on the economics of a project and not solely for the tax benefits of real estate ownership. Development decisions will be based on the market need for space and a reasonable return on equity, not driven solely by a need to generate fees and shelter income. Developers will provide the primary source of growth in the property management industry—new buildings.

What is not known is how the technological revolution will impact real estate. Will office building space requirements per employee continue to decline as they did in the early 1990s? Will shopping from home via television and computers erode sales from traditional retailers, and will that reduce retailers' space needs? Will manufacturers require less production (and warehousing) space because they can operate more efficiently with computerized just-in-time (JIT) deliveries? The answers to these and other technology-related questions will determine future demand and locations for every type of real estate use.

If technology will allow employees to work from their homes, and they can live anywhere, will people choose to move to their dream location—an island, the mountains, by a lake? If this becomes possible and accepted, people could live and work out of two distant communities, one in or near the city and the other in a lifestyle community, which could mean additional real estate development and new management opportunities.

Other changes that have created management opportunities include various government programs for privatizing services—e.g., facility management of housing and other government-owned properties. As some corporate owners move toward outsourcing some or all of their service needs, real estate management companies will find increasing opportunities for expanding their offerings in the areas of facility management and other adjunct services.

Investment strategies also need to be monitored. Will securitization of real estate concentrate the ownership of properties among fewer companies? Will financial institutions and pension funds be major purchasers of medium-to-large commercial and residential properties? Will smaller, specialty buildings be the choice of a society where technology is allowing the populace to scatter across the land?

More to the point, when the real estate market is in equilibrium, will those companies that entered the property management business to generate fees as a means of survival abandon management for their primary source of real estate income and activity? Though it is impossible to know what will happen to real estate management in the future, some things do not change: Real estate will always be unpredictable, and real estate management will always be open to competition because of the ease of entry into the field. In today's world, however, real estate management is a people business—real estate managers do not manage bricks and mortar, steel and concrete; they manage people and relationships. There will always be a need for this type of professional management of buildings.

Because real estate management has become more competitive over the years, and property owners have become more sophisticated, real estate managers must continue their education and capitalize on technological advancements. They must also continue to hone their interpersonal (communication) skills. Successful company executives will manage change to the real estate management firm's advantage.

Operational Issues

2

Starting a Management Business

A fairly common belief among real estate managers who have been in the business a few years is that starting a real estate management company would be easy. Almost every manager with a few years of experience and a love of real estate management has thought about going into business.

There is little doubt that when one compares the start-up of a real estate management company with the start-up of either a retail or manufacturing business, the former is much easier. There is no big expense at the front end, either for inventory as in retail or for raw material and equipment as in manufacturing, and no major location expense. A start-up real estate management business can be operated from someone's home with a well-done business card, some type of voice messaging, and a computer. Before any type of business is launched, however, the aspiring entrepreneur needs to do some homework.

Preliminary Considerations

There are several considerations to be explored before starting a real estate management business. Prior experience on the business side is clearly desirable, and licensing may be mandatory. Evaluation of the market for the service you intend to offer is also warranted. Other up-front issues to consider are how the business will be structured and the advantages and disadvantages of different forms of business ownership.

Business Expertise. Not everyone is cut out to run a company on his or her own. It is not uncommon for an individual to be a first-class real estate manager as an employee but not do at all well as the owner of a manage-

> **Some Characteristics of an Entrepreneur**
> - Willingness to assume authority and accept responsibility.
> - Ability to lead others.
> - Energetic.
> - Self-motivated.
> - Ability to see the "big picture."
> - Willingness and ability to accept risk.

ment business. An employee often has little or no involvement with business development, hiring and firing other employees, leasing space for the business, or buying or leasing equipment. On the other hand, one sometimes discovers talents that have not been called upon previously. Ideally, the potential entrepreneur would have had some prior experience running a management business so there would be some familiarity with the activities and responsibilities he or she will be undertaking. Obviously, if everyone who thought about starting a business was daunted by a lack of experience, there would be no start-up companies in any industry. One can learn from observation and experimentation, and careful planning can help make the challenge more manageable.

Real Estate Licensing. In most states, a real estate management company is required to have a broker's license in order to do business. Generally, anyone who leases space for others, collects rents for others, or manages real estate for others for a fee must have a real estate license. However, many real estate management practitioners are not themselves required to be licensed: Three of the most common situations in which a license is not required are (1) when one manages for another as an employee—so long as the employer is the owner of the property, (2) when one works for a governmental agency, and (3) when one manages one's own property.

In making the decision to go into business, the issue of a real estate license is an important one. Some states have a fast track to a broker's license, but others require specific time as a salesperson before one can become a broker. Still other states have stringent educational requirements before one is eligible to take the broker's examination, although most states recognize a degree in real estate as a basis for a broker's license. Before you make a major commitment to start a third-party management business, you should thoroughly investigate your state's licensing requirements. Some states may also restrict management by entities from other states, which is something you should know if a potential client's properties are out of state. (More information on real estate licensing requirements can be found in Chapter 12.)

Property Market Assessment. Before starting a real estate management business, one of your first considerations should be the market you intend to serve. The most logical market would be the one in which you are currently employed—e.g., shopping centers, office buildings, apartments, condominiums, industrial parks—depending on your expertise and experience as a real estate manager. Even though real estate owners state a preference for the generalist when they are surveyed, it is increasingly difficult to start out as a generalist, especially if a manager is planning to seek clients among the major players—i.e., the businesses and institutions that own and operate the larger investment properties. If you have a niche, you would be well advised to try to start out within that niche market. It is easier to plan for success when dealing with things you already know.

In order to properly evaluate the market, it is important to know what other companies are currently serving it and how well they are doing. The marketplace may be saturated with good management companies at present, in which case your expectations and your initial strategies may have to be adjusted.

Conversely, there may be opportunities, but not in your preferred niche. This raises questions of adaptability and diversification. Can your skills be applied in the area where there are management opportunities? A key consideration may be whether the specific opportunities are within or related to your larger area of specialization. If your experience has been with rental apartments only, would you consider managing condominium properties? They differ from apartments in the amount of paper work and the time commitment (especially attending board and association meetings), as well as the ownership structure, but they are similar in overall property operations and physical components. Likewise, if your experience is exclusively in managing office buildings, could you manage a shopping center? Office and shopping center leases share similarities regarding common area maintenance and pass-through expenses, but retail properties are literally open to the general public, adding another layer of potential customer-clients to be considered. Depending on center size, the manager may also be involved with the tenants in advertising the center to the public.

Real estate management businesses have also been formed at the request of an institution or other owner of a substantial portfolio. This is an excellent way to start a business because there is at least one client from the beginning, which removes some of the risk associated with a new venture. However, most operators of independent management businesses would prefer to start out with several clients rather than have their future depend on a single client.

Management Specialization

Specialization is very important to the start-up management business. A manager is generally ready to specialize after spending several years managing one type of property such as shopping centers, office buildings, or apartments. It is not unusual for a real estate management firm to declare that it manages either commercial or residential properties. However, even this distinction can be too broad.

Once a management company establishes a reputation for quality management service, its clients are likely to ask that the firm manage other types of properties for them. At the outset, at least, the new company will probably do better to promote its services where its principals have been most active in the years immediately preceding the company's formation. If, in addition to property management, the firm can offer leasing, construction supervision, and other related services that can be bundled together as part of management or made available separately, the business can be characterized as offering "full service."

Within the two general categories of commercial and residential properties, there are many subsets of property types, an understanding of whose similarities and differences will help clarify the manager's choices regarding specialization.

Commercial Property Management. Among the properties included in this large category are shopping centers, office buildings, and various types of industrial properties.

Shopping Centers. The shopping center is possibly the most complex type of commercial property to manage, and even with extensive experience working exclusively with shopping centers, it is not likely that most of these managers have sufficient background to manage regional or super regional enclosed malls. Differences in rent structures and the marketing of these large centers direct to the consumer add to the complexity of managing them. Because the owners of these shopping centers can usually afford their own staff and site managers, this type of property generally is not an area of great opportunity for the start-up management firm.

Office Buildings. There is a tremendous difference in management requirements between a small low-rise office building and a high-rise office tower. Geographic location and type (and size) of tenants also play a role: The operational needs of an office building in the suburbs differ from those of a property situated in the central business district (CBD) of a major metropolitan area. Suburban office complexes are often park-like with landscaping and groundskeeping as ongoing maintenance requirements. With the vertical layering of floors in urban towers, there are more complex mechanical systems to maintain (e.g., elevators, communications cabling), and implementation of emergency procedures such as evacuation of the building is made more challenging.

Office buildings whose tenants are predominantly or exclusively health care specialists—physicians, dentists, opticians, and others—are constructed or retrofitted with more extensive plumbing and electrical systems, and they have unique (bio-hazard) waste-disposal requirements. These and other distinctive attributes have led to this type of medical office building (MOB) becoming a separate area of management specialization. Office condominiums are not only rare, but also quite different to manage than a traditional office building because of their different ownership structure.

Industrial Buildings and Parks. Management of industrial properties is likewise differentiated. At the less-complex end of the spectrum is the incubator industrial site tenanted by a few small, perhaps relatively inexperienced, operators—e.g., start-up manufacturers, assembly operations, packagers—most likely in subdivided space in a large building. At the other end of the spectrum is the large, master-planned industrial park. Here there may be single-tenant buildings or spaces subdivided for leasing to two or more tenants or both. This property type also includes large warehouse and distribution operations as well as the self-storage facilities used by both businesses and private individuals.

Residential Property Management. There are several distinctive types of investment residential properties, offering opportunities to manage both rentals (single-family homes, apartments, government-assisted housing) and nonrentals (common interest realty associations). Other types of residential properties are also in need of professional management, but they are extremely specialized uses and are likely to be managed as something other than investment real estate. *Housing for the elderly* that includes services and amenities as an adjunct to independent living (e.g., congregate housing) and *single-room occupancy (SRO)* residences may be owned and operated by nonprofit entities. In major metropolitan markets surrounding large urban centers (e.g., New York City, Chicago, Los Angeles), these types of properties may be owned and operated by governmental agencies—local rather than state or federal. This is not to say there are no real estate management opportunities in these types of properties, but very specialized skills outside the realm of real estate management are often required, adding to the management challenges these properties pose.

Single-Family Homes. One of the easier entrees to real estate management as a business is for a real estate sales office to manage single-family homes as rentals. This type of management is particularly challenging because of the number of sites and their varied locations. Generally, there is a separate management agreement on each house, and often the manager is serving several different owners. Managing this type of property is a lot of work and sometimes very complicated.

Apartment Buildings. Moving up the scale, multiple dwellings come in all sizes. The small apartment property (two, three, and four units to eight, ten, and twelve units in a single building) can be a big challenge. It generally does not have on-site personnel, which means the manager of the property must respond to all calls and deal directly with residents. Once apartment properties reach a given size (e.g., 16 or more units), they may be required by state law to have an on-site manager, which can make the property manager's job a little easier but adds the necessity of hiring, training, supervising, and paying—and firing—site managers. As building size and property complexity increase (hundreds of units, multiple buildings, added amenities), there is also a need for staff in addition to an on-site manager.

Government-Assisted Housing. This subcategory includes *public housing* owned outright by governmental agencies and properties that accept vouchers or receive partial or full rent payments from the federal government under various specific programs (e.g., *section 8* housing for the elderly), as well as affordable housing created via owner subsidies (i.e., *tax credit* programs). Managing assisted housing is very management-intensive and closely regulated, with a burden of extra paper work. Many companies choose to specialize in this type of management, and rightly so. Although some managers may become frustrated in dealing with governmental agencies, once the housing assistance programs are understood and the manager gains experience, managing assisted housing can be very rewarding.

Mobile Home Parks and Manufactured Housing Communities. This is a unique type of real estate management. Usually the resident owns the home and leases the site where it is installed. As a consequence, the residents collectively have as big an investment as does the property owner. This type of housing is highly regulated in many markets via zoning ordinances and licensing of managers as well as other means (e.g., separate landlord-tenant laws). At properties whose residents are mostly elderly retirees, there is often a push for rent control, creating a difficult situation for both the park owner and the manager. For people concerned about housing affordability, these communities provide an opportunity for homeownership at a cost well below construction of site-built houses and the land on which they are built.

Common Interest Realty Associations. Whether a collection of townhouses or a high-rise building—the latter may be built new or converted from rental apartments—*condominium* properties represent a significant proportion of individually owned residences. The shared ownership of common elements, from roof and lobby to a swimming pool and other amenities, means unit owners must pay for the upkeep of these components separate from their individual mortgages. At many condominiums, management is responsible only for the common elements, maintaining overall appearance of the property, collecting assessments, preparing financial statements, and paying the expenses of the property as a whole. (Maintenance of individual residences is the responsibility of the unit owners.) Although the manager should and typically does work directly with the board elected by members of the homeowners' association, this does not preclude interaction with unit owners whose expectations may exceed their entitlements. There is usually also a requirement to attend board meetings, and there may be a need to attend meetings of the homeowners' association. Condominium management differs substantially from apartment management in these particular details, but like apartment management, it can be an area for successful specialization.

Similarly challenging are *cooperative* properties where individuals own shares of the corporate entity that holds title to the property. As a stockholder, each "owner" is entitled to occupy one of the units (under a proprietary lease). A cooperative is similar to a condominium because of the individuals' participating in ownership, and many of its management requirements parallel those of a condominium. However, while owners of condominiums may rent their units to others—if the association permits rentals—cooperative units are exclusively owner-occupied.

A *planned unit development (PUD)* may include single-family homes, condominiums, and rental apartments as well as amenities (golf courses, resort facilities) and services; occasionally nonresidential uses may be included. These entities are governed by community or homeowners' associations comprising unit owners, whether they buy a condominium, a house, or a townhouse. (Renters may not participate in the association but are still subject to its rules.) In this case, the common elements include the green areas (lawns, parks), paved streets, and infrastructure (e.g., incoming utilities) of the development as a whole, in addition to roofs and lobbies of condominium buildings and any recreational or other amenities constructed for use by all members of the community. Where there are rental apartments, these buildings may also be considered part of the "common elements."

It is easy to see that "property management" can be a very broad term and that most managers cannot be all things to all clients. A real estate management business is more likely to be successful if it is launched from an experience base that allows for specialization. As the entrepreneurial manager grows in knowledge and expertise, and demonstrates this growth in a property type specialization augmented with experience as a business owner, there will be opportunities to expand the types of properties accepted for management.

Locational Considerations. In addition to specializing in a particular property type, the new business owner must consider what geographic area will be served. Because of the labor-intensive nature of real estate management, it is not practical to try to serve a very large geographic area unless the business employs sufficient staff to cover it well. Spreading oneself too thin has two downsides: In the first place—and most important—the client whose properties are located beyond a reasonable travel distance is not likely to be well-served. Because the travel time required discourages frequent visits, there is a tendency to do everything by phone. If the property is not visited periodically, the manager cannot know its condition or whether residents or commercial tenants' service needs are being met. However, if the manager makes frequent visits to manage the far-away property properly, the company is likely to lose money on the account. As a general rule, it is not a good idea to take on too many properties that are likely not to be profitable.

On the other hand, if a potential client has several properties, all in the same area some distance away, and the client wants a single firm to manage all of them, there could be sufficient income from management fees from the total portfolio to justify setting up a branch office in the distant city, making the situation work for both the manager and the client. Long-distance management can also be practical if the properties are of sufficient size to allow for on-site management. The distance may be less of an issue because the supervisory activity is generally less time-intensive than direct management would be.

Type of Owner-Clients to Be Served. The type of clients being served will be determined, in part, from the type of properties to be managed and how they are owned in the market being served. Different types of owners have different goals—value enhancement, cash flow, rehab and resale—and the owners' goals will be a consideration in decisions about the management of the real estate. As a management client, each type of owner has advantages and disadvantages. Understanding ownership characteristics should help you in choosing the owner-clients you will serve.

- *Sole proprietors* often have less complicated accounting and reporting requirements and can make decisions more quickly, but they may involve themselves in day-to-day property operations and deal directly with building occupants. The management agreement may be jeopardized if the property owner retires from business or dies, and the heirs decide to sell the investment.
- *Partnerships* can be demanding with regard to operations and reporting requirements, and partners may not always agree on management strategies, slowing the decision-making process.
- *Common interest realty associations* (e.g., condominiums, cooperatives, PUDs) present unique management challenges because of the multiple-ownership. There may be as many "bosses" as there are unit owners, and control of the elected board of directors may change every year, so it is important to establish a primary contact for the manager (preferably the president or another member of the board). Also,

since the property does not have an income stream (i.e., rents), management fees are allocated proportionately among the owners in their regular assessments.
- *Corporations* that own real estate may require the management company to prepare budgets, reports, and other documents in their preferred formats and on their schedule. Third-party managers who work for corporations must be sure they are dealing with someone in authority because it is not unusual to receive ultimate direction from people they do not communicate with directly.
- *Institutional owners* (insurance companies, pension funds) set high standards for operating their properties and typically require use of their preferred accounting software; because of their nature, decision-making sometimes can be slow.
- *Real estate investment trusts (REITs)* present challenges similar to those posed by institutional owners. Because of their dividend requirements, they place heavy emphasis on cash flow. Keeping their properties in good condition is a serious priority as it sometimes helps them gain additional access to capital (i.e., raise additional funds through Wall Street).
- *Real estate owned (REO) properties* often enter lenders' portfolios via foreclosure; as owners, commercial banks may have more extensive reporting requirements, and decision-making can be a slow process.

Financial considerations add another layer of complexity. The size of a business entity that owns real estate is not always the best measure of the availability of cash outside of the revenue generated by the managed property. A sole proprietor may be quite wealthy and generously provide funds to meet operating expenses that are not covered by property receipts. A corporation or institution may have "deep pockets" but expect the property revenue to cover all expenses and generate substantial additional income as profits. The converse is more likely, however: A sole proprietor may be dependent on the property revenue for personal income, and an institution may temporarily make up revenue shortfalls to ensure its property is properly maintained. These are only some of the ways the type of owner can affect the management of a property, but they are important considerations in determining the clientele a management company wants to serve and how its services will be marketed to potential clients. (Owners' goals and concerns are discussed in more detail in Chapter 6.)

Business-Specific Considerations

In starting a real estate management business, there are several issues that are common to all business start-ups. These relate to specific decisions that have to be made about the form of ownership of the business, which has revenue and tax implications. This discussion will also address in-house management and how it might be structured.

Ownership Structure. There are three basic forms of business ownership—sole proprietorship, partnership, and corporation. Each has advantages and disadvantages to be considered. Before making a final decision, the preferred choices should be carefully reviewed by an attorney and a professional accountant to assure that the ultimate goals of the business will be realized within the chosen form of ownership.

Sole Proprietorship. This is a very common form of business ownership, especially in real estate and real estate management. There is almost no set-up cost for this form of ownership. If the company will use a name other than that of the owner, an *assumed name* (a declaration of "doing business as," usually abbreviated d.b.a.) must be filed with the local authorities. There may be a requirement to publish an announcement in local newspapers as part of the proof of business establishment—newspapers that do this routinely know the format and requirements—and you may have to pay a local business permit or license fee. State and local jurisdictions sometimes impose other types of taxes and fees on businesses; dollar amounts may be nominal, but it is important to be aware of and comply with these requirements.

The main disadvantage of the sole proprietorship form of ownership is the unlimited liability. The owner is placing all of his or her assets at risk if there is a large judgment against the business entity in a lawsuit. Also, a sole proprietor can find it difficult to secure a fidelity bond on behalf of a client, but this may sometimes be circumvented if the client is willing to purchase the bond and be reimbursed by the management company. The owner is also responsible to pay the operating expenses of the business—including payroll—and this may have to be funded out-of-pocket if the business is not generating sufficient income.

On the other hand, the sole proprietor is taxed only once (the owner's personal income is adjusted for the expenses of operating the business—IRS Form 1040, Schedule C), and all benefits of the business entity accrue directly to the owner. Another advantage of this form of ownership is control: Only one person is making the decisions and setting the goals for the business.

Partnership. Two or more people may establish a partnership in which participants share in the profits (and losses) of the business. The business entity itself pays no income tax; the partnership distributes profits (and losses) among the participants as taxable personal income. In a *general*

> **Some Considerations Regarding Business Ownership**
>
> The form of ownership of a real estate management business has wide-ranging implications. Different ownership forms may offer advantages in regard to some or all of the following:
>
> - Operating loans (equipment purchases, company expansion)
> - Income taxes
> - Ease of set-up
> - Legal and/or accounting fees
> - Interstate commerce (clients or properties outside your state)
> - Company or employer insurance
> - Sale of the company
> - Succession planning
> - Ease of dissolution

partnership, each partner's share is directly related to his or her level of participation or as otherwise agreed among the individuals. Sometimes a *limited partnership* is preferred; in this type of entity, one individual may serve as general or managing partner with the other (limited) partners only participating financially. The partners' roles and financial participation are spelled out in a *partnership agreement.*

One of the major disadvantages of the general partnership is that each partner is liable for the debts and obligations of the partnership—in their entirety—if another partner should fail to meet his or her share of the obligations. Also, one partner can obligate the partnership without the knowledge of the other participants. In a limited partnership, the general partner has the same kind of unlimited liability while a limited partner is only liable in proportion to his or her investment.

A partnership has the advantage of bringing to the business the talents and experiences of more than one person and the potential to create a stronger company with greater financial capacity and more outside contacts. One partner may enjoy the marketing and business development activities while the other prefers the day-to-day hands-on management. The most important elements of a partnership are respect for each other's abilities and talents and realization of one's own limitations. In order to work together well, partners must also know each others' personalities and share common goals and belief systems. Otherwise, personal incompatibilities can strain the relationship and be detrimental to the business.

Corporation. The corporation as a form of ownership is recognized by federal and state governments as an independent legal entity (established by documenting *articles of incorporation*). As such, the business must pay income taxes on its profits; the shareholders also pay income taxes on the dividends distributed to them. This *double taxation* is one of the disadvantages of the corporate form of ownership.

The major benefit of the corporate structure is that of limited liability. It is possible and even probable that the corporation could sustain a major loss (e.g., from a lawsuit), and that the individual shareholders, being protected by the corporate "shell," would bear no liability beyond the value of their investment. However, the reality is that officers and directors (or trustees) of corporations are frequently named in lawsuits and charged with personal liability. To assure the protection of the corporate form of ownership, great care must be taken that board meetings are held and minutes are kept. This is especially important for very small, closely held corporations.

Federal income tax law recognizes an *S corporation* as an alternative to the *C corporation* described here. In an S corporation, one is afforded the protection of a corporate entity but taxed as a partnership; however, there are many limitations on this form of ownership, and it is not recognized in all states so there may be corporate liability for state income taxes.

Another possibility worth considering is creation of a *limited liability company (LLC)*, a hybrid type of ownership entity permitted under many state statutes. Basically, an LLC offers the limited liability of a corporation with the income tax status of a partnership. However, not all states recognize this entity as yet, and those that allow it have established different limitations and filing procedures. The liability limitation may not apply if the management company is formed as an LLC in a state other than that where it manages property.

In-House Management—Department Versus Company. Sometimes an established real estate or related business (a developer, an investment company, a REIT) will take management in house after years of having third-party managers do the job. The entity benefits from having tighter control over how the property is managed day to day, and retention of the management fees helps contribute to the bottom line. Obviously, start-up of a management business for an ownership entity assumes there is a large enough portfolio to make the effort worthwhile.

One of the biggest decisions that will have to be made with an in-house property management function is whether the new operation should generate a profit or be operated as a service division. The two approaches are very different. If the management entity is set up to make a profit, management fees generally are set at market rates, and services provided to the parent organization are priced accordingly, although there may be intra-organizational conflicts regarding what services are to be provided and the fees to be charged. Such a for-profit entity may be allowed to solicit business outside of the parent organization, offering services to potential clients at competitive rates. It can also decline third-party business that will not be profitable. On the other hand, a management function created as a service division may not be required to make a profit, but it might be expected to be self-supporting. Service is provided on the basis of the parent organization's need. With specific charges being billed, the parent will request services from the service division—for example, work orders, equipment documentation, leasing services, or other items considered "regular" services under a third-party management agreement. Note, however, that property management departments of REITs do not charge management fees to the properties the REIT owns.

If a management business is to be part of another real estate entity, a major decision will be whether to establish a department within the existing larger company or create a separate business entity (e.g., a subsidiary or division). Each approach has advantages and disadvantages. Generally, if the new management function will be providing service and not focused on making a profit, setting up a department is the least complicated approach. All personnel ultimately report to one individual, and it is easier to set common goals and track people's progress in meeting those goals. However, simply shifting existing personnel to the new function may not serve your purposes. You should be asking what you need to do in order to provide quality management cost-effectively.

Frequently there is less cost in setting up a department as compared to the cost of establishing an independent business entity. Also, costs can be allocated directly to the properties to track them effectively apart from the main company's operating overhead. The department approach also minimizes competition within the company to make a profit. It is easy to see how an asset management business and a property management business would consider themselves in competition. The asset management group would want to keep property management fees low to assure that their entity would be more profitable, and the property management group would strive to maximize its fees for the same reason.

Real estate licensure requirements also affect the decision. Most states do not require a real estate license if a person is managing his or her own real estate, and an in-house department is likely to qualify under this type of provision. If this approach is taken, however, it is important to take care not to have a management function with even slightly different ownership than the parent entity because some states would construe this as third-party management and require the management function to be licensed. If the main business entity does not have to have a real estate license for its activities, but the management function does, it may be easier to obtain a license for a separate management company.

One of the main advantages of setting up the management business as a separate entity is that of accountability. It is much easier to track the profitability of a separate company. However, if the management company is to be a separate entity and the goal of that company is to make money, management fees must be competitive in order for it to have a real chance of being profitable. (It is not unusual for an in-house management function to be created with the goal of making a profit, and then, for internal reasons, management fees are set below market rates, which essentially guarantees the function will not be profitable.)

Potential liability is yet another consideration in setting up a management business. It is generally accepted that management is a risky business in terms of liability claims, and it may be desirable to insulate the main company from that type of liability by setting up the management function as a separate business.

Equipping the Management Office. Most businesses today cannot operate without computers, facsimile machines, and other high-technology equipment, and they are likely to embrace future advances in technology that improve efficiency through greater productivity and lower costs. The same is true of real estate management companies. Because almost everything real estate managers do depends on effective communication—from the manager to clients, residents, and commercial tenants; to contractors, suppliers, and employees; to public officials, tenant groups, and public advocacy groups; and back to the manager—it is imperative to have the proper tools to do the job. Although there are other technological tools available to make offices more efficient, the discussion here will focus on the communications-related equipment and services that are a must for the modern management office.

Computers. The real estate management function benefits tremendously from the computer. Real estate managers are now able to collect more data and analyze it more quickly, in more ways, to accomplish their goals. An institutional owner would not even consider a management company that did not have a sophisticated computer set-up. Often clients will require or even provide their preferred software; in some cases, they will actually be connected to the management company computer by modem so they can draw on the program anytime they want.

It is not unusual for a management firm to be running several different accounting programs to accommodate various clients. There are many good accounting packages available on today's market. (The Institute of Real Estate Management publishes a list of programs and minimum standards for property management accounting software.) In addition to accounting software, there are maintenance management programs and systems for tracking rents, occupancy, pass-through operating expenses, rent escalations, and other specifics of the management process, including "tickler" files or reminders. The latter are especially useful for monitoring lease expirations, rent increases, insurance premiums, and other recurring activities. They allow real estate managers to standardize their formats and easily prepare budgets and reports for their owner-clients.

Computers and their adjuncts (modems, printers, networks, software) can be expensive to buy, but they are necessary components of a well-run management office. Because technological advances are introduced with increasing frequency, hardware and software quickly become obsolete. Often the wise course is to lease equipment so that upgrades and replacements can be addressed more cost-effectively. In considering the purchase or leasing of hardware and in choosing software for your company's operations, it is advisable to consult with other knowledgeable real estate managers or with a computer expert.

As this book is being readied for publication there are two basic "platforms" used in business applications—the disk-operating system (DOS) or IBM-compatible professional computer (PC) and the Mackintosh or MAC—each with advantages and disadvantages related to running particular types of software. Many software programs are developed in separate versions for the two platforms, or what is available will work on one or the other but not both. The most important consideration will be compatibility. Hardware and software must be compatible within the company to facilitate sharing of files and data (e.g., via floppy disks or access to a local-area network). Compatibility with client systems and capability of transmitting and receiving data via modem are critical to serving clients' information needs. It may be desirable as well to have one or more portable computers (e.g., laptop or notebook-type models) available that managers or others can make use of outside the office. These, too, must work within the larger "system" for optimum efficiency.

Facsimile (Fax) Machines. The fax is a critical communication tool for the real estate manager. While you may prefer to save a few dollars by having your telephone and fax share a common number, it is really better to have a dedicated line for the fax. There is nothing more frustrating than trying to send a fax and have someone in the intended recipient's office repeatedly pick up the telephone, disrupting the transmission.

In addition, use of the fax tends to imply urgency, and fax messages often receive more prompt responses than those sent via other communication vehicles. It is also a way of ensuring that something is in writing—legally, facsimile transmissions that include signatures are being accepted in lieu of original signed documents, a fact which expedites purchasing and other activities requiring written authorizations.

Cellular Telephones. The cellular (portable) phone is a tool seemingly designed for the real estate manager. It is particularly useful because it can be taken into a vacant unit or out onto the parking lot during an inspection. It allows the manager to call suppliers and contractors while at the property or on the road between the office and a property. It also means the manager can be reached more easily in case of an emergency. Because many models can be programmed with phone numbers that are used repeatedly (speed dialing), it is not always necessary to have both hands free to use a cellular phone. Since drivers using cellular phones while on the road pose a hazard to others, there are also models with voice-activated dialing and speakers instead of handsets, which afford true hands-free calling. Cellular phones are being made smaller and smaller, so they can easily be tucked into a coat or suit pocket, a briefcase, or a handbag.

Although staff members may think they all need such a tool, that is not always the case. Some management companies have only one or two such phones, and managers going on the road check them out when they leave the office and check them in when they return. This allows more people to use this type of phone without incurring the additional costs of units not in use and possible charges for unauthorized phone calls. (Providing a set phone allowance is one way of encouraging responsible use of cellular phones for business purposes.)

There are also cordless battery-operated phones that have one or more lines or can be used with a standard PBX system. These are useful extension phones for in-office and on-site use where a land-based corded phone system is in place. These, too, allow the user to send and receive calls. There are also models with voice mail and other features of a corded phone, and many are configured for hands-free calling. The evolution from analog to digital transmission has added security as well as clarity (digitized phone calls are not "broadcast" so they are not picked up by radio receivers and scanners).

Pagers. Even when a manager has a cellular phone, a pager can be a great accessory. The phone may be off or the line may be busy. A pager allows the person to be contacted and return the call as soon as possible. Some pagers simply alert users to call their office for a message, others show the phone number of the caller—or even a more-extensive written message—so the person who is paged can return the call directly. More sophisticated models use vibrations and sounds other than the traditional "beep," making the page signal less obvious to onlookers while more effectively alerting the carrier to an incoming call. Although many paging services are independent companies, there are combination telephone-pagers and companies that provide dual services.

Incoming 800 Number. An incoming 800 phone number can be set up for local or long-distance calls or both. This can be a competitive advantage as well as a cost-effective business tool. If you manage properties that do not have an on-site manager, an 800 number makes the manager of the property more accessible. The actual cost is comparatively low, and residential and commercial tenants, contractors, and suppliers may be more likely to call if they will not have to pay long-distance charges, so communications are much better. However, to ensure that the service is cost-effective, use of the 800 number should be monitored.

Voice Mail. Another feature of modern telephones, voice mail is either one of the greatest of modern tools or one of the worst things ever foisted on the public, depending on how it is used. There are those who use voice mail to screen their incoming calls—almost never picking up a live call, they selectively respond to the messages callers leave for them. There are also complicated routing programs that give callers a menu of options and buttons to press, making it difficult or even impossible to connect with the right person to respond to an inquiry or complaint. However, used properly to relay information, voice mail helps avoid the problems of lost paper messages and repeated callbacks (so-called telephone tag). When setting up a voice-mail system, including the option to talk to a live operator will increase the likelihood that all callers' messages will be directed properly.

Developing a Business Plan

There are two major areas of planning for a new management business—strategic planning and operational planning—and an analysis of financial feasibility is vital both for planning and decision-making.

Strategic Planning. A strategic plan sets goals, objectives, and guidelines for an organization so that all participants understand their respective roles. In developing a strategic plan for a new management firm, you will need to look at what you bring to the business and what you want the business to accomplish so that you can determine specific strategies for getting there. The information and decisions should be documented as a reference point for measuring accomplishment as well as identifying strategies that need fine-tuning.

In setting goals and objectives for the business, it is imperative to also set time frames for their achievement. Although a common time horizon is five years, the initial plan for a business might set specific goals for a three- to five-year period in one-year increments. A strategic plan should be a working document that can be modified if necessary; having specific time frames commits the planner to evaluating achievements and changing strategies that are not accomplishing the goals—or changing the goals themselves.

The strategic planning process includes looking at all of the issues and considerations mentioned previously in this chapter and creating a well-thought-out plan that states your goals for the business and how you expect to accomplish them. You will also need to look at your actual and potential competitors: What are their strengths and weaknesses? What can be learned from them?

So-called environmental factors—the economic, technological, political, and social factors that are beyond your control but can and do impact the way you do business—must also be evaluated. These include laws and regulations that affect businesses in general and real estate in particular.

Strategic planning is not a static exercise. As a business grows, the size of its staff will increase. Once a real estate management business is no longer a one-person operation—if it ever was—it is imperative for the company's leadership to communicate the strategic plan to its personnel and guide them in accomplishing the vision charted in the plan. The ongoing strategic planning process can be enhanced by working with an outside consultant (i.e., a professional facilitator), benchmarking accomplishments (periodic reviews), and revising as necessary.

Components of a Strategic Plan. A strategic plan should outline the business owner's decisions about how the business will be conducted to be successful. Although it will take the form of a written document, a strategic plan is a *process* that, for a successful business, is ongoing. The resulting document should identify, minimally, a market strategy, a management strategy, and a financial strategy to accomplish the specific goals and objectives of the start-up real estate management business. Most businesses over the longer term set goals based on evaluation of current and potential weaknesses (as well as strengths) and assumptions about emerging or future opportunities. The intent is to improve performance based on measurable standards. Since the future is unpredictable, alternative goals and performance standards are often identified in contingency plans.

A *market strategy* should address what services the management firm will provide and the intended customers for the services. This should also include consideration of pricing and marketing. These decisions require evaluation of the marketplace and, in particular, potential competitors. It also requires determining that there is a need for your services in the marketplace (or if you will have to create the need).

A *business management strategy* should identify the specific functions that will be performed within the company and who will perform them. This requires consideration of the strengths and weaknesses of the individual(s) starting the business as well as availability of additional personnel needed to conduct the business. (On a larger scale, internal communications, cooperation, and individuals' attitudes and beliefs are among the "people issues" that need to be addressed.)

A *financial strategy* should state how the business will be capitalized

> **Considerations in Identifying Your Competition**
> - Who are my competitors?
> - How long have they been in business?
> - Whom do they represent (i.e., who are their clients)?
> - What are their specialties?
> - What are their reputations?
> - Who are their key employees?
> - What are their strengths and weaknesses?
> - What are their vulnerabilities?

initially and how the company will conduct its business in order to be profitable and economically viable over the long term. It should also spell out how needed operating funds will be generated and how profits and excess revenues will be used (i.e., short- and long-term budgets). This requires evaluating cash flow, establishing policies regarding payments (from clients; to suppliers), enumerating and valuing assets and liabilities (including future obligations), and determining the availability and cost of financing from outside sources. The approach to fees is an important consideration. Often people starting companies think they have to compete on price in the early stages, making profitability a challenge and growth and expansion of the business very difficult.

The Planning Process. To start the planning process, you will need to assess your personal capabilities and those of any other participants in the business (partners, intended staff), looking in particular at strengths and weaknesses based on prior performance. For the entrepreneur who is or has been an employee of another management firm, this assessment should explore not only what you have been doing (e.g., managing a particular type of property) but how you have been doing it (your specific successes and failures). You will also need to explore developments in the external marketplace, not only the opportunities (e.g., availability of properties and clients), but also the threats (e.g., specific competition, the overall economic picture) and their potential impact on your start-up and future activities.

The plan itself will consist of *operational strategies* based on your marketing (client acquisition) and management (business-specific) goals—how you intend to accomplish the performance objectives you have established for the business. It will also include a *financial plan* that outlines estimated revenues and expenses.

Initially, a pro forma may be sufficient (this is discussed under financial feasibility later in this chapter). For some situations, it may be appropriate to prepare additional internal financial reports—quarterly (or even

> ### Analyzing Your Competition
>
> An evaluation of your competition should include a service-by-service assessment of each competitor's operations. For each service you propose to offer, a series of questions should be asked and answered. The following are some examples.
>
> - Who offers this service among the competition?
> - How well do they perform the service?
> - How long have they been doing it?
> - Who are their clients?
> - Are they vulnerable? If so, why? If not, why not?
> - Can my company do it better?
> - Can we do it at a lower cost?
>
> This type of competitive analysis is not only important for a start-up business but a key component in considering opportunities that are presented to you or exploring ways to expand your business. It will also help you differentiate your firm from the competition or establish a market niche.

monthly) income statements, an annual (and possibly quarterly) balance sheet showing the evolving relationships among assets and liabilities of the business as well as the owner's equity investment position, and monthly cash-flow summaries showing the firm's cash position. These latter are likely requirements of a larger-scale operation, particularly if such detailed documentation is needed for the real estate management department (or division) of an established business. For the start-up entrepreneur, being able to evaluate performance against the initial pro forma and budget is important but probably not mandatory. This is where computer software that includes a spreadsheet function and allows consideration of "what if?"-type questions can be very helpful.

As the business grows, its strategic plan will evolve. Changes in the marketplace and in your client base will be among the issues that need to be visited and revisited over time. The company that includes a growing staff of real estate managers and support personnel should involve its employees in the planning process. While this may be limited to executive and supervisory personnel initially, the goal should be active involvement of all staff members. Since employees will be charged with implementing the strategic plan, and their individual performance will be measured against the goals and standards set out in the plan, they have a vested interest in making it work. Excluding them can affect their general attitudes as well as their job performance, and these kinds of internal problems can be very difficult to overcome. Asking for employees' ideas and opinions—and using them—will encourage your staff members to buy into the corporate vision. Working with a professional facilitator can help encourage employee participation as well as facilitate integration of ideas into the plan.

> **Some Questions to Be Answered in Developing a Strategic Plan**
>
> - What are the strengths of my new company?
> - What might be perceived as weaknesses of the company and how can I overcome them in the eyes of potential clients?
> - Who are the prospective clients? Where will I look for them and how will I approach them?
> - How will I handle the management of the accounts I already have (if any at this early stage) while also working on the business development activity that is necessary?
> - What are the special talents of my business partners or associates, and how can those talents be used most effectively in the company?
> - How will the business be capitalized? Will we need to borrow money to start up the business?
> - If loans are needed, what sources of funding are available, and what are the prospects of obtaining a loan?
> - What geographic area is realistic for the new business to serve?
> - What services are owners demanding that are not provided in the market?
> - What services do we provide well?
> - Should we specialize in managing a particular type of property?
> - How will such specialization impact the business and its operations?
> - What potential ethical conflicts might arise in prospecting for clients or with my most recent employer and those of its clients whom I served?
> - Who are the strongest competitors in the market and how well are the competitors performing?
> - How will the competition respond if we follow this strategic plan?
> - Do we need advice to make a realistic determination?
>
> It is also important to consider alternatives that could be implemented—or appropriate exit strategies—if the business does not succeed.

Planning enables the company executives to optimize the firm's potential by responding to opportunities instead of merely reacting to problems and crises. Writing a business plan provides an opportunity to analyze every aspect of a company and its operations and to review the company's progress since its inception or over the past few years, reflecting on the goals and objectives of the firm and considering whether the current course of action will achieve these goals. Each draft of the plan should be reviewed by the company's leadership and others charged with responsibility for strategic planning to ensure that it is consistent with the firm's goals and objectives.

The business plan should be easy to read so misunderstandings can be avoided. If it is too complicated, the management team and other personnel may not be able to implement the plan or achieve its objectives. The personnel involved with planning should be able to understand the plan's objectives and measure their own and the company's performance, and everyone should understand their respective roles in achieving the plan's

> ### Developing a Company's Vision
>
> The executive staff of a company has the responsibility of providing leadership, developing a vision for the company, and transferring that vision to the employees. There are three components to a company's vision: (1) core values and beliefs, (2) a statement of purpose, and (3) a mission statement.
>
> **Values and Beliefs** Core values and beliefs are the guiding principles upon which all policies and decisions are based. A company's values and beliefs may include statements regarding employee development, jobs, clients, family, community, rewards, and profit. Values and beliefs are often expressed as several sentences, each representing a specific value, and typically starting with "we believe," "we are dedicated," or "we are committed." A real estate management firm's values and beliefs may include statements regarding clients, residential and commercial tenants, employees, the community, and ethics and integrity.
>
> **Statement of Purpose** The fundamental reason why a company exists is expressed in its statement of purpose. A company's statement of purpose should be succinctly stated in one to three sentences. For example, the purpose of Schlage Lock Company is: "To make the world more secure." That of Stanford University is: "To enhance and disseminate knowledge that improves human kind." A real estate management firm's statement of purpose may address assisting its clients in meeting their goals and objectives, providing a level of service and a professionally managed environment to the building's residential and commercial tenants, and enhancing the building's neighborhood through good management practices.
>
> **Mission Statement** The mission statement serves as the company's focal point of effort. Unlike values and beliefs, mission statements change when the mission is accomplished. The mission statement for the United States that will always be remembered was the one established by President John F. Kennedy in 1961: "This nation should dedicate itself to achieving the goal, before this decade is out, of landing a man on the moon and returning him safely to earth." This statement had a clear and compelling goal and a time period to accomplish the goal. There are four basic types of mission statements:

objectives and gain personal satisfaction from its successful implementation. (Exhibit 2.1 on page 40 outlines the contents of a typical business plan. Each component, including the title page, should be thought through carefully, especially in terms of how the written plan will be used—e.g., to obtain financing for the business.)

A business plan will provide a foundation for the business to be flexible in adjusting and responding to unanticipated changes in the real estate and property management industries and taking advantage of unexpected opportunities. Reviewing the plan on a quarterly basis and updating it annually ensure that the plan will maintain the needed flexibility while continuing to set appropriate goals and provide direction for achieving them.

> **Developing a Company's Vision *(continued)***
> 1. A *targeting* goal would be to accomplish something within a specific time. For a real estate management firm, such a goal might be to double the size of its management portfolio within five years or to become the largest apartment management firm in the state by a certain year.
> 2. A *common enemy* goal would be to exceed or defeat a competitor. For a real estate management firm, such a goal might be to exceed a competitor in portfolio size or amount of office space leased each year.
> 3. A *role model* goal would use another organization as a benchmark for the level of service, profitability, ethics, or other characteristic to be emulated. (Often the model chosen will be outside the company's industry.) The Nordstrom Company is often emulated for the high level of service provided to its customers. Microsoft and Boeing are examples of companies that dominate an industry.
> 4. An *internal transformation* goal would be to implement specific changes. This type of goal is usually set for companies that are in need of reorganization: A large company or major institution or governmental agency may find that it must restructure—i.e., downsize—to operate efficiently.
>
> The employees of a real estate management company, from the on-site maintenance worker to the president, need to believe that the firm has a vision which then becomes the focal point of their efforts. To be effective, a vision must be shared by everyone in the organization. An example of a vision statement is: "To be the company of choice for real estate management service."
>
> A company's values and beliefs, statement of purpose, and mission statement should be framed and displayed in each office, and a copy should be provided to every employee. Some firms include their vision statement on company brochures and letterhead and on the backs of business cards.
>
> [NOTE: This brief discussion can only provide an overview of what is involved in developing a company's vision. We recommend *Beyond Entrepreneurship: Turning Your Business into an Enduring Great Company* by James C. Collins and William C. Lazier as an excellent resource on this subject (see also Appendix C).]

Operational Planning. On the operational side there are several decisions relating to business location, personnel, and other issues that have to be made before you can actually open the doors of a new business.

Where will the new business be located? As mentioned earlier in this chapter, working out of your home is a possibility and may be the least-expensive alternative, but does such a business location project the image desired for the new company? (There are also income tax-related implications to an office in one's home that must be taken into account, and local zoning may be an issue.) The size and location of a leased office will impact the finances as well as the operations of the new company. Is the location suited to the expected management portfolio of the company? Does it show

Exhibit 2.1
Components of a Business Plan

1. **Title Page** The title page should state the name of the firm, the period covered, and the date of preparation and/or adoption.
2. **Contents** A table of contents should identify the major sections and the respective page numbers on which they begin. A list of *exhibits* may be included.
3. **Executive Summary** The first section should provide an overview of the company and its market, its current position and possibilities for the future, and an outline of its goals and the strategies that will be used to achieve them.
4. **Marketing and Business Development Plan** This is where the company and its market would be described in detail. It should include a summary of trends observed in the industry as well as specific threats and opportunities. It should provide a description of the company's client base (actual or intended) and a description of its business development strategy (who will be responsible; current and planned business development efforts; a summary of last year's portfolio gains and losses and a projection of next year's portfolio gains and losses). The business development plan is a dynamic document that needs to be updated throughout the year as changes occur.
5. **Description of Services** This section should identify the firm's market niche and describe its service philosophy and the types of services offered, including the company's capabilities and a schedule of revenue objectives for each type of service.
6. **Organization and Management Plan** This is where operational details are outlined, including: (a) a statement of general management philosophy—including the vision statement and mission of the firm; (b) an organizational chart or outline of lines of authority and reporting responsibility with a description of individual positions; (c) a description or listing of productivity measures (standards and time frames); and (d) the company's employment policies and procedures (addressing personnel recruitment and selection, training and development, and compensation) along with resumes of key personnel (if needed for external purposes).
7. **Financial Plan** This should include the periodic financial schedules developed through the planning process (typically an income statement, balance sheet, and cash-flow statement, with departmental budgets or a composite budget as appropriate—usually showing projections on a quarterly or monthly basis). Financial performance statistics may also be included, with planned financial performance evaluated according to selected indicators such as profitability (profit margin, return on assets, return on equity), cash flow (average collection period), debt management, and liquidity. Because the company's policies regarding debt management, investment opportunities, use of earnings, and profit sharing affect its financial performance overall, these should also be itemized in the financial plan.
8. **Appendices** Although not necessary to every business plan, selected appendices are often included to support the other sections. A plan prepared to obtain financing would include budgets in an appendix rather than in the financial plan. Detailed evaluations of data on the competition and the market are also likely inclusions in an appendix rather than the marketing section.

[NOTE: For those who are unfamiliar or uncomfortable with the planning process, we would commend to you the various publications written on the subject. *How to Write a Business Plan* by Crego et al., published by the American Management Association, is a particularly worthwhile resource (see also Appendix C). There are also software templates available into which company-specific information can be inserted.]

> **Some Questions to Consider in Assessing Progress**
>
> In order to maintain your perspective, from time to time it is a good idea to step back and objectively assess the way the business is performing:
>
> - Are the goals set for the company the right ones?
> - Have we achieved the goals we set for ourselves?
> - Have we accomplished the mission?
> - What do we need to do in the future to maintain or improve profitability?
> - What do we need to know about our competition?
> - Is it sufficient to revise the existing plan, or do we need a whole new direction?

professionalism but still represent a good value to the company? Is there room to expand the company if it grows as planned? Does it provide for signage?

Who will conduct the business? Does the new company have the capability of handling the required activities for a start-up company with existing personnel? If not, are such personnel available either on a contract basis or as employees, and are the funds available to support such personnel? Does the new company have the reporting capability that will be required by the clients it expects to serve? If that capability does not exist in house, have arrangements been made for contracting such services? Will outside services be able to respond in a timely fashion to the requirements of the new company? If outside services will be used to perform some of the required functions, will that arrangement be satisfactory to your clients?

What about communications? If the company is very small, have arrangements been made so the real estate manager can be reached most of the time and can return telephone calls in a timely manner? Voice messaging may be an effective tool for incoming messages, but it cannot respond by calling the manager on a cellular phone or pager. Initially, an answering service may be a better choice for faster responses.

Other details must also be addressed. Are the necessary insurance coverages available and in place? Is a real estate or broker's license required, and have all of the requirements been met with the state agency involved? Does the management company have in place all of the forms and procedures that will be required at the outset? Often forms and procedures will have to be included in presentations to prospective clients, so these should be available immediately.

Because it is possible that the business will be started without any clients in place, you may be tempted to delay some of the operational planning. However, that is not a good idea because it is also likely that many things will take place concurrently. It is much better to be over-prepared than not prepared at all. Prospective clients will have a much better perception of the management company if it appears to have all of the tools in place and ready to use.

Financial Feasibility. Before starting a real estate management company, the prospective entrepreneur should do a feasibility study with a financial projection. (This type of study should also be done before expanding an existing company or in-house department.) There are many costs encountered in operating a business that may not be apparent at the outset. In order to be sure you are being realistic in your expectations, it is a good idea to make projections based on both worst-case and reasonably likely scenarios. Then you will be in a position to evaluate the probability of surviving if new accounts are not acquired as quickly as you had hoped. The sample pro forma in Exhibit 2.2 illustrates several points worth considering. The example is for a company intending to manage commercial properties. A pro forma for a company managing residential properties would show fees based on numbers of units and monthly rental rates (multiplied by twelve months in a year). Except for initial lease-up of a new building or following a period of full vacancy for complete rehabilitation, leasing commissions or fees would not be a separate income item although some sources of property income (e.g., coin laundry facilities, separate charges for parking) might be included in the "gross revenue" for computing management fees.

Income. The example assumes that the new management company will bring in three new accounts in the first year. It should be noted, however, that these new accounts are not likely to come on line from day one, so the income is already overstated. The exception to this situation is one where a developer or investor starting an in-house operation already has a substantial portfolio, in which case there is a built-in source of management income at the outset. For the sake of analyzing the potential income (or loss), we will assume that the three accounts are acquired in the first year and yield a total income from management fees of $99,180. This primary income will be used to pay the operating expenses of the business.

Expenses. In the expense category, the company owner should assign a value to his or her time and talents. (If necessary, this particular expense can be delayed or foregone if the business does not perform as planned. The same is not true of other necessary personnel expenses.)

One of the most important aspects of management today is the accounting function. Clients, especially institutional owners, are very demanding in their accounting requirements, but the start-up company has some options in this area. The pro forma assumes a qualified bookkeeper will be hired to perform all of the accounting tasks. An alternative to this is to hire a less-experienced bookkeeper and send the information out to a service bureau

Exhibit 2.2
Sample Pro Forma—Small Real Estate Management Business (First Year Projection)

Income (at 95% of value):*
1 Office Building (40,000 sq ft @ $15.00 Rent; 4% management fee)	$22,800
1 Shopping Center (60,000 sq ft @ $16.00 rent; 4% management fee)	$36,480
1 Industrial Park (100,000 sq ft @ $12.00 rent; 3.5% Management fee)	$39,900
Total Income from Management Fees:*	**$99,180**

Expenses:

1 Executive	$75,000		
1 Bookkeeper	$30,000		
1 Administrative Assistant	$21,000		
Total Payroll:		$126,000	
Other Payroll Costs (estimated @ 30%)		$37,800	
Total Payroll Costs:†			$163,800
Office Rent (800 sq ft @ $15.00)			$12,000
Insurance (E&O, Liability, Fire & EC)			$7,000
Telephone			$3,600
Utilities			$1,200
Office Furniture and Equipment			$2,000
Office Supplies (stationery, etc.)			$1,000
Travel			$3,000
Professional Memberships			$1,800
Total Projected Operating Expenses:			**$195,400**

Projected Net Income (Loss):‡   **($96,220)**

Potential Leasing Income (assuming three-year terms):

Office Building:	New Leases (4,000 sq ft @ $15.00 × 4%)	$7,200
	Lease Renewals (5,000 sq ft @ $15.00 × 2%)	$4,500
Shopping Center:	New Leases (3,000 sq ft @ $16.00 × 4%)	$5,760
	Lease Renewals (4,000 sq ft @ $16.00 × 2%)	$3,840
Industrial Park:	New Leases (6,000 sq ft @ $12.00 × 4%)	$8,640
	Lease Renewals (5,000 sq ft @ $12.00 × 2%)	$3,600
Total Leasing Commissions:*		**$33,540**

Projected Profit (Loss):‡   **($62,680)**

*Management fee *income* is projected at 95% of value to compensate for variables that normally impact fees (estimated total leased areas and rental rates are average or expected figures; lease terms and actual measurements and rents are likely to vary at a given property). Leasing commissions are projected at full value, but the same kinds of variables can skew these numbers upward or downward.

†Salary estimates are comparable to industry standards, but actual amounts paid may be negotiated lower.

‡A substantial loss is to be expected in the first year of operations because of the first-time costs—initial stationery stock might last two or more years; equipment and furniture, which may be depreciable, is a capital outlay that is not returned directly. Note, however, that if the company executive/owner in this example does not take a salary the first year, the projected loss based on management fees plus leasing commissions would be obliterated and there would be a potential net profit (which would be subject to income taxes).

for preparation of the monthly statements. Still another option is to use an accounting service. While the latter may be the most-economical approach, when work is done by a third party there is some loss of control that could lead to problems for (or with) the client.

Because much of the business aspect of real estate management is paper work, a good administrative assistant is a must. If you want to start out with a very lean operation, this position can be eliminated; however, not having this type of assistance means much of the paper work will have to be handled directly by the business owner, and his or her time may be better spent on business development and managing the properties. A possible alternative is to use a secretarial service for correspondence, but there is often a lag time in this approach, which can be an important consideration in terms of timeliness of response. (While a computer with word-processing capabilities would allow the owner to handle much of the paper work directly, this expense is not included in the sample pro forma.)

Office rent is an item that can be eliminated at the outset by working out of your home, but there are three major problems with this approach: The first is one of personal discipline. Not everyone can maintain good working habits while in the home environment. The refrigerator, family members, and other distractions make it hard to stay focused. The second problem is regarding employees and outside services that may have a need to meet with you. Consider whether you want your home subjected to this kind of traffic. (There is also a possibility that zoning ordinances may limit or preclude such use of your home.) The third problem is one of perception. What kind of image will you project in soliciting business to run a major real estate asset when your office is in your home? On the other hand, many small companies have been started by managers working from their homes, and over time, these have expanded and been quite successful. If you elect to open an office in your home, it should be efficient and professional—most clients of management companies do not expect teak paneling and top-of-the-line carpeting, neither of which will help you manage their property.

Another possibility is to establish your business address in an "executive suite." In the typical arrangement, one can rent a very small office space and have access to a conference room plus telephone answering service, fax and photocopying privileges, and assistance with correspondence, paying only for the services actually used. The rent per square foot is higher than that typically paid for a regular office space, but the overall office operating cost should be substantially less. (If the office is already furnished, there is no investment in office furniture.) This may be the most viable option until the new company is ready to lease its own space.

If you have management accounts established, it may be possible to set up an office in one of the buildings you manage. Some owners will provide office space for the management company at no charge, and your presence serves as an amenity for the building (i.e., on-site management).

Insurance is critical for a real estate management business. At the very least the manager should carry professional liability (so-called errors and omissions) insurance. This type of policy is sometimes difficult to find and the premiums may seem expensive; but weighed against the potential costs in the event of a lawsuit, it is a very cost-effective investment. Most major clients will require the management company to carry a minimum of $1,000,000 in public liability coverage, and many will require as much as five times that amount. Depending on the value of the office furniture and equipment, one may or may not decide to insure the office contents against fire or other loss. Because one of the major expenses in most management companies is the investment in computer networks and software, however, this equipment alone may justify carrying insurance on the office contents. Loss of income and automobile insurance should also be considered.

Bonding of employees who handle clients' rents (e.g., site managers) will be required under the management agreement, and such bonding may or may not be considered an owner expense. Regardless of that specific requirement, all company personnel who will handle clients' funds should be covered by a fidelity bond obtained by the management company. (Bonding and insurance are discussed in detail in Chapter 11.)

Expenditures for telephone services and other utilities must also be considered. If you want to try starting a business on a shoestring, it may be possible to buy used telephone equipment at a considerable savings. However, older equipment may not allow operation of all the adjuncts you need such as a computer modem and a facsimile machine.

Office furniture, especially items that are new and professional appearing, can be very expensive. This is an area where purchasing used items may be the better option. Alternatively, you may want to consider leasing furniture until you can afford the cash outlay to buy it. Besides, you will have a clearer sense of exactly what you need and how it will be used if you can defer this sometimes major investment.

Office supplies (pens, pencils, typing and computer paper) are a must, and there are many economical sources for these items. In fact, most major metropolitan areas have office supply superstores where everything from office furniture and equipment to pencils and erasers can be purchased at discounted prices. The one important investment in office supplies is stationery and business cards that are good quality and present an appropriate image for your business. Since the setup charges are a major component of the initial cost, your first order of stationery stocks may require a substantial investment, but the supply will probably last more than a year. (Small local print shops often provide good quality printing and supportive preparation services at a reasonable cost.)

Travel is an expense that is often overlooked. For purposes of the sample pro forma, the travel expense is the cost of visiting the properties on a regular basis and driving to potential clients' offices to solicit their business. The estimated expense should anticipate an amount for routine servicing and repairs in addition to gasoline and oil.

Managers who have achieved professional designations need to maintain them. Usually there are dues to be paid each year, and the amounts can range from $400 to more than $1,000 per organization. It may also be appropriate to keep in mind the costs of any required continuing education as well as participation in local and national meetings. Some of the latter may be deferred until the business is financially able to support them, but being active in professional organizations is one of the stepping stones of business development (see Chapter 7).

Other types of expenses that may be appropriate to address in a given situation include debt service, legal fees, tax accounting (preparation of income tax filings for the business), and marketing or business development costs (e.g., entertainment, proposal development). Consideration should also be given to specific operational and accounting issues in determining the contents of a start-up pro forma (review of Chapters 3 and 4 in this book will be helpful in this regard).

Measuring Net Income. At this point, a comparison of the fee management income to the anticipated expenses indicates a substantial loss. However, there is another possible source of income—i.e., leasing commissions. If you also have expertise in commercial property leasing, every effort should be made to obtain the leasing contract as well as the management contract on commercial properties. Using minimal figures for the three properties on the sample pro forma in Exhibit 2.2, an additional $33,000 in leasing fees can be generated in the first year. While the amount does not make the hypothetical start-up company profitable, it does reduce the loss substantially.

You may be asking yourself at this point why you would open a business if you are projecting a loss of $62,000 in the first year. It is certainly possible for a start-up company to be profitable initially. However, assuming that you have a viable service to offer and that the market can support that service, it is not unreasonable to assume a period of one to two years to achieve measurable profitability. It should also be noted that if the salary for the executive in the example (the owner of the company) can be deferred or foregone, the business would break even in terms of cash flow in the first year. Obviously, when deciding to go into business, you should

> **Some Things to Keep in Mind When Starting a Business**
> - Start with a business plan.
> - Be prepared to be on your own.
> - Have access to a data base of potential clients.
> - Be prepared financially for your plan to take longer to work out than expected.
> - Understand the commitment required.
>
> Also, family and others close to you need to accept and approve your decision because starting a business is a major time investment and has economic consequences beyond the business activity.

have some personal cash reserves and be able to forego direct compensation for at least a year.

Additional Sources of Income. The management company owner may also want to consider providing additional services to increase the company's income while it is growing. Depending on the manager's background and talents, and those of the other people involved in starting the business, there are several options to consider, including leasing, consulting, construction coordination (if one has the background), tax appeals (this requires a knowledge of the local tax laws), and serving as an expert witness. There may be opportunities as well to provide building maintenance services, operational audits, and brokerage services (sale or disposition of a property). ==There may also be revenue generated from charge-backs when photocopying, postage, and the like are billed to the client as part of the management arrangement.==

Other Financial Issues. The management company owner will have to balance his or her time and efforts between managing—actually earning income—and prospecting for new business. Often the best approach is to set aside some time each day to focus on marketing as one of your high-priority activities. In fact, obtaining new business is one of the most difficult tasks for the owner of a start-up company. (Business development is addressed in detail in Chapter 7.)

An examination of financial feasibility would be incomplete if it did not include consideration of initial capitalization. This might be from liquid assets held by the individual entrepreneur (and others in the case of a partnership), such as savings, or from the sale of valuables or easily converted stocks. There should be sufficient funding available at the start to purchase needed equipment and office supplies and to cover needed licenses and permits. The costs of preparing proposals to obtain management accounts also should be considered. It may be desirable (or advisable) to borrow

> **More Things to Keep in Mind in Starting a Management Business**
>
> - Be realistic in assessing market needs.
> - Choose your business associates (partners and employees) carefully.
> - Be realistic in assessing your skills and talents (and those of any other principals).
> - Start with a realistic budget.
> - Be patient—starting a new business often requires a great deal of time and effort and rewards may be small at first and slow in coming.
>
> Asking for advice from other entrepreneurs and brainstorming with friends and associates can help you develop ideas and affirm your decision as well as identify potential contingencies that may need to be addressed.

funds so that the start-up can proceed smoothly. This step will require consideration of what assets might be acceptable to the financial institution as collateral (e.g., a house, other valuables). Related to this is the need to provide for debt service in the start-up pro forma, a factor which can negatively impact the net revenue projections.

Other Considerations

The way a management firm conducts business and the manager-owner's professional qualifications are points to be kept in mind from the beginning. Personal and professional ethics are necessary to achieving success, and professional designations establish and enhance the individual's credibility.

Ethical Issues. The major ethical issue for the start-up management company is the relationship with the manager's former employer and the clients of that company. Because real estate management is such a personal business, it is not unusual for a client and the hands-on manager to develop a close relationship. If that manager leaves the company, the client may want to follow the manager to a new employer or to his or her start-up company. However, it is unethical to solicit the clients of the former employer in order to set up a new management business. In fact, no discussions regarding such a move should ever take place while the manager is still an employee. Once the manager is no longer an employee, it is still better if the client initiates any discussions about changing its management provider. If the manager, as an employee, has a contract with his or her employer, there may be a time limitation on a non-compete provision, which would thus establish a parameter for future relationships with previously served clients. Regardless of the employment arrangements, however, the manager who is leaving an employer should do everything possible to maintain a good relationship with that company and avoid any appearance of unethical conduct.

Another area of potential ethical conflict is hidden profits. The start-up management business may decide to provide outside services separate from the management function—landscaping, janitorial services, maintenance personnel, etc.—which can result in cost savings as well as more efficient service for its clients. However, the clients should be fully informed that the service entity is owned by the management company and that a profit is included in the charges billed to the property. (No outside service charges should be marked up without the specific approval of the client, and most management agreements specifically exclude such profit-taking.) Nor should there be any add-on fees for payroll or bill processing or for other administrative tasks unless they have been specifically approved by the client. To make sure that there are no future misunderstandings, these approvals should be in writing and signed by both parties. (Ethical considerations are addressed in detail in Chapter 13.)

Professional Designations. While it is quite possible that someone can be an excellent real estate manager without them, achievement of one or more professional designations by fulfilling the established educational and other requirements is evidence to the client community of an interest in the business and a desire to establish and enhance one's professional credentials. It also stands to reason that a client looking at competing management firms is more likely to choose the one whose people have professional designations over the company that has not bothered to participate in such programs. There is also substantial evidence that the income of managers who have achieved professional designations is higher than that of managers who do not.

The start-up management company faces some very difficult challenges in acquiring the first few accounts. Selling a client on the idea that you will do a first-class job when you do not have any properties under management can be daunting. However, when a manager has a professional designation in the field, he or she has demonstrated competence in that area of real estate management, and that fact alone is likely to make the first client more comfortable with having the start-up company manage his or her property.

An additional benefit of having designations is that they help a client justify using the start-up company. This is especially true of institutional investors who tend to be very conservative in their selection of management services. Institutions are very much interested in the background of the company and, more specifically, the person who will actually oversee their property. In addition, they generally want a manager who has prior experience managing for institutional owners so that he or she is aware of the reporting requirements and the need for timeliness and accuracy.

The fact that a manager has one or more designations does not guarantee that he or she will do a good job of managing a property. However, when a real estate owner is deciding between two different management companies, and one has a staff with designations and one does not, it is much easier to justify choosing the management company whose personnel have invested the time and effort to obtain professional designations. (There are several professional designations within the field of real estate management. They are discussed, along with the organizations that grant them, in Appendix B.)

A Sense of Personal Satisfaction

Launching a new management company successfully is a tremendously exciting accomplishment. The chances for success can be greatly enhanced by good planning and an objective in-depth analysis of the local marketplace. One has to consider who is in the market now, what services are or are not being offered (i.e., opportunities to fill a need), and what the chances are, realistically, of capturing a sufficient share of that market to assure success. There is obviously no guarantee of success for any business, but the real estate management business that is based on sound analysis of the market has a better-than-average chance of succeeding.

3

Strategizing Business Operations

The ultimate challenge for a company is to strike a balance between making a profit and providing a service. Most managers will agree that if you do not focus on providing the service, you are not likely to derive the hoped-for profits or have the resources to provide quality service.

At successful management companies, serving the client is the top priority. Clients do not want to hear that you are busy with other problems or that you cannot return their telephone calls until tomorrow. From the level of service to the property and the degree of attentiveness to its owner, each individual client should believe that the firm manages only one property—theirs. When a client needs something done, the real estate manager is expected to respond as quickly and efficiently as possible. However, to best serve the client, it is important to find out exactly what that client's demands are, initially and on an ongoing basis. Many management companies have failed because the clients' expectations greatly exceeded the level of service anticipated in their management proposal.

Apart from clients' specific needs and demands, the management company must also operate as a business. Many, indeed most, of its own operational requirements will be similar to or derived from those of its various clients. Where the company can focus on itself is in regard to profitability. Operating the clients' properties profitably should, one might reasonably assume, make the management company comparably profitable. However, if its internal operations are not efficient or cost-effective, or if the financial checks and balances exercised for the clients are not applied with equal vigilance to the firm's operations, the profits can be drastically reduced or, worse, nonexistent.

Since clients are the lifeblood of the management business, this chapter

> **One Client Versus Many**
>
> While there are often uncertainties when a company has only one client, there are advantages to this situation. With a single client, you work with only one set of policies and procedures, one reporting package, a single management philosophy, and the one owner. This makes everyday operations much easier. It must be acknowledged, however, that when your one client decides to take the property in house or to sell the properties to someone who has a relationship with another management firm, the loss of that client's business has a significant (and possibly critical) impact on your company's income. This type of outcome is avoided when the management company (or function) is a captive of the property owner, but that situation creates other problems.
>
> Most third-party management companies serve several clients. Even some captive management companies may serve "outside" clients, so they must be aware of the needs, policies, and procedures of each owner. The difficulty comes in being sure to "change hats" when you are conducting business for different clients. Some property owners want to be involved in every operational decision while others will be content to approve a budget and let the manager operate within the established framework. On the other hand, most major clients have their own accounting packages and specific reporting requirements. In order to make sure the manager is in compliance with each different management agreement, the particulars of the agreements should be summarized on a form for use as a ready reference in making decisions. If there is a question that cannot be answered from the agreement summary, the client should be contacted for instructions and to be sure everyone involved has the same understanding.

will first address their operational needs. The company's own requirements will be discussed after that.

Focusing on Your Clients

Because real estate management is a service business, its operations will be specifically focused on serving the needs of its various customers—the owners of the properties they manage and the residents and commercial tenants who occupy them. The client's ownership goals provide the primary direction for the management of the property. Everything else that relates to property operations follows from that.

Ownership Goals. Not everyone owns real estate for the same reasons. Sometimes an owner's goal may be immediate disposition (a reluctant heir of a sole proprietor; a property acquired as part of a corporate buyout or merger) or to maintain status quo in anticipation of disposition (properties in receivership or bankruptcy). In such situations, the objective may simply be to generate revenue and minimize cash expenditures until the property can be disposed. In the case of low-income housing, there is often a social

> ### Management Strategies and the Property Owner's Goals
>
> Clients have expectations of achieving their ownership goals. The following are some questions to consider in determining strategies for managing specific properties.
>
> - How do the owner's goals affect the way we will handle the account?
> - What issues can we expect to deal with?
> - What would be the key elements of a management plan we would suggest to the owner for this property?
>
> Also to be considered is how different types of ownership goals are likely to affect the management company's operations.

purpose—the provision of housing to those who may not be able to afford it otherwise.

However, the most likely goals of ownership are cash flow (periodic income), capital growth (investment return), business use, and pride of ownership. In many situations, more than one of these reasons will apply. The owner's goals will determine how the property is managed on a day-to-day basis and how much authority the manager will have in handling fiscal issues. Ideally, the owner's goals will be clearly defined, and the management agreement will establish operating parameters for the property that will allow those goals to be met. (The management agreement will be discussed in detail in Chapter 9.)

- *Periodic Income* The pure cash flow owner generally is living off the income from the property. This might be an individual who purchased real estate to provide income for his or her future retirement or an investor who expects to live off the periodic income from the property exclusively (i.e., has no other source of income). REIT investors may make their investment decision based on the company's track record of providing substantial quarterly dividends.
- *Return on Investment* This type of owner generally is looking for long-term capital growth and is less interested in the day-to-day cash flow. In order to achieve capital appreciation, the owner is more likely to sacrifice short-term cash flow for a bigger long-term gain.
- *Business Use* Typically, this type of owner has a large space requirement. Department stores—and, more recently, supermarkets and drug stores—have often bought their own sites and built their own stores, thereby reducing their occupancy costs. This approach costs them less than they would pay in rent for the same amount of space because they are able to obtain financing more favorably than the developer of a large site can. As owners, they also benefit from the upside potential as the property's value increases over time.

- *Pride of Ownership* Many owners have diverse portfolios that include investment-grade real estate as part of the mix. While these owners may be interested in cash flow or long-term capital growth, or both, they also take great pride in the real estate they own and enjoy pointing out their properties to others. This type of owner generally buys only better properties and then takes very good care of them.

Once the owner's specific goals have been established, it is the manager's job to be proactive in meeting them. Much of the specific direction will be set forth in the management agreement—the result of the negotiation of individual points. Apart from the management agreement, the client—especially an institutional owner—may have an accounting procedures manual to be followed and perhaps an insurance policy statement and an operating policy manual. Finally, some of the specific direction will be forthcoming in the various discussions with the client during take-over of the account. (Specifics of taking over a management account are discussed in detail in Chapter 10.)

The measure of the manager's success in achieving the client's ownership goals is the periodic, usually monthly, reports submitted to the owner. This is another area where owners' requirements can be very different.

Reporting Requirements. The sole proprietor who owns a small apartment property may not want any specific reports other than a general summary of the financial activity—an income statement and explanation. However, that will be the exception. More typical is the owner of a commercial property who needs a variety of data reported, though not necessarily in separate formats. At the other end of the spectrum is the institutional owner who is likely to require a variety of statistical and descriptive reports every month. An operating statement supported by specifics regarding rent collections, delinquencies, marketing and leasing activities, and financial details is the least that might be required. Depending on the type of property and the scope of its operations, there may be more or fewer detailed numerical reports—usually prepared by the accounting department (see Chapter 4). These are accompanied by one or more narrative reports that outline management's accomplishments as well as explain financial shortfalls and suggest solutions for ongoing problems. The narrative portion of the report usually covers some three to ten pages.

Components of the client report package are described in Exhibit 3.1 (pp. 56–57). All these reports are typically prepared on a monthly basis and submitted to the owners on an agreed-upon date. If the books are closed at the end of the calendar month, the reports are generally due by the 15th of the following month. Some owners may want their reports earlier and therefore have the books for their properties closed before the end of the month.

> **Owners' Reports—Some Considerations**
>
> - Issues that impact how the report is formatted—
>   —Type of client.
>   —Number of personnel and internal approvals required.
>   —Costs of preparing reports and impact on management fee(s).
> - What data are needed?
> - Where do the data come from?
> - Who will collect and assemble the data?
> - What is the time frame for delivery to the client?
> - How will it be delivered?
> - How do we protect confidentiality if delivery is electronic (fax, modem)?
>
> Also to be considered are priorities (What has to be done? What can wait?) and how they impact management company personnel (If your personnel work overtime, how are they compensated?). Clients may want special formats or specific software programs utilized, and sometimes they provide the software. If not, the management firm may have to acquire it (Is this a management company cost or reimbursed by the client?).

It is not unusual to close the books on the 25th of the month so the owners' reports can be in their hands by the 10th of the month.

The Annual Property Management Plan. Sophisticated institutional owners require very extensive annual management plans for their properties. Typically, an annual operating budget and management plan is submitted to each property owner during the last two months of the current budget year, discussed in detail, changed as necessary until agreement is reached, and then finalized for the coming fiscal year (the adopted *fiscal year* may be a twelve-month period other than a calendar year). Some institutional owners want these materials presented earlier. Once the expense budget and operating plan for the next year have been accepted by the owner, it is a good idea to have the final approval in writing; such documentation assures that there is no misunderstanding as to the direction to be taken in managing the property. The purpose of the annual management plan is for everyone to look at every facet of the property and determine the best course of action for the coming year. The plan is prepared as a report and includes regional and neighborhood analyses, a summary of the current marketplace, projections regarding lease expirations and resident or commercial tenant turnovers, plus a forecast of capital expenditures and an annual operating budget. Other operational details, including an analysis of the property, are also included. The components of the annual management plan are described in Exhibit 3.2 (pp. 58–60).

Still another consideration in preparing management plans is the personnel who will work on them. How will the work be co-ordinated among

Exhibit 3.1
Typical Components of a Monthly Management Report Package

The monthly management report to the owner typically includes a series of narratives that describe the operations and activities at the property followed by numerical reports that detail specifics.

Financial Narrative Property owners usually consider the financial narrative or *executive summary* the most important section in the monthly management report. Here variances between projected and actual income and expenses for the month and the year-to-date are explained. Some owners require an explanation for all expenses that exceed the budgeted amount by a predetermined percentage or dollar amount (e.g., five percent or two hundred dollars); however, that should not be the only criterion for discussing specific variances, particularly if a trend is becoming apparent over a several-month period. This overview report may be presented first with the various other reports following as backup.

Operations and Maintenance Report This narrative reviews management's actions such as rebidding of contracts (e.g., for janitorial service) or installation of equipment (e.g., a replacement chiller, new energy-conserving lighting).

Move-In/Move-Out Report Although used more often for residential properties than for commercial properties, this information is useful for both. The report shows occupancy at the beginning of the month, move-ins and move-outs during the month, and occupancy at the end of the month. Some owners may want these data reconciled with actual income to see if the two are in agreement. (This may supersede a specific vacancy report or be provided as additional information on the vacancy report.)

Tenant Retention Report In this report, all resident and commercial tenant retention programs—whether implemented or in the planning stages—are reviewed. Although it is preferable to keep this information separate, retention is or should be an extension of the marketing process, and if not budgeted separately, a portion of the marketing budget should be allocated to tenant retention.

Marketing and Advertising Report This is a review of the marketing and advertising activities during the month, with copies of advertisements and promotional materials included. This particular type of reporting is more typical of a residential property; however, if the managed property is a shopping center, activities that promoted the center as a whole (e.g., a sidewalk sale or an arts and crafts show) would be described along with the results obtained.

Leasing Status Report This report is a listing of prospects who are being considered for particular spaces, where lease negotiations stand as of the report date, and whether particular prospects seem to be viable. (The format for commercial properties will be very different from that for residential properties.) This is one way of keeping everyone informed about ongoing lease negotiations. The leasing status report is especially critical during lease-up of a new or rehabilitated property when there are many vacancies to be filled in the shortest time possible.

Commercial Tenant Analysis Retail tenants' sales are analyzed by comparing the current month and year-to-date figures to those from the same month and year-to-date period in the previous year. This report indicates comparative success of individual tenants—or their potential failure. It also compares tenants' sales to those of other retailers on the property and to national data for similar uses (average dollars per square foot).

Capital Improvement Summary This is generally submitted only when there are ongoing capital projects. It sets out the budgeted amounts for specific projects, shows what has been spent to date, and projects total expenditures relative to the original budget. Tenant improvements are often included in this report as well.

Exhibit 3.1 *(continued)*

Litigation Report Unfortunately, some properties seem to have a fair number of lawsuits in progress at any one time. Whether the litigation results from a tenant defaulting on a lease, a landlord-tenant dispute, or a trip-and-fall incident in the parking lot, the property owner will want to know the current status of all ongoing litigation and an estimate of the outcome (whether and how much it is likely to be settled for and when). Although the specific consequences are usually financial, much of this information will most likely be obtained from the legal counsel responsible for prosecuting or defending the individual lawsuits on the owner's behalf. While the types of incidents named here are ubiquitous, residential properties are increasingly subject to lawsuits claiming discriminatory leasing and/or marketing practices, and all types of properties are being sued for liability based on negligence in providing security.

Monthly Operating Statement This will generally be prepared in some detail, showing budgeted amounts and actual receipts and expenditures for both the current month and the year-to-date. Variances from budget are also indicated for both periods (usually showing both dollars and percentages and whether the variance is favorable or unfavorable), and these are explained in the narrative summary. (The budget variance analysis may also be generated as a separate adjunct report.) The operating statement should reflect the accounting method being used—i.e., cash-basis, accrual-basis, or modified accrual.

Current Tenant Roster (Rent Roll) Most rosters include the resident's or commercial tenant's name, the unit or space number, the rental rate, a record of any refundable deposits, and the lease commencement and expiration dates. At commercial properties, option dates and types of options, square footage and rent per square foot, scheduled rent increases, and perhaps even specifics about operating expense pass-throughs (sometimes called billbacks) will usually be included, and other lease terms may be detailed as necessary or appropriate. While some owners ask to see a tenant roster or rent roll only when there has been a change in tenancy, others will want an updated roster provided on an ongoing basis as well as the one accompanying the monthly management reports.

Delinquency Report Generally, delinquency reports are provided throughout the month (e.g., on the 5th, 10th, and 20th), and as a fully aged report at the end of the month. The outstanding amounts are generally broken out in separate categories. The delinquency for a specific tenant at a commercial property, for example, may show amounts for the current month's rent and common area maintenance (CAM) prorations plus outstanding CAM charges (30 days past due) while that for a residential unit might show the current month's rent and parking charges plus other outstanding items. Almost all owners want some explanation of the action being taken to collect the monies due and the likelihood of collecting them in full. (Eviction proceedings may be noted here as well.)

General Ledger Also included with most operating statements is a copy of the general ledger showing the current month's transactions as well as the year-to-date cumulative totals in each category of income and expense. This not only allows the owner to evaluate the amounts of individual expenditures, but also indicates who is receiving payments for what services and materials.

Bank Account Reconciliation One of the more critical monthly reports is the reconciliation of what is actually in the bank (as reported on the bank statement) with what is supposed to be there (receipts deposited versus checks drawn against the account). This report should account for checks written but not cleared and deposits made but not recorded.

If warranted, there may be separate reports addressing contracted services such as leasing or collections; otherwise these activities would be included, respectively, in the leasing or delinquency report. Copies of property inspection reports and other related information may be included in the package as appropriate. (Accounting methodologies and bank account reconciliation are discussed in Chapter 4.)

Exhibit 3.2
Typical Components of an Annual Management Plan

Regional Analysis This section provides an overall description of the current economic condition in the region. Included within the regional analysis are changes that have occurred in past years and apparent or emerging trends, looking at both strengths and weaknesses to arrive at a reasonable assumption about the probable future of the region (e.g., population growth or decline).

Neighborhood Analysis This analysis includes a description of the neighborhood and a listing of new and emerging competitive properties, along with physical, social, political, demographic, and economic characteristics and trends that may affect the future of the subject property, especially changes from prior analyses.

Summary of the Market In order to develop marketing and leasing strategies, a survey is made of competitive properties in the marketplace, comparing them to the client's property and projecting how they are all likely to interface during the coming year. Features, amenities, and rents are among the points of comparison. This report will help determine basic rental rates and lease terms for the coming year and establish the marketing and leasing strategies and occupancy goals for the property.

Lease Expirations This is a list of every current resident or commercial tenant at the property in order of their respective lease expiration dates. Such a listing allows property owners to see when groups of leases will be coming up for renewal. If appropriate, negotiating strategies may be changed for a commercial site in order to retain tenants or seek new tenants who will make the property more successful.

Leasing Assumptions Data from the market survey and lease expiration reports are used to make assumptions about future vacancies and other leasing parameters. This is essentially an estimate of turnovers and periods of vacancy. For a commercial property, the manager will analyze each unit that is or will become vacant during the year, projecting an occupancy date, rental rate, lease term, and tenant improvement allowance, if any. If appropriate, a commission expense will also be estimated. For a residential property, the number of units that will turn over and the vacancy rate for each month would be listed, along with expected renewals and projected rent increases. Unit make-ready costs might also be estimated, especially if any painting or refurbishing is to be done. This report together with the market data and lease expirations may be developed into a separate formalized marketing plan (discussed later in this exhibit).

Basic Budget This is a comprehensive income and expense budget that details each component of the income stream; aggregate figures are used in projecting an *annual operating budget*. In this case, each current resident or commercial tenant is listed, along with the monthly rent to be paid and the revenue expected for the year. Quite often, pass-through expense items such as real estate taxes, property insurance, and common area maintenance (CAM) costs will also be accounted on a tenant-by-tenant basis for commercial properties. For residential properties, however, rental income may be estimated as a lump sum (with an explanation of how the total was derived), although a mix of unit sizes and a wide range of rental rates may warrant a unit-by-unit or resident-by-resident listing. Other sources of income (e.g., parking fees, coin laundry facilities, administrative charges) would be listed separately. Expenses are estimated using last year's actual expenses and adjusting the figures for inflation, changes in contract rates, and/or changing market conditions. This budget may be prepared on a cash or accrual—or modified accrual—basis.

As backup schedules for the basic budget at a commercial property, several additional items may be included—

Exhibit 3.2 *(continued)*

— *Building operating expense recapture*—Generally, there will be a schedule listing each tenant's pro-rata share of the operating expenses of the office building, shopping center, or industrial site (pass-throughs or bill-backs) and how much the manager anticipates will be collected from each.
— *Tax allocation*—This schedule, too, will show, tenant-by-tenant, the tax allocation as stated in their respective leases, projecting the percentage of the overall tax bill that is likely to be collected.
— *Shopping center insurance allocation*—This often requires two separate schedules because liability insurance premiums for the parking lot would be allocated to all tenants at the property, but fire and extended coverage on the building is usually allocated only to the ancillary or shop tenants (anchor tenants frequently insure their own buildings).

Capital Expenditures This report may simply list anticipated capital expenditures for the coming year, itemized by project and the date when the expense would be incurred, or it may be a five-year forecast to give the owner a sense of large expenditures that may be anticipated in the coming years. These expenditures may be paid out of reserve funds that already exist, or it may be appropriate to anticipate an amount to be set aside each month to accumulate the needed capital. In some situations, the ownership may need to fund these expenses out of pocket. (Developers and institutional owners may not establish reserve funds.) A specific capital budget may be included or substituted for this report.

Property Analysis This section presents a description of the property, including the square footage and acreage measures of the site, the number and size of the buildings and other improvements, the type of building construction materials and architectural design, and the building's features and amenities. Depending on the property type, the mix of residential units or the commercial anchor tenants will also be described.

Contractors and Vendors Each existing contract or vendor-provided service is listed with its current cost and expiration date. Assumptions about likely changes in contract terms and costs for the next year (if the contract is extended) are included.

Tenant Retention Programs The next year's resident retention or commercial tenant retention program is described, along with specific costs and the intended impact. Alternatively, this may be included as a discrete section of the marketing plan.

Management and Operations This section is a description of how the property will be managed in the coming year. It includes a discussion of the on-site staff and all contracted services. The past year's major maintenance and capital expenditures are also reviewed, and a capital expenditure and major maintenance plan for the ensuing one- to five-year period is included. (This is narrative and rationale; the numerical data were included in the capital expenditures section.)

Marketing and Advertising The marketing and advertising plan for the coming year is outlined, including strategies and campaigns, the timing of activities, and projected expenditures. This information may be coordinated with anticipated leasing and occupancy results—and tenant retention marketing efforts—discussed elsewhere in the management plan.

Appendix Supporting materials such as photographs, copies of pertinent articles (especially news items about the regional economy and trends manifesting in the local marketplace), bids for service contracts and/or anticipated capital expenditures, etc., are compiled in this section and referenced in the respective applicable sections of the plan.

The order in which particular components of the plan are presented may follow the sequence shown here; however, this listing cannot be considered all-inclusive. The unique needs and challenges of individual properties should determine the particular contents—for example,

Exhibit 3.2 *(continued)*

leasing assumptions might be addressed only in a separate marketing plan. For a commercial property management plan, prorated pass-through expenses (e.g., building operating expense recapture, real estate tax and insurance allocations) might be subentries in the budget section. We would recommend, however, that a set order be established by the management company or agreed-to by the owner-client and the manager and then followed in succeeding years. This will not only facilitate preparation of these management plans each year, but also allow owners and managers to make comparisons more easily over a period of time.

Beginning with a mission or vision statement sets the tone for the entire plan. Inclusion of global and national economic information adds perspective. Legal issues and exposures may also be appropriate components of an annual management plan if there are pending lawsuits or regulatory compliance issues that will have to be addressed during the year. Plans for shopping centers may also include a retail tenant analysis (comparison of each tenant's current year's sales to its prior year's sales and to national averages; projections of percentage rent payments may be included) and consideration of marketing the property to the general public (marketing fund or merchants' association activities).

Usual practice is to include a section itemizing conclusions and recommendations. When appropriate, an analysis of alternatives—including a comparison of costs and benefits—may be included. Special issues that impact the property (e.g., new technologies, changes in measurement standards, metrication) may also warrant separate consideration. The whole may be described in an Executive Summary with many of the analyses and supporting data provided as appendices. This may be done more commonly in a management plan that is part of an initial proposal and in annual plans that address a particular problem or recommend a departure from past actions.

Sources for market-specific comparison data for different types of properties include the following (see also Appendix C):

Dollars and Cents of Shopping Centers published by ULI—The Urban Land Institute includes sales figures (dollars per square foot) for different categories of tenants and typical percentage rates used for calculating percentage rents. In addition to the comprehensive volume, there are compilations specific to different types of shopping centers.

Experience Exchange Report for Downtown and Suburban Office Buildings publishing by the Building Owners and Managers Association International (BOMA) compiles economic data for metropolitan areas.

Income/Expense Analysis® reports for conventional apartments, federally assisted apartments, office buildings, and shopping centers, and *Expense Analysis*® for condominiums, cooperatives, and PUDs published by the Institute of Real Estate Management compile economic statistics for metropolitan areas.

---

the site manager, the property manager, and the company executive? Who will actually write the various sections? What levels of approval will be required? There is also the issue of preparation time and the length of the plan to be considered. A 10-page document is likely to be less complex and take less time than one 100 pages in length.

The annual management plan is similar to the initial proposal that was instrumental in obtaining the agreement to manage the property. Many of the same kinds of analyses are required, and it may be appropriate, especially in the early years of a management relationship, to reference the proposal, recount progress made in accomplishing those initial management goals, and point out how the next year's plan carries the program forward.

Communicating with Clients. Communication is the cornerstone of successful manager-client relations. Two of the standard phrases in the property management business are "no surprises" and "give the bad news first." No one, least of all real estate managers, likes the idea of being the bearer of bad news; but owners must be advised about conditions and incidents occurring at their properties in a timely manner. It is not enough simply to submit monthly management reports on time. Often it is necessary to seek their insights or preferences as well as their approval to take action that may be outside the bounds of what was anticipated in the original management plan or management agreement. For example, a situation may arise that has the potential to be problematic. Even though the manager may believe it will not actually come to that, it is still a good idea to inform the owner and include an analysis of the situation and the steps being taken to ensure that it will not become a major problem.

As real estate managers become more proficient at what they do, they tend to take it for granted that everyone knows what they are doing. Unfortunately, some clients may be thousands of miles away and have no way of knowing what is happening at their properties on a day-to-day basis unless the manager tells them. It is much better to make a practice of over-informing owners. If important information has not been passed along to the owner, and what was originally a minor incident becomes a major situation later, the manager may be accused of trying to hide something or, even worse, not understanding how serious the situation really was. (Communication with owner-clients can encompass a variety of methods and vehicles. These are discussed in detail in Chapter 6.)

Contracting on Behalf of Owners. One of the most common responsibilities assumed by management is that of contracting for services for the property. This is also an activity that has a potential to cause problems for the management company and therefore requires careful handling. The major risk is the possibility that the real estate manager will be held liable if the owner does not pay the bills. For this reason, the best way to contract on behalf of a property owner is either in the name of the property (West Over Apartments) or in the name of the owner (West Over Funds, Ltd.), showing XYZ Management Company, Joe Evans, Vice President, as managing agent (or independent subcontractor). The management agreement should establish the parameters for contracting on behalf of the property owner and state the extent—or limits— of the manager's authority to make particular arrangements (see Chapter 9).

Utility Contracts. Utility accounts can be especially problematic, but it is in the management firm's best interest to be sure they are set up correctly. Because a great deal of information about the business entity is required, a start-up management company may have difficulty establishing credit with a utility. It is inappropriate, however, for a manager to use his or her personal credit in support of a utility contract because it can take several years to remove a name from an account, and that means continued personal liability if bills go unpaid.

Long-Term Contracts. Most sophisticated property management agreements will limit the contracts that can be signed by a real estate manager on behalf of the owner to a term of no more than one year. However, some types of contracts simply cannot be made for short terms (i.e., one year or less), and others require a longer term in order to be financially beneficial. For example, a discount may be provided in a longer-term contract (e.g., 3–5 years). Such contracts should include a 30-day cancellation clause, and they may provide for any discount to be reimbursed or prorated if the contract is cancelled. The most common example that comes to mind is a full-service elevator contract. In instances where it is desirable or necessary for a contract to exceed the duration allowed under the management agreement, the manager should obtain the owner's written approval to establish the contract.

In some cases, it is advisable to have the owner execute the contract personally so there is no question of its being approved. It may be important to know if any restrictions exist regarding the ownership entity's ability to sign long-term contracts. Some institutional owners may limit contractual arrangements for services to a set period (e.g., no longer than two years). We would also point out that it is not unusual for an owner to have the right to cancel such service contracts in the event the property is sold or foreclosed. Most sophisticated owners will also require a blanket 30-day cancellation clause.

The contents of contracts should be scrutinized for specifics. Managers need to be alert to so-called evergreen clauses (i.e., automatic renewals) in longer-term contracts. The original contract may be for a set term (e.g., five years). However, termination may require advance notice (60 days, 6 months), and if such notice is not given in writing, the contract will renew automatically for another full term (i.e., five more years). This is often seen in elevator maintenance contracts in particular.

Bidding Contracts. If a manager were spending his or her own money, it would not really matter to anyone else whether there were several bids on a contract or not. The manager could choose to deal with a relative or a personal friend in that situation. However, when managers spend others' money, they assume a fiduciary responsibility. Either by contract agreement or by moral imperative, they have an obligation to be sure they are getting the best deal for the property and its owner. It should be noted, however, that *the best deal does not always mean the lowest price.*

Most sophisticated owners will insist on at least three bids for all jobs that exceed a given dollar limit. They will also insist on annual contracts being rebid every year or two. The situation becomes even more complicated when a commercial property is being managed because these items are billed back to the tenants. This requirement adds another layer of financial obligation because the manager must also ensure that the tenants are not paying more than they should. The management of condominium associations, where one is contracting on behalf of the unit owners as a group, presents a similar challenge.

Specifications. To be certain that all bids are based on the same requirements, it is incumbent on the real estate manager to write a complete set of specifications for the job to be done and then to be sure that all contractors' bids are written to those specifications. Contractors who think they have a better approach should be required to present their ideas as a separate (or alternate) bid. Handling alternatives this way allows the manager to evaluate all the bids based on the original specifications and, in addition, consider any creative solutions that were not part of the original bid package. Once a vendor is selected, all the other bids should be kept in a file and made available to the property owner if he or she wants to review them personally.

Relations with Residents and Commercial Tenants. The income at residential and commercial properties is derived from the residents and business tenants who lease space there. In the past, there was often an attitude that the resident or tenant was of little importance—if one tenant was a problem or a little difficult, there would always be another tenant to take that one's place. This lax attitude also affected the tenants who often would claim, "The owners don't really care about us; we're just a tax write off." Such comments indicate that the third-party managers of the real estate were not doing their job. Over time, however, real estate owners and managers have come to realize that the best resident or tenant may well be the one that is already in place. When it is an owner's market (the available space is not sufficient to fulfill demand), the real estate manager is doing his or her job if tenants remain in place and rental income is maximized. However, when it is a renter's market (there are more spaces than potential tenants), far more sensitivity is needed because the rent payer can easily lease space elsewhere.

Most property owners do not interact directly with residents or commercial tenants as frequently as managers do, so it is more likely that the latter's dissatisfaction is with the manager and not the owner. Good tenant relations is more than just remembering their names and greeting them cheerfully when you see them. *Tenant retention*—motivating residents and commercial tenants to renew their leases year after year—begins before the

Exhibit 3.3
Tenant Relations Strategies

- View the property from the tenants' perspective.
- Welcome new tenants—orient them to the property, the management company personnel, their immediate neighbors, and the community at large.
- Keep accurate, up-to-date records—make sure billings for extra charges are consistent with tenants' lease terms.
- Maintain the appearance (curb appeal) and general condition of the property.
- Establish and maintain communications—install a toll-free phone number in the absence of on-site management so tenants can communicate with you easily.
- Visit tenants regularly—ask how they are faring and invite their comments about the management of the property.
- Ask what will make your tenants happy—regular surveys keep you informed of individual tenants' problems, perceptions, and preferences.
- Be proactive in relating to tenants—establish programs with a human side; make tenants want to stay at the property you manage.

There are infinite ways of creating goodwill, and the most effective ways often cost nothing. We would also offer this caution: Asking about problems creates an expectation that something will be done about them. You should be prepared to take action if you invite complaints.

---

original lease is signed and should be a continuing effort throughout their entire tenancies. Some helpful approaches to tenant relations are shown in Exhibit 3.3; the strategies outlined there are applicable to all types of properties. Information on other specific strategies can be found in *THE Tenant Retention Solution* and *The Resident Retention Revolution* (see Appendix C).

Focusing on the Management Company

Although clients' needs guide most of the management company's operations, it is also important to focus on the company's specific needs. A well-crafted business plan will include specific policies and procedures to facilitate decisions and ensure that the management office and the managed properties operate efficiently and cost-effectively. The latter is of particular importance because of the impact on the bottom line—the profitability of the management portfolio and the individuals who manage the properties in it. (Business planning is discussed in Chapter 2.)

Policies and Procedures. Policies and procedures can be likened to a road map for your employees—a guide frequently used by new employees and a reference manual used by employees who are familiar with the company when they are confronted with a new or rare situation. They are, first and foremost, a tool to standardize the way employees handle specific assignments. This is especially important when you have branch offices and when managed properties have on-site management or maintenance personnel or both. Usually, the company's policies and procedures are compiled into an *operations manual*. This manual will cover day-to-day operational procedures for the company and its personnel and include forms and sample letters for use in different situations.

In addition to an operations manual for the management company office, a separate manual should be prepared for each managed property. The latter will focus on the particular requirements of the property and may necessarily include components from the client's operating manual or adaptations of the management firm's policies and procedures made to be consistent with the property owner's requirements. Usually the differences are in the details because each property has unique features, and the manager must address them specifically in order for management of the property to be efficient and cost-effective. The discussion presented here covers real estate management operations in general and, as a result, some property-specific components that are likely not to be detailed in the firm's basic office operations manual are included.

The Operations Manual. Once the decision has been made to write an operations manual, there are three basic questions to ask:

1. What are the objectives?
2. Who is the audience?
3. How should it look?

If data in the manual are constantly changing (e.g., technical data), portions of it are likely to require frequent updating, but whole sections (e.g., one that addresses on-site mechanical equipment) may not require updating unless the entire manual is being revised. There are four principal objectives of operations manuals:

1. To inform employees of policies.
2. To instruct employees in procedures.
3. To provide technical data for reference.
4. To define the scope of the job and relate it to the total organization.

The purpose must be clear from the outset since it will dictate content, style, format, and length. The objective will suggest the audience. Carefully segregating or segmenting the audience has several benefits. First, irrelevant information can be eliminated. Second, the manual can be written using the terminology common to a defined group—the style and approach will be very different in a manual for the maintenance department and one for leasing agents whose only need to know about maintenance is what to do in extreme emergencies. A series of streamlined manuals directed to specific audiences is considerably more efficient than a comprehensive general manual.

Once the audience has been defined and the objective established, it will be much easier to decide what topics should be included. The following list represents the more common components of an operations manual and a presentation sequence that has been successfully employed by many companies.

- Company policies
- Leasing procedures
- Maintenance procedures
- Property services
- Accounting and fiscal controls
- Resident and tenant relations
- Employee relations
- Safety and security
- Construction
- Forms (including sample letters)
- Community relations

This list is not meant to be all-inclusive, but rather to serve as a guide in the preparation of an operations manual. The exclusion from the list of categories like marketing and contract negotiations only implies that these activities are most likely to be addressed within a related category—e.g., marketing with leasing, contracts with construction or maintenance. A more detailed break out of contents might include a description of the organization, its philosophy (mission statement) and its personnel. There might also be separate categories for vendor contracts, possibly subdivided by type (e.g., janitorial, landscaping), and compliance procedures (i.e., related to ADA, fair housing, environmental regulations). The needs of your management company and those of the properties in your portfolio should be your primary guidelines.

It is also appropriate to include a "fact sheet" that identifies those sections of the manual that apply strictly to the main office of the management company and ways to access personnel there—e.g., business hours; telephone, fax, pager, and answering service numbers; mailing address (street number, post office box, bank lock box), emergency or after-hours contacts.

Probably the most important objective of an operations manual is to spell out the elements of each function of the business. It should delineate procedures for performing each task and establish a standard against which every employee can measure his or her work. In defining job responsibilities, it is usually best to refer to functions or use position titles rather than employees' names. (Manuals that use names are quickly outdated when employees are promoted or leave the firm.) Titles can also be used in organizational charts linked to the manual; this way lines of authority and responsibility are clearly linked. A single supplementary page listing job titles and employees' names can be updated as required and need not be formally incorporated into the manual.

The appearance of the manual will depend on the format and type style you choose, whether or not you include illustrations, the paper stock and printing and binding methods, and how you index the contents. Most of these decisions will be based on the final size of the manual and the amount budgeted for it. The standard $8\frac{1}{2} \times 11$-inch page size is recommended since it can be easily reproduced on a photocopier. Forms, memos, and letters on company stationery can also be incorporated easily. (Templates for forms and reports that are prepared by computer can also be made available on floppy disks.) Although looseleaf binding (standard three-ring notebook) may be a more costly alternative, especially if you have binders custom imprinted, it is an efficient method of packaging an operations manual and probably the most economical choice in the long run.

The contents of the company's operations manual is often incorporated into management proposal packages, which further commends careful attention to the format and packaging. Also, because you will have operations manuals distributed among the personnel at the properties you manage, a durable, attractive, updatable form is most desirable.

It is indisputable that manuals are more effective when they are clear and concise. The following are guidelines for accomplishing that goal:

- Use direct, concise, active sentences. Readers lose interest quickly when sentences are indirect and long.
- Make it personal. Do not be afraid to use any word that will let the reader know you are talking to him or her (e.g., pronouns: you, yours, we, they, our, etc.); referring always to "the company" and "the employee" is too formal and rigid.
- Use the obvious, natural expression. Convert ponderous phrases to crisp, lean expressions—why say, "in the event that," when "if" does the job?
- Trim the fat. Excess words that merely repeat what you have already told the reader will only weigh down your manual. Four-line sentences can be cut to two lines or shorter; with careful pruning, you can end up with a third fewer words, and the reader will understand you better.
- Use action verbs. Pick out the word that describes the action you want your reader to take; build your sentence around that word.

Company Operations Manual

If not created or anticipated in the business plan for the management company, one of the first actions to be taken is development of an operations manual. This should set out your operating policies and procedures and cover all aspects of the management company's business activities.

- Hiring, training, and supervision of employees.
- Employee compensation, benefits, and "work rules."
- Lines of authority and responsibility for internal decisions.
- Accounting for and disposition of receipts and expenditures—including internal checks and balances.
- Accounting services that will be provided to property owner-clients—within the management fee and as extras.
- An overall philosophy of real estate management—the company's vision and mission statements and goals; its commitment to ethical practices.
- The company's approach to acquiring management business—promotional vehicles, development of management proposals and presentations.
- Records to be kept for different types of managed properties and standardized forms for recording different types of data.
- Record retention policies—which records will be retained for how long and the manner in which they will be disposed when no longer needed.
- The company's commitment to protecting the civil rights of employees, residents, and commercial tenants and prospects who aspire to those roles.
- How performance and profitability of managed properties and property managers will be measured and how often.
- Measures to be implemented to ensure the security and safety of employees and their workplace and the protection of the company's financial assets, including specific emergency procedures.

The goal is to have a smooth-running, efficient organization in which every employee knows his or her unique job and is also an active participant on the management team.

You may well create several operations manuals over time. In addition to a company-wide collection of policies and procedures, it is certainly appropriate to compile the rules that apply to the management office exclusively and ensure that all your employees have their own copies or access to the information they need to perform their jobs. Items related to employees and their employment (hiring and training, wages and benefits, etc.) may be developed into a separate employee manual or handbook (see also Exhibit 5.5).

- Shorten your sentences. Sentences in manuals should not run more than 17 words. A single sentence containing 39 words is about 70 percent harder to grasp than three sentences with only 13 words. Remember: Short, simple sentences are more readable and understandable.
- Build a paragraph around one single point, in a simple progression of statement, elaboration, and conclusion.

Company Operations Manual *(continued)*

Some policies and procedures you establish will apply only to managed properties (e.g., rent collection and what constitutes delinquency). However, even these will require some differentiation between residential and commercial properties as classes and, perhaps, within these larger classes there will be some distinctions for specific property types. For example, the budgeting and collections activities at condominiums and at government-assisted housing properties differ from those at conventional rental apartments and from each other. Tenant improvements are characteristic of commercial properties, but policies regarding them are different for office buildings, shopping centers, and industrial properties. Requirements for qualifying rental applicants is another management aspect that will vary by property type and even to some extent depend on the individual property. Likewise, disaster preparedness policies and procedures should be tailored to and incorporated in the on-site operating manuals for each property or established as a separate emergency procedures manual.

Use of outside services will require guidelines for negotiating contracts and parameters for making decisions. You will also need policies and procedures to guide the outside service personnel, especially if they will be interacting with your staff or with the occupants at managed properties (e.g., janitorial services).

Compliance with applicable laws and regulations has varied implications that should be addressed appropriately in policies and procedures. Fair housing laws uniquely impact residential properties. The Americans with Disabilities Act mandates nondiscrimination in employment practices as well as accessibility of "public" areas and, in that respect, affects commercial properties more directly than residential properties; it also affects the management company and its managed properties as employers. Requirements of environmental regulations promulgated at all levels of government may be expected to influence the management of industrial properties to a greater degree than other commercial or even residential properties, but these others are not without potential environmental problems.

Having policies and procedures in writing ensures uniform training of employees and consistent practices in your business operations, factors which can weigh heavily in your favor in case of a lawsuit or other dispute. They also help ensure fair and consistent treatment of employees within your company. While rules can be bent or even broken on occasion, the fact of their existence establishes boundaries on people's behavior by letting them know what is and is not acceptable. Thus, people's energies can be invested in doing a good job and doing it better instead of trying always to find out just what boundaries apply in any given situation.

Although the company's leadership will have the final say on policies and their implementation, it is extremely important for those who will be using the operations manual on a daily basis to understand the reasons for the policies and willingly follow the procedures. A brainstorming session with employees and other members of the management team to review the manual before its adoption can help identify areas that need clarification and, perhaps, suggest creative alternative approaches that otherwise might not have been considered.

> ## Contingency Planning
>
> Emergency and disaster-handling procedures for a management company have many elements in common with those for managed properties. You need to anticipate natural phenomena and man-made incidents or human events that are likely to occur and develop appropriate responses to preserve the assets of the business—primarily your employees and your records—to maintain continuity. As for a managed property, you need to identify and implement a disaster response team, develop an emergency procedures plan, define evacuation routes, make provisions for first aid, and anticipate extraordinary human needs—e.g., management of volunteers, food service, sanitary facilities. Details of these kinds of preparations have been described at length in publications devoted to the subject. For example, *Before Disaster Strikes,* a video and manual development guide published by the Institute of Real Estate Management, provides general approaches for responding to a wide array of natural and man-made disasters with suggested resources and tips on tailoring the manual to your specific needs.
>
> Assuming your business is located at a site apart from your managed properties, you will need to identify client records and other documents that must be secured at all times and removed from the business site in case of an emergency. This is where routine backup of computer files is essential. Floppy disks—data and software—should be stored securely and easily accessible for removal from the office. (Bulky computer hardware can be replaced more easily than business data and sensitive client records and documents.) Important papers such as contracts, business creation records, and tax information should also be easily removable. A good guideline is: "What do we need to keep the business going at a different site—to be up and running as quickly as possible to minimize any interruption of management services to clients' properties?" To help control the amount of material involved, disaster management professionals recommend "what

Other issues to consider are:

How many copies should be prepared?

What type of binding is best? (Saddlestitching [folded and stapled], hardcover [case] binding, loose-leaf notebook [ring binder], and spiral binding are among the many options available.)

How many pages (estimated)?

How should it be indexed? (Dividers with tabs are one of several possibilities.)

How should it be produced? (Offset printing, four-color process, and photocopying offer different qualities of printed pages.)

Should the manual be illustrated? If so, what kind of illustrations?

What plan will be used to review and distribute the manuals?

How often will the manuals be revised and who will be responsible for revising it?

> **Contingency Planning** *(continued)*
> you can collect and remove in about three minutes" as a guiding principle. In a natural disaster, you may have even less than three minutes, so a plan and periodic "drills" to train your staff will help define what to take, who is responsible, where and how it will be packaged, etc. Storing copies of files and back-up software off site is recommended to help minimize hassle if an emergency does occur.
>
> Even more important than the potential external disaster is the issue of continued operations in general. Business interruption insurance will help pay operating expenses when the company's profits—i.e., income stream—are disrupted because of property damage, but what if the principal of a sole proprietorship dies or is incapacitated? What if something happens to a partner in the firm or the CEO of a corporation? Individual wills, partnership agreements, and the documentation of incorporation are all possible ways to address succession. If a will is the only documentation, copies should be filed with the company's attorney and at the business office. Partnership and corporation papers may include specific succession rights or provide for dissolution of the business under certain circumstances. Legal counsel can best advise you on the preparation of appropriate documents and specific provisions to include. This type of information is extremely sensitive and should be made available only to those who have a need to know it. It also needs to be safeguarded (i.e., stored away from the office and not in computer files).
>
> Life insurance policies on the principals (sometimes called key person coverage) are also advisable. Your insurance agent should be able to develop a policy or policies appropriate to your company's and its owners' needs. Beyond continued operation of the business as such, you should also think about your employees—i.e., their role in such a change and how the change can affect them—and make them aware of whatever provisions have been made for the business. (Insurance needed by the management company is addressed in Chapter 11.)

It is also important to track revisions of the manual, especially when single pages or groups of pages are updated. This can be done by using a simple date code in a footer (or running footnote) at the bottom of every page. Other reference information can be incorporated in this footer as well.

Your operations manual is an excellent marketing tool to use during presentations. Potential clients will be assured that the firm has addressed almost every possible situation. It also signals to clients that all the firm's employees accomplish their tasks within the same company philosophy and that the firm provides a consistent level of service from each of its offices. Often when an institutional client has its property management provider audited, the auditor will ask for a copy of the firm's operations manual.

Economics of Management Companies. One of the most difficult aspects of real estate management is that of striking a balance between managing the property in a first-rate manner and generating a profit for the management company. That is why expansion of the business can be a two-edged sword—on the one hand, the management company has to be ready to take on new business, but if personnel are on board while the product is not, the fact of being ready for more business could be the firm's undoing. (A company that positions itself for growth and states that growth is among its objectives will always have more capacity and staff than it fully utilizes.) On the other hand, when a potential client invites a proposal on a larger portfolio, that prospect wants to know that the management company will be ready to do the job on day one, not take on the account and then try to find suitable personnel, office facilities, and equipment to fulfill its contractual obligation.

While it is perfectly normal to expect a business to grow over time, it is helpful to temper one's expectations of growth and profitability with some real-world facts. The Institute of Real Estate Management Foundation periodically surveys real estate management companies to gather comparison data on how they operate. The data requested include company charactistics—size, basic type of operation (e.g., real estate management exclusively or as a function within another business), numbers of personnel, how long they have been in business—as well as particulars of income, expenses, and profits. The statistical data are analyzed and published in a report titled *The Real Estate Management Office: Income, Expenses, and Profits* (see Appendix C). While it is impossible for the operations of any two management companies to be identical, the operations of management companies, in general, are sufficiently similar that the experiences reported by others can be used to guide some of the decisions and analyses you will make with regard to your company. Data from such surveys give the reader some idea of the range of income and expense amounts that might be expected. Each new edition includes comparisons with prior surveys, and these comparisons are helpful in defining the state of the industry. The report is a useful starting point for measuring a real estate management company's performance.

Real estate management firms may actually have several sources of income. Management fees are the primary source, of course, but as these firms increase their capabilities, they typically offer a number of related services for which they are compensated. The latter will be described after we outline the different ways management fees can be set.

Property Management Fees. Because the mainstay of the management company's income is management fees, it is important to know the various ways those fees can be calculated. No governmental agency, trade group, or association of real estate professionals sets the fees for property management—management fees are competitively based within the marketplace. The astute manager will know what competing firms normally do under given circumstances, but each property is unique and should be considered on its own. The only effective way to set a management fee for a particular property is to account for the costs involved and allow a factor for profit. The following are some approaches to setting management fees.

- *Percentage of gross possible income*—This is a rare basis for setting fees as gross possible income is theoretical, and a property seldom generates the amount that is calculated. The client would be overpaying for management services unless the percentage were lower than it might be for similar properties.
- *Percentage of effective gross income*—This is the most common basis for setting management fees. By using actual collections, the client is paying on monies received, and the manager is getting paid for the monies collected. This approach can be applied exclusively to rents or to both base rents and pass-through expense reimbursements; the latter would only apply to management of commercial properties.
- *Percentage of effective gross income versus a minimum fee*—This is also a very common form of management fee within the industry because it recognizes the possibility of a diminished flow of rental income—e.g., because of a rent strike or a disaster that makes the property unoccupiable temporarily. Lease-up of a new or rehabbed property or an exceptionally high vacancy rate due to turnovers are other possible challenges to management that would warrant having the fee stated this way in the management agreement.
- *Flat fee*—From time to time you may find an owner who is reluctant to base the management fee on the income from the property. One argument often given by owners who do this is that the rents at the property have become so high, a percentage fee would be disproportionate to the work being done. Usually in this situation, the management company can run a cost analysis of the work involved and agree to a fixed amount as the monthly fee, provided the management agreement includes provision for increasing it each year based on something like the cost of living index. It should be noted, however, that the compensation for managing an owner-occupied property (condominium, cooperative) is always a flat fee that is prorated back to the unit owners in their monthly operating assessments.

Leasing Fees. Except for lease-up of a new or rehabbed property or a high vacancy rate to be overcome in a very short time, leasing is usually part of the management of a residential property. When leasing is a major undertaking (e.g., lease-up of a new property), the compensation is negotiated separately since there may be little or no rental income on which to base a management fee.

Assuming the management firm has qualified personnel in house, leasing at commercial properties can be a very profitable adjunct activity. Fees are typically based on the rental rates and lease terms negotiated. (The sample pro forma in Exhibit 2.2 includes income from leasing fees.) Some companies relegate leasing to a separate division of the company while others include leasing in the management operation. In any case, leasing fees can be an important source of income for the management company, and many clients like the idea of having one company do it all.

Construction Supervision. Most real estate managers will oversee minor construction and decorating without an additional fee. Painting or laying carpet in an apartment, minor building repairs (patching a leaky roof), or remodeling are examples. If the manager is also doing the leasing, it is often thought that the total compensation is quite adequate without having to bill the owner for overseeing small projects. However, adding a freestanding building to a shopping center, building a club house at an apartment property, or building out a suite in an office building is generally considered to warrant a construction supervision fee. The amount can be a flat fee (perhaps a few thousand dollars) or a percentage of the total job (this will depend on the manager's capabilities and the scope of the supervision required).

Tax Appeals. In periods of economic downturn, property values decline and tax appeals become a necessity. If the manager is qualified to pursue such an appeal, the result can benefit the tenants as well as the property owner and provide additional income to the management company. The compensation for a successful tax appeal may range from one third to one half of the first year's savings, but the fee for this service is fully negotiable.

Owners' Tax Accounting. If you have the capability in house, you might want to consider offering your owner-clients additional accounting services—e.g., taking their information and carrying it forward to the filing of their personal income taxes—for a fee. This can provide benefits to the client as well as the management company, but most firms are not really set up to do it properly, and the potential liability associated with assuming this responsibility makes it generally inadvisable.

Real Estate Sales. Most states require real estate management companies to have a designated broker and individual managers to be licensed. Because most real estate managers have had some experience with the sales side of the business, it is important to let clients know you are qualified to handle the sales transaction when they decide to dispose of their properties. If you have done your job well as a manager, you have helped create value in the property, and it is fitting that you should share in the commissions when the property is sold. Note, however, that any arrangement to represent the owner in the sale of the property should be established via a separate agreement and not related directly to the management agreement arrangements. (The management perspective on fees is discussed in Chapter 9, and information on other adjunct income opportunities can be found in Chapter 7.)

Analyzing the Real Estate Managers' Portfolios. Each real estate manager can be viewed as a separate profit center, and the income and expenses related to the management of each property can be analyzed as a measure of the individual manager's productivity and profitability. While the residential manager may generate income only in the form of management fees from the properties he or she manages, the manager of a commercial property often has opportunities to generate income from several sources in addition to management fees—leasing commissions, construction supervision, etc. Total income, regardless of the source, must be weighed against the costs of managing the properties. The expenses attributable to each manager are the direct cost to manage the portfolio and a share of the firms' general and administrative (G&A) expenses. The portfolio analysis is helpful in determining which management accounts are profitable, how much to compensate the managers (bonuses, performance-based salary increases), and which managers may be able to assume the management of additional properties.

Because much of what is being considered in such an analysis is difficult to quantify, the analysis of profit or loss from each manager's portfolio is an art more than a science. Many variables must be considered when analyzing a management portfolio, and some of these variables will impact the managed properties even though they are outside the real estate manager's control. For instance, if the local economy takes a turn for the worse or the market is overbuilt, leasing will probably slow down and less commission income will be earned on a commercial building. Changes in the local population (demographic shifts) and a shrinking job market will impact apartment turnovers and rent levels. Other factors over which the manager of a property has no control are more specific: For example, a property manager may assume supervisory responsibilities over new property managers, thus precluding expansion of his or her portfolio of properties. If the owner elects to take management of one of the properties in a manager's portfolio in house, the manager's portfolio income will be drastically reduced. The result could be similar if an owner chose not to improve a property to retain existing tenants or enhance its marketability to new tenants.

Portfolio Income. There are countless ways of determining the profit or loss of a real estate manager's portfolio. The method described here is a good basis for developing a formula for this type of analysis that is specific to the management firm. First the income from each portfolio is determined on a property-by-property basis; then the portfolio expenses (the cost of management including the manager's pay and benefits and a pro rata share of the company's G&A expenses) are totaled. The difference between them is the profit (or loss) yielded by the portfolio. A series of examples demonstrates these calculations.

76   Business Strategies for Real Estate Management Companies

Exhibit 3.4
Sample Real Estate Managers' Portfolio Analysis—Income

Real Estate Manager	Property	Sq Ft	Mgmt Fee Income	Net Comm Income	Other Income	Total Income
Aaron	Newport Center	70,879	30,000			30,000
	Mariner's Cove	141,970	38,720			38,720
	South Hill Court	257,000	49,586	51,019		100,605
	Lincoln Plaza	150,879	34,159	7,370		41,529
	Freeway Office Bldg	51,823	9,750			9,750
	Lakes Plaza	10,200	8,542	4,848		13,390
	Harbor Building	10,273	9,600			9,600
	TOTAL	693,024	180,357	63,237		243,594
	Percent		74%	26%		
Bob	Harbor Village	108,503	24,000	10,800	4,998	39,798
	Vista Center	88,547	48,190	20,359		68,549
	Mission Plaza	116,451	54,658	11,232		65,890
	Seaview Village	163,190	45,532	10,985		56,517
	Woodinville Office	60,100	33,439			33,439
	TOTAL	536,791	205,819	53,376	4,998	264,193
	Percent		77.9%	20.2%	1.9%	
Carol	Woodridge Plaza	161,159	57,078	6,936		64,014
	Northway Village	107,863	41,973	2,588		44,561
	Eastlake Building	90,202	48,772	17,716		66,488
	Brentwood Court	78,128	31,607	16,512	3,516	51,635
	Washington Plaza	97,153	40,835	9,206		50,041
	TOTAL	534,505	220,265	52,958	3,516	276,739
	Percent		79.6%	19.1%	1.3%	
Kim	Pacific Hills	211,217	24,000			24,000
	Library Plaza	227,217	48,000	51,805		99,805
	North Hills	112,592	45,677	29,806	6,444	81,927
	South Hills	115,017	29,839	13,306	7,020	50,165
	TOTAL	666,043	147,516	94,917	13,464	255,897
	Percent		57.6%	37.1%	5.3%	
Trina	Pointe Park Center	94,490	31,490			31,490
	Meridian Village	144,594	39,714	8,039		47,753
	Broadway Med. Bldg	371,895	42,953	1,508	30,000	74,461
	Harbor Med. Court	60,000	42,000	28,000	15,000	85,000
	TOTAL	670,979	156,157	37,547	45,000	238,704
	Percent		65.4%	15.7%	18.9%	
Walter	Eagle Ridge	75,000	40,000	30,000		70,000
	Airport Center	25,000	15,000	5,000	5,000	25,000
	Bear Creek Plaza	185,000	58,100	22,100		80,200
	TOTAL	285,000	113,100	57,100	5,000	175,200
	Percent		64.6%	32.6%	2.8%	
	TOTAL PORTFOLIO	3,386,342	1,023,214	359,135	71,978	1,454,327
	Percent		70.4%	24.7%	4.9%	

Exhibit 3.4 shows an income analysis for Commercial Property Management Company, a hypothetical Midwestern real estate management and leasing firm, whose staff includes six real estate managers, each responsible for several commercial properties. The three income categories shown are management fees, net commissions, and other income. *Net commission income* is the commission the management firm receives after subtracting any co-broker commissions and the real estate manager's share of the commission. *Other income* may include fees for construction supervision, consulting, expert witness testimony, or any other compensable activity of the manager.

The sources of income for each managed property are added together across the line to determine total income, then the totals are added to find the aggregate total for the portfolio. The first portfolio calculation indicates that the seven properties managed by Aaron generated $243,594. For each category of income, the total for each portfolio is calculated by adding down the column, and the result is also shown as a percentage of the total portfolio income. Continuing the review of Aaron's portfolio, the total of $180,357 in management fees represented 74 percent of the total income from his portfolio.

Portfolio Expenses. The portfolio expenses can be determined in several ways. The method used in the example in Exhibit 3.5 combines the cost directly associated with managing the portfolio—the real estate manager's direct cost—with a pro rata (one-sixth) share of the management company's G&A expenses. In Exhibit 3.6, on the other hand, the individual manager's direct costs are considered to be one fourth of the portfolio expense just as the six managers' total direct costs represent one fourth of the firm's total budgeted expenses. The two methods shown yield a difference in profits of $924. The difference can be greater if there is a large variance among the direct costs of the individual managers.

Exhibit 3.4 *(continued)*

Aaron has the most properties in his portfolio, but two of them are very small. Also, the Freeway Office Building is in escrow; the purchaser will assume the management of the office building on April 1—the projected management fee is for only three months.

Kim's portfolio has only four properties; two are large community centers with more than fifty tenants each.

Trina's portfolio income includes $45,000 for supervising tenant improvements and major remodeling of the common areas of two medical buildings. Construction and leasing at these two buildings will prevent Trina from managing additional properties, but the income from these activities is equivalent to the income from managing two or three additional properties.

Walter has also been managing three properties for a developer who assumed the management of those properties on the first of the year. He has room in his portfolio to manage two to four additional properties, each in the 50,000–175,000-square-foot range.

Exhibit 3.5
Sample Real Estate Managers' Portfolio Analysis—Expenses

Each real estate manager employed by Commercial Property Management Company is responsible for leasing all or most of the properties in his or her portfolio. Next year's total annual operating expense for the firm is budgeted at $1,271,041. The budgeted salary, payroll cost, and benefits for the six managers, combined, totals $317,760. All of the other general and administrative (G&A) costs to operate the company total $953,281 ($1,271,041 − $317,760). The G&A costs are divided by the number of managers ($953,281 ÷ 6 = $158,880), and this cost is added to each manager's direct cost, then the total is subtracted from the portfolio income to arrive at the portfolio's profit (or loss). The following calculation uses Kim's portfolio as an example.

Kim's Salary		$40,501	
Payroll/Benefits Cost	+	$12,151	(salary × .30)
Kim's "Direct" Cost		$52,652	(salary + payroll/benefits)
Support Cost	+	$158,880	(pro rata share of G&A)
Cost to Manage Kim's Portfolio		$211,532	
Kim's Portfolio Income		$255,897	
Portfolio Cost	−	$211,532	
Portfolio Profit		$44,365	

A number of other factors also have an effect on portfolio profitability. Client demands can vary greatly, resulting in some properties requiring much more of the manager's time than others do. Also, because potential fees (commissions and other fee opportunities) can vary from property to property, management's control over a property's potential fee income may be limited at best. These and other variables must be taken into account when evaluating the performance of an individual manager's portfolio. Instead of simply distributing the G&A expenses across the number of real estate managers (the results of the approaches shown in Exhibit 3.5 and 3.6), the expense total could be divided by the total number of properties or by the gross leasable area (GLA) of all the properties managed. Furthermore, adjustments can be made for extraordinary and time-consuming financial reporting requirements, unusual travel expenses to visit a property, or any number of variables unique to managing a particular portfolio or an individual property.

Portfolio Profits. Determination of profit (or loss) for each real estate manager's portfolio helps the firm's executives evaluate overall profitability by manager, by portfolio, and across all the properties in the firm's total portfolio. Exhibit 3.7 (p. 80) shows profit as the difference between income and expenses. Profitability of individual portfolios ranged from a low of 8.2 percent (Aaron) to a high of 21.9 percent (Bob); Walter's portfolio showed a loss of 17.7 percent. The overall profit from all six portfolios was 12.1 percent.

Exhibit 3.6
Sample Real Estate Managers' Portfolio Analysis—Expenses (A Second Approach)

A different approach can be taken to calculating overall portfolio expenses using the same basic information: As in Exhibit 3.5, suppose next year's total annual operating expense is budgeted at $1,271,041, and total salary, payroll cost, and benefits for the six real estate managers are budgeted at $317,760. This represents 25% of the total operating expenses for the company. All of the other (G&A) costs to operate the company amount to $953,281 or 75% of the total. In other words, for every $1.00 of real estate manager costs, there are $3.00 of support and administrative costs (including executive compensation and general overhead).

Real Estate Manager Costs	$317,760	25%	($1.00)
Other Company Costs (All)	$953,281	75%	($3.00)
Total Operating Expenses	$1,271,041	100%	($4.00)

The cost to manage each manager's portfolio is calculated by multiplying the manager's direct costs (salary, payroll, and benefits) by 4. (The related payroll and benefits expense is calculated as 30% of each manager's annual base salary.) The cost of management is subtracted from the total income generated by each portfolio to determine portfolio profit (or loss). The following calculation also uses Kim's portfolio as an example.

Kim's "Direct" Cost	$52,652	(salary + payroll/benefits)
Support Cost	+ $157,956	(direct cost x 3)
Cost to Manage Kim's Portfolio	$210,608	
Kim's Portfolio Income	$255,897	
Portfolio Cost	− $210,608	
Portfolio Profit	$45,289	

A Perspective on Operations

When markets are overbuilt, competition becomes fierce, with much too much vacant space chasing too few tenants. Add to this the fact that few commercial operations have to be in a specific location in order to conduct their business and very few residents have to live at a specific property. Over the years, property owners have found that the existing commercial tenant or resident is quite often the most economical one they will ever have, and they understand that keeping these tenants and residents is good for the long-term economic health of the property.

It becomes incumbent on the real estate manager not only to serve the client in all ways possible, but also to serve the tenant or resident who is, in fact, the customer or client of the property. At commercial properties, the array of customers served by the manager of the property is expanded to include the office tenants' employees and clients and the retail tenants' employees and the consumers who are the retailers' customers.

In order to serve its clients and tenants well, the management company must establish performance standards and uniform operating procedures.

Exhibit 3.7
Sample Real Estate Managers' Portfolio Analysis —Profit (Loss)

Real Estate Manager	Portfolio Income, $	Portfolio Expense, $	Portdolio Profit, $	Portfolio Profit, %
Aaron	243,594	223,631	19,963	8.2
Bob	264,193	206,409	57,784	21.9
Carol	276,739	227,224	48,515	17.9
Kim	255,897	210,608	45,289*	17.7
Trina	238,704	204,186	34,518	14.5
Walter	175,200	206,175	(30,975)	(17.7)
TOTAL	1,454,327	1,278,233	176,094	12.1

*Kim's portfolio profit shown here is from Exhibit 3.6. Using the lower figure from Exhibit 3.5 ($44,365) would reduce the total profit by $924 (≈0.4%).

As noted in Exhibit 3.4, three properties in Walter's portfolio were returned to the developer for self-management on the first of the year, which has reduced his portfolio's overall income and, therefore, its profitability.

These not only guide business decisions, but also ensure consistent, high-quality service to clients. Furthermore, a well-managed property is more likely to retain residents or commercial tenants and, therefore, continue to be managed by the same company. The efficiency and cost-effectiveness of the company's operations is translated into profits generated by individual managers from their respective portfolios, and profits are what successful real estate management is all about.

4

Strategizing the Accounting Function

The accounting function in a real estate management company should be designed for flexibility. This is where the company's income from property management and related services will be measured, recorded, and used to pay the expenses of operating the management business. Information developed here will be a critical factor in determining your management fees. Control of your internal operating costs is necessary to maintain a competitive edge in bidding for management business as well as to assure that your company makes a profit for its owners.

Real estate managers are familiar with the budgets, charts of accounts, and accounting records required for the management of different types of properties. For a management company, the principles are the same, but the contents will be very different. In particular, you will be paying rent—or a mortgage—for the space occupied by the management firm's offices. Wages, salaries, other forms of compensation, and employee benefits will be part of your company's cost of doing business as a business. The secretary or administrative assistant who works with and for the management company's chief executive is not likely to provide specific services to owner-clients in the realm of property management. Nor is the receptionist who answers your telephones. However, the income derived from management fees must cover these individuals' salaries as well as the wages and benefits of other management company staff members who are directly involved in managing properties. Expenses directly related to managing each property must be accounted separately from the management company's operating overhead, although the latter may be apportioned to managed properties for purposes of balancing the firm's internal accounts.

This chapter begins with an overview discussion of accounting principles and their application to the management company. The need for flexibility will become apparent as we discuss the accounting function in relation to the management of different types of properties.

Accounting for the Management Business

The primary interest of the accountant is the manner in which data are collected and recorded—i.e., financial accounting. This type of accounting is done for external use (e.g., to borrow money from a bank, to report to investors). It should follow generally accepted accounting procedures (GAAP).

Management company executives, as users of accounting information, are concerned primarily with evaluation and interpretation of the data in making effective management decisions—i.e., managerial accounting. (Most property accounts are managerial accounting records; for tax purposes, the data are converted to financial accounting statements.) Both perspectives are important to the operation of a real estate management company.

Financial Accounting. Financial accounting documents the financial position of the business in the form of a balance sheet and a profit and loss statement. These are the "hard numbers" that show the company's financial status and operational results, respectively, and can be verified by an audit. A cash flow statement that discounts depreciation and amortization and factors in principal payments (on loans) and balance sheet adjustments is a necessary tool for medium- to large-size companies.

Balance Sheet. A balance sheet is a statement of the company's assets and liabilities and the owners' equity. Under assets might be listed cash and items of value belonging to the business (e.g., land, buildings, office equipment, automobiles). *Current assets* are items easily convertible to cash, including bank accounts and receivables (monies owed to the company). *Fixed assets* comprise equipment, fixtures, and other items used in the business, most of which are not readily convertible to cash and, because they wear out and have to be replaced, diminish in value over time—i.e., they depreciate. Also on the assets side of the balance sheet, there is usually a category called "other," which includes items with specific value (e.g., investment securities) as well as intangibles (specifically, goodwill).

Liabilities represent amounts owed by the business. *Current liabilities* are expected to be paid out of current assets. These include short-term notes, interest due, employee wages and withholdings, and accounts payable. *Long-term liabilities* are items that will mature more than one year from the date of the balance sheet. Mortgages, long-term notes, and bonds are examples. *Owners' equity* is divided among contributed capital invested in the business, retained earnings or net income from prior years re-invested in the business, and net income generated during the current period.

Profit and Loss Statement. A profit and loss statement provides vital information about the operation of the management firm that can be used in making business decisions. Also called an earnings report, an income statement, or an operating statement, it provides a measure of the company's financial success. The statement compares operating revenues (income generated from providing management services) and operational outlays (including depreciation); the difference between the two—the net income—represents net profit if the balance is positive or net loss if it is negative. Profit and loss data are used to determine profit margin, operating cost ratio, and net profit ratio which, if reviewed annually, indicate the financial soundness of the management company. (More detailed discussion of financial accounting is beyond the scope of this book. A professional accountant is the best source of advice on setting up balance sheets, profit and loss statements, and other reporting formats for the management business and the various calculations required.)

Managerial Accounting. Managerial accounting is used to make intelligent projections about what will or may happen. Because these forecasts are not actual transactions, managerial accounting is not auditable.

The tools of managerial accounting are *cost accounting,* which measures expenses incurred as a result of actual operations, and *budgeting,* which is the development of a financial plan for the management firm. The two must be compatible; the financial facts of the company's operations must be understood in order to budget appropriately for its future operations. Budgets are created for a fixed period, usually one year or less, and often reported and evaluated monthly or quarterly as well as annually. (A forecast for more than one year is a long-range plan.) Cost accounting measurements—per-unit costs, per-person costs, percentage of gross income—must also be for the same period of time as the budget (i.e., one year) so that the records are consistent. Since the major cost of real estate management is people, most cost measurements will revolve around salaries and other payroll costs, usually on a per-person or per-function basis. Because the bookkeeping function is a major service to clients, costs allocated to it will include not only the personnel expense, but also computer equipment and operations and a pro-rata portion of the overall operating costs of the business.

Company Chart of Accounts. Cost accounting isolates the costs associated with operating the business, and there must be a systematic method of assigning these costs. A *chart of accounts,* usually including account codes or numbers, is just such a tool. Because its purpose is to facilitate analysis of business operations by providing unit cost information, specific accounts should be those needed by the company to document its activities. With that in mind, it may be appropriate to establish a minimum dollar figure for specific tracking of recurring expenses; occasional expenditures in amounts under a certain dollar amount can be handled via a petty cash account. (Petty cash funds should also be tracked and reconciled on a regular basis—e.g., weekly or monthly.)

The number of account categories will vary with the size and complexity of the management operation. Payroll and personnel expenses are likely to be itemized into subcategories for different operational functions (departments) or individual employees, or both, while the break-out of other operating expenses may combine several types of activities in a single category. The goal is to have each individual account be meaningful to the management personnel who use the information for making decisions. (Minimally, it may be worthwhile to consult with an accountant on income tax reporting requirements so that extra work will not be necessary to differentiate classes of deductible operating expenses at tax time.)

The list of items suggested for a chart of accounts in Exhibit 4.1 is intended to identify major categories likely to be utilized by a start-up management firm. As the business grows in size and complexity, the various listed categories can be divided into subcategories to identify major components of a class of income or expense. Usually each account category is assigned a number; subcategories are then numbered within the series—for example, the payroll category might be account number 200, and the five subcategories shown in the exhibit might be numbered, respectively, 201, 202, 203, 204, and 205.

Income Accounts. The primary source of income for the firm will be *management fees,* so they are differentiated in Exhibit 4.1 from other income. (If the firm manages both residential and commercial properties, the two types of fees would likely be accounted separately.) Even though a lump sum will likely be used for most analyses, it may be desirable to subdivide the management fees category from the very beginning and assign individual account codes to each property (or client) from whom a specific fee will be earned. This differentiation will facilitate budgeting for the next fiscal period as well as allow tracking of individual payments received.

Other income is revenue derived from leasing commissions and other fees (e.g., for supervising construction or rehabilitation projects). Here again, it may be worthwhile to itemize specific sources of income into subcategories by class if not by individual source. Other possible sources of company income include interest and reimbursement of expenses charged back to clients. If management agreements provide for adminis-

Exhibit 4.1
Suggested Components of a Management Company Chart of Accounts

Income Accounts
  Management Fees
  Other Income
Expense Accounts
  Payroll
    Executive
    Property Managers
    Bookkeeping
    Administrative
    Other Payroll Costs
  Automobile
  Business Acquisition and Retention
  Data Processing and Computer
  Equipment and Furniture
  Insurance Premiums
  Legal and Audit Fees
  Office Expense
  Postage and Shipping
  Professional Memberships and Education
  Rent
  Taxes and License Fees
  Telephone
  Travel
  Utilities

trative charges (e.g., rental application processing fees, late fees) to be retained by management as compensation, there should be categories for tracking them as well.

Expense Accounts. The number of separate categories for expense items will vary, and some classifications may warrant subcategories initially. While the categories listed in Exhibit 4.1 are rather broad, they account for the major types of expenditures common to all businesses and to real estate management companies in particular. As noted in the individual discussions that follow, some items may be accounted in different categories. The goal of any chart of accounts is to provide a systematic classification of costs.

Under *payroll,* individual categories are shown for specific functions, so that those expenses which would be evaluated as part of the cost of managing individual properties (e.g., property manager, bookkeeping) can be easily accessed for determining management fees and measuring profitability. Often it is necessary or desirable to account for each employee individually.

Other payroll costs include workers' compensation insurance, unemployment insurance (FUTA), employer payroll taxes (FICA), and employer-paid employee benefits such as medical insurance, as well as costs of contract or part-time labor and employee recruitment. Here again, it may be worthwhile to create subcategories for the individual payroll costs being accounted.

The *automobile* category would include all company-paid costs of operating automobiles, including employees' own vehicles. However, if employee parking is paid along with your office rent, the combined expense should be accounted in the rent category.

Business acquisition and retention encompasses promotion of the business (marketing and advertising), development and presentation of management proposals, and other activities required to gain and maintain management accounts. (Subdivision of this category to capture costs of acquiring individual accounts may be advisable if the costs are expected to be recouped over the course of the management agreement term.) Although entertainment might be included here, it would be accounted as a travel expense for income tax purposes.

In the category of *data processing and computer* would be itemized such costs as service bureau fees, computer lease costs (or depreciation, if the equipment is owned), and software costs. Maintenance and support of the equipment would likely be included here, although it may warrant its own category. These items are separated from the general office equipment expense because of the specific relationship to accounting and preparation of reports to clients.

Equipment and furniture is all the other business machines (calculators, photocopiers, facsimile machines, cellular phones, etc.) and office furnishings that are needed to operate the business.

Under *insurance premiums* are recorded such expenses as professional liability (errors and omissions) policies, business income coverage, property loss (damage, theft), liability insurance, employee fiduciary bonds, and life insurance on company executives. (Employee insurance benefits and workers' compensation coverage are accounted as payroll costs as noted previously.)

Legal and audit fees are a necessary cost of doing business. If legal counsel or an accounting firm is on retainer, those expenses would be accounted here.

Office expense is typically a catch-all category that includes office supplies and stationery items, business and accounting forms, coffee service, and photocopier and computer paper. Printing of things like stationery, some types of forms, and marketing materials may be accounted separately, but photocopying has effectively supplanted printing for many less formal (e.g., non-stationery) requirements. However, if the costs of printed or photocopied forms are to be charged back to individual property accounts, these expenses should be categorized separately.

> **Depreciable Property**
>
> The physical assets of a business are depreciable for income tax purposes, and loss of value is also calculated for insurance reimbursement in case an item is damaged or stolen. Because the physical assets represent value to the business, the chart of accounts and periodic balance sheets should account for depreciation of business property. Items with an expected use life of more than one year may be depreciated for tax purposes based on precalculated tabulations. However, for some items, it is better to consider the purchase as an expense. Vehicles (automobiles, trucks), if cared for, may be operated for many more years than the five-year depreciation period. Computers, on the other hand, may not wear out physically, but their value diminishes as newer, faster models become available, and they may have to be upgraded or replaced at intervals of two to five years (or more often) in order to guarantee adequate operating capacity and the capability to run the software programs needed by the business or required by management clients. Whether to buy or lease and whether to buy new or used can be important economic decisions for a start-up management firm.

Although they are typical office expenses for most businesses, *postage and shipping* are accounted separately because they are, in part, costs of managing individual properties. Many companies have accounts with overnight shipping services or with local messenger services, and those expenses would be accounted here as well.

Real estate management personnel, especially property managers, need to maintain their skills. Costs of seminars and other training as well as dues and fees related to maintaining professional designations or memberships are accounted under *professional memberships and education.*

In the *rent* category, the cost of leased office space, maintenance of that space, and possibly employee parking would be accounted. If the building is owned, mortgage expense and real estate taxes would be accounted in this category, although it may be appropriate to name the category differently in that case. Utilities (e.g., electricity, heat) may be included here as well, although they are usually differentiated for income tax purposes.

Taxes and licenses is where municipal business license fees or taxes are accounted. Some municipalities may also require permits for signage. Real estate taxes (which are accounted under rent) and income taxes (which are not considered a business expense) would not be included in this category.

The *telephone* category is where telephone equipment rentals, local and long-distance charges, and answering services are accounted. Because this particular cost is often related to the management of individual properties, separate accounting can facilitate redistribution of the costs. However, Yellow Pages advertising billed by the telephone company would be charged to business acquisition.

All costs of travel (by air or train), meals, and lodging incurred in the conduct of company business are accounted in the *travel* category. (The amount reimbursed to employees should be a stated company policy.) Note that for income tax purposes, meals (and entertainment) are not fully deductible, and the difference impacts overall profitability.

Utilities—e.g., electricity—may be categorized separately since the high-tech equipment usage makes this a major expense item. For many businesses, telephone expenses would be categorized as utilities, too.

A more comprehensive chart of accounts might also provide for items that are recorded on the balance sheet (assets, liabilities, etc.) and differentiate between mortgage principal and interest. Maintenance services and supplies might be a separate category if the business pays for these services itself. It may also be desirable to establish categories or subcategories that allow for recapture of other specific operating costs, especially if such "overhead" expenses will be needed for establishing fees for management and other services provided by the company.

The chart of accounts for a management business will be substantially different from those created for individual managed properties, in which the type of property and the owner's reporting requirements will dictate specific categories of income and expenses. (Residential and commercial property charts of accounts are discussed later in this chapter.)

Accounting Methods. There are three basic accounting methods:

1. *Cash-basis accounting,* which records income as it is received and expenses as they are paid;

2. *Accrual-basis accounting,* which records income when it is due and expenses when they are incurred, regardless of whether monies have actually been received or paid; and

3. *Modified accrual accounting,* in which items that repeat at regular intervals might be accounted on a cash basis while those requiring accumulation of funds toward a large dollar payout would be accounted on an accrual basis.

While cash-basis accounting offers the advantage of simplicity in recording cash receipts and outlays and allows some flexibility in tax planning, accrual-basis accounting provides a more accurate determination of the actual financial experience of a business enterprise for a given period because it shows amounts owed *to* the company and amounts owed *by* the company. Because management fees (income) are almost always received during the period earned, and most of the expense of operating the business is its payroll, the costs of which are also paid in the accounting period, cash-basis accounting has long been used in real estate management companies. However, the ease with which computer programs can accept, track, and analyze data encourages the use of accrual accounting.

The method you choose for the management firm has wide-ranging im-

> **Management Company Accounting Methods**
>
> Regardless of the accounting method or methods you must use to serve your clients' needs, the choice of accounting method to be used for the real estate management business is an important one. If you occupy rented office space and lease office equipment, most of your business income and expenses are likely to be easily identified and accounted, and a cash system may serve your needs quite adequately. If the business owns the building that houses its office, mortgage payments and accumulation of funds to pay real estate taxes may commend the use of an accrual system. In dealing with lending institutions—e.g., if the business needs cash to meet a payroll or takes out a loan for a major equipment purchase—you may well be required to provide both cash-basis (statement of income and expenses) and accrual-basis (balance sheet showing assets and liabilities) accounting information in order to secure the needed financing.
>
> The choice of an accounting method should be given careful consideration so that you can develop consistent records for income tax purposes as well as account for income and expenses in a manner that satisfies your own and other business participants' need for financial information.

plications. A management company might preferably use cash-basis accounting for its own record keeping while clients' requirements may be for predominantly accrual or modified accrual accounting. (The size of the business and its information needs are important considerations.) Also, the U.S. Internal Revenue Service (IRS) requires identification of the accounting method on business income tax returns, and once elected, any change in method requires IRS consent. The form of ownership of the management company will also impact this particular decision. The IRS requirements differ for sole proprietors, partnerships (general partners, limited partners, and limited liability company members are differentiated), and corporations (profits are taxed to the corporation and dividends paid to shareholders are taxable as personal income). An S corporation is exempt from federal tax itself; like a partnership, its income must be distributed to the shareholders who are then liable for income taxes on their proportionate shares. If the management activity is a function within a real estate investment trust (REIT), or a division or department of a larger corporation—whether in the real estate business or not—there are likely to be specific tax requirements for these arrangements as well.

Many states impose income taxes, and some municipalities levy personal income taxes, real estate taxes, and/or personal property taxes. There may even be local employer taxes to be considered. Advice of legal counsel and a certified public accountant (CPA) should be sought regarding the form of business ownership and the tax advantages and disadvantages for a particular business venture. A professional accountant can also help guide your choice of accounting method and advise you on forms and procedures to assure compliance with tax and employment law requirements.

Company Bank Accounts. While trust or agency accounts, or both, may be established for holding clients' funds, the management firm will need to set up separate accounts for itself. You may want to explore with your bank the best, most cost-effective, type of checking account for the business. While one requiring that a very low minimum balance be maintained may be preferable, accounts with a specific minimum balance requirement often include additional bank services or customer perquisites, or they may have only minimal service charges. Your business's cash flow needs should also be considered in deciding whether to tie up funds in a required minimum checking account balance.

Your checking account needs may change as the business grows, and this fact may be a consideration in your choice of bank along with the services offered by the institution. Bank service charges often vary, depending on the size of the account, and they may be waived when the account balance exceeds a certain threshold. Sometimes banks require establishment of savings and/or checking accounts with them if they lend funds to a business so this, too, should be kept in mind.

Employer's are required to withhold income taxes and social security contributions from employees' wages, and these withholdings along with the employer's portion of employees' social security must be paid to the government periodically (frequency of payment depends on dollars involved; tax return forms are filed quarterly). It may be necessary or appropriate to hold these funds in a separate bank account along with required amounts for unemployment taxes and workers' compensation insurance.

In addition, insurance premiums for policies covering the owners of the business, vehicles used in the business, and employee benefits (medical, disability, and life insurance are common employee coverages) are likely to be paid quarterly or semi-annually. Establishment of any kind of pension funding is another example of a potential periodic payment. Since these types of payments represent substantial dollar amounts, it may be necessary or appropriate to accrue the funds on an apportioned basis each month and use an interest-bearing account to hold them.

Various types of savings accounts and interest-bearing checking accounts are available, and you should explore the options your financial institution makes available to businesses. It is imperative that these funds be immediately accessible for withdrawal to make the specific set-aside payments. An emergency "capital" account, again preferably interest-bearing, is another possibility to consider.

Consultation with an accountant and/or an attorney may be advisable with regard to financial and record-keeping requirements for the business with respect to its own needs and those of its clients. As with bank accounts for property operations (discussed later in this chapter), it is important to reconcile the firm's bank accounts promptly.

> **Separation of Clients' Accounts**
>
> Improper handling of the client's funds by the third-party manager could be a violation of state laws. Most states require third-party managers to have a real estate license in order to manage properties in which they have no interest and when they are not employees of the property owner. Within the real estate laws, there is a requirement that the client's funds must be accounted separately. One of the most serious offenses is that of *commingling of funds*—the mixing together of two or more clients' funds or of a client's funds and the manager's personal funds so that ownership of the monies is unclear.
>
> Regulatory agencies are inclined to take a dim view of a master account that contains the funds of several clients, even if the funds are accounted separately on paper. Most managers maintain separate bank accounts for individual clients to avoid this potential problem. In many instances, separate accounts are even maintained for individual properties when a client has more than one property under management by the firm.

Company Budgets. Real estate management firms often do a better job managing someone else's business (e.g., their client's properties) than managing their own business (i.e., the management firm). Every year, real estate managers develop for each managed property an annual "management plan"—the operating budget. Data obtained from the properties' annual budgets—i.e., management fees, leasing commissions, and other ancillary sources of income—are needed to develop the firm's budget and cash flow projections. The firm's annual operating budget is one of many tools available for monitoring its income and expenses and for measuring its success as a business.

Real Estate Owners' Accounting Requirements

With more and more investment real estate being owned by institutions, the accounting and reporting requirements have become more sophisticated. As a consequence, real estate management companies are spending more time on the accounting function, and it is not unusual for a firm to be working with several different accounting software programs. Institutional owners generally require that management reports conform to their programs. Some are even connected to the management company via modem and can access management information directly at any time.

Financial Reporting. Much of the basis of management planning is related to the financial records of a property. While a single rent roll or tenant roster might be sufficient for some owners, others may require general rental information to be documented separately from lease expiration dates. For commercial properties, there may be a separate listing of common area operating expense pass-throughs (sometimes called bill-backs) and possibly another one differentiating credit and non-credit tenants. Operating statements are generally issued on a monthly basis, but it is not unusual for an institutional owner to require a combined statement every quarter in addition to the usual monthly statement.

Typically, institutional owners will provide the management company with an accounting procedures manual that sets forth all of the institution's requirements. The procedures will include—but are not limited to—the setting up of bank accounts, selection of banks (or other financial institutions), signatories on the accounts, and when the accounts are to be reconciled. Usually the institution will also provide a chart of accounts and establish the format and timing of the monthly accounting reports. Budgets are generally required on an annual basis, also in the format defined by the institution. The procedures manual will also dictate whether accounting will be done on a cash or accrual—or modified accrual—basis and set forth the cash balance to be carried. An appropriate (fiduciary) bond will generally be required to protect the client in case of manager dishonesty. Additionally, separate schedules will most likely be required to track security deposits, and deposit funds may have to be held in separate (trust or escrow) accounts.

For the management of commercial properties, the procedures manual may indicate when common area or pass-through expense budgets are prepared, when tenants are notified of adjustments, and when and how the year-end reconciliations are to be handled. Rent increases will be covered, and the manager may be required to compute any increases, submit them to the owner-client for approval, and then forward them to the tenant. Retail properties will have additional requirements for handling of percentage rents.

Methods of Accounting for Clients' Funds. Cash, accrual, and modified accrual methods have specific applications in accounting for the funds related to managed properties. Usually the owner's reporting requirements will dictate the method to be used. While all three methods of accounting are commonly found in the management of investment real estate, the most important thing for the manager to understand is that the accrual and modified accrual methods take more time and effort to administer—in effect, everything is accounted twice, first when it is due and again when the cash changes hands.

In *cash-basis accounting,* theoretically nothing needs to be accounted until money actually changes hands. The tenants' rent may be due on the first of the month, but it does not impact the record-keeping system until it is received, and that may be on the fifth of the month. Real estate taxes may be paid only once or twice a year, so there would be large entries for taxes in the months when the payments were made. If an application of blacktop in the parking lot was done in June but paid in October, the accounting records would reflect the latter date.

The theory behind *accrual-basis accounting* is that a transaction has occurred when it is due or when it has become a commitment. This system has many practical applications in real estate management. A tenant's rent due on the first of the month would be accrued at that time; when the payment is received—e.g., on the fifth—the accrual account would be credited (cleared). At a retail property, for example, percentage rent may be computed monthly but paid quarterly. An accrual system would show this as a receivable item until it is paid or written off. Real estate taxes might be paid in two installments, say in April and December, but the accrual system would record one twelfth of the annual amount as an expense each month; when the payments are actually made (April, December), the account would be debited. Similarly, the parking lot application mentioned earlier would be shown as a payable item in June when the work was done, and the account would be debited in October when payment was made.

While most institutional owners will want the benefits of accrual accounting, they generally do not want the additional complications of that method. For that reason, many institutions will use a *modified accrual system* in which the major components of income are accrued. This would apply to rents in all types of properties and to common area maintenance (CAM) and other pass-through expenses paid by tenants in commercial properties, but not to such things as late fees or minor miscellaneous income items. On the expense side, real estate taxes and insurance premiums would almost always be accrued, and so would major repairs or replacements above a dollar amount set by the owner—e.g., $10,000—but smaller items would probably be handled on a cash basis.

An accrual system gives owners a better view of the property's financial status on a day-to-day basis than does a cash system. It also reduces the likelihood of monies being "lost" in the system. From the real estate manager's perspective, however, cash-basis accounting is preferable because cash is needed to pay the property expenses—accrued income means little if the monies are not collected. In fact, most accrual and modified accrual systems also require preparation of a cash statement periodically so everyone knows the property's cash position at a given time.

Bank Accounts for Clients' Funds. The client will almost always designate the types of bank accounts to be maintained although the choice of institution may be left to the manager. This issue is usually addressed specifically in the management agreement (see Chapter 9). Usually two bank accounts will be maintained for each property or each client. One will be an interest-bearing (deposit) account to be used as the repository for all income so it will accrue interest from the day it is received. The other is a

> **Trust Accounts**
>
> A trust account is a fiduciary account established by the real estate manager to hold funds that belong to another party—the property owner. Trust accounts are regulated by state law, and therefore the rules governing them vary on a state-by-state basis. In most states, all monies belonging to property owners must be deposited in a trust account. The same is true of security deposit monies collected from residents and commercial tenants—most states consider that these monies belong to the tenant. (Security deposits are regulated under landlord-tenant laws in a number of states.) It is advisable to include in the management agreement a description of how trust accounts are to be handled, regardless of whether there are specific laws in your state. Where laws exist, your procedures should comply with them.
>
> Usually funds must be deposited in a federally insured financial institution within the state. Often management firms establish two trust accounts for a client to separate security deposits from operating funds belonging to the owner. The requirements regarding interest-bearing accounts vary. Some states permit trust accounts to be interest bearing provided the management agreement states that this is to be done and disposition of the interest is stipulated. An interest-bearing account is particularly desirable in locales where landlords are required to pay interest to tenants on the security deposits held over from year to year.
>
> The downside of trust accounts includes the requirement, in most states, for deposits to be made within a very short period after monies are collected. In some states, deposits must be made immediately, before the end of the next banking day, or within 24 hours; elsewhere the timing is related to business (banking) days. The range extends to seven days in some states.

disbursement account. Usual procedure is for a batch of invoices to be collected periodically (e.g., once a week), and the money needed to pay them is transferred from the deposit account to the disbursement account, against which individual payment checks are written. Sometimes a client may have the right to "sweep" excess funds from the interest-bearing account electronically so that monies can be consolidated in the home office to maximize investment income. Regardless of the details of the client arrangement, a real estate manager is likely to work with two basic types of accounts—trust accounts and agency accounts.

Trust Accounts. The typical trust account is one set up by the broker (real estate manager) on behalf of the client. The broker and/or the broker's designated personnel are the only signatories on the account, and this type of account is subject to very strict state regulation. Clients sometimes ask to be signatories on trust accounts, but such an arrangement should not be allowed because it will jeopardize the broker's standing with state agencies.

A client's funds should not be commingled with those of other clients or with the manager's personal funds. Any interest earned belongs to the

> **Trust Accounts *(continued)***
> The most serious violation regarding trust accounts is commingling of funds. Although *specifics vary by state,* the following are considered to be instances of commingling of funds:
>
> - Management company funds or personal funds are deposited in a trust account set up for the property owner's funds.
> - Funds held in trust for the property owner are deposited in the agent's general or personal bank account.
> - The agent conducts his or her personal business through the trust account.
> - Funds of one client are used to make payments for another client's property.
> - Commissions or fees are left in the account longer than the allowable time.
> - Security deposits belonging to tenants are used to cover operating expenses of the managed property.
>
> Clients' trust accounts having a negative balance may also be considered commingling.
>
> Along with all the other regulation of trust accounts, there are often requirements for how long records of the transactions on the account must be retained. It is common to require that records be retained for at least three years after the account has been closed, although some firms may opt to keep records for longer periods consistent with their other record retention practices. Trust accounts are also subject to auditing by the state; some states audit all accounts on a regular rotating schedule (e.g., every two years), while others may conduct audits only when a complaint is received. Since questions raised about trust accounts also relate to the agreement between manager and property owner, the management agreement is clearly the place to spell out the details of trust account requirements for a particular management arrangement.

client, not the manager, and all funds must be fully accounted at all times—funds cannot be held outside the account or borrowed by the manager against future fees without approval of such actions by the client.

In most states, such trust accounts are audited routinely by a state representative, and disciplinary action can be taken if discrepancies are discovered. Depending on the severity of the infraction, the disciplinary action may be only a letter demanding compliance with account requirements, or it could be suspension or loss of the broker's license. If you take on a trust account without prior experience with this type of entity, it is a good idea to check with state authorities about their specific requirements, which can be more exacting than those of your client.

Agency Accounts. An agency account serves the same purpose as a trust account without the same state requirements. It should be noted, however, that the manager still has a fiduciary responsibility to the client that requires funds to be handled prudently. An agency account is generally set up with the same requirements as a trust account, except that the client is often a signatory in addition to the manager and/or the manager's representatives. While funds can be withdrawn from the account by the client at will, this is seldom done without first consulting the manager about the need for funds to operate the property.

Chart of Accounts. The chart of accounts for a managed property is generally dictated by the client, and it may not be consistent with the charts of accounts of other clients or with the basic system in place at the management company. Since most accounting systems are computerized, it should not be difficult to accommodate these differences and fulfill the requirements of individual property owners.

The income and expense categories in the chart of accounts will also vary with the type of property, depending in part on the features and facilities made available to the residents or commercial tenants. More comprehensive charts of accounts include categories for capital expenditures and debt service (if paid by management) and may also provide accounts for assets and depreciation.

Among the income categories are several items in addition to monthly rents. An apartment property is likely to itemize parking charges, late fees, interest, and income from coin-operated laundry equipment and vending machines. At a mobile home park (and some rental apartments), utility charges are billed separately to residents. On the other hand, condominiums and cooperatives generate no income as such—unit owners pay a monthly assessment that is a prorated portion of common area operating expenses and may include an amount for capital reserves. However, there is "other income" to be accounted from such sources as recreational facility or "guest suite" charges, interest, and late fees.

Commercial properties will have income categories for base rents and reimbursements—i.e., payments for operating expenses passed through to tenants. Late fees, utilities, parking, and interest are other common categories. For shopping centers, there is typically a category for percentage rent and separate categories for different operating expense reimbursements (e.g., real estate taxes, insurance, common area maintenance).

Expense categories will differentiate the entire array of expenditures common to rental properties—i.e., real estate taxes, insurance, management fees, building and grounds maintenance, common area utilities (electricity, heat), waste disposal, municipal utilities (water and sewer), and business permits. Apartment properties will also have separate categories or subcategories for maintenance of apartment interiors (plumbing, electrical, appliances, and carpet cleaning, repair, and replacement) and common areas (window washing, swimming pools, recreation rooms, security systems); marketing costs; and, if there is an on-site staff, payroll and personnel expenses.

At commercial properties, expense categories may be differentiated between costs borne by the property owner (e.g., the management fee) and those passed through to tenants for reimbursement. Real estate taxes, property insurance, and common area expenses, including maintenance and utilities, are typical pass-through expenses. (Common areas may include the roof in addition to the building exterior, parking lot, security systems and services, and landscaping.)

The main complication in commercial property accounting is the exceptions built into the leases of individual tenants, especially at shopping centers. It is not uncommon for one tenant's lease to exclude waste disposal because the tenant has a separate arrangement in place. A pad or outlot tenant may negotiate to obtain its own insurance coverages. Often there are differences in tenants' prorations of administrative costs, requiring special billings for each exception. If the property includes different uses (e.g., retail in an office building or offices in a shopping center), an additional set of subaccounts may have to be established.

It is desirable to have as complete a chart of accounts as is necessary to account for and analyze income and expense information. However, it should not be so large or so detailed as to increase the accounting expense without a commensurate increase in benefits. (Books that address the management of specific types of properties, such as those published by the Institute of Real Estate Management, are excellent sources for examples of property-specific charts of accounts and detailed explanations of their components; see Appendix C.)

Operations of the Accounting Department

The most common method of handling accounting functions in a real estate management business is to establish an accounting department. This may be only one person in a start-up business; however, if the clientele includes owners of large portfolios of residential or commercial properties, or both, the accounting department may employ a very large staff. (An in-house management department that is part of another business entity may have its own accounting function, or personnel in the accounting department of the main company may be assigned specifically to the management department's accounting needs.)

Depending on the size of the management business, and its in-house capabilities, the firm may contract for accounting services for part or all of its requirements. In particular, if a client's accounting software requires more sophisticated hardware than the firm has available, or if a client's turnaround time is radically different from that of other clients and the capabilities of the management firm's systems and personnel, use of a service bureau might be a worthwhile stopgap measure. However, service bureaus are seldom used because of the extended turnaround time required and the fact that most clients want the accounting function tightly controlled by the manager.

Internal Controls. Of the many functions of the accounting department, none is more important than the handling of funds. Because monies belonging to clients are received and paid in the name of the managed property or its ownership, it is imperative to establish specific policies and procedures for handling receipts and disbursements. Supervision of accounting personnel and others who handle the funds of the company and its clients is a primary safeguard. Financial activities are generally assigned within the office so that one person is responsible for collecting the funds, but another will make up the bank deposit. Payments are approached similarly: When invoices are received, one person will approve the payment and another will prepare the check. Often a third person will actually sign the check.

These types of internal checks and balances reduce the possibility of theft or misappropriation of funds as well as minimize the potential for accounting errors. Most management companies will also institute an internal audit system in which a supervisor reviews prior transactions for irregularities. If an unusual charge shows up, for example, the supervisor will question those who approved the expense and may even contact the vendor to determine what product or service was provided (and, when applicable, how it applies to a specific property). Obviously if everyone's answers are satisfactory, the audit will be considered closed. However, if the answers are unsatisfactory, the supervisor will have to continue the investigation until he or she is satisfied or the problem has been corrected or eliminated.

In most companies, authorization to sign checks for the business is limited to the principal (the business owner) or the executive responsible for accounting and finance (the controller) or an accounting supervisor. Particular authorizations to sign, as well as dollar limitations and a need for more than one signature, would be arranged with and on record at the bank on which the account is drawn. (In most situations, checks that exceed a set amount must be signed by two individuals; this reduces the chances of error and averts the potential for misdirection of funds.) Specific arrangements should be in place for the management business in particular. Accounts established for clients may require the signature of a management company executive or, in some cases, a representative of the client. Accounting personnel need to know who is authorized to sign checks for company and client accounts and understand the limitations on individuals' signatory authority.

The handling of clients' funds requires insurance to protect the funds. Most management agreements will require the management company to provide a *fidelity bond* in an amount sufficient to cover the largest balance of the clients' funds that the firm is likely to have on hand at any time. Providing for electronic "sweeps" of clients' accounts can help reduce the amount of money on hand and, thus, lower the amount of the fidelity bond required. A large management company may employ a full-time internal auditor as an added safeguard.

Strict adherence to the internal controls you establish and implement will not only minimize problems within the accounting function, but also help assure that there will be very few problems uncovered in any performance audits requested by clients. Because the accounting department also serves the accounting needs of the management company, the internal controls must be applied to the handling of the company's financial transactions as well as those of its clients.

Payments Received. Incoming funds must be accounted accurately and promptly. Cash in any amount can tempt a potential thief, whether that person is a staff member or comes in off the street. Negotiable forms of payment (checks, money orders) can pose a similar risk in some situations. Although residential properties may have to accept cash from time to time, it should be company policy that checks or money orders are the *preferred* form of payment. Even so, if rents are paid on site, rather than mailed directly to the management company central office, there is a potential risk. At commercial properties, there is little opportunity for theft of cash because payments are almost always made by check and mailed to the management company. It is extremely rare for a payment to be made at the property, and cash transactions are almost nonexistent.

However, a clever bookkeeper could manipulate incoming checks and convert them to personal use. For this reason, it is critical to have in place a system of checks and balances that will serve as an early warning system if funds are not being handled properly. An accrual or modified accrual system is also helpful in this regard because monies due are set up as receivables, and that posting can only be reconciled by incoming cash or a specific write-off. If a receipts-handling system is set up properly, a supervisor should be able to detect any irregularities with a superficial review and take action immediately to correct the situation. (Institutional owners have annual audits performed to ensure that the accounts balance properly.)

Funds should be deposited as soon as possible and practical, preferably the day they are received, but not more than a day or two later. It is not unusual for clients to demand daily deposits even if the amount is not large. As a security measure, it is best not to let it become common knowledge that a property keeps large amounts of cash or checks on site. (See also the discussion of Trust Accounts earlier in this chapter.)

> ### Performance Audits
>
> The management agreement provides for the owner of the real estate to audit management company records related to the managed property. Because of this provision, it is best to keep accounting and other records of a property's management activities up to date. If you have been doing your job right, the audit will confirm this. Sometimes an owner only wants to validate the legitimacy of budget variances or specific disbursements. An institutional owner may have an obligation to its stockholders that requires periodic audits of all accounting records, including the real estate management function. Sometimes, however, there may be a serious problem that needs to be addressed. Regardless of the need or reason, you should be prepared to work with the auditor to obtain the desired information and to provide answers to questions that arise.
>
> You should be notified in advance when an audit will be made. This is not just a courtesy—it may be necessary to collect information from the on-site management office as well as to prepare a work space for the auditor and adjust your schedule so you can spend some time with him or her as necessary or appropriate. Ideally, the notice will come from the client and include the record-keeping period the audit should cover. It may also signal whether the client has a particular concern or indicate that the audit is purely routine. Either way, it should allow you ample time to gather records and make sure those for the period to be audited are complete and up to date.
>
> If the notice does not contain these particulars, the client should be asked for a letter of authorization that identifies the auditor and states the intended scope of the audit. (A check against the management agreement clause will indicate whether the audit is within the parameters defined there.)

Deposit Controls. It is not unusual for all funds to be sent to the main office of the management firm rather than being collected on site. This allows for a more-sophisticated accounting system and personnel and removes temptation and the potential for error at the site level.

An alternative approach is to have a bank "lock box." All monies are sent to a local bank where an account for the property has been established, and the funds are deposited directly to the account by the bank. Note, however, that there may be a significant time lag between receipt at the lock box and when the management company knows who has or has not paid their rent.

If monies are collected on site and deposited locally, a copy of the deposit slip is generally sent to the main office—by fax—immediately after the deposit is made. A supervisor is then responsible for checking the deposit records to be sure they agree with the tenant payment records and that everything will reconcile properly at month's end.

Bank Account Reconciliation. One of the most important tools in accounting is the bank account reconciliation. Generally bank accounts are

> **Performance Audits *(continued)***
> The auditor may contact you, but it is better if you take the initiative and ask the auditor to provide written details of the time period to be covered and any specific documents needed for the review; whether the audit will be done in your office, at the managed property, or in both places; when the auditor will be there (dates and times), and what provisions need to be made to accommodate him or her (office space, equipment, etc.).
> Professional auditors are people, too, and they, like everyone else, respond to a welcoming environment. Introductions to accounting personnel and others from whom they may need information are a must. A tour of the office, including areas where coffee and other refreshments are available, is also in order. A cleared desk in a quiet area and the records to be audited should be ready when the auditor arrives.
> Apart from the initial welcoming tour and introductions, you may want to offer an early meeting opportunity—perhaps over lunch—so you can try to discover what the audit is expected to uncover and let the auditor know you are willing to answer questions. Otherwise, the auditor should be left alone to conduct the audit. However, a meeting after the audit has been completed is also in order. You should be prepared to answer questions and explain your approaches and practices.
> Finally, keep in mind that your client is also the auditor's client. Kind words are appropriate, but they should not be overblown. You can expect anything you say to be presented to your mutual client in the context of the auditor's report. Nor should you take a defensive stance. Often there are details of real estate management accounting procedures that are peculiar to a property or are accepted industry standards even though they may be somewhat at variance with standard accounting practices. An explanation of this difference may be all that is required.

set up so they and the accounting records have the same cut-off date so that complete reports can be in the owners' hands on time. (Timing of account closing dates is discussed later in this chapter.)

Using a form similar to that shown in Exhibit 4.2, the accountant will take the account balance shown by the bank, add to it deposits made after the account closing date, and deduct checks that have not yet cleared the bank. The result should agree with the account balance on the check register. If the two amounts do not agree, the accountant must identify the item or items that comprise the discrepancy—e.g., an outstanding check, an unrecorded deposit—and make the amounts agree. Usually outstanding checks will be recent issues, often with consecutive numbers, but occasionally a payment from the previous month or even earlier may not have cleared the bank. Likewise, a deposit may not be recorded in the check register if more than one deposit was made the same day or a bank holiday required a deviation from the usual practice.

Because of the potential for errors as well as confusion, clients' bank accounts should be reconciled promptly each month. The bank reconcilia-

Exhibit 4.2
Sample Bank Account Reconciliation Form

Property:		Date:
Account Balance per Statement		$
Less Outstanding Checks		
Check No.	Amount	
		$
Plus Deposits in Transit		
Date	Amount	
		$
Other Adjustments		
Description	Amount	
		$
Adjusted Cash Balance		$
Cash Balance per General Ledger		$
Less Adjustments		
Description	Amount	
Adjusted Balance		$

> ### Preventing Employee and Officer Fraud
>
> One of the most important responsibilities of a management company is to safeguard the funds, supplies, and other personal property that belong to its owner-clients. As in any business venture, the issues of theft and fraud (by employees or officers) require implementation of specific preventive strategies. The most basic precautions against the mishandling of funds involve company policies and procedures for handling receipts, especially cash. Recommended policies include:
>
> - Keep cash and checks out of sight and locked away at all times.
> - Use a safe with a slit for depositing sealed envelopes containing cash.
> - A master key should be necessary for obtaining access to accumulated funds (dual key system).
> - If the amount of cash is large, an armored car service may be used to transfer funds.
> - Encourage residents or commercial tenants to pay rent and other charges with checks or money orders to minimize the amount of cash on site.
> - Deposit cash and checks daily.
> - Make night deposits to a bank lock box.
> - Limit the number of people assigned responsibility for handling funds.
> - Require written records of all transactions, signed by the responsible employee and including the date and time.
> - Give receipts for all monies collected and keep a copy of those receipts in the office.
>
> Receipts should match payments required as shown on leases and amounts recorded in residents' and commercial tenants' ledgers. Reconciliations should be performed by a different employee from the one charged with accepting payments and making deposits. As an added safeguard, site records should be audited periodically.

tion report is one of the first items sophisticated clients will review to be sure their accounts are in order. An astute business owner will personally reconcile accounts from time to time to be assured that they are in order. This discipline should apply to the company's accounts as well as the clients' accounts.

Approval of Invoices. Processing of incoming invoices is a critical component of the accounting function. Bills must be paid on time to assure the continued availability of products and services and to maintain the reputation of the property. It is also important to be sure the correct amounts are paid and allowable discounts are taken whenever possible. Incoming invoices should be marked with the date received (by hand or using a date stamp) and directed to the proper person for approval. This not only expedites timely payment but allows the entire payment process to be tracked. It also facilitates communication with vendors regarding payment timing.

> **Preventing Employee and Officer Fraud** *(continued)*
>
> Equipping the office with blinds or other window coverings that can be closed when money is being counted makes this activity less apparent. You can also install an alarm system in the management office that alerts police to any break-in or disturbance. A code should be required for each individual who has to access the management office. This will allow the alarm system to be deactivated and reactivated each morning and evening. These codes will have to be changed when employees leave the company, although newer technologies allow for personalized access codes, and you need only cancel the one person's code when he or she terminates employment. Electronic locks, timing devices, and monitoring via closed-circuit television (CCTV) are other options you may want to explore for business security.
>
> It is good business practice, in general, to store blank checks in a locked file or a safe. (Periodic review to ensure that checks are used in sequential order is also advisable.) Specific staff members who use the checks should be given sole access to the storage area via keys or other access-control devices. The same safeguards may be applied to other office supplies, in which case it is a good idea to take inventory regularly. All files and business records, especially those regarding the company's and its clients' finances, should be kept under lock and key, and employees should be reminded regularly of their responsibility to keep such records confidential.
>
> Requiring regular financial reports to compare results to a realistic budget will help identify significant variances that may be early warning signs. Use of purchase orders for all supplies and services will facilitate internal tracking of deliveries and payments and frequency of re-orders. Other safeguards include maintaining a list of authorized vendors and not allowing purchase orders to be issued without prior authorization and designation of accounts to be charged.

The best invoice-handling procedures require that supplies or services are accounted when they are ordered, using either a numbered purchase order (see Exhibit 4.3) or a specific contract. When the merchandise is delivered or the service is rendered, the person who placed the order should ensure that the item or service is what was ordered and the price is as agreed. That person should then approve the invoice and forward it to the accounting department for payment. Any shipping documents that came with the merchandise should be attached to the invoice as additional verification. (The same procedures apply to purchasing for managed properties, and the manager of the property or other designated individual would be responsible for the required approvals.)

Exhibit 4.4 shows the information typically included on a payment approval stamp used at a managed property. Note the inclusion of spaces to indicate accounts and amounts for distributing the charges. In the absence of this type of rubber stamp, approval can be signaled by writing the following minimum information directly on the invoice.

- Payment approval ("OK to pay")

Exhibit 4.3
Sample Contents of a Purchase Order Form

- Purchase order number
- Order date
- Vendor name and address
- Name of the person placing the order
- Delivery address and required delivery date
- Billing address
- Space to list the quantity, item description, unit price, and extended price
- Spaces for signatures of the originator and approving supervisor

Standard blank forms can be purchased from office supply stores, and these are often satisfactory for general purchases because they have ample space to write or type detailed descriptions. Some mail order office supply houses offer property management-specific forms in a variety of formats. Often these are carbonless (NCR paper) or carbonsets (three or four copies per set) that can be crash-imprinted with the firm's name and address.

If the company has personalized forms prepared, blanks might be added to indicate disposition of delivery charges, the account number to which it should be charged and, when applicable, the building or the tenant or space for which the purchase is being made (names or number codes). Spaces may also be included to indicate a vendor number and to itemize sales taxes and negotiated discounts. Purchase order forms usually have "terms of purchase" printed on the reverse, and this type of information should be developed with the guidance of legal and/or accounting professionals. Such forms are often carbonsets providing copies for the accounting department and the originator—the original is sent to the vendor or service provider. Additional copies may be warranted to satisfy the requirements of the accounting function (i.e., one for attachment to the invoice in the approval process) or the property owner-client (e.g., to accompany the monthly reports).

- Authorized person's signature and the date
- Property name or code
- Vendor number or code (if required and known)
- Account number to be charged

If the expense is to be charged to more than one account, the specific dollar amounts (or percentages) chargeable to each different account number should be indicated.

It is the responsibility of accounting personnel to check that the amounts on the invoice are properly extended (quantity multiplied by unit price) and that it has not been paid previously. Requiring that payment be made from invoices only and not from statements is one assurance that billings do not include prior balances or amounts not related to a specific purchase. Once the items and amounts have been verified, the invoice should be recorded and paid.

In a small company, one person in the accounting department may

Exhibit 4.4
Sample Payment Approval Stamp

APPROVAL FOR PAYMENT

Property No. _____	Process Date _____
Invoice No. _____	Invoice Date _____
Account Code _____	Amount ($) _____
Account Code _____	Amount ($) _____
Account Code _____	Amount ($) _____
Vendor No. _____	On-Site Manager _____
Property Manager _____	
Accounting _____	

Custom-made rubber stamps such as this can be ordered from local office supply stores. Lines can be added for additional levels of approval or to accommodate more specific accounting notations (e.g., payment date and check number). A stamp for management company internal use might include spaces to identify the people responsible (ordered by, approved by) instead of site and property managers and, possibly, a purchase order number.

---

match orders and invoices, verify the invoice calculations, record the payment, prepare the check, and (possibly) sign it. This is not an advisable practice because of the risks it poses—there are no checks and balances. It is much better altogether if the person who prepares the check generally is not the one who will sign it. This allows for at least one additional person to verify, to the extent possible, that everything regarding the payment is in order. It is not unusual for clients to insist that any check drawn against their accounts in amounts exceeding a preset dollar limit (e.g., $1,000.00) bear two signatures. This is a recommended practice regardless of clients' requirements because it provides a safeguard against mishandling or misappropriation of clients' funds.

Accounting Systems. There are two types of accounting systems in common use—manual and automated (computerized). While manual systems are generally not sophisticated enough to meet the accounting requirements of owners of complex properties, they are still useful for some types of record keeping. Because the manager is often required to provide a comprehensive analysis of the numerical data as well as make projections, a computer spreadsheet analysis program is often necessary. This type of tool is also essential for evaluating the success of the management company's operations.

It is very important to create and maintain backup files of management company financial data as well as information and reports related to the managed properties, regardless of the system being used. This issue is addressed in the discussion of Contingency Planning in Chapter 3.

Manual Systems. Some records in real estate management continue to be recorded by hand, at least in the preliminary stages, because data often are accumulated one number at a time. Leasing traffic reports and a roster of vacancies are examples. While manual recording systems can be time-consuming and cumbersome, they offer the advantage of easy changes and corrections and accessibility for direct supervisory review. However, they have the disadvantage of being subject to human error in terms of both numerical entries and computations, and it can be difficult to read another person's handwriting.

A one-person start-up management business intending to serve a small number of clients whose reporting needs are uncomplicated may be able to utilize some type of manual system initially. For many purposes, a one-write system that creates a systematic record of cash received and at the same time generates a written receipt for the payee may be adequate. Entries in a cash receipts ledger and a disbursements ledger are often handwritten, as are the annotations on individual residents' and tenants' ledgers. Straight-forward reports for the property owner can be typewritten neatly in a format that differentiates entries as necessary or appropriate. It is possible, if not desirable, to start out simply and acquire more sophisticated systems and equipment as your business needs grow. Most accounting calculations can be verified with an adding machine or electronic calculator; a machine that generates a printed tape is preferable because it produces a written record that can be kept with the handwritten reports. However, many would argue that, compared to computerized systematization, the time required to perform accounting tasks manually could be more effectively spent managing and supervising the properties.

Computer Systems. Most real estate management companies use computer systems to maintain their accounts. They may utilize a PC (professional computer microprocessor) with a simple software program to create a record and enter specific data, then have a service bureau prepare the owners' monthly statements. The data might be transmitted to the service bureau via modem or delivered to them on a "floppy" disk. This type of setup is more common in the management of a small portfolio of residential properties whose owners' reporting requirements are fairly simple. If a firm manages large properties, whether they are residential or commercial, it will be expected to have or have access to a state-of-the-art computer system with integrated systems for tracking receivables, payables, and pass-throughs and for preparing invoices and operating statements.

Before purchasing any kind of computer system, it is imperative to know what your accounting needs are so you can find a system that will meet your needs. Buying a system and trying to mold your accounting requirements to its capabilities is counterproductive. Clients' software requirements (and compatibilities) are additional considerations. Generally, it is recommended that you choose the software first and then seek out appropriate hardware to run it efficiently. Talking with other managers who have had happy and unhappy experiences with computers and asking to see samples of reports and formats are important components of the decision to purchase a computer. Talking with someone who is using the system you prefer and, if possible, trying it out *before* you make a commitment to purchase—perhaps a short-term lease can be arranged—should help answer your questions and alleviate your concerns.

There are accounting software packages suited to very small residential properties; these may cost only a few hundred dollars. A very sophisticated system that will integrate all the functions needed for a complex portfolio of commercial properties could cost tens of thousands of dollars. The costs reflect, in part, the hardware capabilities (memory capacity, operating speed) necessary to support particular software packages and may not include upgrades of electrical and telephone cabling to accommodate the equipment. Frankly, it is unlikely that there is a standard accounting package available that will perform all the functions one desires in the manner in which they need to be performed. However, the cost of having custom software developed is likely to exceed the resources of any but the largest management firms. If your clients are committed to specific accounting software, it is more important for you to be able to have hardware that will run that particular program.

It should also be understood that a particular computer accounting package will not educate the newcomer to the accounting function. In order to use the computer program properly, one must fully understand the accounting function in the first place. When making a purchase decision, the costs of training key personnel should be included in the calculations. Ideally, a properly trained accountant or someone whose background includes experience in accounting and bookkeeping would be charged with learning to operate the computerized program and supervising the preparation of the accounting reports for your owner-clients.

You may find that your needs for the management business are sufficiently different from those of your clients that you will want to acquire specific software packages for your own use. You should also consider other potential uses for this equipment, which is often a major capital investment for a business. There are software programs for tracking inventories of supplies as well as monitoring maintenance work orders. A good word-processing program will facilitate preparation of correspondence and narrative reports. Sophisticated spreadsheet programs are available for conducting investment analyses, and graphics imaging programs facilitate in-house preparation of presentation materials. Desktop publishing software, while not mandatory for the use, can make it easy to generate newsletters for circulation to clients, residents and commercial tenants, and your employees. There are also specific programs that provide templates and therefore facilitate development of things like business plans and operations manuals.

While software programs usually can be written to address unique business needs, this can be very expensive and time-consuming. Modification of an off-the-shelf program that comes close to fulfilling your requirements may be a more practical approach. Consultation with a computer expert should help you determine the basic hardware appropriate to your intended use, and you can add specific software applications as your business needs and your budget permit. (Examples of other types of software programs are described in Chapter 2.)

[NOTE: Because computer technology is constantly changing and improving, a more detailed discussion is beyond the scope of this book. However, the Institute of Real Estate Management conducts periodic analyses of computer systems and software, publishing comparison data on the features and uses of different programs. The *Journal of Property Management* publishes current review data on computer software at least once a year, as well. These sources are recommended for more definitive information on accounting software. Also, the cumulative supplement to our book, *Managing and Leasing Commercial Properties,* published by John Wiley & Sons, Inc., includes a discussion of converting to another software system and selecting accounting software.]

Accounting Personnel. The number of people responsible for the accounting function will depend, in part, on the size of the company's management portfolio and the degree of reporting sophistication required by individual owner-clients. There may be a single bookkeeper who literally does all the accounting work, in which case it may be advisable to cross-train others who can perform the accounting function if the bookkeeper is ill or takes vacation time. (Cross-training also adds to your internal controls.) Other staff members may be assigned to specific accounting tasks on a part-time or as-needed basis, but the costs of these personnel should be considered. It may be more practical to bring in temporary accounting personnel to ensure timely accounting and report preparation. Having a relationship with an accounting firm or a certified public accountant (CPA) who understands the management firm's operations is advisable regardless of company size. This would not only provide for back-up accounting services on an as-needed basis but also serve as a resource in regard to specific accounting practices.

Full-Charge Bookkeeper. In a small company, the accounting department may consist of a single full-charge bookkeeper who performs all of the accounting functions necessary to the operation of the managed properties in addition to keeping the books for the management company and, perhaps, even performing the business owner's personal record keeping. There are many advantages to this arrangement. In particular, at least one person generally knows the system's capabilities and fully understands the owner-clients' requirements for their individual properties.

The danger in this situation is the fact that this person is usually the only one who understands the system, which means only he or she can perform the accounting function. This person is also in a position to manipulate the system for personal gain or to sabotage a manager-client relationship if he or she were so disposed. This prospect can be averted, however, by instituting a system of checks and balances: The individual's work should be reviewed periodically to catch inadvertent errors and discourage dishonesty. If the bookkeeper makes out checks, someone else in a position of authority (e.g., a company executive) should have to sign them. Invoices should be reviewed and approved by someone other than the bookkeeper—there should be no exceptions to this—and someone in authority should review the bank account reconciliations and verify income items against tenant records from time to time.

Accounts Payable Function. In large companies, the functions within the accounting department are compartmentalized. The accounts payable function may be assigned to one or more people who have no other responsibility. These individuals can become very adept at evaluating invoices, analyzing them for accuracy, and making sure they are not duplications of prior bills.

An invoice that comes into the management office should be pre-approved for payment by the person who ordered the product or service. The approved invoice is checked by accounting personnel for accuracy, discounts allowed, merchandise not delivered (i.e., back orders), etc., and prepared for payment. (If the approval does not include the account to be charged, this information must be noted on the invoice, or it should be returned to the person who approved it for the information.) The person who prepares the check should not sign it.

Accounts Receivable Function. The accounts receivable function is responsible for receiving and recording the company's income from management fees and other sources. However, its major activities are property related because it is also responsible for the income from the managed properties. This person usually maintains the tenant records, and working from lease summaries, he or she sends out monthly invoices for the rent (if applicable). Rent checks are also logged in and checked to be sure tenants have paid the invoiced amounts. This person also monitors tenant rent increases, tracks percentage rents that are due, and prepares a delinquency report. He or she is generally responsible for making sure that all accounts are balanced and in agreement with the bank statements (bank account reconciliation).

Rent Collections Function. In many companies that manage commercial properties, the manager of the property is responsible for rent collection. He or she knows the tenants better than anyone else does, and often there is no one else to assume this responsibility. At residential properties, rents are usually collected in either of two ways: If there is a site manager in residence, he or she is responsible for collecting the rent, and only those situations requiring legal action (e.g., evictions) are handled by other management company personnel. At small properties where there is no on-site management, the manager who supervises the property's operations would be responsible for collections. Alternatively, residents may be required to mail their rent payments to the management office. In all situations, collections should be a specific responsibility of one person; this assures that they are being handled properly and in a timely manner.

As the management company grows and the accounting staff is increased, it is not unusual for accounting personnel to assist with or take over the collections function. This is a logical activity of the accounting department, and the change has the added advantage of removing the manager of the property from the collections function, which has the potential to generate hard feelings when a tenant is being pressured to pay what is owed. Large firms may even employ someone who does nothing but collections. Having a collections specialist on staff relieves both accounting and management departments of this difficult and sensitive task.

Records and Reports. The accounting department also has a role in maintaining various financial records for the managed properties, in particular to assist in the preparation of budgets and management plans for succeeding years, as well as the monthly financial reports on property operations. At commercial properties, pass-through expenses and percentage rents based on retailers' sales are important sources of operating revenue (these reports are described on pages 113–115). The types of numerical reports that accompany the owner's monthly operating statement are listed in Exhibit 4.5. (Other components of the monthly management report are described in Chapter 3 and Exhibit 3.1.)

Exhibit 4.5
Typical Monthly Accounting Reports—Numerical Data

- Income Statement
- Budget Variance Analysis
- Bank Account Reconciliations
- General Ledger
- Rent Roll
- Delinquency Report (including action taken to collect monies due)
- Vacancy Report
- Lease Expiration Summaries
- Market Surveys
- Traffic Reports (marketing and leasing activities)
- Turnover Reports and Evaluations (resident/tenant retention)
- Shopping Reports (residential property comparison data)
- Inspection Reports (summaries)
- Operating Expense Pass-Through Report (commercial property prorations and payments)
- Sales Reports (retail tenants' percentage rents)
- Bad Debt Reports

This list comprises the items typically submitted along with the narrative explanation of activities at a particular residential or commercial property. In some situations, reports may be combined (e.g., delinquencies and vacancies may be tracked on the rent roll).

A *balance sheet* may be prepared periodically showing assets and liabilities of the managed property; this is not ordinarily a regular component of the monthly operating statement. Particulars of a marketing plan and examples of advertisements and promotional pieces may be occasional inclusions; ongoing marketing *results* should be reported regardless.

Budgets. There are too many variables in both income and expenses to allow the financial outcome of a property to be left purely to chance. While many things are outside the manager's control, it is possible to plan and, hopefully from that plan, to be ready for the most likely occurrences. Although it is extremely rare for real estate managers to budget for more than a single year at a time, some institutional owners require the manager to prepare an additional five-year budget. In this approach, each expense item is increased by an inflation factor for each year, and estimates of major maintenance and capital expenditures for each year are usually included.

The manager typically prepares the next year's operating budget for a property late in the current year. Much of the information on which the budget is based is from what has happened in the current year (and immediate past years). Most often the accounting department will provide operating statements for the current year as well as those from past years to be included as appendices in the budget package that is presented to the owner. Many times a summary of previous years' operations is all that is needed, however, and the operating statements may simply serve as a reference for the manager in developing a rationale for specific dollar items. For example, if the landscaping maintenance cost for the past three years

> **Commercial Property-Specific Reports**
>
> **Pass-Through Expenses** The practice of prorating operating expenses and passing them through to tenants for reimbursement is unique to the management of commercial properties. Commonly referred to as pass-through expenses or bill-backs, these billings can become a source of disagreement between landlords and commercial tenants. If not handled properly, the result can be a loss of income that impacts not only the property's income stream but also its value.
>
> In small management firms, the billing for these expenses is often prepared by the manager of the property and sent to the tenants, with a copy to the accounting department for the property records. There is little doubt that the manager must be part of this billing process because he or she is usually the one who orders most of the maintenance and repairs at the property. However, it is a good idea to have a second person review the figures before these bills are sent.
>
> Ideally, each tenant's lease will have been analyzed to determine exactly what the tenant is obligated to pay and how it is to be paid. (Each commercial lease should state the common area expenses that are to be billed to the tenant, the tenant's pro rata share, and the basis for the proration—e.g., the percentage of a shopping center's gross leasable area, in square feet, represented by the tenant's gross leasable area, or such other basis as may be appropriate for the individual property.) From this analysis, a master list of the individual prorations should be developed for use in preparing the monthly billings. As new tenants lease space at the property, the master list should be revised so it is current at all times. This list should also indicate specific exceptions, as when a tenant does not pay for waste disposal.
>
> It is also a good idea to maintain a master file for accumulating all the items that are to be billed back to the tenants. This not only makes the information available for review when bills are prepared, but also serves as the data resource for periodic account reconciliations. Often the pass-through billings are estimates—for example, payments made by management for real estate taxes and insurance may be made only twice a year—and the actual expenditures will require adjustment of the amounts owed by tenants.

has been around $21,000 each year, it is safe to estimate a similar amount for the coming year, assuming nothing has changed; the figure should, however, be adjusted for inflation as appropriate. As part of the process of estimating the landscaping costs, the existing contract and the costs of landscaping materials (sod, shrubs, chemical treatments) should be scrutinized, and the landscape systems that are in place should be analyzed to see if they should be upgraded in the coming year. With computer accounting software, it is easy to generate a three-year analysis of all income and expense items to guide the manager in making budget projections.

The accounting department should be able to prepare an analysis (or trend report) for the past year and the year preceding it to serve as a basis for the next year's budget. Lease data regarding rents and rent increases should be entered in the computer system so the accounting department

> **Commercial Property-Specific Reports** *(continued)*
>
> It is not unusual for anchor tenants or major space users to be billed for one set of operating expenses while ancillary or shop tenants are billed differently for the same items or charged for additional ones. Anchor tenants often have exclusions or limits on expenditures that do not apply to the shop tenants (e.g., a cap on expense pass-through increases). Administrative expenses may be charged differently to different merchants.
>
> In office buildings, there usually are no such variances between types of tenants. However, in buildings where base years are part of the operating expense billing calculation, it is possible to have several different base years to be accounted, which can complicate the billing process. (Sometimes stop clauses in tenants' leases have to be considered.) If these billings are not handled properly, the property can lose a great deal of income, and the office tenants may lose confidence in the management of the building.
>
> The most common approach to pass-through expense billings relies on monthly estimates and a *year-end reconciliation*. For example, suppose the budget for an industrial property indicates that a paint shop tenant will owe $1,200 for common area operating expenses for the year. The tenant would be billed $100 each month throughout the year as an estimate of its share. Then, if the year-end calculation from actual expenditures indicates a $1,300 share, the tenant would be billed for the $100 difference. Conversely, if the year-end total came to $1,100, the tenant might be given a refund or the $100 difference could be credited to the tenant's account for the coming year.
>
> Because these year-end reconciliations are important to the tenant as well as the landlord, they should be accurate and timely. The accounting for the reconciliations is the same as for the monthly expense billings, but with the added requirement of reviewing all the expenditures for the year to be sure the amounts are reasonable and consistent with conditions in the market. It is not unknown for a landlord to pay some of these expenses out-of-pocket rather then pass them along to tenants who may be having difficulties making ends meet because of market conditions or other situations outside their control. Such actions might be accounted for as a loan and, depending on the lease terms, collectible with interest at a later date.

can run a lease analysis for the coming year. This should show the existing tenants, their lease terms, and any changes that will come up during the year. Many commercial leases have built-in rent increases, with the amounts and due dates stated specifically. For tenants whose rent adjustments are based on increases in the Consumer Price Index (CPI), the due dates on the computer printout can be used with current CPI data to estimate the amount of those tenants' rent increases. Other analyses that can be provided by the accounting department include rents received under *new* leases in the preceding year or six-month period and historical data on income from operating expense pass-throughs, utilities, and other sources. These numbers, tempered with anticipated changes in the marketplace, become the basis for projecting next year's income.

Once the manager has completed the budget for a property, it is impor-

> **Commercial Property-Specific Reports** *(concluded)*
>
> **Sales Reports** Accounting for sales reports and percentage rents is common to shopping centers and also to other properties where retail and/or service businesses lease space (e.g., office buildings and industrial sites). Sales reports are important for two reasons: First, they indicate when percentage rent is due, and second, they are a means of measuring the success of retail tenants.
>
> To assure that the required reports are received and properly processed, a master list of all tenants should be prepared, including identification of those who are required to submit sales reports. It should also show when reports are to be submitted and when percentage rents are to be paid. (Some managers may choose to account solely for those required to report, but having a complete list reduces the chances that a tenant is inadvertently omitted.)
>
> It is not unusual for the accounting department or the manager of the property to send every tenant a supply of sales reporting forms at the start of each year so they will be encouraged to comply with this requirement. When reports are received, they must be checked for accuracy and to determine any monies due. (Sales may be verified by having tenants submit validated copies of sales tax reports filed with a state or municipal authority.) If payment is submitted with the report, it is important to verify that the amount is correct. When reports are not received on time, someone has to follow up with the tenant; when payments are not received on time, they are accounted as a receivable, and the tenant must be contacted to arrange payment.
>
> Typically a sales report and analysis is prepared so that management can review the income and evaluate the progress of the merchants. In large shopping centers and malls, monthly as well as annual reports are prepared showing each tenants' sales and comparing the current figures to past periods, with projections of next year's figures.

tant for the accounting department to verify the accuracy of the numbers and check the format to be sure it can be integrated into the system once it is approved by the client.

Monthly Management Reports. Monthly management reports are the client's main link to the property and how it is faring under management. Consequently, timely and accurate reporting is critical to the effective management of a property. Furthermore, institutional clients generally have a large portfolio of properties that includes the one under management. If the reports are late or if they are incomplete or inaccurate, the asset manager's reports will be delayed, or possibly invalidated, and this can create severe problems for the property owner.

Each month, the client receives a number of specific accounting reports (see Exhibit 4.5) accompanied by a narrative description of what has happened during the month and the impact of those occurrences on property operations. Account closing and reporting dates should be carefully coordinated with the accounting department to be sure there is sufficient time, not only to close out the records for the month and issue the numerical reports, but also to allow the manager of the property sufficient time to analyze the data, prepare the narrative report, and present the package to the owner as agreed. Typically, it takes 15 days to complete these reports and deliver them to the client. If the client is to receive reports on the 10th of the month, the books for the property should be closed on the 25th of the preceding month. (Bank accounts should close on the same date so that the account reconciliation covering the same period is included in the report package.) Many large institutions are driven by financial reports, and the importance of their being on time, complete, and accurate cannot be overemphasized.

As reporting requirements become more sophisticated—use of computers permits all types of analyses to be run, and each new capability tends to spawn a report that utilizes it—accounting departments are being asked to reconcile more information each month, and this requires ever more time and effort. The data themselves often need explanations that require research as well as analysis. For example, if $48,600 was budgeted for income from rents in the current month, and the amount collected was only $43,500, most clients will want to know very specifically why less money was collected and which tenants did not pay their rent. It is not enough to indicate that there is a delinquency or that an amount is being disputed. Especially in large companies where much of the detail work is compartmentalized, it is incumbent on the manager of the property to monitor the accounting function throughout the month so the month-end results do not come as a surprise or require a rushed analysis.

It is also a good idea to have the accounting supervisor review the final reports to be sure they are accurate and complete before they are sent to the client. Nothing is more frustrating for a client than receiving incomplete or inaccurate reports because often he or she will be incorporating the management company's report data into other reports that go further up the line, and that process must be halted until the management report is corrected.

Disbursement of Net Cash Flow. When a property generates positive cash flow, the manager of the property is responsible for its disposition. The manner in which it is to be handled should be spelled out in the management agreement. Generally, the manager is allowed to retain sufficient cash to cover normal operating expenses. Any balance over that amount is disbursed to the owners on a fixed schedule (e.g., once or twice a month), often via electronic transfer. Many times the prior month's proceeds will be sent to the owner with the monthly management report, in effect "netting out" the previous month. In rare instances, however, the manager may deposit the proceeds in an interest-bearing account until the owner asks for specific disbursement. It is also commonplace for owners to "sweep" the property bank account, removing the additional funds any time the balance exceeds a prescribed amount. This is done by electronic transfer, and the "trigger" number is agreed to in advance by the client and the manager—and presumably stated in the management agreement—so both parties know and understand when the funds are likely to be transferred.

On-Site Accounting

On-site accounting is fairly commonplace at residential properties. However, at commercial properties, it is rarely seen unless the property is locally owned and managed completely on site. Where the owner has other interests or the property is managed by a third party, rents are collected and bills are paid out of a central management office. Different property types require different approaches to on-site accounting.

Residential Properties. Often a residential property will have some management personnel on site, and at larger properties, there may be an accountant or bookkeeper as well. From the property manager's perspective, this is an excellent arrangement because all the records are maintained on site, and all the manager has to do is review and analyze the material. As accounting costs rise, accounting and record keeping are increasingly likely to be performed on site. However, this move also increases the potential for mistakes in record keeping and misappropriation of funds, and safeguards must be built in when on-site personnel perform the accounting function.

As real estate management has become more sophisticated, on-site accounting systems have become computerized, and they are often linked to the computers at the management company office. The computer records can be checked at any time, replacing a visit to the property to check the resident ledger cards against bank deposits and other records.

Although electronic data processing offers certain safeguards, cash-handling policies are also needed. Cash payments should be discouraged, and all checks should have to be deposited daily or more frequently (e.g., when a certain dollar total is reached). Checking accounts established for properties or any on-site cash boxes should be audited regularly, and all cash disbursement records should have to be accompanied by a receipt showing the phone number and address of the recipient.

Commercial Properties. When monies are collected on site at a commercial property, the same precautions apply as were mentioned for residential properties. Often it is helpful to use an accrual or modified accrual accounting system because either one has built-in advantages for tracking income in particular. From the property owner's point of view, it is also

> ### On-Site Accounting Records
>
> Although the monthly financial reports sent to owner-clients may be prepared in the management company's main office, certain records must be maintained at the respective managed properties. In general, the support documents on which the reports are based—rent rolls; delinquency and vacancy reports; marketing, leasing, and traffic reports; budget variances and analysis; and those reports specific to commercial properties (CAM and other pass-through prorations and payments, retailers' percentage rents, and shopping center promotions under the auspices of a marketing fund or merchants' association) as well as receipts and disbursements ledgers—are generated or at least initiated at the site. Many of these records may be handwritten first and entered into the computer system later. Depending on the level of staffing and the types of equipment available, the data may be keyed into the on-site computer and transmitted via modem (or a network linkup) to the central office. On-site personnel are usually in the best position to analyze, comment on, and explain the numerical data, and they should be required to provide their insights for the report sent to the property owner.

helpful for all reports dealing with monies to be fully reconciled. If income was budgeted as one amount and there is a shortfall, the account records must not only report the lower figure, but state why the shortfall occurred.

Reconciliation of year-end CAM or other operating expense pass-throughs should balance against the expenses charged to the property. At most commercial properties, some expenses are charged to the building owner and some to the tenants, and this complicates the accounting procedures. For example, a client may require all expenses of the property to be shown in the aggregate as well as allocated by category to the proper entity (owner or tenants). Subsequently, the portions attributed to CAM or tenant pass-throughs would be reconciled against each tenant account, and any amounts not accounted would have to be explained. The on-site accounts for both income and expenses would also be audited on a regular basis.

The problem of differences in accounts is not always one of theft or misappropriation. Large losses are often the result of personnel not knowing what they are doing or simple carelessness. For example, in paying bills, such things as not checking to see if prior balances have been paid, not reviewing extensions to be sure the arithmetic is correct, and not taking allowable discounts can lead to large dollar losses for a property. If NSF (not sufficient funds) checks are not handled properly, the revenue they represent becomes a loss that is increased by bank charges for returning them.

The Cost of Accounting Functions

The accounting function can and usually does represent a significant portion of the cost of managing a property. As reporting becomes more com-

Exhibit 4.6
Sample Calculation—Accounting Costs

Given:
Property (size/type): 100,000-square-foot shopping center
Average rent: $15.00 per square foot per year
Management fee: 3.5%
Accounting costs: $1,155 per month
Profit goal: 12%

Find the amount available to cover non-accounting costs of management.
Monthly rent (total): 100,000 SF × $15/SF/yr = $125,000
Management fee: $125,000 × .035 = $4,375
Profit: $4,375 × .12 = $525
Cost of management (fee − profit): $4,375 − $525 = $3,850
Accounting costs (% of management costs): $1,155 ÷ $3,850 = .30 (30%)
Non-accounting costs (management costs − accounting costs):
  $3,850 − $1,155 = $2,695

The $2,695 would have to cover the remainder of the general and administrative cost of managing the property (the property manager, the management company executive's time, prorated administrative and office costs, insurance, education, travel, etc.).

---

plex and computers are used more and more, the costs are slowly growing. Typically in a medium-size management company, the cost of operating a separate accounting function will be approximately one fourth of the cost of managing the property, and it can be much larger. The management fee must be adequate to cover the cost of management and a profit (management firms generally aim for a profit level between ten and fifteen percent). Exhibit 4.6 shows a representative calculation.

If the accounting function is involved in collecting rents and other charges, and possibly also involved in budgeting for the property, accounting costs can be as much as one third of the cost of management. As can be seen from the example in Exhibit 4.6, the proportion is disparate. The conditions at the managed property can be a complicating factor that adds to the accounting costs. For example, distressed properties with large accounts-payable balances can consume several hours of accounting personnel time simply talking to unhappy vendors about amounts owed to them. Similarly, the cost of collections at this type of property can make its management unprofitable.

If accounting costs rise much above the range noted here, and if the accounting function is handling no more of the overall process than has been described, it will be very difficult for the management company to earn a reasonable profit. Specific accounting costs need to be kept in mind when setting the management fee.

A small management company that is starting up may choose to hire a full-time bookkeeper or accountant, thus representing a higher percentage of the management cost than would be desirable over the long term. However, having a dedicated staff member to focus on the quality and timing of reports and statements—and control them—would give the company a tremendous advantage in making an impression on clients by demonstrating that it can do as good a job (or better) as established management firms. The alternative—subcontracting the accounting function to a service bureau until the portfolio of managed properties is sufficiently large to support a full-time person—carries the risk of not being able to deliver reports on time or in the formats required by the clients. How the accounting function is to be handled is an extremely difficult call for the new management company that is striving to create an appropriate image in a very competitive market.

There are always advantages of scale, of course. A large management company with an extensive portfolio is likely to be able to reduce the percentage of its costs that is attributable to the accounting function and still provide first-class service to its clients. There can certainly be an economy of scale if the firm is managing several properties for an individual owner-client. Furthermore, very large companies can compartmentalize and specialize various functions, making them more efficient.

Regardless of the size of the management company, the accounting function is a critical element in the management process, and it should not be treated lightly.

An Added Perspective on the Accounting Function

The accounting function has other responsibilities not discussed in this chapter. A particularly important internal function is development of cost allocations for determining management fees. Profit center reporting, along with a consolidated company report, is another possibility. In a large company, income and expenses may be differentiated by divisions or departments (leasing, property management, etc.) within the company.

Operational reports similar to some of the management reports prepared for your property owner-clients each month should also be submitted to the management company executives. This should include a statement of receipts and disbursements—and net operating income (NOI)—itemized in sufficient detail to allow early identification of potential expense overages and income shortfalls. At a minimum, personnel, payroll, and accounting costs should be accounted as line items, as should any other significant categories of management company expense. A budget variance analysis should also be prepared, and regular performance analyses of individual properties and their managers should be performed as often as necessary to adequately monitor the management function. (The latter are described in Chapter 3.)

At the very least, the accounting function will be involved in preparing the payroll for the firm's employees and may handle payroll accounting for property site staffs as well. Even if the payroll is prepared by an outside service—usually these services are better-equipped to comply with all the applicable nuances of income tax laws and payroll deductions—the information on who worked when and for how many hours must still be assembled in house. There is also the matter of payments of withholding taxes to the government and filing of the requisite returns, all of which would be accounting responsibilities.

In the realm of collections, the accounting department may issue notices to "pay or quit" or otherwise be involved in initiating eviction proceedings, especially with regard to records of delinquency and nonpayment. If the company's management portfolio includes government-assisted housing, it is necessary to bill the U.S. Department of Housing and Urban Development (HUD) or other agency for tenant (resident) subsidies and other reimbursements (using the required forms) and maintain the back-up records related to these billings.

Electronic transfer of funds is increasingly popular. Utilities invite automatic deductions from their customers' checking accounts, and automatic deposit of payroll checks has been available for many years. Payments to governmental agencies by this means—as well as filing of many required returns—is encouraged more and more. Payments from the government are also being handled electronically. (The Tenant Rental Assistance Certification System—TRACS—is a computerized payment voucher processing system used by HUD.) It may even be possible to arrange for rent payments to be collected via automatic electronic transfer, although the option may not be adopted universally by all residents or commercial tenants. This method of exchanging funds adds a whole new dimension to accounting as more sophisticated approaches to record keeping are required. Note that this alternative payment mode rarely replaces the traditional check transaction completely because some entities the management company does business with will not use it.

Because accounting costs are likely to be an increasing proportion of the cost of managing real estate, management company executives should encourage cost accounting for all management activities and analysis of accounting and reporting costs in particular. In order to be fairly compensated for the amount of work that is typically required in this area, it may be appropriate to set an hourly rate (based on the accounting cost information) to be multiplied by the number of hours required to prepare the requisite reports for a given client and then use the result in establishing the management fee. Some management companies attach a rider to the management agreement that identifies services *not* covered by the management fee along with the amounts that will be charged for them.

As the text of this chapter indicates, the accounting function is extremely important to the real estate management company. It is the clearing house for all the financial data related to the firm's operations and the properties it manages. Analyses of these data are the foundation of the monthly reports to owner-clients and the annual budgets and management plans for the properties and the measure of the firm's overall profitability.

5

Strategizing the Personnel Function

Employees are a company's most valuable asset. While this applies to every business, it is especially true of real estate management, which is more demanding than most other kinds of businesses. Through its management agreements, a firm establishes what are expected to be long-term, mutually profitable relationships with its property owner-clients. Relationships are fostered by one-on-one interactions, and the firm's employees are often the pivotal reason for continued renewal of established agreements. Developing loyalty to your company and to the clients you serve requires the firm to choose employees carefully, train them properly, and reward them generously.

General Staffing Considerations

In a start-up operation, the business owner may be the lone property manager, perhaps supported by a part-time administrative assistant and an accountant-bookkeeper. With increased business, the company will need additional personnel and different skills to accomplish its goals. The generalist positions established initially will evolve into separate specialized functions. The one accountant-bookkeeper is likely to become a department supervised by an accounting manager, with accounts payable and accounts receivable functions, and possibly a collections function. Payroll may also be a separate function. Each of these functions may eventually be staffed by several people. The part-time administrative assistant may become a staff of general administrative support personnel who answer the telephone, type correspondence, and prepare reports. The property management department may eventually include "regional" managers (senior or supervising property

> **Fostering Employee Loyalty**
>
> Productivity requires more than physical (and mental) labor. Efforts to increase the measurable components of productivity yield a better response when they include incentives to be loyal to the employer. By this we mean treating employees as valued customers—your *internal customers*. While you will have to define the types of incentives to be implemented for yourself and your business, the following are some ideas to consider.
>
> - Make sure employees know what is expected of them and ensure that they receive training on an ongoing basis, starting with company procedures (how) and policies (why).
> - Find out your employees' expectations regarding authority, supervision, compensation, and other particulars and, within reason, try to meet those expectations—or at least provide an explanation of why certain things cannot be.
> - Make your employees part of the "team"; invite and reward—and implement—employees' suggestions for improvements in business operations and programs. The people who do the work are much closer to it; with a little encouragement, they are likely to come up with efficient, cost-saving, time-saving services and procedures to increase their productivity and the company's bottom line.
> - Support your employees' decisions and actions, especially in the public arena—i.e., in front of their co-workers and others—or countermand them gracefully and address the consequences one-on-one: ==Praise in public; criticize in private.==
> - Set realistic goals with your employees and then let them find creative ways to fulfill those goals. Performance guidelines that include acceptable alternatives build in flexibility that fosters achievement.
> - Give employees the authority to respond to complaints and address concerns of owner-clients, residents, and commercial tenants—your *external customers*—on the spot.

managers), who have responsibility for overseeing other property managers and managing several properties in a defined portfolio, as well as site managers who handle day-to-day operations of single properties.

If the management company will also provide maintenance services, it may be desirable (or advisable) to create a separate department or division for this function. Such an arrangement will allow you to track—and better control—the costs of providing specific maintenance services. It may also make it easier to set up this function as an independent business entity at a later time. The maintenance function will likely require creation of several levels of responsibilities (e.g., supervisors, technicians, assistants or helpers) with specialized job functions or skill requirements differentiated for each position.

Managing a growing staff requires a standardized approach to hiring, training, and supervision. You should also be thinking from the beginning about how an individual employee would gain the skills and expertise to

> **Fostering Employee Loyalty** *(continued)*
> These and a host of other strategies are outlined in countless books on the subjects of customer service and employee empowerment. Those you adapt or adopt will need to be considered carefully in light of the firm's goals and means. Although it is imperative to have rules in place, occasionally making exceptions to them to accommodate an individual employee (e.g., allowing time off or flexibility in work hours to take care of a personal crisis or illness in the family) will foster the kind of loyalty from employees that will help the company overcome an economic or other crisis.
> Encouraging your staff members to give something back to the community at large is an extension of this principle. Membership in charitable and service organizations (e.g., Lions Clubs, Kiwanis, Rotary International) as well as volunteer activities on the part of both employees and management and executive personnel send a message to the community that you are and want to be a part of it. One way to demonstrate the firm's commitment to the community is for a company executive to volunteer to help with one function of an employee's charity each year. Some of these types of community participation can and should involve the properties you manage—with the owners' approval, of course. A crime prevention community watch program at a residential property can include outreach to neighboring properties. Allowing social agencies or local charitable organizations to promote their services at a shopping center is another possibility.
> Most such activities have little or no dollar cost, and they develop a wealth of goodwill over time. They also create positive perceptions of the company and its people, which can be a valuable asset in your favor in the event zoning or taxes or other issues of local governance require "popular" support.
> These kinds of activities also provide material for news releases and present opportunities to foster positive perceptions, not only of the firm and its people, but of the real estate management industry as a whole. These are all important building blocks in developing a company's reputation.

progress from an entry-level position to higher level jobs in the same department. Although your initial hiring may encompass different levels of skills, ultimately a program that promotes employees within the organization will foster employee loyalty. Besides, if other internal efforts encourage personal growth and professional development, you need a way to capture and retain these "improved" employees.

This chapter will explore the various aspects of the personnel function. While particular emphasis may be given here to the property manager position, most companies also employ a variety of personnel whose job functions support the property manager either directly or indirectly, and much of the discussion is generally applicable to these positions as well. Among the issues that need preliminary consideration are determinants of individual workloads, development of a training program, and strategies for averting employee turnover.

Determining Individual Workloads. There are no rules or industry standards for the number of properties that can be handled by individual

> ### Staffing Considerations and Challenges
>
> When a company is growing rapidly, the need to have more seasoned, competent staff means you will have to bring in new employees and train them quickly. Timing is a major complicating factor in this regard. Clients and their sensitivities are also considerations in employees' assignments. Sometimes you will not know that your management proposal has been accepted until a few days before you are expected to assume management, yet you may be expected to name the personnel who will be assigned to the property in the proposal you submit. If current staff members were named and their present responsibilities are to be expanded (or superseded), the change can have a negative impact on existing clients. (They may not appreciate having the people who were assigned to their properties taken away to work for a new client.) Existing employees and their capabilities have to be continually evaluated as part of business development planning, and the need to increase staff has to be anticipated reasonably in advance so that new personnel are ready to assume assignments when new accounts are acquired.

property managers and accounting personnel or the number of property managers an administrative person can support. There are several variables that will determine workloads, and these are specific to the company and the management portfolio.

The first variable is the level of service the company will provide. A management firm's reputation is determined by the types of services it provides its clients. Not all property owners need the same level of service. A management firm's client base will also be a factor in determining the employees' workload. Another company-specific variable is the standard of technology it has implemented—the firm's software, computers, and other equipment.

There are several other variables that can be either company or portfolio specific. One is the distance between the managed properties and the management office. Anything more than a two-hour drive or a short plane ride away from the management office will require a full day for each site visit. Someone who manages a number of office buildings in a closely defined downtown area can visit several properties in one day. Properties that do not have on-site management or maintenance staff require more time of the property manager and administrative staff than those that have either or both. The number of rental occupants (residents, commercial tenants) will also affect the number of properties a property manager and a bookkeeper can handle.

Property type is another important variable. Shopping centers and office buildings are more management-intensive than industrial properties. A property manager with leasing responsibilities for a commercial portfolio will not be able to manage as many properties as one who does no leasing.

> **Variables That Determine Employees' Workload**
>
> **Company-Specific Variables**
> - Level of service to be provided
> - Client base
> - Available technology
>
> **Company- or Portfolio-Specific Variables**
> - Property type
> - Number of occupants (residential or commercial tenants)
> - Distance from office to managed properties
> - Presence of on-site management staff
> - Responsibility for commercial leasing
>
> **Employee-Specific Variables**
> - Personal experience, knowledge, motivation, work ethic
> - Level of staff support available
>
> **Other Factors**
> - Location of the property (e.g., high-crime versus low-crime neighborhood)
> - Problems with rent collections or excessive turnovers
> - Client demands for extra reports
>
> The number of properties being managed, the type and frequency of meetings with clients, and other factors may also impact an individual's workload.

Even though commercial properties may be in operation only 10–12 hours a day, their managers are on call for emergencies around the clock.

Residential properties are in use around the clock, and they need someone available 24 hours a day. Large apartment properties and some condominiums may have a resident manager or maintenance personnel (or both) living on site to handle emergencies as well as day-to-day operations (more often the manager will live off site). If the management company provides services from an off-site location, however, the supervisory and support staff workloads may be increased. Depending on company policy and practice, leasing based on resident turnover may be heavier at certain times of the year or an ongoing process. This, too, will affect staffing requirements and workloads.

Other factors that become considerations relate to the properties themselves and their owners. Properties that have rent collection problems or extremely high turnover rates or are located in crime-ridden areas will require more of a manager's time. An owner may require additional analyses, market data, accounting reports, or other paperwork, and such demands limit what can be done for other clients.

The experience, knowledge, motivation, and work ethic of individuals also determine their work capacity. Another important consideration is the level of administrative and accounting support in the main office.

The company's executives establish the firm's level of service. Then, based on the variables discussed here, the executives determine the workload for each staff member and monitor their performance to ensure that each employee's workload allows sufficient time to provide the desired level of service while working at full capacity.

Developing a Training Program. Real estate management is a business; as such it encompasses a variety of activities that include marketing and leasing (sales), business and real estate law, governmental regulations, financial analysis and reporting, maintenance management, emergency procedures, human resources, and administrative issues. Few managers can develop solid expertise in every one of these areas; most acquire expertise in a few areas, at best, and a working knowledge in the remainder. Other staff members whose support roles are specialized (accounting, maintenance) also need to know something about property management as well as their own areas of responsibility.

Only through continual education and training of its staff can a management company maintain its competitiveness and operate on the cutting edge. Governmental regulations, landlord-tenant laws, management techniques, and communications technologies are just a few of the fields that are constantly changing and must be mastered. Accounting and administrative personnel need to be trained in new company procedures, software upgrades, and the requirements of new clients.

The company's executives are responsible for ensuring that the firm's personnel maintain the knowledge and expertise necessary to provide the level of service established by the firm. To do this, they will have to monitor industry trends, evolving management and leasing techniques, and new governmental regulations, incorporating changes into an ongoing training program that will maintain the firm's leadership position in the real estate management industry. Although some very large organizations have created "corporate universities" and have full-time training staffs on board, this is not always an option, even for large companies. Depending on the company's size, range of activities, and internal educational needs, it may be more cost-effective to use outside sources whenever possible, especially for small- to medium-size companies.

A company's commitment to training its personnel is an effective means of ensuring the entire staff performs at the highest level of professionalism. Its program can be divided into three areas: company training, departmental training, and individual training. Company training consists of in-house education sessions for the entire staff. Usually these are one to two hours long, and the topics discussed during these sessions are of interest to everyone—e.g., new company procedures, software upgrades, office safety, and employee insurance benefits.

Training related only to specific departments, such as accounting or

> **Some Factors that Contribute to Employee Turnover**
> - Dissatisfaction with the job or the workplace.
> - Dissatisfaction with the pay or other aspects of the compensation package.
> - Lack of opportunities for promotion.
> - Lack of training.
> - Lack of Motivation.
> - Feeling unappreciated.
>
> These kinds of "feelings" affect employees at all levels. Perceptions are also important. The lower the pay and perceived value of the job and/or the employee in that job, the more rapid the turnover.

property management, is usually addressed in sessions lasting one to four hours. An attorney may speak about negotiating office building leases or changes in residential landlord-tenant laws for leasing and property management personnel. Roofing and parking lot consultants may conduct sessions for maintenance workers and property managers. The firm's insurance agent might be asked to discuss different types of insurance coverages and the correct procedure for filing a claim for accounting personnel as well as site managers, property managers, and others involved in risk management. In-house training sessions may be supplemented by short seminars presented by local chapters of professional real estate organizations.

Individual training usually consists of one-on-one training on the job supplemented with local and national seminars. An entry-level property manager may be assigned to an experienced manager for guidance and supervision, or company executives may assume responsibility for training new property managers. Supervisors may be responsible for training new staff members who work for them. This type of training introduces the employee to the company culture, the firm's policies and procedures, and the specific duties of the job.

Some large management companies have a committee that works with the executives in developing the firm's training program for each year. There may be regularly scheduled sessions or presentations on an as-needed basis using senior staff members or guest speakers as instructors. Also useful in this regard is a year-end review, which may be either an all-company or a departmental meeting where employees can evaluate the past year, comment on current operating practices, and offer suggestions for future improvement. (It is also a good time to recognize staff members' personal accomplishments in addition to those of the company as a whole.) This might be presented as a two-hour session, beginning at noon and including lunch, allowing for a formal agenda to be covered in an informal setting.

Exhibit 5.1
Hidden Costs of Personnel Turnover

In addition to the direct costs of hiring replacement personnel (advertising, training, etc.), employee turnover has a number of hidden costs:

- Decreased productivity—The person who is leaving tends to be less efficient in the weeks immediately preceding separation, and other staff members who fill the gap may perform poorly, not only because they are overextended, but because they are less knowledgeable or less well trained for the position. The longer a position is vacant, the greater the loss due to decreased productivity.
- Lost opportunities—When a firm is understaffed, it cannot assume additional new business.
- Intangible factors—The loss of goodwill due to disruption of continuity of business operations, the decline in morale among the remaining staff members, and the quality of departing employees (they may be the company's most valued human resources) may not be measurable in themselves, but they do have economic consequences.

It is especially expensive and time-consuming to replace management-level personnel, professional staff, and employees who have unique skills. Because these are the types of job categories characteristic of the real estate management business, management firms need to be proactive in combatting employee turnover.

Without an ongoing training program, a management company will slowly lose its competitive edge. That is in addition to potential economic losses due to errors and omissions when staff members are not given adequate on-the-job training or encouraged to test and refresh their skills and knowledge. Providing a variety of opportunities for training benefits individual staff members and the management company as a whole. To do this effectively requires a commitment to excellence, development of policies that encourage individual learning, and an adequate budget to pay for such a program.

By providing opportunities to acquire education and supporting professional memberships and training, you will be helping real estate managers grow within the industry as they grow in their jobs, and your company will benefit directly from having better-educated, better-informed, more-involved employees. These employees will also be loyal to your company and to your clients.

Averting Employee Turnover. A property manager may stay with a company, on average, about four years. People in other staff positions may be with a company even less time—only about two years. This is unfortunate for company owners. It also has hidden costs (Exhibit 5.1). Some employees, managers in particular, will receive offers that cannot be matched or exceeded by their current employers while others may simply want a

Exhibit 5.2
Some Components of a Compensation Package

In addition to salary, there are a number of "benefits" that are frequently provided to employees and considered part of a total compensation package.

- Vacation time
- Paid holidays
- Floating holidays
- Paid sick days
- Various types of "health" insurance coverages (major medical, dental, long-term disability)
- Life insurance
- Pension plan (e.g., profit sharing, 401K, ESOP)
- Performance incentives for achieving company goals (e.g., bonuses, gain sharing)
- Tuition reimbursement program

The employers' contributions to social security and workers' compensation and unemployment insurance programs would be included in a determination of the value of a compensation package. Sometimes employees pay part of the premiums for medical insurance, especially for dependent coverage, and it is common for them to be able to make voluntary contributions to the company pension plan. Monetary or other awards for long service (e.g., increased vacation time), provision for unpaid leaves of absence (under the Family and Medical Leave Act), and compensatory time off in lieu of overtime are other types of benefits that might be considered, depending on the level of individual positions (overtime is usually only paid to employees whose wages are hourly) and current practice in the local market.

---

change. A certain amount of turnover is healthy; but there is always some percentage of turnover that is a result of employee dissatisfaction, and much of this type of turnover is preventable. Some strategies that can be part of an employee-retention program include:

- Select qualified employees—Define specific positions, advertise them appropriately, match applicants' qualifications to the job requirements, and carefully check application information and references. Include testing of skills and attitudes as necessary or appropriate.
- Provide orientation and training—New employees need to learn about the company's policies and procedures and its goals and objectives (mission) as well as the details of the job they are to perform.
- Design an equitable pay system—Having job descriptions that define the required skills and qualifications and state the duties and responsibilities will allow a firm to classify jobs at different levels and establish appropriate compensation for each position (Exhibit 5.2).
- Provide a supportive work environment—More than the tools to do a particular job (e.g., computers), employees may need administrative or other assistance in addition to supervisory leadership and

---

Exhibit 5.3
Components of an Exit Interview

- Type of termination—resignation, retirement, discharge.
- Reason for leaving—areas of dissatisfaction such as hours, pay, working conditions, type of work, supervisor.
- Perceptions of the job and/or the company—how the individual feels about his or her progress with the organization.
- What it would take for the employee to stay—the things he or she would have liked to change.
- Personal expectations—whether the employee's job expectations were met.

---

mentoring. Opportunities to improve their skills and advance their careers are also important.

Because all turnover cannot be avoided, it is a wise policy to conduct exit interviews with departing employees. These may be in the form of a one-on-one conversation or a written questionnaire, or both. (Some points to be covered are identified in Exhibit 5.3.) Although there are instances of general dissatisfaction, usually there are specific reasons people leave a job. These may include things like lack of feedback from their supervisor, performance problems, difficulty adapting to the company culture, lack of opportunities for advancement, and job stress. The employer's and the employee's expectations of the job are also considerations. Because it can be difficult to obtain objective information from departing employees, it may be worthwhile to hire a public relations or employment consultant to conduct exit interviews. Often they are able to elicit more objective responses that can be helpful in evaluating retention alternatives.

Strategizing Employment Practices

Hiring qualified personnel is a major responsibility. There should be a detailed job description for each position within the company, and these should be included in the company's operations manual. A good job description will identify the position that supervises the job and any positions that are supervised by the person in the job, as well as the specific duties and responsibilities of the position. Exhibit 5.4 is an example.

Usually the skills and educational requirements are included, and specific fiscal responsibility may also be stated. The latter may only relate to positions with authority to approve purchase orders or payments up to a dollar limitation, above which additional approvals are required. As a general rule, each job description should include in the duties section a statement that precludes employees from saying, "That's not in my job

Exhibit 5.4
Sample Job Description—Regional Property Manager
(Highlights)

Basic Function
- Responsible for maintaining the integrity of the physical asset and maximizing the returns from the asset in accordance with the Company's mission, vision, and objectives.
- Responsible for training and development of all personnel assigned, either directly or through others.

Relationships
- Reports to Vice President of Property Management.
- Supervises all on-site personnel at properties assigned.
- Maintains relationships with peers and all other departments within the company.
- Maintains relationships with suppliers, vendors, and others serving the Company or the property.

Activities
The activities listed here are not all-inclusive; rather, they indicate the types of activities normally performed by this position.

- Maintaining the physical asset—
  - —Supervises employees and contractors.
  - —Assures adherence to specifications (contractual; operations manual).
  - —Conducts formal site inspections of building interior and exterior.
  - —Makes recommendations for physical repairs and/or replacements.
  - —Ensures observance of safety regulations.
- Marketing and leasing—
  - —Supervises leasing personnel.
  - —Regularly evaluates market conditions and property comparables.
  - —Implements marketing plan.
  - —Periodically reviews rental applications and lease forms for accuracy and compliance with established policies and procedures.
  - —Makes recommendations to improve marketing and leasing programs.
- Rent management—
  - —Supervises rent collection in accordance with policies and procedures manual.
  - —Approves and monitors rental rate recommendations for new leases and renewals based on current market information.
- Financial reporting and control—
  - —Reviews and helps develop annual operating budget and supporting business plan.
  - —Reviews all monthly financial reports.
  - —Approves payments (payroll, invoices).
  - —Approves expenditures in accordance with Company policy and procedures.
- Administration—
  - —Handles employee selection, training, and control, and assures that all supervised employees comply with the appropriate policies and procedures.
  - —Interfaces with outside professionals regarding legal, accounting, insurance, tax, and other matters, as appropriate.
  - —Ensures property files and records are maintained.
- Continually improves management and technical skills.
- Spends agreed-upon percentage of time on obtaining market knowledge, community relations, and asset evaluation.

Exhibit 5.4 *(continued)*

Qualifications *(Ideal)*

- Minimum of five years experience at site and supervisory levels.
- Real estate license (if applicable).
- Strong leadership and motivational abilities.
- Exceptional communication skills and ability to interact with wide range of people.
- Attentive to detail.

This example is suggestive of the array of requirements for a supervisory or regional property manager position. If the individual will be responsible for a specific type of property (residential, commercial), it may be appropriate to incorporate property-specific details (e.g., inspection of apartment unit interiors might be a component of maintaining the physical asset). Because personnel in supervisory roles have extensive contacts off site and outside the company's offices, community and industry involvement might be an added component under relationships.

Job descriptions should be clear in regard to lines of authority and communication, specific duties and responsibilities, and requisite qualifications. In the latter category one might also identify required (or preferred) professional designations. It may be necessary or desirable to include information about the physical demands of the job and the general work environment. This type of information is important for compliance with the Americans with Disabilities Act.

Adapted with permission from a job description used by Magnuson Management, Inc., in Tacoma, Washington.

---

description." Language such as the following is typical: "And such other duties as may be assigned from time-to-time by the supervisor."

You should also have in place a procedure that specifies, minimally, how jobs will be advertised, who will interview candidates for different positions, and how offers of employment will be tendered. Want ads in local newspapers are commonplace for administrative, maintenance, and professional positions. However, professional journals or trade association publications may be appropriate places to advertise for property managers, accountants, or skilled tradespeople. Networking with fellow professionals, especially other members of associations you belong to, can be another helpful resource. Executive positions might be advertised in business or industry newspapers or the *Wall Street Journal*. There are also many executive search firms that specialize in recruiting for high-level management positions. Whenever possible, openings should also be posted on a staff bulletin board so your employees can apply for promotion from within. (The operations manual is discussed in Chapter 3. Descriptions of key property management positions can be found in Chapter 1.)

Recruitment and Hiring. However you approach personnel recruitment, you are likely to receive applications from more individuals than you can begin to interview, especially in a market where there are more qualified personnel than there are jobs. For this reason, advertisements

Understanding the Employment Market

Management company executives should always be aware of what is happening in the local employment market. It helps to know if the local market is currently saturated with job seekers and whether the available personnel are entry-level workers with limited knowledge and skills, experienced workers with some expertise, or executives who may be over-qualified for most positions. Also important is whether salary and wage levels are going up or down or if they are stagnating.

There are many good sources for this information, professional and trade associations among them, and the astute executive will be tuned-in to all of them. It takes time to monitor the local and national markets, but the information you can acquire is worth it. The help-wanted ads in local newspapers are almost always a good indicator of what is happening in the industry. How many ads are there for "property managers"? Are they for entry-level positions? Are there more or fewer such ads as time passes?

Another indicator is the numbers of phone calls and resumes received from people who are looking for work in the field. More of these signals a general tightening of the job market for real estate managers. The number of calls from employment agencies trying to place a manager or asking for possible candidates for a search they have underway tells a similar story. Talking with these job search personnel can prove enlightening as to what is going on in the marketplace at any given time—types of openings, salaries, benefits, etc. Being helpful to placement personnel can be similarly instructive: Often they can tell you how the market looks for personnel in the real estate management business, including the wages being offered and the general terms of employment.

Attending meetings of professional organizations is a good way to find out what is happening nationally and regionally in the area of employment. Simply talking with members and guests of the organization can be informative.

Trade magazines often have articles on the state of the industry, including what is happening in the employment market. Huntress Real Estate Executive Search firm publishes an annual report of employment changes for the past year, listing salary levels and other pertinent information of interest to everyone in the business.

Networking with other real estate managers and property owners is one of the best sources of current information. These people know what is happening right now, while a magazine article may reflect what was happening six or more months ago.

If the management company also hires people to work on site as maintenance, janitorial, or security staff, or as site managers, the firm's executives need to be aware of those markets as well. Information about types of positions, required qualifications, and wage structures can be gleaned from want ads. Employment agencies and companies that place temporary help are other possible sources of this information. There are professional and trade associations for most types of workers, and these organizations may offer placement services to their members. Trade schools, community colleges, and local universities are other potential sources of entry level personnel. As for defining specific jobs, one useful reference is the U.S. Department of Labor publication *Occupational Outlook Handbook*.

requesting that resumes be sent to a blind box are often preferable. They allow you to select potential candidates without having to reply to all respondents. The downside, however, is that the company name is usually omitted so you are unable to attract prospective job candidates based on the firm's reputation. It is also fairly common to request a salary history or salary requirements and, for many clerical positions, to require computer skills (e.g., facility with specific types of software).

A good strategy for narrowing the field of candidates is to quickly glance at each resume to identify which ones meet all (or most) of your advertised criteria. This is where a salary history is helpful; someone who is already compensated well beyond the salary range of your job opening might become a low-priority candidate or not be pursued at all. Your goal at this stage is to identify the half dozen or so candidates whom you wish to interview. If the skill or experience requirements are at a high level, you may want to create a second "tier" of potential candidates in case no one in the primary group becomes a finalist.

Everyone who is invited to your office for an interview should be required to complete an employment application form. This is not only a good business practice; it organizes the information about every candidate in the same manner and facilitates comparison for your hiring decision.

Although the individual who has primary responsibility for human resources may handle the recruitment activities, it is appropriate for the supervisor of the position to actually conduct the personal interview. This one-on-one session should be sufficiently structured so that the same kinds of information are being collected from every applicant. It is appropriate to have a list of questions to be asked, and these should focus on things like the applicant's job skills, work history, and attitudes. (Applicants should be given an opportunity to review the job description and ask questions about it.) Ideally, most of the interview questions will be open-ended, asking WHAT and HOW and WHY questions that require an explanation—i.e., a simple yes or no will not be a sufficient answer. Using a prepared list assures that all applicants are asked the same questions and, like the application form, creates a bank of comparison information for consideration.

Personnel who are charged with responsibility for interviewing job applicants must understand what comprises discriminatory practices. It is illegal to discriminate in hiring on the basis of race, religion, national origin, age, gender, or disability. (Some local jurisdictions may include other "protected classes.") Just as fair housing laws require identical treatment of all rental applicants, other civil rights laws require the same treatment of all job applicants. (The various labor laws administered under the U.S. Equal Employment Opportunity Commission are discussed in Chapter 12.)

It is rare in today's business environment to hire an individual after a single interview. For some positions, especially administrative office positions, it is desirable to test math, computer, typing, and filing skills. Most companies narrow the field to two or three candidates whose qualifications best match those of the job, and these individuals are brought back for a second interview or testing (or both). Test results provide additional comparison data for differentiating among two or three closely comparable candidates. Second interviews may be conducted in less depth; at this stage, the interviewer's goal is usually to clear up uncertainties, address any still-unanswered questions, and generally to assess the personal "fit" between the applicant and the company. In many fields, the department manager may also interview applicants at this stage. Depending on the level of the position and the responsibilities attached to it, executive personnel may also conduct an interview. In some situations, other departmental personnel may be asked to speak briefly with a prospective co-worker. Insights gathered from the "peers" of a position can help determine the degree of a prospect's "fit" with the company.

Before a final hiring decision is made, it is important to check the applicant's references. Some firms may check out every detail of an applicant's education and work history; others may rely more heavily on personal references and a check on the most recent one or two positions held. Sadly, some people do misrepresent the level of education they completed, the position they held with a previous employer, or their salary, or all of these. At a minimum, it is important to verify the most recent employment. (It may not be practical to contact all previous employers due to company mergers, relocations, or name changes, or because of business closings.) Credit reference and criminal background checks are becoming accepted practice for some positions.

Employees who will handle the firm's or its clients' funds should be bonded, and this will require additional background information. For some positions, criminal background checks may be less important for financial reasons than to screen for potential violent behavior; however, this can be a good practice in general where it is allowed by law. Previous employers will not always provide complete information, especially in situations where they terminated employment for reasons of unacceptable (read: violent or potentially violent) behavior on the job. It is important for potential employers to be satisfied with the credentials and the character of the person they are about to hire. It is also important to be consistent in the application of specific pre-employment screening checks (i.e., to all candidates for a particular position) in order to avoid claims of discrimination in hiring. This can be an especially sensitive issue in regard to a criminal background check.

Having satisfied yourself that you have identified the one candidate you wish to bring into the company, the next step is to extend an offer of employment. Until this point in the proceedings, it is usually considered inap-

> **Employer Recordkeeping Requirements**
>
> For each employee, there should be a personnel file that includes his or her employment application form, resume (if appropriate), results of pre-employment testing (if performed), documentation of work eligibility proofs and reference and other background checks, a copy of the written offer of employment (or contract), and records of periodic performance reviews and pay increases. When employment is terminated by the employee, the resignation and exit interview (if conducted) will complete the file. If the company terminates employment, documentation of the reason for the termination would also be retained in this file. Other information specific to the individual employment arrangement should be included as appropriate. (Forms authorizing payroll deductions for income taxes and other withholding items would be retained in appropriate accounting files along with records of employees' hours and wages.)
>
> Many personnel and employment records have to be retained beyond the period of employment. Employee service records and paychecks may have to be kept permanently, while individual time cards may only have to be kept for five years. Income tax requirements, state statutes of limitations, and the potential need to defend against a lawsuit are among the criteria that guide development of a specific records retention plan. A professional accountant or an attorney can provide additional guidance regarding the records your company should retain and specific periods of retention. (*Guide to Record Retention Requirements,* published annually by the U.S. Government Printing Office, outlines specific federal requirements.)

propriate to discuss salary. Once a candidate has been selected, however, the offer of employment must include salary and a start date. Often the employee benefits provided by the employer, including those such as medical insurance for which both employer and employee may share the premium cost, are also indicated. Although the offer may be tendered by telephone, it should always be confirmed in writing.

Before establishing your company's employment policies and procedures, some research may be in order. There are many publications that address particulars of the employment process. *The Complete Do-It-Yourself Personnel Department* is an example of a resource that provides sample personnel forms, including a template for creating job descriptions. *Manual of Personnel Policies, Procedures and Operations* is another resource. In addition to a model personnel manual and information about employment laws, it includes sample job descriptions for numerous positions common to a variety of industries (e.g., maintenance technician, clerk-typist, accountant, personnel manager). Although property manager and similar real estate management jobs are not addressed in either of these, a description of the roles of property and real estate managers including the nature of the work, working conditions, and qualifications can be found in the *Occupational Outlook Handbook* published by the U.S. Department of Labor. This publication, which is updated periodically, describes all the types of jobs for which statistics are compiled by the U.S. government, including job outlook and compensation data. (See also Appendix C.)

It is also appropriate to seek advice of legal counsel regarding equal employment opportunity laws as well as state and local laws that may impact the hiring process and the firm's relationship with its employees. You will need to consider full-time versus part-time or temporary employment. Some job categories are exempt from overtime wage requirements while others are not, and the differences are not always clearly delineated. People who are hired as independent contractors must fulfill certain criteria in order to be exempt from employee status; this affects both the individual and the firm that employs him or her. (More information on the legal issues related to the employment process can be found in Chapter 12.)

Orientation and Training. New employees should be given an orientation. At the very least this might be a tour of the firm's offices and introductions to their new co-workers. However, a thorough orientation will include a review of the firm's employment policies and procedures, an opportunity to become familiar with the company's operations manual, and an introduction to the company culture and mission. Many elements of an orientation can be reinforced by presenting new staff members with an employee's handbook and reviewing the contents with them. Usually this provides background information on the company and spells out the policies and procedures that apply to all personnel, including details of employee benefits such as vacation time, insurance coverages, the pension program, etc. (Exhibit 5.5, p. 142, is a list of typical contents of an employee handbook.) One of the most effective training tools, especially for new members of the staff, is a well-thought-out, complete set of policies and procedures—a company operations manual. All new employees should be required to read these, with special attention to the sections pertaining to their activities within the firm. They should also be given some time to ask questions so they can better understand how the company works and what is expected of them in most situations. (See Chapter 3, especially Company Operations Manual, for a detailed discussion of this business tool.) Access to industry information, opportunities to participate in seminars, and attending meetings of professional organizations are also aspects of training.

Industry Information. One of the least-expensive sources of training and information for employees is trade publications such as the *Journal of Property Management*. Supervisors should be encouraged to maintain an awareness of what is happening in the industry. Recent articles in journals, trade magazines, and newspapers that would be helpful to their employees should be circulated to everyone who might be interested. Most real estate

> ### Employee Versus Independent Contractor Status
>
> The relationship to the employer is more likely to be interpreted as that of an employee—
> —If the company sets the hours of work.
> —If the company dictates how the task is to be performed.
> —If the company pays the person an hourly wage.
> —If the company supplies materials and tools for the task.
> —If the company provides office space and/or equipment and/or support (e.g., secretarial) services.
> —If the company defines the geographical territory in which the work is performed.
>
> For each of the above items that is true for your company, an individual worker is *less* likely to be considered as having independent contractor status. In a court of law, economic reality usually prevails over technical definitions.

professionals receive or subscribe to more magazines than they can easily read each month, and it is helpful to have specific articles brought to one's attention. This does not mean a supervisor has to read every article in print, but from a review of the titles and considering the publication source, articles that appear germane can be scanned to see if they would be helpful, and the few that are can be circulated to those who would be most likely to benefit from reading them. The fact that a supervisor took the time to call an employee's attention to an article—even one of limited interest or importance—is a statement of the supervisor's and the company's commitment to keeping employees up-to-date.

Seminars and Courses. There is a wealth of opportunities for real estate management personnel to attend seminars that provide meaningful education. Local and national seminars on real estate management and leasing are offered by the Institute of Real Estate Management, Community Associations Institute, Building Owners and Managers Association, International Council of Shopping Centers, and other real estate organizations (see Appendix B). These seminars are the best formal education a real estate manager can receive. Not all employees need to attend a particular seminar. It is often just as productive to send one employee and have him or her share with other staff members the salient points of the discussion and copies of the information handed out at the seminar. Sending different individuals to different seminars allows each of them to feel more involved while spreading around the opportunities to attend such programs. The information exchange afterward develops and hones presentation skills and fosters team spirit.

College courses are another possible avenue for specific training. Local community college offerings typically include a variety of business subjects,

> **Employment Contracts**
>
> Some states require the use of employment contracts for certain personnel who work for real estate companies (e.g., real estate managers, site managers, maintenance workers). It may be desirable to have a contractual agreement in place even if it is not required. A contract spells out the respective roles of the employer and the employee and the terms of the employment arrangement. It also states the compensation to be paid and the basis for that compensation. It may address rules of conduct and issues of confidentiality as well. This is an area where advice of legal counsel should be sought. Not only is there a need to comply with applicable laws (federal, state, and sometimes local), but if a problem arises in the employment arrangement, you will want the documentation to be upheld in a court of law. Legal counsel can also advise on employment policies and procedures.

from accounting to real estate management. Usually these are evening or weekend courses; tuition is relatively inexpensive, and classes are conveniently located (i.e., close to the student's home or work).

Professional and Trade Association Meetings. If the company is supporting affiliations with more than one professional organization, it is often helpful to "assign" an employee to be active in a specific association and share information gained from that source with his or her co-workers. In such an approach, one staff member might attend national meetings of the Institute of Real Estate Management, another would participate in meetings of the Building Owners and Managers Association, and a third could be the contact with the National Apartment Association, while all might be encouraged to attend meetings of the local chapters of these organizations. (Information on professional memberships as business development opportunities can be found in Chapter 7.)

In-House Training. One effective approach to specific training and education is the in-house seminar. It can be quite disruptive to send several employees or your entire staff to off-site seminars, but an expert can be brought in as a guest speaker very cost-effectively, especially if a large number of employees would benefit directly from the information provided. For example, bringing in an expert on a type of computer software (e.g., WordPerfect for Windows or Lotus 1-2-3) allows for company-specific dialogue as well as individual learning. This is usually more effective than sending employees out for training one at a time or their trying to learn the system exclusively from the software manuals provided.

The education you choose to provide in this format will depend on your employees' needs and the availability of qualified speakers or trainers. The company attorney might give a seminar on eviction and its legal rami-

Exhibit 5.5
Sample Contents of an Employee Handbook

The Company
Work Environment
Company Profile
Mission Statement
Equal Employment Opportunity Policy
General Employee Classifications
Employee Communications
Nonsolicitation
Company Visitors
Safety Program
Substance Abuse

Your Job
New Employee Orientation
Work Periods
Time Reporting
Pay Procedures
Overtime
Employee Travel
Travel Expense Reporting
Personal Status Changes
Performance Planning and Appraisal
General Work Rules
Problem Review Procedure
Attendance
Appearance and Attire
Use of Company Telephones
Rehiring of Former Employees
Employment of Relatives

Outside Employment
Smoking
Anti-Harassment Policy
Religious Observance
Layoff and Recall
Confidential Personnel Information
Exit Interviews

Your Benefits
Vacation
Holidays
401(k) Plan
Workers' Compensation
Group Insurance Benefits
Medical Insurance
Dental Insurance
Life and AD&D and Long-Term Disability
Sick Leave
Care for Sick Children
Leaves of Absence
Medical Disability/Pregnancy Leave
Military Leave
Jury Duty
Bereavement Leave
Tuition Reimbursement
Bulletin Boards
Suggestions
Questions

Building access and security, parking assignments, and a form for the employee to acknowledge receipt of the handbook are other possible components. An organizational chart may be included but is often distributed separately.

---

fications. A session on stress management may be a tremendous benefit to property managers in particular because most of them face subtle stresses every day. Other topics that may be of interest or problematic for the staff are fair housing, ADA compliance, and environmental laws.

Before launching a program of seminars in house, it is a good idea to poll the staff to see if there are topics of common interest that could be presented this way. Possibly one or more of the property managers may have an expertise worth sharing with the other managers. Tips on preparation of annual budgets, calculation and allocation of common area pass-through charges or rent escalators, leasing of store fronts, or marketing apartments are some examples. Having a staff member present a seminar is not only economical; it enhances the self-esteem of the person conducting the session while it builds a shared knowledge and information base for the rest of the staff members.

Supervision and Communication. Ideally, supervisors will have either an "open door" policy or specific times when an employee can ask questions or seek direction. Because the real estate management business does not have pat answers for most problems, it is often necessary for the manager of a property to consult with the client or a supervisor to determine the proper course of action in a given situation. If the manager has a question but does not have access to the answer, the problem may not be addressed until he or she is given the needed direction. Although it might be argued that the manager should take the initiative in such a situation and make a decision, the decision-making authority most often rests with either the client or the supervisor, and the property manager would be taking too great a risk by assuming that authority. As property managers become familiar with their supervisors and with the clients they serve, they often learn how those individuals would react and may become comfortable making some decisions without consultation; but in many situations, such initiative would be inappropriate or even risky.

On the other hand, it is quite possible that the property manager is being pressured for an answer by a contractor, another employee, a tenant, or the property owner. When the answer is not given in a timely fashion, the manager may be perceived as not taking action—or, worse yet, not being able to take action—and his or her effectiveness is diminished. Timely decision making is a very important part of the day-to-day activity of real estate management. (Company policies are an effective way to define the responsibilities of property managers and other staff members, including their authority to take action and whom to contact for information and decisions that exceed their authority.)

Communications with employees can take many forms—conversations, formal meetings, written memorandums. Regardless of the form of communication, you should always put yourself in the position of the recipient and try to imagine how your message may be perceived. Because each person responds differently, their individual differences bear consideration. You need to evaluate each situation and decide on the best way to communicate your message to obtain the results you desire.

Timing of communications is important. If you arrive on site and find a maintenance worker at the top of a ladder trying to fit a heavy air conditioner in place, and the installation is not going well, this is not the time to point out another problem that needs attention.

Word choices are also important: If a supervisor called a staff member on the phone and said, "We have to have a meeting this afternoon in my

Education and Employee Retention

Once employees are on board and you have given them a proper orientation to the company, the next consideration should be their training and education within the real estate management industry. The business is constantly changing and becoming more sophisticated. If newly hired real estate managers do not keep up with the industry, they will always be a little bit behind the curve—and while they may see the need for education, without help and encouragement they will probably choose not to pursue it. Employees are not going to develop a great deal of loyalty to a company that is indifferent to their personal and professional growth. The fear among those in higher positions in the business is that the company will lose good employees who have improved themselves. What is more likely, however, is that employees who are given opportunities to acquire education, training, and professional credentials will appreciate what they have and, if there are opportunities for advancement internally, are likely to remain with the company. While some employees are always ready and willing to move along and easily become disenchanted with their employment, most people in real estate management would prefer to work for a company where they can grow personally and professionally and have a career. Changing jobs is as disruptive for the employee as it is for the employer.

There are several ways the employer can help employees become better educated on the job and recognize the individual's gains in the industry. The type and amount of help will depend on the company's ability to share the cost of external programs and adapt to the employee's absence from the workplace for the periods of time necessary to complete various programs. The feasibility of different approaches will, of course, depend on the number of employees involved. What may be necessary or desirable for the individuals among a staff of six whose responsibilities are varied may not be practical or cost-effective for a large group in which several employees have the same kinds of responsibilities. In the latter case, group discounts may be available to help reduce costs.

Obtaining professional designations can be expensive; but the cost is generally spread out over several years, and it represents an investment in the company's most important asset, its people. The designations themselves are an asset to the company. Many prospective clients are interested in the qualifications of the personnel who will handle their accounts, and they will ask how many of your staff members have CPM®, CSM, PCAM, or RPA designations.

The Certified Property Manager® (CPM®) designation is one of the most recognized in the industry. In order to become a CPM member of IREM, one has to meet certain criteria that include work experience, education, and minimum portfolio requirements. Having on staff one or more people who hold the CPM designation is a selling tool for the company; having personnel that have a higher level of education in the industry is a plus. Each company should consider developing an educational program for employees that will be mutually beneficial. One approach is to allow each employee to choose a designation related to his or her specialty. Assume for the moment that the employee has chosen the CPM designation and his or her specialty is apartments. The employer might agree to send the employee to a certain number of courses each year with the eventual goal of achieving the designation.

> **Education and Employee Retention** *(continued)*
> Many employers who have such a program pay for the entire cost of each course. Some require the employee to pass the examination for the course in order to be reimbursed for the expense, while others may agree to pay some percentage of the cost (perhaps a 50:50 split). Some employers allow the employee to attend class anywhere in the United States; others require the class to be close to home—in the same city or near enough that the employee will not have to fly out of town or stay in a hotel. The more the employer is willing to underwrite, the more the employee will be encouraged to participate. Regardless of the extent, the important thing is for the company to take an interest in the betterment of its employees.
>
> The same approach would apply to courses toward the Professional Community Association Manager (PCAM) designation awarded by the Community Associations Institute, the Real Property Administrator (RPA) designation granted by the Building Owners and Managers Association, and the Certified Shopping Center Manager (CSM), Certified Leasing Specialist (CLS) and Certified Marketing Director (CMD) designations from the International Council of Shopping Centers. Most companies will not underwrite two or three designations at a time, but helping employees pursue one at a time is likely to benefit the company as well as the individual. (For more information regarding professional designations, see Appendix B.)
>
> Many real estate practitioners need continuing education credits to maintain their professional licenses or designations; these requirements have built-in incentives. However, staff members in other areas may need incentives from their employer to pursue more education. Job advancement, tuition reimbursement (in part or in full), or special recognition may be offered. Support for employees' outside education may be provided as a component of your company's employee benefits program. Many companies will pay for tuition and books for a specified number of college classes or credits over a given time period. The employee's goal may be an advanced degree, specialization in a given area of business or real estate management, or to complete an associate or baccalaureate degree. Here, too, the total cost of all educational programs must be weighed to determine the potential benefits to the company, but helping employees to grow personally as well as professionally is itself a benefit to both them and the company. (Sometimes a company may ask employees to sign an agreement to remain with the firm for a period of time if it substantially underwrites education that is not directly beneficial to the company. The time period may be commensurate with the educational costs.) In the field of real estate management, individual career development is consistent with company growth and success.

office," there would likely be some fear or concern as to what was going to be discussed. On the other hand, if the supervisor had said, "Can you drop by my office for a chat this afternoon?" the request is likely to be perceived as less "threatening."

If it becomes necessary to chastise or discipline an employee, such communications are best handled in private. There can be no valid reason for embarrassing anyone in public. If it is necessary to discuss a concern immediately, you should find a private office or a secluded spot where you

> **Some Tips for Improving Communication Skills**
>
> - **Listen carefully** One of the most important aspects of good communication is being a good listener. What is the person really saying? It is important to let the other person tell his or her story. It is very easy, especially if you think you know where the speaker is going, to cut the person off and provide an answer before the story has been told. This often leads to an improper answer and to frustration on the part of the employee because it is obvious you are not willing to listen.
> - **Distinguish main points** When listening to another person, try to distinguish the main points of what is being said. Often people have difficulty speaking clearly and succinctly. They may give too much detail or not enough. You may have to ask specific questions to nudge a speaker back on track so his or her main points do get addressed.
> - **Consider the speaker's perspective** Employees may come to you with problems that seem to you to be unimportant but are really quite important to them. Patience and some gently probing (i.e., open-ended) questions can often help them find a solution to the problem for themselves.
> - **Be aware of nonverbal cues** Observe the speaker's facial expressions and other body language to help you interpret what is being said. Often someone will be saying they agree with you, but their body language may indicate that they have reservations or doubts they are not willing to verbalize. Such cues suggest a need for more explanation or a desire to be given a more sound rationale for agreeing fully with your words.

will not be overheard. A public "dressing down" will only create resentment and provide further blocks to good communication.

Caution is also advisable when communicating with staff members in writing. A company memo may be addressed to "all employees" in an effort to correct a recurring problem. However, some employees may resent the communication, thinking that the memo was directed to them—perhaps because they may have a slight sense of guilt about the problem, they think they are being singled out for a reprimand.

You also need to look for ways to compliment and praise people for a good job. Too often it is taken for granted that a job will be done well and correctly and nothing needs to be said. However, everyone likes to know that others see and appreciate what they are doing. When something requires a joint effort, completing monthly management reports for example, some sort of group reward may be in order. You might occasionally take the group out to lunch as a thank-you or present a gift certificate to each member of the team after a particularly trying session. The important thing is to let them know you are aware of their efforts and accomplishments so your personnel will not feel unappreciated. (See also the discussion of Communication Basics in Chapter 6.)

At one time, the boss may have been allowed and even expected to be autocratic and results-driven, with little concern as to how employees or

> ### Communicating Nondefensively
>
> Communication is often made more difficult by defensive feelings. A question may be perceived as a criticism. If you ask someone why something was done in a particular way, the person may assume you are not happy with the results. You may be trying to understand the rationale behind the approach that was taken, but rather than accept your question at face value, the listener reacts defensively. You need to be aware of these kinds of defenses so you can deal with them effectively. There are five nondefensive approaches to communication:
>
> 1. **Inquire** Ask if there is a problem—let the other person know his or her response is uncharacteristic. Try to find out the reason for his or her particular reaction. Your interest will likely build better communication.
> 2. **Empathize** Try to put yourself in the other person's place. Why has he or she reacted in this way? Is there a problem at home, or is the person under a lot of pressure at work (e.g., to complete a report that is due)? Is he or she late for a meeting, and are you adding to that lateness?
> 3. **Disclose** Let people know why you acted as you did. An angry response is likely to be accepted more readily if others understand that you have a headache or an angry client is on the phone waiting for an immediate answer.
> 4. **Depersonalize** Focus on the work that is being done and not on the person's character. It is important to indicate the nature of the problem and how you want it solved. It is not helpful to say that the person did not get the job done because he or she is lazy or has a tendency to procrastinate. Such accusations will only set up a defensive reaction, and the issue is not likely to be resolved at all. If there is evidence that the person is lazy or puts things off, those issues should be dealt with separately and as objectively as possible.
> 5. **Disengage** Tactfully end the discussion with the agreement that you will take it up again at a mutually agreeable time. Take time out to think about where the conversation is going wrong and what can be done to put it back on track.

others might react. In a more-enlightened business environment, however, managers realize they can communicate more effectively and humanely by taking into account the other person's point of view and trying to be more understanding of that person's feelings and perceptions.

Setting Goals and Evaluating Performance. In addition to helping employees improve themselves through education, the employer also has an obligation to provide the employee with ongoing performance evaluations and general encouragement. Every employee's performance should be thoroughly evaluated at least once a year. In the process, both the employee and the supervisor express their points of view, and the employee is given an accurate assessment of his or her standing within the company. This is generally done as part of an annual compensation review, although the latter may be a separate process. Additionally, however, employees should be given encouragement when they are doing things well; and when they are not, their shortcomings should be discussed along with suggestions for overcoming them. It is not fair to be dissatisfied with an employee's performance but say nothing about it and then fire the employee without ever having given him or her an opportunity to correct the problem. Employees are usually eager to please and want to do the job the way their employer wants it done. Unless they receive feedback from the employer and there is an opportunity for dialogue, it is hard for employees to know whether they are meeting the company's expectations and vice versa. In the best of situations, expectations are spelled out at the beginning, along with the employee's duties and responsibilities, and everyone is traveling the same path.

In fact, it is fairly common in some industries to bring in new employees on a "probationary" basis—usually the first 60–90 days of employment—which allows employee and supervisor to evaluate each other. (This particular practice should be discussed with your attorney.) During this time, there may be a greater degree of supervisory support and scrutiny, with the employee being given specific feedback on his or her performance and progress. At the end of this period, a poor "fit" between employee and employer may be reconciled by mutual agreement to terminate the employment, while a good hiring decision would lead to a mutual decision to continue employment. Regardless of whether new hires have "probationary" status, conducting a formal performance review after the first six months of employment gives the supervisor an opportunity to share constructive criticism and recommendations. It also opens the door to mutual goal-setting for the next six months (toward the one-year anniversary).

For some if not all positions in the company, goals may be established within the annual performance evaluation. Initially, the supervisor may specify what an employee is expected to accomplish, but best practice is for both supervisor and employee to agree, in writing, about the individual's performance goals. For a property manager, major goals might include achievement of specific occupancy or rent levels. Development and implementation of policies and procedures for a newly assigned property might be another type of goal. A property manager's goals may be linked directly to his or her current compensation (e.g., a bonus) or future salary increases. (Analysis of an individual manager's portfolio, which is one measure of a manager's job performance, is discussed in Chapter 3.)

Goals for other staff members would be consistent with their duties. An accounts receivable clerk might aim to complete monthly billings a day earlier than in the past. A leasing specialist might commit to closing a set number of leases per month or other specified period. A maintenance technician might be expected to increase the number of work orders completed in a day. Regardless of whether individuals' goals are linked to compensation, setting goals and achieving them—and having one's accomplishments acknowledged and rewarded—are part of what motivates employees to do a good job and to remain with their employer.

Salary increases are not mandatory, but they are expected—and given—as acknowledgment of good performance and motivation for continuing one's employment. It is a good idea in general to establish a policy regarding raises, when or how often they are given, and how the amount is to be determined. Most businesses look at their expected revenues for the coming year and budget for salary increases accordingly. If company policy dictates a range of percentage increase, there should also be provision for exceeding the maximum to reward exceptional performance and a requirement to justify not giving an increase or giving less than the full amount. In many companies, a salary range is established for each position. The minimum might be the least you would offer for an entry-level position if the person being hired has only minimal skills. At the other extreme would be the maximum you are willing to pay a highly qualified individual to perform the duties of the position. Promotion to a higher level position with more responsibility would be required to increase an employee's salary beyond the established range. For purposes of hiring, some companies prefer to start low, with the midpoint salary or a lesser amount being offered initially. As a new employee proves his or her value to the firm, that increased value can be reflected in appropriate salary increases.

Internal Opportunities for Promotion. There is little doubt that the chance for upward mobility within a company is a strong influence on employee retention. Most employees are hard working and have a desire to succeed. The longer they are with a company, the more knowledgeable they are about how the company functions, how things are accomplished within the organization, where they fit in the hierarchy, and therefore, within limits, what their future with the company may be. Few things will discourage employees more quickly than their believing they are ready for promotion and the job they thought would be theirs being given to an outsider instead.

It is in the best interest of any real estate management company to look to its own work force before going to the outside to find employees. There is always a possibility that no one on your staff is truly qualified for a new or open position, and if that is the case there really is no choice but to look elsewhere. However, if any staff members are likely to think they are qualified for a job opening, they should be given a chance to discuss the position with a supervisor, and if they are not promoted at that time, they should be told why. If they lack a critical skill or need additional training, the situation affords an opportunity to counsel them on how they may become better prepared for a future opening. If the difference is marginal, perhaps a provisional promotion would be workable, with a requirement that the employee prove himself or herself in the new position within a specified time period—say, three to six months. For most employees, including property managers, the chance to grow within a company with which they are familiar is preferable to changing jobs and perhaps having to start all over again.

The Work Environment

In order to be productive and do their jobs properly, employees need the proper tools, including a good working environment. This does not mean a corner office with a commanding view and teak paneling. However, a property manager should have a work space that provides some privacy for making telephone calls, working on budgets, and handling personnel issues. For managers who are required to be in the field frequently or for long periods, having a portable (cellular) telephone available facilitates staying in touch with suppliers, contractors, and others as well as the office. (Cellular telephones and other technological tools and their uses are described in Chapter 2.)

Some large companies back up their property managers with in-house specialists in collections, construction supervision, maintenance oversight, and other areas so the managers can spend their time managing their assigned properties. Obviously, the manager who has staff support in these areas should be able to handle a larger portfolio than one whose duties include these responsibilities.

Proper administrative or clerical support for the property manager will also ensure that correspondence is answered in a timely fashion and papers are filed properly so they are available the next time they are needed for reference. It is short-sighted to hire a property manager and expect him or her to take care of clerical details. Exceptions to this would be during start-up of the business and entry-level management positions in which understanding of the administrative details will facilitate their property management efforts. This does not mean that every property manager must have a private secretary or administrative assistant, but it can be very cost-effective to have one secretary or clerical support person available to assist three or four property managers on an as-needed basis.

Because much of the property manager's activity concerns financial issues, he or she needs access to accounting records and personnel. A commercial tenant may ask about a rental rate increase or an escalation billing. A contractor may want to know when payment will be made or why the amount paid was different from the amount billed. If the manager of a property does not have ready access to these answers, a lot of time can be wasted, and his or her effectiveness will be diminished in the eyes of the inquirer.

A Perspective on Personnel

Attracting people who will be successful in managing real estate for others is a major challenge. Without qualified people to manage the properties profitably and account for the clients' and the company's finances accurately, a management firm cannot operate at all, let alone be successful.

A real estate management company's personnel are one of its most important assets. The company must help its employees grow and prosper or they will seek opportunities elsewhere. If a company continually ignores its employees' potential for growth, it will repeatedly experience costly turnovers. It is in the best interests of both employer and employee for the company to encourage staff members to acquire additional education and training and, to the extent it is reasonable to do so, to underwrite or share the cost of that training and education as an investment in the company's future and its reputation.

6

Strategizing Client Relations

The real estate management industry has always been subject to business turnover. A property owner may decide to take back the management function. If the property is sold, the new owner may prefer to use a management firm with whom he or she already has an established relationship. A long-term client can become dissatisfied with the management company's performance. Sometimes the management company may elect on its own not to renew an account. Because business turnover is disheartening as well as costly, it is worthwhile to invest time and money in retaining the clients you already have.

Client retention begins even before the management agreement is signed because all of the contacts and negotiations leading up to documentation of the management arrangement create impressions that can make or break the management-client relationship over the long term. To avert problems, you need a clear understanding of what property owners consider important. You also need to be able to address their unique interests and communication needs. In a very real sense, client retention is an extension of your marketing and business development activities.

Understanding Clients' Concerns

Property owners have large numbers of management firms from which to choose. However, their choices are narrowed by the abilities of these firms to meet their needs and the relationships they have developed already. The property owner's concerns relate to three issues:

1. Fulfillment of their ownership goals and objectives,
2. Ability to provide desired services, and
3. Potential conflicts of interest.

These issues will be part of the decision to accept your management proposal and will remain considerations throughout the duration of the management arrangement.

Ownership Goals.   Property owners have different short- and long-term goals and objectives. It cannot be assumed that every owner's goals and objectives are to enhance the value of their properties. While value enhancement is an important consideration, many owners will have additional or different goals and objectives. An owner who lives off the cash flow from an apartment building may be more concerned with the monthly distribution of proceeds than with long-term appreciation. A wealthy owner of a shopping center may value the property's appearance (pride of ownership) more than either cash flow or long-term appreciation. An owner planning to sell a property in the near future may be more interested in making cosmetic alterations than investing in capital improvements that will only produce a return over the long term.

It is imperative to discuss ownership's goals and objectives when management is being assumed and to maintain a dialogue with the owner throughout the term of the management agreement so any changes in those goals can be determined and addressed. One of the best times to discuss goals and objectives with the owner is prior to writing the annual management plan for the property.

Long-term management-client relationships are built on the performance of the management firm, which can be measured in a variety of ways. The best measure is how well the firm was able to meet the owner's goals and objectives or assist the owner in achieving them. Unrealistic ownership goals will not yield a realistic measure of the firm's performance. Management should evaluate the owner's goals based on factors that will impact the probability of those goals being realized. For instance, achieving an occupancy level 10 percent higher than the norm in a weak real estate market, exceeding the area's projected office space absorption rate by 50 percent or more, or selling at a high price when property values are declining may not be achievable goals. It is incumbent on management to provide data that will either support or refute the possibility of achieving the owner's goals, and the owner must agree that the goals and objectives established for management are, in fact, achievable.

Service Capabilities.   Some owners prefer to have one firm provide all the necessary services for a property. While it may be possible to do this in some situations, more often than not you will need to call upon consultants or other real estate experts to handle specific assignments. If a management firm does not have the expertise in house to achieve all of an owner's goals, it may be desirable to recommend another service provider. For instance, if tax appeals or construction supervision services are components of the property's management plan and your firm is not qualified in these areas, it is best to recommend a firm that specializes in such tasks. Alternatively, it may be possible to partner with other firms that have the needed expertise or to outsource selected tasks or activities so the services desired by the owner can be provided competently and professionally. Property owners will respect a management firm that does not try to provide a service it cannot perform at or above industry standards. Recommending the best firm for a specific assignment will assure clients that your company places their best interests ahead of an opportunity to earn additional income. Loyalty to a client often generates loyalty in return.

Conflicts of Interest. Conflicts of interest are a major concern, especially for institutional owners. Owners from out of state or outside the local area may not be aware of a firm's management and leasing portfolio. A particular concern is whether a firm might be managing or leasing another property that competes directly with the owner's property, thus creating a potential conflict of interest for the management company if it would be marketing or leasing the two properties at the same time. This can happen if the firm is managing two competing office buildings, for example, and a prospective tenant is considering both buildings as a possible business location. Though the manager may not encourage the prospect to choose one building over the other, the owner whose building is not chosen may question the manager's actions.

The best way to avoid potential conflicts of interest is full disclosure. This should occur first in the discussions about entering into a management agreement. Providing the prospective client with a list of properties managed and/or leased by the firm and discussing any of the properties that are in close proximity to the prospect's property is the best way to identify this type of potential conflict of interest. If the prospect's property is near one from an existing account and the possibility or perception of a conflict of interest exists, both owners should be made aware of the other property the firm is managing or proposing to manage. The property owner who is fully apprised of any actual or perceived conflicts of interest will be better able to make an informed decision whether or not to hire the management firm.

Often it can be explained to everyone's satisfaction why managing and leasing each property is a benefit to both of the owners. However, if the management company executive believes there may be a potential conflict of interest in managing the prospect's property, it is better to say so up front and not pursue the management or leasing opportunity further.

Other areas of the management firm's business activities may also be perceived as or become a potential conflict of interest. Contracting service to a company owned by the management firm or any of its employees is an example. For instance, sometimes it is to the client's advantage for a management firm to use its subsidiary company for contract maintenance. The price of the services may be lower than that of other maintenance companies. Also, the maintenance company has an already-established loyalty to the property owner via the management firm, and the service response time will usually be superior. However, the management company executive is obligated to make a full disclosure to the property owner of the interest the firm has in the maintenance company. (More information on the importance of full disclosure is presented in Chapter 13.)

Addressing Clients' "Hot Buttons"

Every real estate owner has areas of particular interest, which can be in marketing and leasing, operating the physical plant, financial reporting, or anything else related to the management of their properties. An owner's interests are usually also very specific—negotiation of maintenance contracts, the appearance of the rental office and model apartments, reviewing financial reports—and that is why they are called "hot buttons." The manager of the property needs to place additional emphasis on handling these particular responsibilities and to address them specifically in his or her written and spoken communications with the owner. Real estate managers also have special interests and capabilities, and these should be considered when personnel are being assigned to particular accounts so their accomplishments will achieve personal goals as well as serve the priorities of the property owner.

Apart from property owners' personal interests, their information needs vary with the type of ownership. Institutional owners and their advisors have a restrictive environment in which to operate the property, especially as fiduciary relationships and federal laws place additional responsibility and burdens on the asset manager and advisor. Also, institutional owners often have specific financial reporting format requirements that must be met; they are less flexible in negotiating management agreements and more demanding about qualifying prospective tenants, both residential and commercial. In fact, such ownership decisions are often made by a committee.

At the other end of the spectrum is the owner who lives near the property, has no partners, can accept the management firm's standard reporting formats, and is familiar with the area and the market conditions. Usually this type of owner requires less formal market data, is more flexible about evaluating prospective tenants, and can make decisions on the spot.

Due to the competitiveness of the real estate industry and the need to meet financial projections, all types of property owners are more demanding. It is therefore imperative for the manager of the property to find out the extent of the property owner's or asset manager's experience and his or her particular needs.

- What types of information does the property owner need?
- How extensive does the information need to be (level of detail)?

- What is the decision-making process?
- How familiar is the property owner with the market and competing properties?

A property owner who has little or no direct experience or knowledge in this area may need to learn about real estate and its management from the start of the relationship.

There is also greater emphasis on long-range planning. Owners require more information so they can make more-educated decisions. Strict deadlines for specific financial reports are the rule rather than the exception. Ability and willingness to provide special reports on short notice is a particular requirement of managing for institutional owners. (More information on clients' reporting requirements can be found in Chapter 3; clients' accounting requirements are addressed in Chapter 4.)

Communicating with Owners

Often the only difference between the level of success of two competent real estate management firms is the effectiveness of their communications with their clients. If the manager is not keeping the owner of the property informed about management, operations, and leasing activities, the owner may question what the management firm is doing to earn its fees. Because property owners have different communication needs, you will have to develop—and implement—a communications plan to meet the specific needs of each owner-client.

The frequency and type of communications will depend on several variables. One is the owner's location in relation to that of the property. An owner who lives in the area where the property is located will be familiar with local economic conditions and the local market and will probably visit the property regularly. An out-of-state owner, on the other hand, will need to be informed of changing market conditions and other local activities that will impact the property.

The type of ownership is another variable. An individual owner who has no partners may prefer meetings and telephone conversations and require few written reports other than a basic monthly accounting. At the other extreme are institutional owners and asset managers who usually need more numerous reports, including documentation of recommendations and more extensive financial accounting. Regardless of the way the property is owned, it is most desirable to have a single person representing the ownership entity in the owner-management relationship. In a partnership, one of the general partners may serve this role; in a condominium or other homeowners' association, the president or another member of the board may be delegated this responsibility.

Conditions at the property must also be considered. If the property has a problem, such as high vacancy or disgruntled occupants, the manager will need to be in contact with the owner more frequently than when everything is running smoothly.

Also to be considered is the personality of the property owner. Some individual owners prefer to be involved with the daily activities of their properties while others do not. One asset manager representing an institutional owner may need every detail explained while another might not. In part, the type and frequency of communication will depend on developing trust between the ownership entity and the management firm.

One of the best ways for a client to follow the activities of the property manager and the progress of the property is written reports. These include the monthly management reports that chronicle day-to-day property operations and measure progress in achieving the goals of the annual management plan. (Components of monthly report packages and the management plan are discussed in Chapter 3.)

However, the most effective means of communication is a business meeting in which the property owner and the management team can engage in a dialogue regarding issues and recommendations and arrive at a mutually agreeable plan of action. (Some property owners may prefer to have regularly scheduled telephone conversations with the manager in addition to or instead of in-person meetings.) Preparation for these communications includes making a list of issues to be discussed and having related information readily available.

On the other hand, situations that require immediate attention are best handled in a less-formal way via direct personal contact. This is also a way of keeping the client informed in the periods between monthly reports and scheduled business meetings. Clients also need to know about what is happening in the community surrounding their properties, and there are many ways to provide this type of information to them. All of these elements should be considered in developing specific client communications strategies.

Regardless of the form of communication, real estate managers must always practice full disclosure even though they sometimes are the bearers of bad news. Owner-clients cannot make the best decisions for their real estate investments unless all the necessary information, regardless of whether it is positive or negative, is provided as soon as possible.

Meetings with the Client. Although meetings with clients are usually held at the management office or the property (a preference of some absentee owners), a local owner may sometimes prefer meeting at his or her office—or possibly in a more casual setting (e.g., over breakfast, lunch, or dinner). If an owner resides out of state, the manager should offer to travel to the client's office. (Travel expenses and who pays for them would be considerations in making such an offer and deciding who would attend the

> **Communication Basics**
>
> Most day-to-day communications rely on the spoken word. Some encounters will be face-to-face, but a very large proportion of the real estate manager's spoken communications will be by telephone. Generally, when one is able to speak with others face-to-face, there is the added advantage of body language—so-called nonverbal communication. A smile and a friendly tone of voice create a relaxed environment that facilitates communication of your message while a stern expression is likely to imply disapproval (or dislike). The problem with body language is that it can send an altogether different message to the listener and observer than the words are intended to convey.
>
> The listener's body language is important, too. Speakers become frustrated when they are trying to explain a complicated situation to someone else, and a listener is looking at his or her wristwatch (a sign of impatience) or otherwise seems inattentive. These not-so-subtle clues make it obvious to the speaker that the person is not really listening and wants to be doing something else.
>
> Because the telephone removes the benefit of body language, words will have more weight, but so will tone of voice. A monotone or "flat" voice (no inflection) is likely to imply boredom. A harsh tone may suggest anger. Because these nuances affect the way spoken messages are received, you need to be aware of how you sound to others.

meeting in addition to the manager of the client's property.) The goal should be to have a productive discussion in an environment that is conducive to agreement, wherever that may be. (If it is not possible to set up a face-to-face meeting, a videoconference may be a desirable alternative since it provides an opportunity for dialogue and discussion.)

The client, with management's input, sets the agenda for these meetings, and the management staff should do everything possible to be prepared for them. Ideally, you will be advised ahead of time about the client's intended agenda and expectations and can prepare folders that include all the necessary information for everyone who will be present.

One or two days prior to the meeting, the company executive should get together with the manager of the property and review all aspects of each issue. One way to maximize this review exercise is for the executive to assume the role of the owner and ask specific questions. In addition, the annual management plan, recent monthly management reports, site and floor plans, and any other relevant data—i.e., all information about the property and its operations that will help facilitate the meeting—should be assembled.

Other preparations include making a telephone available for the client's use, having coffee and other refreshments available, and ordering a meal brought in, if appropriate, rather than interrupting the discussions. Asking clients about their food preferences beforehand or immediately after they arrive will ensure that everyone is accommodated. Such arrangements are

> **Communication Basics** *(continued)*
> The written word can be even more difficult to interpret. In the absence of voice inflections and other nonverbal cues, a written message may seem harsh when that was not the writer's intent. A busy executive may send out a letter intended to resolve a situation, but in the desire to act quickly, he or she may choose words or construct sentences which give the reader a perception that the problem is more serious than either of them had thought. In fact, such a letter can cause more problems than it solves. Recognizing this, effective communicators will dictate this type of letter but delay sending it for a few days, reading it again to see if it really sends the message they want to communicate. On reflection, it may be desirable to revise parts of the letter or rewrite it completely. Alternatively, someone else in the office can be asked to review the letter and see if they agree that it should be sent. Often a second (or even a third) perspective on the letter and the situation that inspired it can help guide the writer to tone down the language or write a more appropriate response.
> Most relationships in real estate management are ongoing, and an angry or ill-timed communication can damage or destroy a relationship that has been nurtured carefully over a period of months or years. In addition to owner-clients, real estate managers form relationships with building occupants (residents, commercial tenants) and others who provide services to the property or the management firm. It is important to keep in mind that, even though office and retail tenants and contractors may actually be business entities, you will be dealing directly with their representatives who are people much like yourself. Demonstrating simple consideration for people's feelings will not only foster goodwill but enhance the manager's reputation as a good communicator.
> Real estate managers also deal with tradespeople, attorneys, and others whose specialized expertise may encompass profession- or trade-specific terminology. Making an effort to learn the "language" of those you must work with will pay off in more effective communications with them because you will better understand what is being said by the other person.

usually very much appreciated by busy clients, although they may prefer to eat out because it can provide a much-needed break.

Client meetings are likely to be convened for several reasons: Discussion of next year's budget, marketing planning, and visits to the managed property are among the most common ones. Regardless of the purpose of the meetings with clients, careful notes should be taken, and at the end of the meeting, the real estate manager should try to summarize the decisions and assignments so everyone understands what the client and the management company expect from each other. A written memo to all the participants as a follow-up to the meeting will help clarify future assignments.

Annual Budget Meetings. These usually take place after the first round of budget adjustments. The goal is to fine-tune the figures and finalize the spending plan. A copy of the proposed budget in its current revised stage should be available to each participant. Back-up information should be included in the folders along with any other pertinent information.

Usually the manager who prepared the budget will lead the meeting, but it is helpful to have accounting personnel there as well. Any extraneous material that might have an impact on the budget—market surveys, building surveys, etc.—should also be available so valuable time will not be spent waiting for someone to find and copy needed information. If others of your staff members will be expected to provide input, they should be available and fully prepared to step in and respond when they are called.

Marketing Meetings. Marketing is always a critical operations issue, but it receives even more attention during difficult economic times. Proper positioning of a property within its market (target marketing) is being given more and more emphasis. For marketing meetings, copies of the latest market survey should be available, along with the most up-to-date information available on the property's competition. Current reports from local brokers, market analysts, or competing management companies can also be very helpful.

If the client wants to tour the market area, preparations should include careful planning of the route to be taken so the driver will know exactly where to go. If the entourage is large, plan to provide a comfortable vehicle to accommodate the entire group. Often the most important marketing discussions occur while "on tour." It is also an excellent opportunity to demonstrate the management firm's unique expertise.

The leader of the tour should be familiar with each of the comparable properties that will be visited. He or she should also be aware of other similar properties in the area and have available pertinent information about them. If the desired tour turns out not to be feasible—e.g., because of inclement weather or time constraints—a good slide or videotape presentation may serve the purpose as well or better.

Site Visits. Some clients visit their properties infrequently, and the less often they visit, the more important each visit becomes. The property must be at its very best because whatever the client sees may be his or her only impression of the property for the entire year. When the client arrives at the site, the manager of the property should have keys available for all spaces or be able to access the keys immediately if the owner should ask to see specific areas.

Site personnel and any contractors expecting to work at the property should be made aware of the client's impending visit and their respective roles in any scheduled meetings. If they are likely to be asked for information, they should be told that and, if possible, advised of the likely context. For example, at a residential property where elevator renovations are being discussed, the manager might have the elevator company representative available to outline the options being considered and discuss some of the projected costs. Residents and commercial tenants should also be informed that the owner will be visiting.

Direct Personal Contact. Contemporary businesspeople generally expect instantaneous communication. Telephone calls are personal and informal; they can facilitate agreement through conversational give and take. A phone call to the client, letting him or her know about changes at the property is always appreciated. However, it can be difficult to connect with clients if they are on one coast and the management company and their property are on the other. With voice mail and answering machines, detailed spoken messages can be left, and these efforts may be satisfactory if a reply —or specific approval—is not needed urgently.

On the other hand, one of the most effective methods of communication today is the fax machine. It is not disruptive, and even though it implies urgency and is somewhat impersonal, it does allow specific details, such as contract language or cost information, to be communicated quickly and accurately. Written approval, if needed, can be sent by return fax. (This is valid documentation in case a question arises and there is no other "paperwork" indicating formal approval.) If what is being sent is just for informational purposes and no reply is needed, that fact can be stated on the fax sent to the client.

Electronic mail (e-mail) is an alternative that affords instantaneous communication. However, technology is not the answer to every problem. Consider that some issues which are highly sensitive may best be addressed in spoken conversation—one-on-one—while the more traditional vehicles of letters and memorandums should not be ignored when formal documentation of a communique is desirable or required. Also, certified mail (USPS) and various overnight delivery services automatically generate proof of delivery (if needed) and permit lost items to be traced.

Electronic communications have their limitations. In the case of faxes, digitizing breaks up text and images. Very small type (as on a contract) may not be readable at the receiving end, and photographs or other images with differing degrees of contrast may lose much of their impact. E-mail is often converted to and from DOS files for transmission, and this will alter the format of documents sent that way. Attached files can get lost or not be accessible by the recipient because of computer incompatibilities. We would also offer this word of caution: Fax, e-mail, and other electronic media should only be used for transmitting messages that do not involve issues of confidentiality unless appropriate security measures (e.g., encryption) are also employed.

Other Communications. Regular communication with owner-clients apart from scheduled meetings and formal written reports is good business

> **Client Satisfaction Surveys**
>
> The best surveys are short—a dozen or fewer questions. Usually they include response scales or multiple-choice answers and some blank space for comments. In requesting performance feedback from real estate management clients, however, it may be more appropriate to include a mix of open-ended questions that allow for a detailed response along with some questions that include choices of answers. Among the issues that can be addressed in client surveys are:
>
> - What clients like most (and least) about doing business with you.
> - Clients' preferences for communications about their managed properties.
> - What types of problems clients have encountered with your company or your personnel.
>
> Questions that can be answered yes or no can have these choices listed. However, for some yes or no responses, it may be important to ask "WHY?" and provide space for an explanation. Examples of different types of questions include:
>
> **Questions for Use with a Satisfaction Scale**
>
> How satisfied are you with the services provided by [*Name of Management Company*]? (Scale choices might be: Very satisfied, Satisfied, Slightly dissatisfied, Very dissatisfied)
>
> How would you rate the real estate manager assigned to your property? (Scale choices might be: Excellent, Good, Fair, Poor, Unacceptable)

and a key client retention strategy. Some managers subscribe to local newspapers and have them sent directly to their clients' offices. Others may peruse the papers, clipping out items of interest and sending them to clients. Local economic and political issues are likely items for clipping in addition to specific mentions of the property, advertisements promoting the property, and events or incidents in the neighborhood, especially if they may impact the client's property.

Another such source is articles in trade journals. Quite often real estate journals include articles on various regions of the United States. When there is coverage of the region where their property is located, owners will certainly be interested. Some journals even list current and/or pending deals (e.g., real estate sales and/or leases), and owners are always interested in the nature of current transactions in the marketplace. Individual articles can be clipped out (be sure the source has been identified), or the intact issue can be forwarded. You may want to subscribe to extra copies or acquire multiple copies of some issues that would interest several clients. Because photocopying for such distribution should be done only with the publisher's permission, it may be worthwhile to arrange permission to make multiple copies through the Copyright Clearance Center. (Your local library should be able to provide information on this service and its fees.)

It is always a good idea to be on the mailing list to receive the agendas

> **Client Satisfaction Surveys** *(continued)*
> **Open-Ended Questions**
> How can we better serve your real estate management needs?
> What additional services would you like [*Name of Management Company*] to provide?
>
> An important question to include, in general, is whether the client would recommend your company and your services to others. The answer to this question may be more telling than any rating scale or explanation.
>
> It is a good practice to repeat the survey periodically. If you mail to all clients, you should probably distribute the survey at least once a year. If you are looking for particular feedback, it might be worthwhile to time your information request in relation to a specific event or activity (e.g., expiration of the management agreement term, completion of the budget planning exercise, after a massive marketing and leasing effort).
>
> Although statistical data from surveys are compiled anonymously, client satisfaction surveys require identification of the respondent, which will help the management team address a client's concerns specifically. On the other hand, especially favorable comments can be very effective when quoted in marketing materials and annual reports to stockholders. (The client's permission should be obtained, in writing, before any such "testimonials" are published.)

for meetings of the city council and other local groups (e.g., chamber of commerce). Often there are items of some interest to clients, even though there may be no direct impact on their properties. Sending them copies of the meeting agendas when the information is likely to be of interest keeps clients informed about local government actions and other relevant issues.

Another vehicle is a regular newsletter that can address a range of topics from real estate market data and trends to general business issues that are likely to be of interest. If management company personnel write for real estate industry publications, reprints of appropriate articles can become part of your client communications. Copies of news releases can also be mailed to clients when appropriate. (These strategies are discussed in detail in Chapter 7.)

Two forms of communication that property owners seldom receive are thank-you letters and surveys. Sending a letter to each of your owner-clients expressing appreciation for the opportunity to manage their properties is a nice touch at year's end or on the anniversary of the management agreement. Surveys sent to property owners asking them to rate the service received from the different departments of the management firm is a way to identify problems and obtain recommendations for improving your internal operations. It is especially important to seek these types of feedback from clients who have terminated a management arrangement. However, personal interviews of former clients may be more effective for this purpose than a written questionnaire.

Dealing with Difficult Clients

One of the biggest challenges in real estate management is working with a difficult client. Such individuals can consume an enormous amount of the manager's time, requiring excessive numbers of special reports and having a negative influence on the morale of the entire management team. There is no standard or ideal way to handle this type of client. Best practice is for company executives to immediately attempt to determine if the client is unhappy with the service provided by the management firm:

Is the management firm not meeting the owner's expectations?

Does the manager understand the client's goals and objectives?

Are the client's expectations realistic?

The answers to these questions can only be discovered by meeting with the client and reviewing the elements of the management arrangement, including the annual management plan, the progress made toward achieving the owner's goals and objectives, the performance of the property manager and the accounting department, and any special reports or tasks required by the client. The problem may be that the client and the manager of the property have different business styles or personalities, or both; in which case, it may be necessary to assign a different person to manage the property.

Sometimes the client is the "problem." Some people are not good communicators, so their requirements and expectations may not be clear from the beginning. It is also possible that the management plan and agreement may have been interpreted as promises that have not been or cannot be kept, and consequently the client is disappointed or dissatisfied. Sometimes, you may simply have to accept the fact that a particular client will always be difficult to work with, especially if the account is important to the management company. The alternative is to exercise the cancellation right in the management contract. While it is painful to lose a management account, the disruption in the office and the impact on employees' morale that can arise from having an unhappy client may necessitate such drastic action.

A Perspective on Client Retention

Clients are extremely valuable assets. The vast majority of the firm's income derives from management contracts, which are the primary consideration in determining the company's value or worth. The value of management accounts can be expressed in several ways. Each account provides an income stream needed to sustain the management company—its income stream is its value. The combined income streams are a measure of the firm's value. Management accounts also establish a company's reputation

> ### Adding a Personal Touch
>
> Some owners enjoy socializing with the manager of their property, and this type of interaction can take many forms. You might want to develop a mini-profile on each of your owner-clients. Whether they enjoy tennis, golf, or other recreational activities can be noted along with personal data (birthdays, anniversaries, information about family members). It is especially helpful to know food and beverage preferences or if someone does not smoke or drink.
>
> Consider appropriate activities or entertainments both owner and manager can enjoy. An owner from out-of-town might welcome a tour of the city, a visit to a museum, or a baseball game. Other clients may prefer an early dinner with the manager and the company executive and time alone to prepare for their next property visit. Sometimes including clients in a holiday party or a summer picnic with management company personnel can bring them into closer touch with the human side of your staff.
>
> An issue that is debated within the industry is whether or not to give gifts to clients during the holiday season. Some institutional owners have a policy that prohibits their employees from accepting gifts. Other companies allow their employees to receive gifts that are under a specific dollar value or are not considered "substantial." If it is a management company practice to give holiday gifts, you should find out your owner-clients' policies regarding acceptance of gifts, and the value of anything given should allow no one to infer that favors are expected in return. Food gifts are festive, consumable, and often inexpensive. They are usually suitable for giving the same gift to every member of a group. In fact, they can be repeated year after year, perhaps becoming a "signature" gift from the company. An especially nice choice is something unique to the area where the property is located (e.g., smoked salmon from the Northwest; fruit from California).
>
> Personal interactions with clients require an added word of caution: One client's perception that another client is being treated better or entertained more lavishly could create hard feelings, and the potential ill will this might generate can be problematic to overcome. Knowing the client is key to implementing these types of strategies.

and position within the industry. Another measure of the value of a management account is the disruption created by the termination process. The cost of acquiring a new account is yet another indicator of the value of an existing account.

A firm's ultimate growth depends on its ability to retain existing clients while adding new ones and expanding its management portfolio. While client retention is rightly an extension of the firm's marketing and business development activities (see Chapter 7), this chapter has focused on ways to retain clients once they have been acquired. All of your firm's interactions with prospective clients, as well as the ongoing relationships with the owners of properties you manage currently, need to be examined from a client's perspective. Your operations, your accounting services, and the personnel you hire to operate your business and service your property management accounts are all part of what makes clients want to do business with you in the first place and continue doing business with you over the long term.

There are three reasons why management accounts are lost—a change in the ownership of a property or an owner taking the management function back in house or dissatisfaction with management's services. When a property is sold or foreclosed by a lender, the new owner may have its own management company or department or prefer to contract with another firm with whom it has developed a relationship. The management agreement often provides for termination of management in the event the property is sold because the management contract is not usually transferred to a new owner automatically. An owner may take management back in house for any of several reasons but mostly to be able to retain the management fee. The property owner who is dissatisfied with management's performance may seek improvements or simply not renew the agreement when it expires; in an extreme situation, the agreement may be canceled outright if it has been breached. Though a lost management account is often replaced, the income stream generated by a specific account can never be recaptured.

Account turnover is inherent in the real estate management business. Although turnover due to an owner taking management in house cannot be avoided, an active client-retention program can help avert the loss of an account due to client dissatisfaction. Such a program should include, at a minimum, monitoring of manager performance as well as property performance and frequent communications with the client.

A satisfied client becomes a source of referral business. Because long-term relationships are necessary as well as desirable, every effort should be made to nurture the firm's relationship with a client. It behooves everyone in the firm to focus on serving and retaining clients, even though client retention is primarily the responsibility of those assigned to the property or the account. Each member of the company has an important role in meeting clients' needs, from the receptionist who represents the company to callers and visitors, to the bookkeepers who are responsible for accurate and timely financial reports and the administrative staff who support the real estate managers. Everyone in the organization must understand that real estate management is a service business, and the "product" the management firm offers is their time, their professionalism, and their expertise.

Business Development

7

Strategizing Business Development

The lifeline of a third-party real estate management company is a continual stream of new business. To generate new business, a company must have a marketing plan. Without an effective marketing plan, a company will not prosper. In fact, it will eventually fail. A company's ability to grow and prosper is dependent on its leadership's commitment to marketing.

Although adding new management accounts will be its main growth strategy, a real estate management company is often qualified to provide a variety of adjunct services in addition to property management. Usually these are specialized activities in which the firm or some of its personnel have developed expertise, and they may be marketed (and contracted) separate from the firm's management services.

Marketing Strategies

Marketing is an investment that drives company revenues. Among the keys to successful marketing are commitment, consistency, and patience. Commitment is the choice to pursue a specific course of action: Develop a plan, follow through with it, and measure the results. Consistency requires persistence: Contacting a prospective client only once, occasional attendance at meetings of professional associations, or sending out only one press release will seldom produce positive results. Patience is needed because profits only come after one's services have been sold to the client, and being consistent in fulfilling the commitment to the chosen plan of action takes time.

Marketing is not a one-time thing. Markets change and people forget. Your competition will not go away. Marketing must be an ongoing activity to strengthen your identity, maintain your credibility, and give you an advantage over competitors who do not actively market their services. Business that is acquired today is often a result of marketing efforts initiated two or more years ago, and today's marketing activities may not generate business until sometime in the future. A good marketing plan will provide strategies that can be implemented immediately and in succession over a period of time.

In targeting potential clients, you may utilize an assortment of marketing strategies. Your success in acquiring new business is the measure of the effectiveness of those strategies. However, business is retained by developing and sustaining clients' confidence in your company and by continuing to provide the services your established clients want and need.

Establishing a Market Niche. Few service companies are of sufficient size to serve an entire industry, and this includes real estate management firms. The first step in developing a marketing plan it to define the company's market niche. Once that is known, prospective clients can be identified and contacted.

Each management firm needs to define its market niche in terms of property type(s), geographic area, level of service, services offered, and client base—i.e., how its services and capabilities match the market's needs. This is done by appraising the firm's current and potential resources, defining its competitive advantages, assessing its competition, and identifying business opportunities.

Resources. A company's resources are its people, its reputation, available capital, and technology. A key consideration is the expertise of the management *personnel*. If the group comprises five property managers, four of whom have worked in apartment and condominium management for their entire careers and one who has had limited experience in office building management while also managing apartments, the company's prevailing expertise is in residential management. In order to serve clients who own office buildings or shopping centers, commercial real estate management and leasing expertise will have to be developed among the existing personnel or added by hiring managers who have appropriate commercial experience. Alternatively, it may be possible or practical to develop a strategic alliance with a firm whose strong suit is commercial management and leasing; in such an arrangement, the companies together could offer management services for both residential and commercial properties.

The company's *reputation*—how it is perceived by others in the real estate industry—is built on the quality of the service it provides and the type of property it specializes in managing. Often a firm will have a reputation for managing a particular type of property and be overlooked for opportunities to manage other property types. Seldom will a firm be given an opportunity to submit a proposal for a property type with which it has limited management experience. The quality of its service, on the other hand, relates to fulfilling clients' service expectations and clients' perceptions about the way they are treated by the firm and its personnel.

Evaluation of the company's *technology* should include:

- The capacity of its computer hardware—Is it capable of operating multiple software programs?
- The capabilities of the company's software programs—Can they handle multiple property types?
- The company's ability to compete based on state-of-the-art technology—Are personal computers available for the administrative staff? Do the real estate managers have pagers, portable phones, laptop computers, voice mail, and other current technologic tools?

The company's technologic capabilities also define its ability to meet the financial reporting requirements of institutions and other sophisticated property owners.

Capital is necessary, not only for expansion, but for maintaining a competitive edge and surviving downturns in the industry and to be able to endure a loss of one or more major accounts. Appraising the company's strengths and weaknesses will give you an understanding of its capabilities and what is needed to overcome its weaknesses.

Is there sufficient capital available to operate the business?

What is the amount of cash reserves?

Do the partners or principals have the ability and the willingness to invest funds in the company?

Can the company obtain a line of credit to invest in upgrading equipment and expanding its services?

A specific financial philosophy and strategies for managing (and taking advantage of) its banking relationship are additional considerations.

Competitive Advantages. The company's strengths are the key to defining its competitive advantages. Which property types does the company excel in managing? Is yours only one of a few firms that specializes in managing and leasing a specialty property type such as medical buildings? In what geographic area does the company have a strong presence? In which services and specialized expertise does the company excel? How does your service compare with that of other management companies? In essence, what distinguishes your company from its competitors?

The Competition. After you have a complete understanding of your own company, your competition must be evaluated. How many firms are managing the same type or types of property as you do? Do they specialize in a property type? What are their primary strengths? How are they perceived by others in the industry (their reputation)? Are they locally based or a division of a national brokerage firm? Are they associated with a national developer who has ventured into real estate management? What technology do they have? Which software programs do they operate? Do they have resources to acquire new technology and respond to different property owners' demands? Evaluating the competition allows you to assess your firm's ability to compete in the marketplace.

Business Opportunities. In order to establish a market niche, you will need to identify opportunities. What is the client base? What types of properties are managed for a fee? Where is there a need? For instance, medical office buildings are often owned by groups of doctors who have limited knowledge of real estate and limited time available to manage their investment. A firm specializing in managing suburban office buildings may take advantage of limited competition in the field and develop a specialty niche in managing and leasing medical buildings.

Look for growth areas. Developers create real estate management opportunities. Will there be a surge of development of a particular property type? Consider other geographic areas. A company can expand its services into a nearby community less expensively and with fewer logistical problems than it can expand to the other side of a state or into another state hundreds of miles away. Are investors in a small community a few hour's drive from your metropolitan area being served poorly—or, perhaps, not at all—by local management companies?

A real estate management firm may expand its services by accepting challenges. In an overbuilt market with high vacancies and depressed rents, creative marketing and leasing strategies are needed to prevent distressed properties from being foreclosed by the mortgage holders. When such properties are foreclosed, they become part of the lender's real estate owned (REO) portfolio, and financial institutions frequently seek professional assistance in managing their REO properties. In addition, real estate managers often serve as court-appointed receivers to safeguard properties while the property owner and the lender resolve the status of the loan. As major corporations downsize and look for ways to reduce overhead, they often outsource some or all of their real estate services. Such outsourcing, especially of facility management, is another business opportunity for real estate management firms. (Outsourcing is discussed in detail later in this chapter.)

A comprehensive analysis of your company, its competition, and the marketplace will help you determine if the firm's present market niche is correct and explore opportunities to enlarge its client base by broadening its market niche.

Developing Credibility. Credibility is something of a conundrum: Like the chicken and the egg, a company must have credibility to acquire clients, but credibility only comes after it has established a clientele. The reputation of the individuals who started the business will establish the firm's credibility initially.

Property owners, especially institutional owners and their advisors, need to know that the decision to hire a specific management company is not only the *right decision,* but also the *safe decision.* They want the management company they select to be capable of managing the property in a professional manner and not create any problems that will reflect poorly on the person responsible for making that selection. A management firm and its staff must be well known for their excellent reputation and expertise. This in turn will give potential clients a level of confidence that enables them to feel secure in the selection of a particular firm.

A management firm's credibility is best established by the performance of its real estate managers. The general public takes a property's management for granted and often becomes aware of it only when a property is poorly managed or if the owner is neglecting the property or an incident at the property is publicized. The real estate community is usually no more informed about the level of management of a specific property or the array of properties in a management company's portfolio than is the general public. Property owners, especially those living in other states, are unaware of the performance of firms that are not managing their properties. A visit to a property conveys only limited knowledge of how it is being managed. Usually only the owner of the property is aware of the performance of its management.

If a firm's clients are not telling others about its excellent performance, few people, if any, will be aware of the expertise and capabilities of the management company. The credibility and name recognition enjoyed by many real estate firms is partially based on longevity. A long-established firm will promote itself as a client's safe decision based on its name recognition and its track record. A local firm that is not well known and does not have name recognition, especially on a regional or national level, must market its staff's expertise to gain credibility.

Promote Your Expertise. A firm needs to develop and implement a strategy to establish and enhance its credibility. One of the best means of establishing credibility is to become known as an expert through such activities as *public speaking, teaching, and writing.* These techniques provide exposure within the real estate community for a firm and its leaders because the audience they reach (listeners and readers) will include potential clients and people who refer management companies to property owners. Ideally, the listener or reader will form a favorable opinion of the speaker or writer, and his or her company and their expertise, as well as acquire specific knowledge from the presentation or article.

Speaking, teaching, and writing are the most cost-effective means of marketing a company to groups of businesspeople. The out-of-pocket expense is usually nominal although there is a cost in terms of the time invested in these activities. The benefits of writing and speaking can be doubled because the information is easily recycled: An article can be the basis for a speech, and a speech can be rewritten for publication. Similarly, professionals who teach real estate courses—whether for the local real estate board, as part of an adult or continuing education program at a community college, or for academic credit at a college or university—gain name recognition for themselves and their companies. Word of mouth is one of the most powerful forms of advertising.

Published articles can also be used in direct mail promotion of the company's services. Copies of an article can be mailed, along with a brief cover letter, to the management firm's clients (present, past, and potential), lenders, appraisers, and other business contacts. The out-of-pocket (direct) costs for such mailings are the postage, plus the costs of the envelopes, the letters, and the reprints. Depending on the postage rate, mailing 200 reprints can cost less than $150. There is also the indirect expense of the time the author devoted to writing the article and the staff spent to accomplish the mailing. However, both the direct and indirect expenses are insignificant compared to the credibility and exposure gained by the management company and the author. Articles can also be included in the firm's presentation package for acquiring a management account.

One's accumulated knowledge and expertise may even warrant publishing a book. Being a published book author enhances a writer's credibility and can lead to invitations to be interviewed about the book or to speak on related subjects. The management company that employs a published author benefits from book promotion that includes the writer's credentials and business affiliation. A book can also be used as a marketing tool. A publisher may grant an author a special discount that makes it possible to purchase a large number of copies that can be sent to selected clients and contacts.

Another possibility is to become a *resource* for other real estate professionals. The real estate business thrives on information and statistics. Lenders, appraisers, brokers, developers, and others in the industry need data about markets, trends, and operating expenses. In the management, marketing, and leasing of individual properties, real estate managers collect a wealth of information on a variety of subjects—e.g., rental rates, concessions, vacancies, operating expenses, apartment residents' amenity prefer-

> **Public Speaking as a Business Development Strategy**
>
> In every community, there are numerous opportunities to speak in public throughout the year. Though the primary purpose is to convey information to the audience, the benefit of public speaking as a business development technique cannot be denied: Public speaking enables the speaker to target and command the attention of a select audience.
>
> Local chapters of national real estate organizations frequently offer half-day, one-day, and two-day seminars. These may comprise a series of one- to two-hour educational sessions presented by panels of two or three experts. Serving on such a panel is an excellent way of getting involved in public speaking. Whether at the podium or seated at a table, you have the company and support of the other panelists, and you present only a portion of the program.
>
> Another excellent opportunity is to be the guest speaker at the monthly meeting of a professional association or a community or business organization. Everyone in real estate needs to know current market information and future trends. For example, you might speak to the local appraisal association about market trends relating to a particular property type. Because case studies are always intriguing, a property turnaround would likely be of interest to any group, as would the marketing and leasing of a new building or one in development. Service clubs may be interested in a more general perspective—the real estate market or the real estate management industry. For an audience comprising the general public, a discussion of the advantages or disadvantages of membership in a homeowners' association would be an interesting topic. College instructors often seek out guest speakers on specific real estate topics. Speaking to a small group of students in a real estate class or novices in the profession is one of the best ways to develop confidence in your speaking ability.
>
> The keys to successful public speaking are understanding what interests your audience, providing information of value, keeping within the allotted time, and being well prepared. There are numerous books, audio- and videotapes, and seminars on public speaking that can help you get started in this direction. These programs not only discuss developing the presentation, they also address posture, humor, and attire—the intangibles that can enhance or detract from the presentation and the person.

ences. Other real estate professionals often have only limited access to these types of data. Offering to share particular data, along with your perspectives on the market and future trends, creates goodwill within the real estate community. It can also lead to referrals as those real estate professionals develop confidence in your firm's information and a rapport with its real estate managers.

Often there are opportunities to be an industry resource for the local print media. Real estate editors and reporters working for local business journals and daily newspapers need contacts within the real estate industry who can provide facts and opinions on issues and market trends. Being

> **Teaching as a Business Development Strategy**
>
> Teaching at all levels provides enormous credibility and personal satisfaction. Teaching a course or seminar enables a real estate manager to discuss an issue in depth. A half-day or full-day seminar affords the opportunity to meet some of the students, while an extended course will enable the instructor to get to know everyone in the class. Most students will remember their real estate instructors years after the course was completed, especially if they are impressed with the instructor's knowledge and presentation skills, and that could translate into future business or referrals. Although most real estate managers who teach do so in their local area, some will also serve on the national faculty of a real estate professional association such as the Institute of Real Estate Management (IREM).
>
> One of the best opportunities to start teaching is at a community college. In most metropolitan areas, there is at least one and possibly several community colleges (or vocational technical schools) that offer a real estate curriculum. However, the need to develop the course content is a potential obstacle. College instructors often prepare an outline summary or syllabus for a course based on a particular textbook or resource. In the field of real estate management, there are only a small number of textbooks that are supported by instructor materials. In particular, IREM has developed a series of courses that are designed to be taught primarily at the community college level. This series is comprised of three introductory courses, a general overview course and separate courses on apartment management and commercial property management. The textbooks are supported by instructor manuals, overhead transparency masters, and banks of examination questions. (The course materials are available to college instructors at

quoted for publication gives one credibility as well as exposure to a large audience. You can reach out to these editors and writers by inviting them to a one-on-one lunch, during which you can provide them with statistical data and tell them about your firm's expertise and your willingness to be a resource for them.

Public relations (PR) and publicity can be used to enhance a firm's reputation and create community awareness. Press releases are both information sources and filler copy for local print and broadcast media. Cultivating a relationship with real estate writers and editors not only encourages them to seek you out as a resource but predisposes them to publish information you send to their attention. (Specific PR strategies are discussed later in this chapter.)

Networking. Real estate management is a service business that is built on relationships. Because people prefer to do business with people they know, one of the fastest ways to become known and to develop a reputation within an industry is by networking. Building and nurturing a network within the real estate community is one of the most-effective and least-expensive business development techniques for a management company.

> **Teaching *(continued)***
> no charge.) Some community colleges use the series of courses as the basis for property management certificates or as part of the curriculum for a certificate or degree in real estate; they are also used in continuing education courses (usually as electives) for real estate licensure and relicensure. Although IREM chapters sometimes partner with local colleges to co-sponsor courses based on these materials, knowledgeable professionals who are contacted by the schools and invited to teach may be asked to recommend instructional materials. In the latter situation, the instructors usually review their intended courses with the real estate coordinator at the educational institution. Alternatively, you can approach the school and offer to teach a course based on the IREM materials.
>
> Other local teaching opportunities include entry-level property management courses offered by the Board of Realtors, Real Property Administrator (RPA) courses offered by local chapters of the Building Owners and Managers Association (BOMA), and property management courses offered by proprietary real estate schools as one of their continuing education courses for real estate licensure.
>
> One of the best opportunities to come in contact with potential clients is as a member of the national faculty for a professional association, such as IREM or the Commercial Investment Real Estate Institute (CIREI). However, the requirements are rigorous: IREM requires extensive experience in real estate management and in-depth knowledge of the subject to be taught; you must also pass a course content interview and a presentation to their faculty committee and successfully complete their faculty training program. Once accepted, instructors must maintain acceptable ratings from students to remain on the faculty.

Networking is an organized method of linking people you know to each other via an ever-expanding base of contacts. A network grows each time you meet someone. As more people are brought into the group, their contacts are added to the network. Although the discussion here is focused on real estate industry contacts, involvement in service and charitable organizations in one's local community also provides opportunities for networking.

Networking is an acquired skill, and one's networking activities must be planned and managed. The most effective networking arena for real estate managers is a professional association. Most national organizations have local chapters throughout the United States. Active membership in the local chapter of a real estate organization is an excellent way to network on a local and regional basis. Becoming active at the national level is usually the only way most individuals can network on a national basis. The benefit of the contacts and referrals generated by networking often exceeds the cost of attending the national meetings and conventions of such organizations as the National Apartment Association (NAA), the Community Associations Institute (CAI), the Building Owners and Managers Association (BOMA), the International Council of Shopping Centers (ICSC), and the Institute of

Writing as a Business Development Strategy

Writing is another cost-effective means of marketing a company. The unique aspect of writing as a business development technique is its potential to reach a much larger audience. Unlike an advertisement that conveys a message about a company, which may only be of interest to a limited number of people, an article in a local publication may be read by hundreds or even thousands of people. An article in a national publication may be read by tens of thousands of people. In a society where information is valued and professionals are seeking ways to perform at a higher level, published articles provide a welcome service to others in the industry.

Every real estate manager has knowledge that can be the subject of one or more interesting articles. The editors of real estate publications are always searching for articles with good content. If an author has an interesting subject, can organize his or her ideas and opinions well, and expresses them clearly and concisely, professional editors at the publications will correct the spelling, grammar, and punctuation.

Editors of real estate publications need information that is interesting *and* current. A manager's daily experiences can often suggest ideas for potential articles—e.g., helpful tips or shortcuts. Topics for articles abound:

- How to retain commercial tenants.
- Amenities preferred by today's apartment residents.
- How to lease strip shopping centers.
- Checklists for assuming management of different types of properties—an office building, a shopping center, an apartment building or condominium.
- How to prepare for a specific emergency.

A unique management or leasing experience can become a case study that informs the reader about a solution to a specific problem or challenge.

Real estate managers regularly conduct market surveys, and data from such surveys can yield articles on market conditions for a specific property type in a particular geographic area—e.g., apartments in the northern part of the county, downtown class B office space, or suburban shopping centers in all their myriad forms. This kind of article can even be updated on a quarterly or annual basis. Local and regional newspapers, business journals, and real estate magazines regularly publish market survey data and interpretations. When a real estate manager writes this type of article on a regular basis, both the writer and the writer's firm become known as experts.

The scores of real estate publications mean there is always a need for good articles of either local or national interest. Locally, especially in large metropolitan areas, there are likely to be daily business journals, monthly newspapers of local real estate organizations, and periodic newsletters in addition to newspapers with a general circulation. Publications with a business focus and daily newspapers often have a weekly real estate section.

Among the dozen or more national real estate publications, the *Journal of Property Management* from IREM is of particular interest and value. Each fall, *JPM* publishes a calendar of subjects that will be the focus of the next year's issues. Real estate managers who have experience or a case study related to one of these subjects can contact the managing editor to discuss a proposed article. Other national real estate journals often send out a "call for papers" on a particular subject.

> **Writing (continued)**
> There are two approaches to writing an article. One is to write the article and submit it to the editor of a publication. The other is to discuss an idea for an article with an editor before writing it. Each approach has advantages and disadvantages. In the first instance, the author can write the article at his or her own pace without concern for a deadline. However, the article may have to be submitted to a number of publications before it is accepted, and it may not be published. In the second approach, the article is not written until the subject has been accepted, but the deadline will be determined by the editor.
>
> Once you have an article published, you can use it as a marketing piece. So there are really two audiences for your article, the reader of the publication in which the article appears and the people to whom you send copies of the article. Publishers usually can provide the author with a Velox paper proof of the article, either free or for a nominal charge. This black-and-white proof can be used by a local printer to generate copies of the article. (Alternatively, the publisher may make reprints available to authors when the issue goes to press. This service may be provided at no charge, or there may be a sliding-scale fee based on the quantity ordered.)
>
> Writing a book is the ultimate accomplishment. It takes dedication and discipline. Before writing a book, which can take six months to a year or longer to complete, you should obtain a commitment to publish it. This requires submission of a proposal to a publisher who will want to know what you will write about, the perspective or viewpoint you bring to the subject, the range of topics you expect to cover, and the level of detail (outline and chapter descriptions), the audience to whom it will be addressed (who will buy it), and your qualifications to write on the subject (resume or curriculum vitae). One or more sample chapters should also be included so the publisher can gauge your writing ability and evaluate your approach. (Copyright is usually transferred to the publisher under an agreement that compensates the author in royalties from book sales.) Here again, you may submit a proposal to several publishers before it is accepted. As an alternative, you can publish it yourself, but self-published books are difficult to market on a regional basis and almost impossible to market nationally.

Real Estate Management (IREM). Since it may not be possible or practical for every real estate manager within a company to attend the meetings of several organizations, individual managers may be assigned to attend and be active in a particular association on behalf of the management company. This will enable the firm to maintain a presence in several different real estate organizations.

Still another excellent networking opportunity is one-on-one meetings, usually over lunch. Such get-togethers provide an opportunity for real estate professionals to become acquainted on a personal level while they compare their experiences, discuss their real estate activities, and provide each other with referrals. They may even become involved in business opportunities together. This particular strategy can be fostered by encouraging managers on your staff to develop a list of real estate professionals they

> **Association Networking Strategies**
>
> Real estate professionals miss one of the primary benefits of association membership—i.e., networking—if they do not participate in the organization's meetings and other activities. The benefits of networking can be maximized by meeting as many people as possible at each of the association's events.
>
> Because attendees at meetings tend to stay with the same small group of people, you should make a concerted effort to meet and interact with new people at each event. Getting to know the leaders of a professional association is an excellent strategy. They are usually the most respected people in the organization and have large numbers of contacts in the industry.
>
> One of the best ways to become known within a professional association and gain the respect of its members is to volunteer to serve on a committee or to chair it. The ultimate leadership position and the one that provides the greatest recognition is to serve the organization as one of its officers, especially as its president.

would like to invite to lunch during the coming year. The list might also include lenders, bank trust and REO officers, architects, appraisers, developers, and professionals from other allied industries.

Networking is most successful when information and referrals can be shared. Information about such things as building operating expenses, vacancy trends, and leasing situations that real estate managers take for granted is often valuable to other real estate professionals and difficult for them to obtain. Successful networking requires a commitment, a plan with targeted goals, and faithful execution of the plan.

Advertising. Most management firms do little *promotional advertising*, as such, because it is not particularly effective in generating management business. (Seldom do property owners look for a management company in a newspaper or real estate magazine.) However, *institutional advertising* can be used to create name recognition and enhance a firm's identity. Announcements of new accounts and similar major achievements as well as *image ads* help put the company's name in front of potential clients. To be successful, an image advertising campaign must have consistency—repetition increases exposure; an ad placed once or twice has only a limited chance of producing results.

Public Relations and Publicity. *Public relations* encompasses all of a company's activities in dealing with the public, other industry professionals, and its clients. *Publicity* is the technique of drawing attention to a person or a company by telling a story. Real estate management firms use pub-

> **Advertising Adjuncts**
>
> One advertising opportunity that should not be overlooked is signage on the managed property. Usually management agreements can be negotiated to include a provision that the management company will be permitted to install signage on the premises announcing that the property is "Managed by ABC Management Company." Sometimes this information may also be incorporated into signage that identifies tenants (the directory in an office building or at a shopping mall or strip center). Installation on the exterior of the building may be preferable over internal signage if both cannot be done. Having one's company name appearing on buildings whose ownership is known in real estate circles can lead to additional management business. A side benefit is that tenants who have been satisfied with your management will seek opportunities to lease at other properties you manage. Word-of-mouth advertising will be recalled as property owners and potential tenants see your company's name, leading to additional management and leasing opportunities.
>
> Stationery is yet another advertising tool. A simple identifying icon or logo may be included on business cards and other stationery items, but it is not absolutely necessary to have one. All stationery should include, at the very least, the company's name, address, telephone and facsimile numbers, and e-mail address if appropriate. Sometimes it is possible or appropriate to include a "tag line" stating the types of properties the firm manages or the types of services it offers. Firms that obtain the AMO® designation from the Institute of Real Estate Management may incorporate the AMO logo on their stationery or simply add "AMO®" after the company name. Choices of paper color and printing ink should be consistent with the image you wish to project over the long term. Consider that every letter sent to a prospective client and every business card handed to someone as you network with colleagues should be an ambassador advertising your company.
>
> Other, less-specific, forms of advertising also can be effective in creating name recognition. These include things like sponsoring a Little League baseball team or a local charitable event. (Sponsors are named in materials promoting the particular activity.)

licity techniques to establish and enhance their position in the local market and the industry at large, to build name recognition, and to enhance their image. Publicity is also used to overcome negative perceptions.

Publicity consists primarily of mailing news releases to the print media; however, uninvited media attention should also be viewed as an opportunity. If the firm or its personnel have established specific expertise, there are likely to be requests for interviews and statements of opinion on issues their expertise addresses.

The effectiveness of a publicity program is built over time with a steady flow of news releases. Published stories make potential clients aware of the firm, its management personnel, their expertise, and the company's management portfolio. The subjects of press releases can include:

- Announcements of new management accounts—The story should identify the property (including its size), the individual assigned to manage it, and possibly the property owner.

- Specific successes—Progress on or completion of the remodeling or rehabbing of a property, a property achieving a high occupancy in a soft market, and sales and leasing transactions are examples.

- A change in the business—Announcements of this type include opening of a branch office or relocation of the main office or the purchase of or merger with another firm.

- Announcements of achievements, awards, and promotions—A press release can be sent out when the firm receives an award such as the Accredited Management Organization® (AMO®) designation; when an individual achieves the Certified Property Manager® (CPM®) or Real Property Administrator (RPA) designation or some other professional recognition such as Certified Public Accountant (CPA); or when an individual is promoted or hired.

- Stories about management company employees' involvement in the community—Assuming a leadership role in a service organization, serving on a committee or the board of a social agency, or volunteering time to work for an organization such as the Boys and Girls Club or a food bank reflects well on both individuals and the companies that employ them.

Good news may be the preferred substance of publicity, but negative events, which are the substance of news, demand an appropriate response. That is why it is a good idea to prepare a crisis public relations plan to be implemented in the event of a major incident or catastrophe at one of the firm's managed properties. A firm that specializes in crisis public relations can provide a list of the information to have readily available in case of an emergency. One person—usually an executive of the management firm or the property owner or a representative of the public relations firm—is designated as the only person to communicate with the media in such situations. In that way, a consistent, appropriate response will be prepared and distributed, and negative repercussions from the event and the media attention to it can be minimized. (Some news release preparation tips are provided in the accompanying box.)

The best way to get your news release published is to have contacts at the publications on your mailing list. You may be able to meet the real estate editors at local newspapers and professional journals (serving as a media resource was discussed earlier in this chapter). Although it is not always possible to meet the editors of publications outside your area, you should

> **Preparing News Releases**
>
> A news release should be concise and brief. A long news release is likely to be edited, and important information may be omitted when it is published. The following are some tips for preparing news releases:
>
> - Note the date of issuance in the upper right-hand corner.
> - Follow that with the release date at the left (or just say, "For Immediate Release").
> - Include the name and phone number of the person to contact for more information.
> - Start the release with a short catchy title that states the subject of the announcement.
> - Type the text double-spaced and leave wide margins.
> - Include a black-and-white glossy photograph whenever possible (and appropriate).
>
> News releases should be prepared on $8\frac{1}{2} \times 11$-inch paper. Some companies have special news release letterhead printed, or they type the release on company letterhead for duplication. Copying on only one side of the paper was once preferred, but it has become acceptable to use both sides of the paper to minimize postage costs, especially when mailing photographs flat in large envelopes. Although photographs may be large (8 × 10-inch prints may be preferable to show building or construction details), pictures that show only one or two people can be duplicated in a $3\frac{1}{2} \times 5$-inch size that will fit into a standard (#10) business envelope.

be able to obtain their names from the publications' mastheads. For wider distribution, it may be more productive to hire a public relations firm to use its expertise and influence in getting news releases printed. However, good PR firms' services cost money, so it is a good idea to make sure you are their only real estate client and that you receive the service for which you are paying.

Copies of news releases can also be mailed to the firm's contact list; or as an alternative, you can print and mail an announcement card with the same message, accompanied by a photograph of the person or property.

Newsletters. A newsletter used to communicate regularly with clients, prospective clients, and industry professionals can be a valuable marketing tool. Newsletters provide name recognition, enhance a firm's image, and reenforce its position in the industry. However, while the firm's activities—new accounts, successful lease-up of a building, awards received—and its employees' accomplishments are worthwhile topics, they are best presented in news releases. The main purpose of a newsletter directed to this audience should be *to provide readers with useful information about the*

> **Starting a Newsletter**
>
> The first step in developing a company newsletter is to assemble a team of volunteers who will be responsible for selecting a design, writing the material, editing the stories, and publishing (printing) and mailing the newsletter. The team should develop a list of topics to be addressed over several issues—at least a year's worth. (A survey of owners' information needs would also be helpful at the start.) Case studies and property success stories provide real-world examples of management and marketing strategies and their implementation. A market update column might be a regular feature—each issue could include market data on a specific property type so that every major type of property is discussed at least once a year. Industry trends and management and marketing tips might also be regular features. Guest columns addressing legal issues, preventive maintenance strategies, and other specialized topics may be invited from experts who do business with the firm. Emphasis should be on providing information that will have value to the intended reader.
>
> Computers have made it relatively easy to produce a professional-looking newsletter. Desktop publishing programs allow you to incorporate photographs and line art in the pages as they are viewed on screen, and the finished copy can be sent to a printer on a computer diskette. Even a word-processing program and a laser printer can generate high-quality originals for photocopying.
>
> Producing a newsletter can be a time-consuming activity. Also, while a large regional or national management company may be able to hire an advertising or PR firm to create and publish its newsletter, a small- or medium-sized firm may not have that option available. If the work is done in house, which is the usual situation, staff members will have to commit blocks of time to writing the articles and columns and publishing the newsletter. However, the product of these efforts will be a marketing tool for the company as well as a means of communicating with clients and others. Working on the in-house newsletter will also hone the writing skills of real estate managers and other staff members, perhaps encouraging them to write for publication in industry and professional journals.

real estate industry. (Information about starting a newsletter is presented in the accompanying box.)

Creating and Using a Contact List. Building a database of potential clients—i.e., owners of the type of property the firm manages—is an investment in business intelligence. (For practical purposes, such a database may be limited to properties above a predetermined size, such as apartments of twenty units or more.) The database should include contact names, addresses, and telephone and fax numbers. Particulars about the properties they own should be part of the information collected. This database will have many uses, not the least of which is as a mailing list for the firm's newsletter. The property owners can also be contacted by phone and in person, and they can be sent marketing materials (including copies of news releases and reprints of articles) on a regular basis. The contacts on this list should include owners from whom you want to solicit business as well as those who have invited you to present a management proposal or are likely to do so. It goes without saying that it should also include all of your current clients.

Contact lists have a tendency to grow, and that adds to the cost of individual mailings. It is important to review your lists periodically to ensure that names and addresses are correct and to delete those that are no longer valid. Use of computers not only facilitates this updating but permits lists to be coded and segmented so that selected individuals or groups can be sent a particular mailing.

Solicitation. Direct solicitation of a property owner can be an effective means of generating business, or it can be an expensive, nonproductive activity. While some owners are receptive to solicitation, asset managers and institutional owners with large portfolios usually do not have time for it. A person who is hired as a paid solicitor will spend most of his or her time traveling to visit property owners, often receiving compensation in the form of a salary and a commission (typically a percentage of the management fees earned for a property for a set time—e.g., two years). Such a solicitor should have experience in managing real estate and be familiar with the market conditions and operating expenses for buildings in the area where the firm manages properties.

Requests for Proposals. Management firms are often asked to submit a specific proposal for managing a property. When such a request for proposal (RFP) is received, the first question that should be asked is, "Why is the owner making a change in management?" The answer to this question can help shape the proposal and its presentation.

Since each such RFP is an important opportunity for the company, the presentation team must be prepared to perform at its best. The management company executives must select the members of the team, gather information regarding the prospective client and the subject property, analyze the property and its position in the market, assemble presentation materials, and direct the team in rehearsing and making the presentation.

The presentation team should include, at a minimum, a company executive and the real estate manager who will be assigned to the account. (Criteria for selecting the manager include expertise in managing the type of property, ability to assume the management of the additional property, capability of addressing the property's specific problems, if they are known, and a management style that will create the best working relationship with the client.) Depending on the prospective client and the proposal requirements, the firm's controller or other management-level personnel may also participate. If the firm has a separate leasing division, the person who will be responsible for leasing the property should be included. Others who might be added are the property accountant and the real estate manager's administrative assistant. Prospective clients may be asked if they have any preferences for who should be present or an interest in a particular type of information, and those preferences should help guide the team assignments.

A separate "manual" should be prepared for each presentation, with the information tailored to the prospective client and the subject property. The package typically includes a variety of materials that assist the team in making its presentation and help the prospective client assess the qualifications of the firm and the capabilities of the management team. (The contents of a proposal package and presentation strategies are detailed in Chapter 8.)

Company Brochure. One component of a proposal presentation that has other uses is a company brochure. Since competition for management business can be fierce, it is important for a company brochure to make a good impression. It may be worthwhile to invest in the services of a marketing professional to help in selecting appropriate words and images and effectively utilizing the space on the printed page. A well-thought-out brochure should include color photographs of typical properties the firm manages, a description of the firm's services, a brief history of the company, and information about the company's vision—i.e., its mission statement, values and beliefs, and statement of purpose. It may also be desirable to include pictures of key company personnel, but this is not always practical. (It is expensive to revise a brochure each time there is a change in the staff, and an individual's appearance changes over time.) The result should be a multipage, full-color booklet that can be used in a variety of marketing strategies, including as a mailing piece.

Developing Ancillary Sources of Income

A prospective client may not need property management, as such, but may be a candidate for related services. Adjunct services (consulting, leasing, etc.) have the potential to become an important source of revenue. Often the profit margin on these services is substantially larger than that for management services because the latter have already covered the company's fixed costs.

Before offering any adjunct service, you should evaluate the benefits and the costs of such a change.

- Does the company have the expertise to provide the service?
- What type of fee structure can be established?
- What additional operating expenses will be incurred?
- What will be the company's competitive edge in providing the service?

- Who are the firm's competitors and what are the opportunities in this field?
- Are there any special licensing or insurance coverage requirements?
- Will the firm need to purchase any equipment?
- Can the existing staff provide the service?

The foregoing are only some of the questions that must be answered to determine whether you should pursue such a venture. The following sections describe the more traditional services a management firm may provide. (Information on appeal of real estate taxes and owner's tax accounting, which are also potential adjunct services, can be found in Chapter 3.)

Consulting. Real estate management expertise encompasses a broad range of activities that include marketing and leasing, maintenance management, the daily operations of a property, and developing long-range management plans, each of which can be the basis for offering services as a consultant. A property owner may have a generally competent on-site staff, but these personnel may lack expertise in a particular area or not have time to tackle specialized problems. Preparing a comprehensive management plan, negotiating a complicated lease with a major commercial tenant, or analyzing the market to determine rental rates and possible concessions are examples.

While these tasks may not require the ongoing, full-time attention of the owner's staff, it would be difficult—if not impossible—to hire someone qualified and willing to do such work on a part-time or short-term basis. In addition, hiring such a staff person may not be cost-effective because of the associated expenses of additional office space and backup administrative or accounting support. In such situations, hiring a management firm to perform specific jobs on a consulting basis may be the answer. Among other things, a real estate manager-consultant may be called upon to:

Train or reorganize an in-house leasing or management staff,

Offer advice and recommendations for a change of property use,

Analyze the tenant mix in a shopping center, or

Evaluate a property for purchase or sale.

The consultant is task-oriented and brings to the situation the expertise and experience to address the property owner's problem. Because the consultant knows how the job should be handled, he or she can provide an estimate of the time needed to complete the task as well as the maximum cost that is likely to be incurred. The owner pays only those costs that are directly associated with resolving a specific problem. (Some tasks, such as negotiation of a complicated lease, may be difficult to cost out firmly; but an experienced consultant should be able to provide a reasonable estimate.)

There are many benefits for a real estate management company in providing consulting services. The most obvious is the increased revenue of another profit center. Consulting also provides exposure that can lead to additional management accounts. If consulting becomes a major activity of a real estate manager, he or she should consider applying for the Counselor of Real Estate designation, which is awarded by the Counselors of Real Estate, an affiliate of the NATIONAL ASSOCIATION OF REALTORS (see Appendix B).

Leasing and Brokerage Activities. In the management of commercial real estate, leasing is not always included among the agreed-upon management services. The nature of commercial leases (e.g., multi-year terms, escalating rents, variable pass-throughs—the dollars involved) and the fact that every detail is potentially negotiable has created a niche opportunity for those skilled in this specialized art. For these and other reasons—a manager may not be able to devote sufficient time to the leasing activity in addition to his or her management responsibilities—the leasing of commercial space is a separate consideration.

It is not unusual for a company that manages commercial properties to just break even or lose money on its management services. The company's profits are more likely to come from its leasing and/or brokerage commissions. Commercial leasing and brokerage can be a very lucrative business. (The role of management and its compensation for leasing commercial space directly and in situations where the property owner hires another firm to handle the leasing activity are considered in the context of the management agreement in Chapter 9.)

If leasing services are to be offered for properties other than those the firm manages, it is important to decide which property types and geographic areas you will serve. Unless the firm has a large leasing staff, it is not possible in a large metropolitan area to acquire the expertise, develop the contacts, and have the time to lease all types of commercial properties across the entire region.

An important leasing issue to be resolved is how the real estate managers will be compensated for leasing. People who are willing to do extra work to lease a building are often motivated by the opportunity to earn additional income. Because managers receive a salary and often have most or all of their expenses reimbursed, they may receive less than 50 percent of the leasing commission paid to the management firm. (Several companies pay their managers substantially less—in the range of 10–20 percent of a renewal commission and 20–30 percent of a new lease commission.) When a manager exceeds a performance goal that is portfolio specific and based on either leasing a predetermined amount of space or generating an agreed amount of commission dollars, the commission split for subsequent leases may be increased for renewals and new leases. Separate goals are established for new and renewal leases, and there is no standard commission compensation formula.

Selling a property is a very rewarding but time-consuming activity. Seldom does a real estate manager have the time to pursue multiple sales, but when a client wants to sell its property, the manager may be the best person to represent the seller and find a buyer. In such a situation, the manager will need support and marketing tools to effectively market and sell a property. It is also important to monitor the manager's activities to ensure that management duties are not being neglected to pursue commissions. The manager must balance the time spent fulfilling management responsibilities and leasing or selling the property.

Sales or brokerage commissions related to a managed property should be negotiated and documented in a separate agreement. When a management company is not positioned to broker a sale, it may be possible to partner with a brokerage firm to share responsibilities and commissions. A similar stance can be taken with a mortgage broker in refinancing a property. Still another approach is to form a strategic alliance with a commercial broker—e.g., an individual who is a Certified Commercial Investment Member (CCIM) designee of the Commercial Investment Real Estate Institute. Having such an individual on board will allow the company to take advantage of sales opportunities that present themselves apart from the management arena.

Maintenance Services. A separate maintenance function can be a profit center as well as provide a valuable service to the management company's clients. When maintenance services will be provided by a separate company, the charges must be within the range of competitive rates. More important, the ownership of the maintenance company and how its fees compare to those charged by other maintenance companies *must be disclosed* to the management firm's clients. (A wholly owned subsidiary of a management company represents a potential conflict of interest.)

To be successful, a maintenance business must have strong leadership, a qualified staff, an efficient operation, and tight fiscal controls. It must also provide superior service at competitive prices. The competitive edge for the management firm is that there is little selling and collections cost in operating a separate maintenance company. Often the volume and timing of the work can be determined months in advance, allowing maintenance tasks to be scheduled efficiently and cost-effectively. There are several types of services a maintenance company can provide.

- A roving maintenance staff can respond to maintenance needs of several properties (charges based on an hourly rate).
- Janitorial service can be provided for office buildings (charges based

on a cost per square foot) and for cleaning vacant apartments (charges based on a cost per unit).
- Landscape maintenance can be offered for all types of properties. This requires employing a qualified landscaper to provide technical knowledge and supervise the landscape maintenance crew.
- Painting apartments and office suites as an independent service can minimize downtime between occupants.
- Providing building, plumbing, and other repairs can save a client the cost of skilled labor.

One of the key components in the success of a maintenance company is being able to estimate its operating costs accurately. The costs of purchasing and replacing equipment, purchasing and maintaining vehicles, and insurance and bonding are often underestimated. It is also important to price the different types of maintenance services correctly. When the fee is to be based on an hourly rate, workers' salaries must be grossed up properly. To do this effectively requires monitoring the rates the maintenance industry charges. Pricing of maintenance services is a particular concern because the subsidiary maintenance company may be competing against service providers who price their services very low. (Often they can do this because they pay low wages. They also may not be appropriately licensed and bonded, and they may not pay all of the required taxes.)

Construction Supervision. This type of service consists primarily of contracting for tenant improvement work, and renovation, remodeling, or rehabbing an existing property. Tenant improvement opportunities are usually limited to office and medical buildings. Industrial properties may offer some limited opportunities in this area while most shopping center spaces are re-leased in as-is condition. Construction supervision is usually compensated by a percentage of the cost of the work.

Renovation, remodeling, or rehabilitation opportunities exist on all types of properties. A decision to pursue these types of opportunities depends on whether construction supervision is a service the firm is qualified to offer. Some points to consider are:

- Does the firm have the expertise to serve as a construction supervisor? Most real estate managers have a working knowledge of construction, but not all have the expertise to supervise construction activity.
- Is a state contractor's license required? Some states require prior experience, passing a general contractor's exam, and evidence of a construction bond before they will issue a contractor's license.
- Will the firm have to purchase a construction bond and additional

insurance? Even if these are not requirements, it is advisable to have the protections they provide.

Construction supervision can be very time-consuming, and the person assigned this responsibility must have time available in his or her schedule to provide this service. If a management firm does not meet the state's qualifications to be licensed as a contractor or is otherwise not qualified to supervise construction, you can consider offering the firm's services as a *construction coordinator*. The latter entails serving as liaison between the general contractor, the architect, residents or commercial tenants, and the property owner. The person in this role serves as the leader of the construction team and provides accounting services and financial reports.

Accounting Services. Some property owners prefer to manage their own properties, but they do not have the expertise or the equipment (computers, software) to properly prepare the necessary accounting and financial reports. A management firm can offer property owners an array of services in this area. It can provide full accounting and financial reporting or selected individual services, or it might accept a special assignment developing an annual budget or calculating and billing commercial tenants' common area maintenance (CAM) charges. For these types of services, clients often prefer a fixed fee or a flat rate, which is feasible because the management firm's controller can accurately estimate the time required to complete different tasks. This type of adjunct service will only be viable if the management company has broad accounting capabilities and uses computer programs that are compatible with the potential client's needs.

Expert Witness Testimony. Many real estate disputes are resolved in arbitration, if not by litigation. Serving as an expert witness provides an opportunity to use your skills and expertise to assist in resolving an issue. There are numerous situations in which a real estate manager's knowledge can enhance the case of a defendant or plaintiff, among them offering an opinion as to:

- The value of a leased or leasable space,
- The mitigation efforts of a landlord when a commercial tenant vacated its premises prior to the expiration of the lease, and
- The impact on the value of a property when a municipality condemns part of it (e.g., a parking lot) to widen a street.

There may also be opportunities that do not involve formal testimony. A law firm that specializes in real estate disputes may need information and advice regarding accepted real estate management practices to help the attorneys determine the issues and formulate an approach in a particular case.

Contacting real estate attorneys, especially those who handle litigation,

> ### A Perspective on Adjunct Services
>
> There are many considerations that must be addressed before expanding the services you offer. These include how the services will be marketed, the fees that should be charged, contractual arrangements, and reporting requirements.
>
> **Marketing** Adjunct management services are best marketed on a subtle, low-key basis because the list of potential clients is as broad as the real estate field itself. It includes developers, lenders, REITs, investors, pension fund advisors, asset managers, trust department officers, redevelopment agency officials, appraisers, attorneys, brokers, and anyone else who has a real estate problem or opportunity.
>
> The best source of new business is referrals from existing, satisfied clients. Positive word-of-mouth is priceless, and a letter of recommendation for a job well done is a valuable selling tool. Teaching and writing for publication—especially if these activities showcase specialized expertise—are ways to promote consulting and other adjunct services indirectly. Membership and active participation in professional organizations and having achieved one or more relevant professional designations also increases one's exposure.
>
> **Setting Fees** Fees should be based on the manager's experience as well as the market. The fee for a particular service may be an hourly rate, a fixed sum, a retainer, or a combination of these. An *hourly rate* might be charged for negotiating a lease, analyzing and reorganizing a leasing or management office, or finding qualified personnel for a property owner's staff. A *fixed fee* may be charged for developing a management plan, analyzing a distressed property, or determining market rental rates.
>
> A *retainer* would be called for when the manager's responsibility involves performing an ongoing assignment, as when an owner has an in-house department and prefers to have specific accounting or other management functions performed in its main office but requires someone to supervise site personnel working at a distant location. It is not unusual in such cases to charge an additional reorganization or set-up fee during the first month or two. Typically, this is double the regular monthly retainer.

and making them aware of your qualifications (experience and expertise) and your interest in serving as an expert witness is one way to gain this type of opportunity. Another is to inform your clients that your firm provides expert witness testimony.

Before accepting a case, several factors should be carefully evaluated. First and foremost, you must determine the nature of the case.

- Do you have expertise in the particular field?
- Can you defend the plaintiff's or defendant's position without hesitation?
- Could this case cause problems for you in the future?

> **Adjunct Services** *(continued)*
>
> **The Service Contract** The manager who provides adjunct services should take great care to define the client's exact needs and expectations in a written contract. In this way, there can be no misunderstanding at a later date. The parties should carefully discuss the specific tasks the manager is to perform and the purpose behind each task. They should outline the ways in which the owner's goals will be accomplished, the type of information and reporting that will be required, and how the reports are to be formatted. Since each opportunity is unique, the agreement should be tailored to the particular situation.
>
> Once everyone is in agreement, the details should be set forth in a written contract signed by both parties. Because consulting and other service agreements have great potential for misunderstanding, the contract should provide protections for both the manager and the client. (Although there is no standard agreement form, networking with other local fee managers and real estate professionals can help you identify someone who has contracted for a particular service previously using a form that you may be able to adapt.)
>
> **Reporting** Both parties should have a clear understanding—and agree in writing—about the required documentation. It is most important that the client outline specifically what the services to be provided should include and what types of written reports will address each aspect of the work performed. Reports may range from a brief summary to a comprehensive management plan that exceeds 100 pages. (Often the reports generated from a consulting assignment—the outline for the rehabilitation of a shopping center or a market survey used to establish apartment rental rates—can be used as a marketing tool to promote the management firm's services. It is a good idea to seek the property owner's approval before using materials in this way, however.)

You need to consider whether representing the plaintiff in a slip-and-fall case might lead to your statements being used against you if a similar incident occurs on a property you manage. Geography may be another factor to consider. For example, it may be easier to distance yourself from potential repercussions if your expert witness services are being utilized in a city a hundred miles or so from your business location.

The most important asset of an expert witness is credibility: Is this an area in which you have expertise? Can your particular expertise withstand the kind of scrutiny it will receive? You also need to consider whether you have the time to devote to preparing for the case, meeting with the attorney, being deposed, and attending all or part of a trial.

Another very important consideration is conflict of interest: Do you know or have you had business (or other) dealings with or for either of the parties in the case? A conflict of interest may disqualify you from testifying. Also, on a personal level, you need to consider whether you are prepared to have the opposing attorney try to discredit you.

There is considerable demand for credible real estate experts who are willing to prepare for a case. Expert witnesses are paid well for their services, usually on an hourly basis. Serving as an expert witness adds to the real estate manager's and his or her firm's credibility.

Outsourcing and Insourcing. Corporations seeking to operate more efficiently and reduce their overhead frequently consider *outsourcing* some or all of their real estate activities, utilizing professional resources to supplement (or supplant) an in-house real estate department. Outsourcing has been fueled by several things, among them:

- Competitive pressures in the marketplace (i.e., a need to reduce operating costs).
- Acknowledgment that adjunct business activities are not necessarily well managed.
- Promotion of business theories that address change (i.e., focusing on core competencies and encouraging process re-engineering).
- Changes in the industry that have forced commercial real estate companies to aggressively seek out new sources of revenue.
- The dynamics of a changing real estate market (i.e., increasing complexity of addressing what were once straightforward management tasks and an emphasis on the bottom line).

The number of corporations using outsourced real estate professionals and the extent to which they are used will depend on the condition of the economy and trends in corporate management. Among the services frequently outsourced by corporations are janitorial, maintenance (including furniture and utilities), and groundskeeping; architectural design, space planning, and facility engineering; construction management; office operations, secretarial services, purchasing, shipping and receiving, and mail service; health and safety, security, and environmental operations; and lease acquisition and site selection. Other similar opportunities include management of branch banking facilities and provision of maintenance management services. Many corporations need *insourcing* rather than outsourcing services. These include training employees in their in-house real estate departments.

Compliance Surveys. One of the most far-reaching civil rights laws is the Americans with Disabilities Act (ADA). Its goal is to make buildings that are open to public commerce accessible to disabled people. Some management firms have looked on this as an opportunity to provide an adjunct service to property owners. They will evaluate a property, *usually one they are not managing,* to see if it is in compliance with ADA requirements and determine what modifications or additions are needed if it is not. This type of service can be especially valuable when recommendations are made as a disinterested third party. (Several professional organizations, notably IREM and BOMA, have published guidelines on ADA compliance.)

The future is likely to bring other laws and programs that will provide opportunities for real estate managers to assist owners in assessing their properties' compliance with governmental regulations. As management firm personnel have experiences with regulatory agencies (e.g., HUD, OSHA, EPA), the firm's pooled expertise in this realm will increase and suggest other compliance-related opportunities that can be sought.

A Perspective on Business Development

As can be seen from the preceding discussion, business development is a continuous process. A company's leadership has the primary responsibility for generating new business. These individuals will devote a greater percentage of their time to business development—25–50 percent or more is not uncommon—than will anyone else in the firm.

Although acquisition of new business is an all-the-time proposition, it should not take precedence over retaining the clients you already have. Growing the business—not merely replacing accounts but increasing the size of the firm's portfolio and its income and profitability—is the goal of business development.

8

Strategizing the Management Proposal

Each opportunity to present a management proposal should be approached as if the company's future depended solely on that proposal. Most often the prospective client will suggest the items to be covered, but the astute company executive will go beyond that and consider the prospective client, the property, and the marketplace in determining any other information that may be important to include in the proposal. For instance, if a similar property is being planned for development in the immediate area of the property proposed for management, this fact should be mentioned even if such things were not suggested as items of interest by the prospective client.

This type of disclosure raises a question of what is appropriate to include in a proposal. The prospective client may not even be aware of the property that is being developed nearby, but it represents competition for tenants and could impact your approach to managing the prospect's property. It is often said that company executives must be cautious about giving away information at this stage because the prospective client might take advantage of the information without using the management firm's services. However, prospective clients must be convinced that a particular company is the one they want to manage their property, and they are not likely to be convinced of that if information that might be beneficial to their property were excluded.

The cost of developing the proposal information is also a consideration. Keeping track of the costs of preparing various management proposals helps to identify strategies that are—or are not—cost-effective. In most instances, preparing a videotape documenting the situation at the property, then putting together a 500-page proposal document and bringing a staff of ten to the proposal presentation is not warranted. If such an extreme approach were to be used for every proposal, the likelihood of this being a cost-effective activity would be substantially reduced. In other words, the proposal and the presentation should be appropriate to the potential of the account.

Cost-effectiveness has to do with what is required to sell a particular property owner on your management services. You will need to be aware of possible competitors, including the nature and extent of their typical proposals and the fees they are likely to charge for their management services. You also need to be aware of their strengths and weaknesses.

If for any reason the property up for bid is not worth an all-out effort to prepare a comprehensive proposal, it is better to decline the opportunity to bid than to make a half-hearted effort that will reflect negatively on the management company for both this and possible future opportunities. It is not unusual to make a proposal and not acquire the management account—only rarely does an owner invite a single bid on property management services. However, the opportunity to bid allows the management company to demonstrate its capabilities, and the professionalism of its presentation can position the firm as a contender for future management opportunities.

Preliminary Considerations

A management proposal must demonstrate understanding of the property owner's requirements. Usually these are outlined in a specific request for proposal (RFP). Extensive research and evaluation of the property and its market will have to be done in order to gather data and formulate a management plan. The firm will also have to examine its capabilities as they relate to the particular property and the RFP requirements.

Although the prospective client will expect the company executives and the manager assigned to the account to be knowledgeable about the property and its market, all members of the presentation team should be familiar with the property. With the owner's permission, the team should visit the property and conduct an inspection. This should include taking photographs of deferred maintenance, the condition of vacant spaces, and areas in need of renovation, as well as the positive features of the property. The photographs will accompany a written report that will become part of the presentation.

One question that is likely to be asked by the property owner is, "What should my rents be?" To answer this question, representatives of the management company will have to visit competing properties and conduct a market survey to determine the range of market rents in the area and establish rental rates for the subject property. The presentation materials may include data on comparable or competing properties (a market survey or comparison grid), along with photographs of those properties, in support

> **Components of a Request for Proposal (RFP)**
>
> - Introduction or statement of objectives—the reason the RFP is being sent out.
> - The specific services being sought—property management or other service.
> - Required components of the proposal—what the property owner requires from the bidder.
> - Evaluation criteria—the basis for making a decision.
> - Submission procedures—how, when, where, and to whom the proposal should be submitted.
>
> The RFP may include background information necessary to facilitate preparation of the proposal (e.g., identify a problem or pose a challenge). It may also indicate how information is to be presented (if a specific format is required). Particulars to be addressed in the submitted proposal—i.e., what the property owner requires from the bidder—usually include WHAT the bidder proposes to do, HOW it would be accomplished, WHO will do the work, and HOW MUCH the work would cost (the management fee). Information about the company's and/or the individual's qualifications to provide the proposed services is also required, sometimes in a separate request for qualifications (RFQ).

of recommendations for rental rates and concessions. If appropriate, the rental rates may be itemized for each commercial space or for each type of residential unit. From the property visit and market survey, it should also be possible to evaluate the subject property's strengths and weaknesses and identify what is needed to improve its position in the market and maximize its net operating income and value.

The team must also understand the prospective client's needs and idiosyncracies. If possible, company executives should talk to people from other firms that have managed properties for the particular owner. These conversations may reveal important information such as:

- Issues that are of primary concern to the owner,
- Any problems the owner may have had with prior management firms,
- What requirements, if any, are imposed on the prospective client by others (e.g., business partners), and
- The owner's so-called hot buttons.

The goal is to discover what types of experiences other management companies may have had with the prospective client and vice versa. The prospect may have unusual requirements for accounting or other reports or a special interest in marketing and leasing or, perhaps, in operational issues such as landscaping and curb appeal. Information on the person's background and interests is often helpful in developing a rapport with the individual. Financial and other pertinent information on the ownership entity may provide additional insights. Also a consideration is the management firm's ability to address the property's needs. If its primary problem is high vacancy, a marketing team can be assembled to prepare a marketing and leasing plan. If the property is a major multi-tenant industrial park and the firm does not have a strong presence in industrial leasing, a qualified leasing company may be invited to work with the management firm in submitting a joint management and leasing proposal. Alternatively, an experienced industrial leasing agent might be added to the management firm's staff, or an industrial leasing firm might be recommended to the client to provide its services separately.

It is also important to assess the competition. Although it is not always possible to know who you are competing against, it is often possible to determine fairly accurately who else may (or may not) have been asked to bid on the management of the property. By understanding the competition, it should be possible to develop a presentation that will highlight your firm's strengths and downplay its weaknesses.

The Contents of a Management Proposal

The finished proposal should be professional in appearance and tell a complete story—who is going to manage the property, how they will go about accomplishing that activity, and what tools and personnel they have available to make sure the job is done properly. It should also address any issues or circumstances that are specific to the potential assignment.

While it is not likely that one will be awarded a new management account based on an attractive proposal alone, the first impression of the reader is likely to be positive if the document looks professional. An attractive cover and index tabs for easy identification of different portions of the proposal serve this purpose. The size (thickness) of the finished proposal should be dictated by the required information and not by any desire to make the proposal look more impressive. The reader who finds a lot of "fluff" in the text is likely to be less than enthusiastic about a management company that has so little respect for a prospective client's time. Obviously copied "boilerplate" material is likely to generate a similar response.

On the other hand, if there is relevant information to be conveyed, the proposal should be as large as is needed to tell the whole story. Often the "details" (statistical information, some of the calculations) can be compiled into one or more appendices at the back of the document so the proposal is complete while the proposal text presents a clear line of reasoning to be followed. Inclusion of a concise Executive Summary in the front of the proposal document can be helpful if the amount of material is likely to seem daunting to the prospect. (Printing and packaging of management information were described in some detail in Chapter 3 relative to the firm's operations manual, and many of those stated parameters apply to proposal packages as well. See also Creating Winning Proposals later in this chapter.)

Either the cover of the proposal or the page immediately behind the cover should contain the full name and address of the property, including the city and state. This page should also include the names (properly spelled) and the full and proper titles of the individuals and the company to whom the proposal is being made, as well as the name of the company making the proposal, the name of the individual within the management company who prepared the proposal and is likely to answer questions and make the actual presentation. This person's full title should also appear there, along with the company's full mailing address and the telephone number of the presenter. Finally, the cover page should show a date, preferably that of the presentation but, minimally, the date it was prepared.

It is usually desirable to include a current color photograph of the subject property, either on the cover or on a page very near the front of the proposal. This says that you took the time to visit the property and focuses the reader's attention on it.

The order of the remaining materials included in the proposal can vary, and items that are not applicable to a particular proposal can be omitted. It is more important for each presentation to be complete and well organized in itself. The goal is to "sell" the prospective client your management or other services. It should present the "features" of your company—the particular services you offer and, more specifically, how and why they are the best available—and tell how your services will "benefit" the property's ownership.

Company Information. This section of the proposal should include some background information about the management company—who started the business, when it was founded, and why. Information about the size of the portfolio under management should be included to let the client know the extent of your current activities. This is also a good place to include the company's *mission statement* and its goals in terms of service and commitment to its clients. The goals can and should be tailored to the potential client and the property that is the subject of the proposal—e.g., helping the property owner realize a higher return on his or her investment, stabilization or turnaround of a troubled property. If yours is a start-up business and there are no properties under management yet, this is the area to make a statement about what the company will be as well as its philosophy. The prior experience of the principals of the business would also be detailed here, along with the various types of properties the company intends to manage.

Since information about the company will be included in every proposal package, it is a good idea to have all the particulars in one place. Setting up computer files will allow individual documents to be updated as

> **Typical Components of a Management Proposal**
> - Company Information
>   —Personnel and Operations
>   —Properties Managed
>   —Client References
> - Services Offered by the Company
>   —Property Management
>   —Marketing and Leasing
>   —Maintenance
>   —Accounting
>   —Budgeting
> - Analysis of the Property
> - Proposed Management Plan
> - Proposed Contract Terms
> - Exhibits
>
> Other items may be incorporated into a specific proposal based on the property to be managed and the service capabilities of the management firm. Leasing might be a separately specified service for a commercial property. Construction supervision would be an appropriate addition if the proposal recommends rehabilitation or renovation of the property or, perhaps, a change of use. If the client's specific goal is periodic income, the management plan is likely to focus on income maximization and cost controls rather than address any enhancements to the property (unless improvements to the property are necessary to increase cash flow).

information changes. This will also facilitate compilation of proposals, allowing the preparer to select specific components and control the amount of detail without having to start over each time.

Personnel and Operations. An established management company may have a large number of employees. If so, the company information might include brief biographies of each of the major players, starting with the principals and including the real estate managers, the accounting supervisor, and the heads of other divisions or departments. For a very large organization, it may be more appropriate to provide substantial biographies for the personnel who would be directly responsible for the particular account and simply list the names and titles of those who would provide other specific services. The purpose is to show the specialized expertise available within the management firm (e.g., landscape architect, environmental engineer) or accessible via alliances with specialty service providers. (An organizational chart might be included in the appendix to give the reader an idea of the size of the organization as well as its internal structure—i.e., levels of authority, division of responsibilities.) On the other hand, if the company is very small—only one principal or two partners—there should be a more complete resume on each of the owners.

Pertinent information about the company's operations should also be included. Most potential clients, especially institutional owners, are very interested in the depth of the personnel, the level of sophistication of the management program, the policies and procedures that govern the activities of the company, and the computer programs (particularly accounting software) in place. Internal financial controls would be a major concern to most property owners—this section should tell how the company is structured to assure the potential client of checks and balances in approving and paying invoices.

Although prospective clients will differ in their needs for and expectations from fee management, most will be interested in the following types of information about your services and capabilities:

- *When and how reports are prepared and distributed*—The reporting function is of critical importance to most property owners, and this would be an area in which to discuss both the timeliness and accuracy of the monthly reports. A statement of their importance within the management company will help build confidence. If the company has an in-house incentive plan for getting reports out on time, that fact should be noted, too.

- *The management firm's maintenance capabilities*—Is work done in house or contracted? Do you have any special programs for the organized bidding of larger jobs? Is special emphasis placed on supervision and follow-up? If the management company has capabilities and contacts that would result in cost savings for the property, these should be detailed.

- *Unique or detailed programs the company has in the area of resident and tenant relations*—Tenant relations is a critical item in the management of all types of income-producing properties. A description of any special resident or commercial tenant retention programs and past successes will help sell your management services better than a mere discussion of the company's attitude toward tenant retention.

- *The company's in-house capability in the area of credit and collections*—Does the company have a specific policy of conducting credit checks on all potential residents or commercial tenants? Is there a person on staff who has a strong background and expertise in collections? Such policies and personnel are good selling points for a management company. A specific history of collections successes can also be outlined here.

- *How you interact with your management personnel*—Do company executives have regular meetings with real estate managers to discuss property operations and how to improve on them? Is there a regular program in place for sending managers to special seminars to improve their capabilities? A description of the firm's commitment to continuing education of its management personnel is an appropriate addition.

- *The company's in-house capability for construction, contracting, legal backup, etc.*—Is there specialized expertise within the company related to regulatory compliance (for example, environmental concerns, ADA considerations)? What about real estate tax analysis and appeals? What are your leasing capabilities? Is there brokerage capability for the ultimate sale of the property or for finding potential properties for purchase? An itemized listing of the types of adjunct services you can provide directly or can access readily on behalf of clients should conclude the operations segment. (More information on adjunct services can be found in Chapter 7.)

It is especially important to disclose the nature of in-house capabilities in maintenance, construction, etc., in order to avoid the appearance of a conflict of interest.

Properties Managed. If the company has an extensive portfolio of similar properties under management, they should be listed in a special section of the presentation package. The name of each property, the city and state where it is located, and its size (number of rental apartments or square feet of office or retail space) will be helpful to the prospective client in understanding the types and sizes of properties currently under management. (For a start-up management company, this section might include a listing of properties that have been managed previously by the principals of the business or by other staff members.) A brief description of property conditions and specific achievements in their management may be appropriate as well. If any of the properties had special features or if specific expertise was required for their management, such details should also be noted.

Client References. Seeing a list of the types of owners served by the management company will tend to give the prospective client more confidence in the firm's capabilities based on its current and past experience. In particular, institutional owners like to know that a manager has experience in dealing with institutions because their requirements are very exacting and they tend to be more demanding than a local partnership or an individual owner. The client list should include the name of the contact at the client's office, the client company, its full mailing address, and a telephone number—preferably the direct line to reach the contact person.

The reference list should be carefully checked each time a new proposal is prepared to be sure it is current. If an asset manager who is a very good contact has left the original client company, you may still want to list the person as a reference, but with his or her new company information.

(In such a situation, the replacement person at the original client company should also be contacted to be sure that he or she knows about your prior or current services and will give you a *positive* reference—an indifferent response in this case is likely to have the same impact as an unfavorable one.) For companies that manage commercial properties, tenant references can also be an important inclusion.

Services Offered by the Company. This section of the proposal can be set up on your computer as a generic description. The sequence and level of detail are likely to be different each time, depending on the needs of the prospective client and the property for which the proposal is being prepared.

[NOTE: The headings in the following sections are used to differentiate topics for purposes of this discussion; the subheadings and contents of individual proposals can be tailored to the property or its ownership as needed. Reference to policies and procedures in these discussions is consistent with the notion and practice of including the company's operations manual as a component of the proposal package. See Chapter 3 for detailed information on operations manuals.]

Property Management. This segment should outline how the company manages different property types, with particular emphasis on the type of property for which the proposal is being made. The following additional information should be included:

- The average number of visits made to each property. This should include a caveat that the actual number of visits will depend on the needs of the property under management.
- The number and types of physical inspections conducted—and the reasons for them—with reference to the specific form to be used and a copy of that form included in the exhibits at the back of the proposal. Apart from the goal of maintaining the property in first-class condition, concerns for safety, security, and liability are strong supportive arguments and selling points.
- The manner in which on-site employees will be hired, supervised, and trained for the subject property (if this will be a management responsibility). In a particular proposal, this portion may contain very specific information about site employees to answer the needs of the prospective client.
- The number, type, and frequency of reports to the property owner. This is an opportunity to reiterate the importance of—and your firm's commitment to—timeliness and accuracy. In addition to the normal monthly, quarterly, and annual reports, there should be an indication of the management company's commitment to good communication with its clients at all times.

Marketing and Leasing. The management company's approaches to marketing and leasing should be described. (This should include how the market survey was conducted for the property, who performed this task, and how the data were compiled and analyzed.) The firm's commitment to gathering accurate market information and identifying realistically comparable properties should be emphasized, along with the importance of these data in formulating marketing and leasing strategies. Your experience with marketing and leasing similar properties should be detailed, and sample analyses can be included (usually these would appear as exhibits in an appendix).

Maintenance. How the property will be maintained is a critical part of any management proposal. Key points to address in this section are:

- Procedures for bidding, contracting, and supervising maintenance work—This should spell out how you ensure that owners will receive optimum service for the money spent. Internal controls such as purchase orders and a bill-paying system that includes checks and balances to verify that invoices are correct and that a bill is not paid twice will be impressive to the prospective client. Carefully crafted maintenance contracts being required for all service providers will show the professionalism of the management company, as will a policy of meeting with contractors on a regular basis.

- Supervision and oversight—If supervisors or management company executives (or both) visit managed properties on a regular basis to evaluate progress, this would be an additional benefit to the property owners that can be stated.

- Additional "monitoring"—Many managers have worked out a system in which contractors report back on anything they see that may lead to problems or appears to need attention at the time they are at the property. This is an additional set of "eyes and ears" on the property and a benefit to the property's owner.

Accounting. Accounting is a critical area of property management. The lack of capability in this area can prevent a company from acquiring a management account or lead to its losing an existing one. Many real estate managers have little specific knowledge of the accounting function; because the work is done by others, all the manager may see is the monthly operating statement. (Since many asset managers to whom proposals are submitted have an accounting background, management personnel could easily be embarrassed if they have not learned the basics of accounting.)

Management companies are often required to use the same accounting software as their clients, and it is not unusual for them to be running several different software packages. Being connected to the client's main office by modem may also be required. This portion of the proposal should indicate the standard system the management company is currently using and include a statement of the firm's capability of working with different types of accounting software, including the prospective client's software (if known).

This is also the place to indicate a strong commitment to collection of all funds due and to timely and proper payment of all bills. For example:

- *How funds will be collected and deposited*—Here one might indicate that funds will be deposited in an interest-bearing account on behalf of the subject property (naming the property specifically) so they will be earning interest at all times. (It is both desirable and appropriate to indicate the name of the prospective client and the property throughout the presentation.)
- *How monies will be disbursed*—This might be a list of the policies and procedures that will be followed to ensure that all discounts are taken and only the proper amounts are paid for goods and services.
- *How tenants will be billed*—Here you might describe the company's capability of billing for tenant charges (e.g., operating expense pass-throughs at commercial properties). Even though an owner may not require it, he or she will want to be assured that everything to be billed will be billed and, within reasonable limits, collected.

Budgeting. The budget for each property generally represents the operating plan for the coming year. The management company must demonstrate a sophisticated budgeting capability, including provisions for an internal timetable and review process and for budget meetings with the owners (if they are so inclined), as well as a commitment to timeliness in the budgeting process. Sample budgets can be included in the exhibits section at the back of the proposal, although it is likely that most (if not all) prospective clients will have their own budgeting formats.

In addition to the initial budget, this section should include a statement of the company's commitment to an ongoing evaluation of the property's progress and how it relates to the budget (e.g., variance analysis). This may be handled in the monthly reports, additional quarterly reports, or special narratives, but the potential client must be assured of being fully informed on a regular basis about the financial position of the property.

Included in the description of the budgeting process should be a statement of the management company's ability and willingness to handle all reserve fund calculations and deposits as well as all capital programs, both short term and long term.

Analysis of the Property. This section should include a complete analysis of the subject property, some comparisons with competing properties to show rental rates in perspective, and a statement of the property's position in the marketplace. (More specific information on this section of the proposal is included in the separate discussions of proposals for the management of commercial and residential properties later in this chapter.)

Proposed Management Plan. This section should indicate who will actually manage the property (if the person has already been assigned), and give a brief biography and reasons why he or she is the best person in the organization to handle the assignment. Familiarity with the marketplace because of having managed properties in that geographic area would be an especially good reason. Any specific credentials of the real estate manager, such as a professional designation—e.g., the Certified Property Manager® (CPM®) designation from IREM—should be noted. A very strong record in turnarounds, collections, upgrading of maintenance standards, etc., are other individual qualifications that may be good selling points. Other management company personnel who will be assigned responsibility for the property should be named here as well, along with a brief recapitulation of their qualifications.

Here is where you should outline the specific way in which your company proposes to operate the prospective client's property. It should also identify any observed problems (photographs should be included) and tell how the firm would deal with them. Where solutions require specialized expertise, the capabilities of in-house personnel can be pointed out. The firm's ability to call upon outside experts by partnering with other firms to provide select services can also be noted in this section.

Changes in the property's operations can have immediate economic impact, and the proposal can and should include estimates of improvements expected from operating efficiencies (reduced expenses) or stepped-up collections (increased income). Renovation or rehabilitation of a property or replacement of capital equipment will require major investment by the owner, and recommendations for these types of changes should be supported by cost-benefit analyses and pro-forma projections of the costs and the payback period. (If the company has the resources to provide access to capital for such improvements, this should be mentioned here.)

While it is generally not a good practice to criticize the current management, it may be necessary to point out deficiencies in order to make the point of what has to be done to improve the situation at the property. (Any specific criticisms should be presented in a professional manner and only to the extent necessary to make the point.)

Once the problem has been identified, however, the proposal should outline the steps considered necessary to correct it, indicate how the proposed changes will be implemented, identify the specific results you expect to achieve, and tell why your company is the best one to accomplish the solution. (If there is more than one problem, each should be identified and a specific solution proposed for it.) If possible during the bidding process, there should be ongoing discussions between the management company and the prospective client to help you understand what the property owner is seeking and tailor the proposal to his or her expectations.

Great care must be taken when a property owner has one perception and the company making the management proposal has another. Whenever possible, the two different positions should be fully discussed prior to finalizing the management proposal—there should be at least some agreement as to where the proposal is heading. It is not hard to understand that, if a proposal comes as a complete surprise and is in opposition to the property owner's perceptions, it is going to have an uphill battle because the prospective client not only has to buy into the management company's perception of the problem, but also be sold on the solution. The more that can be settled prior to the formal presentation of the management proposal, the better the chances of the proposal being accepted. (Management plan specifics are addressed in the separate discussions of residential and commercial proposals later in this chapter; see also Exhibit 3.2.)

Proposed Contract Terms. Here should be outlined the proposed terms of the management agreement. This should include the compensation desired (e.g., a percentage of the effective gross income or a percentage versus a minimum fee), the expected duration of the contract, any incentives the management company considers appropriate to this assignment, and any special requirements of the property owner that would be stated in the agreement in order for management to meet the goals outlined in the management plan. This section should not be a statement of the contract terms as such; rather it should indicate the "usual" services compensated by the management fee, the range of rates or fees for additional or exceptional services, and how these relate to the property being proposed for management. More importantly, it should repeat the philosophy behind the recommendations in the plan and state, in reasonable detail, the actual activities that will be undertaken by the management company to accomplish the stated goals.

A statement as to *why* the management company is the best and safest choice to manage this particular property should also be included in this section. The reasons might be any or all of the following:

- Your firm is the only one in the area specializing in this type of property.
- Your firm has the largest presence in this marketplace.
- Your firm has had great success in handling the particular situations or conditions that are evident at the property.
- Your firm has a successful track record of leasing up the type of property.

The reasons stated should be factual and verifiable. However, this is not a time for modesty. You are selling your services, and it is important to point out your strengths and what they will mean to the prospective client's property. Support your claims of success with specifics—dollar savings, percent occupancy increases, etc.

Exhibits. Exhibits should be carefully prepared to represent the array of management tools (mostly forms) used by your company to accomplish the required tasks. However, one has to be careful not to include everything. The proposal would be much too long to be read during the presentation, and the reader would quickly realize that much of the material is not likely to be germane to the particular property. The Exhibits section should open with a list of what is included so it will be easy for the reader to focus on those items that are of particular interest. (A listing of the more relevant forms is included in the specific discussions of residential and commercial management proposals.)

The property analysis, the proposed operating management plan, and the array of exhibits are the principal differences between the two types of proposals, and these are addressed in the following discussions.

The Residential Proposal

Many factors will be considered in developing a proposal to manage a residential property. The type of property—rental apartments, owner-occupied condominiums or cooperatives, a mobile home park, etc.—and the particular management challenges it poses will determine the level of detail in different sections of the proposal. The example here is more specific to an apartment property.

Property Analysis. The proposal should include a comprehensive analysis of the subject property and its environs. The following types of information are used in developing a targeted marketing and leasing plan.

- Where it is located.
- How many units—total and by different types (e.g., studio, one-bedroom)—and their square footage.
- Whether the units are a good size for the target market (i.e., if two-bedroom apartments are popular, are there two-bedroom apartments at the property?).
- Whether the amenities within the units are proper for the market.
- The features and amenities of the property as a whole and whether they are appropriate for the likely resident.
- The characteristics and conditions of the neighborhood and whether

it is supportive of the residential complex (i.e., compatible with the property and the likely residents).
- The types of transportation available for the residents (e.g., buses, trains).
- The freeways and major arterial roads nearest to the property and whether they are conducive to commuting to work and residents' other daily living activities (shopping, schools, etc.).
- Employment opportunities available in the general area of the property and whether the wages offered are commensurate with the rents being charged.
- Potential problems at the property (or in the neighborhood) and the impact they might have on its overall operations.

Within this section of the management proposal it is helpful to include a map of the general area or neighborhood indicating the location of the property. A larger area (regional) map showing freeways, schools, shopping, airports, etc., may also be a desirable inclusion. (If the manager thinks it will help sell the firm's services, an updated demographic analysis can be quite impressive, and these are easy to obtain.) A plot plan of the property and floor plans of the various units may also be included.

Inclusion of a comparative analysis of similar properties in the area lets the prospective client know that you have investigated the market and that you understand how the subject property fits into it. To make an effective comparison, four or five properties should be identified and visited. Unit sizes, rental rates, amenities, typical lease or rental terms, and special offerings or concessions should be presented on a comparison grid along with the same types of information about the subject property to show its relative position in the marketplace. A map indicating the locations of the comparable properties in relation to the subject property will also be helpful to the prospect's understanding of the proposal. Each comparable property should be described individually on a separate page, complete with current photographs. The information should include street address, number of units, their size and mix, rental rates (and rates per square foot, if known), the array of amenities available at the property, and any special lease terms or concessions.

Management Plan. This section describes how your management company would operate the residential property and identifies the manager responsible for carrying out the plan, along with his or her qualifications. The physical and financial condition of the property would determine the extent to which maintenance, collections, and other issues would be addressed. However, specific leasing strategies are likely to be a major component of a residential management proposal regardless of market conditions.

Because apartment leases are often for only a single year, lease renewals are usually offered at a nominally higher rent—a dollar amount or a nominal percentage rate increase to offset increases in operating expenses. However, if the property is *superior* to its competition, it should be able to command substantially higher rents. Based on that information, your proposal might advance an aggressive marketing and leasing plan to achieve this goal. When there are more potential renters than available apartments, such a plan might include an announcement to all residents that leases will be renewed at larger-than-usual increases, with an explanation of the superior value they receive for their rent dollars. However, if the market is soft and turnover and vacancies are high, an appropriate lease renewal program might recommend little or no increases in rents.

Ideally, a leasing plan would include a specific program aimed at resident retention. Such a program might offer a variety of incentives for renewal that enhance the rental unit, with specific options linked to rent adjustments and the renewal lease term. For example, painting one room or shampooing carpets might be offered with a modest rent increase, while major redecorating or replacement of cabinets or appliances might require a substantial increase to "amortize" the costs over the term of the renewal lease. In this way, the resident benefits from an upgraded apartment, and the market value of the individual unit has been increased.

On the other hand, if the property is *inferior* to its competitors, the management plan might recommend systematic renovation or rehabilitation to make it more competitive and better able to command higher rents. In the latter instance, the firm may want the management arrangement to include responsibility for overseeing the required construction work and appropriate compensation for such oversight. In addition to the company's qualifications for managing and leasing the residential property, this type of proposal should list its experience and expertise in supervising the type of construction work that would be undertaken.

Exhibits. The following are suggested exhibits for a residential property proposal. Where appropriate, specific forms (e.g., leases) should be accompanied by a caveat that their adoption is subject to review and approval of the property owner's attorney.

- A sample residential lease (or rental agreement) form. This is especially important if the current management is using a form that is outdated or has built-in problems. (You should include the date of the review and name of the attorney who reviewed and amended the agreement. Incorporation of the move-in/move-out inspection form and/or security deposit agreement as an addendum to the lease is also appropriate.) Showing that your lease forms are appropriately comprehensive and in compliance with current landlord-tenant laws and local ordinances and practices is very important.

- Representative rules and regulations (if separate from the lease) and examples of resident communications demonstrate the professionalism of the management company and indicate that the ideas presented are not just theoretical or developed exclusively for this proposal, but rather a proven program that will also be used to benefit the particular property. In evaluating the proposal, the prospective client should be able to gain confidence in the management company from these materials.

- Examples of marketing brochures, classified and display ads, etc., are also quite important, especially if some of the types of materials have been particularly effective at other properties managed by the company. Notes about how these materials increased occupancy, helped gain higher rents, or reduced turnover will be impressive adjunct information. (The information should be verifiable and relative costs should be noted.)

- If the marketing or site personnel are required to visit the competition on a regular basis and prepare a report, a sample of the type of report they would prepare should be included in the exhibits. Again, this will show that there is in place a well-thought-out report format that will help in evaluating the competition and using that information to keep the property competitive.

- Most sophisticated residential property managers keep a log of the traffic for rental prospects. The typical log indicates where prospects learned about the property, what type of apartment they were seeking, some indication of whether they were qualified prospects, and whether a rental application (or lease) resulted from the inquiry—or, if they did not pursue the rental, the objection that was raised. These logs are used by the manager of the property to evaluate the site personnel and their approach to leasing prospects. They are also a means of deciding whether people or procedures should be changed in an effort to capture a higher percentage of the prospects seen. A representative traffic report with interpretive notes is an appropriate inclusion. If weekly traffic reports are consolidated into a monthly report, both styles should be shown.

- If the firm uses an exit questionnaire to find out why residents move out, this is another good item to include. It is important to know why people are moving away, and although nothing can be done about the individual move outs, it is not unusual to detect a pattern among the reasons given by departing residents. The problems that are identified may be addressed by changing the approach to management and maintenance, the amenities of the property, or the rental structure, all to the property's benefit.

- A set of sample monthly reports should be included. While it is likely that prospective clients will want their reports in a specific format, they will be interested in the level of sophistication of the company's reporting capability. (Typical components of a monthly report package are described in Exhibit 3.1.)

Examples of any other reports that are likely to be of interest in the particular situation should also be included. Discrimination lawsuits, construction or retrofitting of equipment to comply with new or existing environmental laws, and insurance losses are items that might require monitoring and be included in the monthly reports to the owner. The choice of inclusions may best be guided by the recommendations in the management plan. For example, if you are proposing renovation or rehabilitation, this would be an item to report monthly while the construction work is in progress. In this case, copies of forms for bidding the contracts and other related documents used as "standard" practice by the management firm should be appended as well.

The Commercial Proposal

A proposal for the management of a commercial property will be very different from one for a residential property. At commercial properties, common area or building services are typically provided by the management firm, but the costs are billed back to the tenants under their respective lease agreements. The provision of janitorial and repair services in office buildings is a potential source of major problems between management and the building occupants. Quite often there are issues of operating agreements between different owners of parts of a shopping center. The tenant mix and marketing of the shopping center can be sources of management-tenant problems. The accounting function has to be able to track tenants' sales (for collection of overage or percentage rent) as well as prorate the common area maintenance (CAM) expenses and anticipate rental increases that are built into tenants' multi-year leases. These complexities must all be addressed in the specific management proposal.

Property Analysis. The property should be clearly defined on an area map and again on a localized map that shows more detail of the surrounding streets, residential areas, etc. The locations of competing properties may be indicated on either of these maps, depending on how far apart they are. If a physical inspection was completed prior to preparing the management proposal, a summary of that inspection should be included. (An inspection of the property is particularly important because the results can have a major impact on the specifics of your management proposal.) Along with the summary of the problems found during the inspection, there should also be proposed solutions—i.e., things the management company would do to correct the problems. Another added touch is inclusion of color photographs of the property showing its major features and, if relevant, the deficiencies found during the inspection.

The analysis should include a plot plan of the property, and if it has multiple owners (as when a supermarket owns its own site), that fact should be noted. The total square footage that is proposed for management should be indicated on a schedule showing the number of buildings, the number of occupiable spaces (e.g., stores, office suites), and the square footage of each building. (It may be desirable or appropriate to include metric equivalents—i.e., square meters—for the areas, especially if U.S. governmental agencies are in any way involved with the property.)

Information about the market—vacancies, absorption rates (for office buildings), new construction or proposed development, etc.—and about properties that compete with the subject property, directly or indirectly, will add context to the property analysis and help demonstrate why the changes you propose are necessary or desirable.

If there are known deficiencies in the accounting or record keeping for the property, they should be noted in this section as well. These functions are of continuing concern and can easily lead to the changing of a property's management. In commercial properties, it is not uncommon to find common area or escalation charges that have not been billed properly or consistently (including disputes over square footage charges—actual area versus specific billings), rental rate increases that have been missed in the past, lease files that are incomplete, and similar administrative problems.

If conditions in the neighborhood or trade area are having an adverse effect on the property, they should be described in this section of the proposal. An office building may have had four new competitors open in the last year, depressing the market for office space. Downsizing of a major company in the area may have forced people to move elsewhere or changed the income range of consumers who shopped at a strip center or enclosed mall. Major street construction may have reduced the accessibility of an industrial park, bringing leasing to a standstill and making renewal of existing leases more difficult.

The property analysis section should be used to present a complete picture of the property as it exists at the time the proposal is being made. The goal here should be to set the stage for the operating recommendations that will be presented in the management plan section of the proposal.

Management Plan. This section should present the operating plan that will correct the problems stated in the property analysis. Each problem should be summarized here along with its proposed solution. For instance, if the lease files are in poor condition, there should be a statement as to exactly how this will be corrected. Such a statement might read as follows:

> XYZ Management Company will review all lease files to ascertain that there is a file for each tenant. A lease summary will be prepared for each lease, and that information will be compared to the accounting records to be sure all rents and charges are current and being billed in accordance with the agreements. A follow-up "tickler" file will be prepared indicating all future events on the individual lease to be sure they are handled in a timely fashion. Lease information will be confirmed with the respective tenants as necessary to assure the accuracy of future transactions.

The statement of what is to be done must be complete because other people in the prospective client's office may read the proposal but not have the benefit of seeing and hearing the presentation.

Leasing is often a critical aspect of the overall operation of a commercial property, and it should be addressed in the management plan section unless the potential client tells you specifically that leasing is a separate function. This section should also identify the manager and any other personnel who will be responsible for the account.

All areas of concern to the prospective client should be touched on in this section—accounting, record keeping, management reporting, tenant relations, maintenance, insurance, tax administration, security, etc. Even if there are no particular problems, the proposal should state how the company handles the various management functions to provide a complete picture of the services being offered.

Exhibits. Exhibits should help the reader understand how the management company will manage the property. Typically these would be:

- A sample budget format, especially if it will differentiate the owner's expenses from those passed through to tenants and separate base rents from common area, tax, and insurance income (tenant pass-through expenses)—and from percentage rents (from retail tenants)—and include capital items and debt service (if necessary).
- Copies of common area work sheets that show how the allocation process is handled by the management company.
- Record-keeping forms for computing and collecting percentage rent —sales report, calculation of monies due, sales comparisons for the entire center, and auditing procedures.
- Copies of the typical monthly management reports prepared for commercial properties (see Exhibit 3.1).

> ### Commercial Leasing and the Management Proposal
>
> Because the leasing of commercial space has become a time-intensive activity requiring specialized expertise, the leasing function is usually segregated from the management of the property. Commercial leasing involves targeting specific businesses as potential tenants, aggressively wooing them and selling them on the benefits of relocating, and then negotiating the economic terms and other aspects of the lease. For shopping center space, there are national and regional tenant prospects to consider as well as locally based businesses. The tenant qualification process is complicated by the need for information about the merchant's success as a retailer—i.e., the demand for its goods or services—as well as the credit status of the business operation. For their part, businesses often hire a broker to find properties and lease terms that fulfill their space requirements and are within their price range. (This is more common among national companies that are major space users at many different locations.) If the management company expects to contract for the leasing as well as the management of a commercial property, the proposal should not only identify leasing strategies and anticipated outcomes, but also spell out the firm's qualifications for taking on the leasing assignment—i.e., its experience, expertise, and personnel.
>
> Obviously, the best approach for the management company is to handle the leasing in house because it is often one of the most profitable activities in the management arena. Additionally, there is always potential for the development of friction between an outside leasing agent and the management company, making it more difficult to manage the property effectively. However, there is also the consideration of whether the management company has the capability to do a first-rate job of leasing. While the additional income is nice, if the leasing is handled poorly, the management contract could be put at risk.

If the management company is recommending use of a different lease form, a sample lease should be included as an exhibit to show the client the level of sophistication of the replacement form—or how it is more comprehensive or up-to-date—compared to the lease currently in use. (As noted earlier, there should be a caveat that adoption of the recommended lease form is subject to review and approval by the property owner's attorney.)

Presenting the Management Proposal

Before the proposal is prepared, you should find out how many copies will be needed so that everyone attending the presentation can have their own copy and there will be one for the permanent files of the management company. It is advisable to make at least one extra copy in case someone is invited to the presentation unexpectedly. By preparing a sufficient number of copies at the outset, you avoid having to reproduce photographs and other proposal components at single-copy prices.

The presentation team should assemble a few days before they will see

> **Commercial Leasing** *(continued)*
> If the management company considers itself the best and safest alternative, the proposal should outline a complete leasing program that includes the current space available, suggestions of potential tenants for the space, likely leasing rates and terms, and a timetable for completion of the leasing effort. If turnover leases are involved as well, the proposal should address all those that are due to expire in the near future and outline an approach to renewing or replacing specific tenants and the rationales for these recommendations. If someone other than the manager will be responsible for the leasing, that person should be named along with his or her qualifications.
> If the leasing will be done by an outside leasing agent, the management company should indicate how leasing companies will be interviewed, what criteria will be used to evaluate them (selection process), how communications between the management company, the property owner, and the leasing personnel will be handled, and how results will be reported. Also, if the management company expects to share in the leasing commissions or receive an extra fee for overseeing the leasing activity, that should be mentioned as well.

the property owner. During this pre-meeting, the team members should discuss the content of their presentation and decide who will be responsible for which parts of the plan and the order of presentation. This will allow team members to look for flaws in the presentation and marketing materials (while there is still time to overcome them) and determine which points should be emphasized.

The date the prospective client will require the proposal is critical. Real estate managers are often asked to submit an extensive proposal for managing a property but given a very short time in which to prepare it. You must not only be prepared to meet the prospect's needs, but also be sure you will be able to meet any due date that is agreed to initially. A late proposal is likely not to be considered at all, unless there are no other realistic bids. That is too much of a risk to take.

You should make every effort to be allowed to present the proposal in person. The typical management proposal on a large property is very complex and can be better understood with some additional comments. In particular, your analysis of the property as the background and context of your proposed plan for its management should be part of the discussion. It is not necessary for the hiring decision to be made during the face-to-face meeting, but it is most important to be given the opportunity to explain the salient points of your proposal and "sell" your services. It is also an opportune time to find out if anything is missing from the proposal—or if there is any additional information the prospective client would like to have—and arrange to have it provided as quickly as possible.

As part of the presentation, it is also a good idea to mention any properties in the area that the company has managed or is managing currently.

Creating Winning Proposals—Another Perspective

Since a management proposal is directed to a single prospective client and addresses the management needed by a unique property, the place to start is with the property. A thorough inspection of the property coupled with a comprehensive review of its operating history and interviews with building personnel is one aspect of the research to be done. Repeatedly "shopping" the property will give you better insights. Review and analyze the data you have gathered, looking for possible weaknesses that your approach to management can correct.

From your research and analysis, develop questions to ask the prospective client and try to arrange an interview. (Focus on major issues only.) At this stage, your objective is to gather information so you can better understand the prospective client's goals and expectations. The best way to find out what they are is to ask, point blank, "What are your goals for the property?" and "What do you expect from the firm that is awarded the management account?"

Assuming the prospect's goals and expectations are consistent with the capabilities of your company, your next step is to determine what to sell and how to sell it. Find out who else is competing for the account and evaluate your company against these competitors. Try to identify ways to set your company apart from the competition—look for creative, cost-effective solutions to problems; step outside the bounds of the traditional approaches. If possible, shop your competition: Find out how your company's strengths and weaknesses compare to theirs.

Although the proposal should be informative, it should be designed, above all, to persuade the prospect to give you the account. Use language creatively and confidently—from title page to appendices, hold to a theme. If the goal is to attract upscale renters to an apartment property, the proposal might be titled: "XYZ Apartments—Segmenting the Market to Attract Upscale Renters." Similarly, throughout the executive summary, refer to strategies that "will" segment the market, that "are likely" to attract renters with incomes in a stated range (and do state the dollar range), and on and on. Selling your company also requires specific terminology. Provide measures of the quality of your service: "We consistently maintain higher occupancy rates than are usual in the area."

Since pictures convey more than words, use graphics to demonstrate statistics. A chart takes up less space than a complex table, and it makes differences immediately apparent—e.g., for a comparison of income and expenses, numbers and percentages in a table have to be assimilated, but a pie chart shows instantly which amount is larger. If you can use color, that is even better. However, do make sure the data are available as backup—they can be presented as tables in the appendix.

The executive summary should be carefully crafted. Here, in brief, you need to spell out all the problems you expect to address in managing the property and the specific strategies you would use to overcome them. This is the heart of the proposal and the part everyone will come back to, whether or not they read all the details of the analyses. Start with a strong statement, such as: "Aggressive marketing to 'baby boomers' can attract upscale renters to XYZ Apartments within 90 days." Then identify individual problems that preclude achievement of the desired goal now (i.e., under the current

Creating Winning Proposals *(continued)*

management) and offer specific solutions to overcome them. In fact, offer more than one solution—presenting options not only reflects creative thinking but also gives the prospective client more reasons to favor your particular proposal. You also need to spell out the benefits that will accrue from the implementation of particular solutions—e.g., a 12-percent increase in gross rental revenue the first year, a 20-percent increase in property value, etc.

Others who regularly develop account-winning proposals offer this additional advice: Focus on the property and its needs and on the owner's specific goals. Ask the prospective client, specifically, what should be covered, in how much detail, and what types of examples should be included. This is especially important if the original request for proposal (RFP) does not spell out the potential client's requirements and expectations. Use this information to guide your development of an overview perspective on the goals of management. Support your recommendations with data from your research and analyses—market surveys, property analyses, and other details can be compiled in appendices along with sample forms that are consistent with the particular proposal—but omit data and forms that are not relevant.

There are also some pitfalls to avoid. Offer and describe only those company services that fulfill the mission of the proposal. (You can always offer additional services once a contract is signed.) Provide biographical information on the individuals who would directly manage the account or interact with the property owner—these should be brief resumes, preferably in the form of bulleted lists. (An organizational chart or comprehensive discussion of qualifications, especially of people not involved with the account, will only be a distraction.) Obtain the account before you try to negotiate the terms of a management agreement and a specific fee. (The prospective client will likely want to know what *range of fees* you charge for different services, and this information can be stated; but it is unwise to commit to a fee until the details of the assignment are settled since the specific duties determine your operating costs.) While the proposal should be as large as is necessary to address the owner's requirements stated in the RFP, a general rule of thumb is: Shorter is better.

Each proposal also warrants a suitable "package." However, while color graphics and substantial binding may be expected if not mandatory in competing for the management of institutionally owned properties, a sole owner of a mid-sized apartment building is likely to be overwhelmed by such sophisticated packaging and perhaps even concerned that the enhancements inflate your management fee.

Most of all, you should learn from the proposal development process what works best for your company. Ultimately, some components can be designated as "standard" or "boilerplate" copy for all proposals. The company history, for example, and people's resumes should need only minor updating for future proposals. A format for presenting market comparisons or property analyses can be standardized so that only the particulars—property identification, numerical data, and interpretations of those data—need to be incorporated into a "template." Computers and word-processing programs allow numerous options, and you can not only develop standard formats, but also tailor them to the needs of the potential client as set forth in his or her RFP.

This will provide added verification that your firm understands the particular market as well as help you ascertain whether there is a perceived or an actual conflict of interest involved—some prospects will see your work with other properties in the area as a benefit, but others may see it as a conflict.

Letters of recommendation from owners of similar properties that you have managed in the past can also be supportive, especially if the firm is fairly new and has only a limited portfolio. Such letters can help assure the prospective client that the management company (i.e., the individual involved) has been successful previously in dealing with the type of property—and ownership—involved in the current proposal.

Once the management proposal has been presented or submitted, it is a good idea to check back in a few days to see if there is anything more the prospect needs to make a decision. No one wants to be perceived as a pest, but it is important to show that you are interested in the property and the proposal, rather than just sit back and wait for the decision. The presentation itself might conclude with an indication that you will follow up with the prospect in two or three days. If there are any questions or if additional details would be helpful to him or her in making a decision, you should want the opportunity to respond.

If you are awarded the management contract, your next action will be to present a specific agreement form for negotiation. (That is the subject of the next chapter.) However, if you are not awarded the contract, it is reasonable to ask why and whether there is anything you could have done differently that might have helped you win the account. It is also important to let the prospective client know you are still interested in doing business with him or her. The goal is to have another opportunity to make a proposal the next time the property's management will be bid or whenever management proposals are sought for other properties in the prospect's portfolio.

Proposals in Perspective

Management contracts are most often placed as the result of the proposal process. The management proposal that is submitted must not only respond to the particulars of the RFP, but also "sell" the management company and its services to the prospective client. This chapter has identified and described the kinds of information that are commonly included in management proposals, indicating some of the major differences between proposals prepared for residential and commercial properties. Within each of these large classifications, there are differences that must be considered for individual types of properties—management of condominiums is substantially different from that of rental apartments, and office buildings offer different challenges than shopping centers. Because each property is unique, there can be no single "standard" list of proposal components. Rather, the property owner's requirements are usually spelled out in a specific RFP, and these requirements along with the characteristics of the property determine the approach to preparing a particular proposal.

Institutional owners especially must be sure they have considered the firms in the area who are specifically qualified to manage their properties and that they have chosen the best and the safest management company for the job. For this reason it is critical that each opportunity to submit a proposal is taken seriously. This means doing the best possible job of compiling and interpreting the property and market data and, from that information, making recommendations for managing the property that will make it financially successful and fulfill the owner's goals. If you treat the proposal lightly, the prospective client may develop a poor perception of the management firm's capabilities or, worse, decide that the company does not really care about acquiring the account.

9

Strategizing the Management Agreement

Real estate management, as a business, is based on relationships with property owners—relationships that must be established, nurtured, and maintained. They may begin with an owner's decision that his or her investment property should be professionally managed and the resulting choice of the management firm based on its expertise. Bonds of mutual trust and admiration, and sometimes friendship, are often forged over years of working together to make a property successful.

Most management arrangements are entered into with both parties intending to establish a long-term relationship. Over time, however, any relationship can become strained. The fact that the real estate being managed is a source of income for both the owner and the manager subjects property management relationships, in particular, to misunderstandings. Any issue that arises can easily become a point of contention between the parties. In order to minimize the possibility of misunderstandings and the problems they can cause, the relationship between property owner and management company should be documented in writing in the form of a management agreement, and no work should commence until the agreement has been signed. A written management agreement provides a checklist of items that have been agreed to in establishing the relationship between the management firm and the property owner. Used as a reference point, it should prevent misunderstandings from occurring and provide a basis for settling disputes.

[NOTE: Many states require a written contract when real property is managed by a third party. Violations of this statute can subject the management firm to disciplinary action by the state's real estate commission. In some states, a property manager must have a written contract (i.e., a management agreement) in order to sign contracts, maintenance agreements, and leases on behalf of the property owner.]

Management Agreement Considerations

The *management agreement* is a legal contract between the management company and the property owner. It defines the manager's duties, authority, and compensation and states the property owner's obligations. Because the agreement establishes the management company as a legal *agent* of the property owner, there are many specifics of the relationship that have to be addressed and documented. A standard management agreement should be drafted for the firm by an attorney, and any significant changes to the standard form that are negotiated with a particular property owner should be reviewed by legal counsel before the document is signed.

In establishing a management agreement, there are many issues that are concerns for the management company, and these differ from the concerns of the property owner. In discussing these differences, we will also address how some types of problems can arise in the manager-client relationship and suggest strategies for dealing with these situations.

Management Company Concerns. A real estate management company has three primary concerns regarding the management agreement—payment for services it renders, reduction of its risk, and specifics of operating the property.

Compensation. The *management fee* is only one of several fees that can be charged for a variety of services provided by a management firm. Seldom is there a dispute regarding the payment of the basic management fee; however, problems can arise regarding fees for additional services. The typical management agreement will list specific duties of the manager, such as collecting rents, paying expenses of the property, maintaining the property, and reporting to the owner. Usually, the agreement will also list "other services" that are to be provided by the manager and the separate fees to be charged for them. These other services may include things like leasing, tax appeals, and supervision of major maintenance, renovation, or tenant improvement construction. Because it is not possible to anticipate all the services that may be requested or required by an owner in the course of managing a particular property, the management agreement should clearly define what "management services" are to be compensated by the management fee. It should also include a separate provision that allows the management firm to charge for services that are beyond the scope of the basic property management services and not specifically listed in the agreement as "other services."

It is important to understand that the property owner and real estate manager may disagree on which services are outside the realm of basic property management. A good relationship between the manager and the owner may or may not prevent such conflicts from occurring or allow for an equitable resolution of the disagreement. It may be necessary to survey other firms to determine the basic management services provided for a specific type of property. This is better done before a management agreement is set. The more specific the written agreement is regarding "basic services," the less potential there will be for misunderstandings. It is also important for both parties to discuss their respective expectations during the negotiation of the agreement.

Another issue relating to fees is early termination of the management agreement. The manager should be compensated for the additional work required to set up a management account if the agreement is terminated early. For example, if the agreement is terminated during the first year, there should be provision for a cancellation fee to be paid to the management firm. [NOTE: The amount should be negotiated and stated in the agreement—one third of the fee for the remainder of the current year may be an appropriate place to begin these negotiations.]

Risk Reduction. The second concern of management firms is their potential liability for others' actions. Management company executives will want the owner-client to indemnify the management firm against lawsuits relating to activities or incidents at the property that are either beyond the firm's control or are not included in the specific duties of management. To address this concern, the property owner may be asked to include the management company as an additional named insured party on the insurance policies for the property and agree to inclusion of an indemnification or hold-harmless provision in the management contract.

This is one of the most difficult provisions to negotiate satisfactorily, especially for small management firms. Many sophisticated owners of investment real estate—banks, insurance companies, REITs, and partnerships—are likely to balk at some inclusive indemnification language. Because of who they are, they know they are likely to be seen as a "deep pockets" resource—i.e., having large amounts of capital available, presumably it will be easier for them to recover from a lawsuit. The owner may expect the manager to be included in such responsibilities and insist that indemnification language include a reference to the manager's duties. For example, the manager might be indemnified to the extent that he or she performed all assigned duties in a competent and professional manner. If the manager were *not* to perform in this way, liabilities and problems could arise putting both the manager and owner at financial and legal risk. Most owners do not want a manager held harmless for incomplete work, incompetence, or illegal acts.

Operational Issues. The primary operational concern is whether the property owner has (or will make available) sufficient funds to operate the property. Maintenance being deferred and contractors not being paid on a timely basis can affect how a property is managed and how it is perceived in the real estate industry and the local community. These factors can have a negative impact on the management company's reputation. There are other consequences as well. Payment concerns can affect the property's and the management company's credit standing. Also, fielding telephone calls from angry vendors takes a great deal of time and is damaging to staff morale.

There are many other issues that can strain the relationship between management and ownership, and each one presents challenges that must be addressed and resolved. Special requests for additional financial analyses or reports on short deadlines can disrupt the orderly operations of the management firm's accounting department and affect its ability to produce all of its reports on a timely basis. Another potential concern is whether the property owner will respond promptly to the manager's recommendations and inquiries. Issues that cannot be resolved amicably will threaten the relationship between the parties and jeopardize the management agreement. Some issues—e.g., ethical and legal questions—are so serious that the management firm may elect to terminate the management agreement. However, most potential conflicts between management and ownership can be resolved through effective dialogue.

Property Owners' Concerns. The real estate owner is contracting for management of an investment property based on his or her *goals and objectives*. The goals can vary among managing the property for immediate cash flow or long-term appreciation, to preserve ownership or prevent a foreclosure, or to effect an immediate sale, to name just a few. The owner's first concern is that the real estate manager understands his or her goals and objectives for the property. Next in importance is that the manager and his or her support staff have the capabilities and resources to implement a plan to achieve the owner's goals and objectives. (A discussion of the importance of various characteristics of property management firms and specific property management tasks is presented in Chapter 1, and property owners' rankings of them are shown in Exhibits 1.1 and 1.2.)

Property finances are a major concern. Since net operating income is a determinant of the property's value, the real estate manager is expected to maximize income through diligent rent collection. Real estate owners also want their properties to be managed as economically as possible by controlling costs. This means not only seeking multiple bids for service contracts but ensuring that vendors do not overcharge for the services they provide. (The increasing sophistication of owners' financial reporting requirements has been addressed in earlier discussions of company operations and the accounting function; see Chapters 3 and 4 in particular.)

A concern of all property owners is their potential *liability* arising out of the actions of the managing agent. Many owners are requiring management firms to carry errors and omissions insurance and liability insurance in addition to having fidelity bonds, sometimes with higher limits than the firm already has in place. Some owners are requesting—even requiring—

that they be listed as additional named insured parties on the management company's fidelity bond and liability insurance policy. (When this occurs, the management firm may be successful in negotiating for the property owner to pay for the requested increase in the insurance coverages.)

When the market is soft or a property has a high vacancy rate, the owner's primary concern is *leasing:* Most of the conversations between the owner and the manager will focus on marketing and leasing, and the manager may be required to provide additional leasing reports and market surveys. As part of the preparation for negotiating the management agreement, the management firm should anticipate this and design a marketing and leasing program that will achieve the maximum results possible, along with a reporting system that keeps the owner aware of market conditions (including leasing activity in the market) and the progress being made at the managed property.

Other Potential Problems and Solutions. Often problems that arise between the owner and the management firm are due to *poor communications*. The manager may not understand the property owner's goals and objectives, or the owner may have failed to communicate them effectively. Sometimes owners have hidden agendas that prevent them from informing the manager of their true problems and goals. Management company personnel must assume the responsibility for developing and maintaining a constant and effective flow of communication between themselves and the property owner. This starts with meetings between the parties prior to the execution of the management agreement. These meetings are an opportunity to discuss the owner's goals and objectives, the type and frequency of management and financial reports, the issues and tasks that are of particular importance to the owner, and his or her preferences for type and frequency of communication. These meetings also provide an opportunity for the owner and manager to get to know each other's personalities and interests and to develop a working rapport.

The *frequency of communication* will depend on the needs of the property owner and specific problems that exist at the managed property. The manager should ask how often the owner needs or wants specific types of communications and set up a system to accommodate the owner's requirements. These communications are in addition to the annual management plan and the monthly management and financial reports prepared for the owner. (Owners' reporting requirements are addressed in Chapters 3 and 4. Communications and other aspects of client relations are discussed in Chapter 6.)

An important item for many real estate owners is *special reports*. Institutional owners regularly analyze their portfolios, and the asset manager often needs additional data from the management firm in order to complete a report. The request may be to revise a budget, provide a five-year projection, or analyze the impact of a major renovation. It is common for the asset manager to give the firm only a few days to prepare such a report. These

Strategizing the Management Agreement 227

Preparing for Negotiations

Successful negotiations require knowledge of the property and the market, understanding of the prospective client's needs, and an assessment of your negotiating position and that of your competition. Convincing the prospective client that you can meet his or her needs also requires an effective presentation and appropriate pricing of your services.

Research has shown that negotiators who set targets obtain more favorable results from their negotiations than those who do not. Some potential targets for negotiating a management agreement include specific fees, the period or term of the agreement, cancellation penalties, the exclusive right to sell the property, and the exclusive right to lease a commercial property.

Before negotiations are begun, the importance of this potential management account to the firm must be determined.

- Will it establish the firm's position in a new geographic area?
- Will it add a new property type to the firm's portfolio?
- Will it strengthen the firm's current portfolio of a property type(s)?
- Will it create a relationship with a specific property owner or asset management firm?

If the property or the management relationship will accomplish certain goals for the firm, greater flexibility in negotiating fees and non-monetary provisions of the management agreement may be appropriate.

Because the management agreement contains both monetary and non-monetary provisions, it is a good idea to list the negotiable provisions and fees in the particular agreement and establish priorities. It is important to establish a fee structure, know what minimum fees are acceptable for the management firm, decide what concessions can be made, be able to offer modified or alternative positions on negotiable items, and know which issues are non-negotiable. You also have to be prepared to terminate negotiations if the best interests of the management firm are not being served, either because the fee structure is inadequate or because provisions required by the property owner are onerous. (More information on proposal contents and presentation strategies can be found in Chapter 8.)

---

types of requests can create havoc for the management firm, yet the client's needs must be met. The asset managers, themselves, often are not given much advance notice of the analyses they must perform, so they have to make their special requests to the management company with short deadlines. This situation cannot be avoided; however, a discussion with the asset manager or property owner regarding the content of the report and requesting an extension of the due date may alleviate some of the disruption. [NOTE: Asset manager turnover is another factor that can complicate the relationship with an institutional owner—e.g., if the new appointee has different expectations of the management company and its staff or is favorably predisposed toward another firm that would like to acquire the management account.]

Additional services—items not specifically mentioned in the management agreement—are a potential area of conflict between the management

> **Negotiation Positions**
>
> In preparing to negotiate a management agreement, you will need to identify:
>
> - Your ideal position—the best possible deal for the management company (maximum),
> - Your fallback position—the terms you are willing to accept (minimum),
> - Concessions you are willing to make—which points you can yield and which are non-negotiable, and
> - When to bow out—the point at which continuing negotiations would no longer be worthwhile.

firm and the property owner. It is usually difficult and often not advisable to say no to a client's special requests—service companies, including real estate management firms, routinely provide services beyond the scope of their contracts to maintain a good client relationship. As clients' requests escalate, however, the management company must decide when to charge extra for the additional service. There are approaches to this sensitive issue that can avoid conflict or disappointment. First and most important is to distinguish between standard and additional services in discussions with the property owner prior to executing the management agreement. On the other hand, services provided and charged for may be perceived as a *conflict of interest* if the intent to charge is not disclosed properly. Use of a subsidiary maintenance company to provide property maintenance services without disclosing the management company's ownership role is an example discussed in Chapter 8.

The Issue of Fees

A continual and predictable income stream is necessary for the survival and success of a real estate management firm. The majority of its income is earned from activities associated with managing the firm's portfolio. There are no standard management fees or leasing commissions in property management. However, there are several factors that determine the types of services provided and the fees to compensate for them.

The first variable to consider in determining an appropriate fee is the *owner's goals and objectives*. The amount of time that will be spent managing a property is often influenced by the property owner's short- or long-term investment goals. For instance, if the owner is planning to sell the property within the next twelve months, the property may need a major renovation. If that is the case, the management firm will be called upon to coordinate a major remodeling and/or construction project during the initial term of the agreement and raise rents quickly to increase NOI and value, and there is no assurance that the firm will be retained to continue managing the property after it is sold. Such a potential short-term management agreement with a major time investment by the real estate manager may require a higher management fee than would a property where less management time is required and there is a better possibility of a long-term contract.

The second variable is the *level of service* the management firm will provide (e.g., on-site management or the frequency of visits by the real estate manager; the frequency and complexity of reporting). A high level of service requires more time from the entire management team than does a moderate or low level of service. A property owner who lives near his or her property, is familiar with the market, and needs only a basic monthly accounting report, will often prefer a lower level of service than an out-of-state institutional owner does.

The *complexity* or difficulty of the management and leasing assignment is one of the most important variables in establishing a management fee. Deferred maintenance, criminal activities in the neighborhood and possibly on the property, a building renovation, marketing of a troubled residential property, or hiring and training new site personnel will require more of the manager's time than would a property that has none of these problems.

The *location* of the property in relation to the management office is a variable that is easy to overlook. However, when a property is more than a two-hour drive from the manager's office, each visit to it can consume a half day or a full day. Other properties may be only a short distance from the manager's office, and some will have an on-site manager. Excessive travel time adds to the cost of managing a property.

There is also a great deal of *competition* for management accounts. The number of REITs has increased rapidly, and these entities have taken almost all of their management in house. This strategy has been a two-edged sword, creating competition for fee management companies on the one hand and employment opportunities for real estate managers on the other. Likewise, many developers, brokerage firms, syndicators, and institutional owners have entered the property management business, either to offset income lost from their primary real estate business or to create a new profit center or to have more control over their properties. This has meant existing properties being taken off the market for fee management—often at a time when real estate development was slow or nonexistent—and the universe of properties available for third-party management being shrunk as the number of entities providing property management services grew.

While evaluating the *cost to manage* a property, one must also be cognizant of market conditions and market fees. Market conditions create a fee range for all properties. In addition to knowing the range of market fees, you need a reliable estimate of what it will cost the firm to manage the particular property at breakeven. Once this cost is known, you can determine an appropriate fee to propose. The minimum acceptable fee for services should cover the salaries of the staff member or members assigned to the property exclusively. It should also reimburse the costs of compiling

> **Factors That Determine Management Services and Fees**
> - The property's owner's goals and objectives.
> - The level of service provided by the property management firm.
> - The complexity of the management and leasing assignment.
> - The location of the property.
> - Competition for the management business.
> - The expected cost of managing the property.
> - The management company's cost of doing business.
> - The importance of the account to the management firm.
> - The firm's relationship with the property owner.
> - The property owner's perception of an appropriate fee for managing (and possibly leasing) the property.

accounting data and preparing monthly reports to the owner and carry a proportionate share of the firm's general and administrative overhead (i.e., the costs of operating the management company). Consider, too, the nature of the arrangement. For example, if an established client is offering an additional property for management, and the client's property which you have already managed for five years is operating efficiently, it may be prudent to propose a more competitive fee to acquire the additional business or offer to negotiate a lower fee within the existing arrangement (because of the efficiency).

Another variable in establishing the management fee is the *importance of the account* to the management company. A firm may be willing to manage a property for a small profit or even a breakeven (minimum) fee in order to establish a relationship with a particular property owner, or to enter a new market or add a new property type to its portfolio. The property might also offer the opportunity to earn leasing or sales commissions, which could offset low compensation for management—i.e., a trade-off. Note, however, that such a trade-off has inherent risks. If the manager fails to lease or sell the property as contracted, the loss will be greater because there will be no commission to offset the lower management fee. A wiser move might be to negotiate a standard management fee set off against the commission or a flat fee for marketing the property regardless of whether it is sold. If the management firm already has a relationship with a property owner—perhaps managing other properties or providing other compensable services such as leasing—it may be willing to manage the property at a smaller profit margin.

The final variable is the property *owner's perception* of an appropriate management fee. There may be an opportunity to influence the owner's opinion of a fair fee prior to negotiation of the management contract, during the early discussions of the particular challenges of managing and leasing the owner's property.

> ### The Base Management Fee
>
> The primary fee for most management accounts, and the greatest source of income for the management company, is the base management fee. It serves as compensation for those activities necessary to operate the managed property on a day-to-day basis. These services generally comprise accounting and financial reporting, resident or commercial tenant relations, maintenance management, marketing and leasing of residential properties (including prospect screening and selection and compliance with applicable laws), and administrative activities, although other services required under the management agreement may be included as well. Usually, the base management fee is a percentage of the gross rental income collected (i.e., the property's effective gross income). However, it can also be a dollar amount per unit (sometimes referred to as a dollars-per-door fee for residential properties), a cost per square foot of building area, or a fixed amount (flat fee) per month.
>
> Many property owners prefer to pay a percentage of the income collected. Since this type of fee grows as the amount of rental income increases, it serves as an incentive for management to collect all of the property's rental income on a timely basis. On the other hand, an owner may prefer a fixed monthly fee, especially when a large increase in the property's income is expected, and that increase is not due to the management firm's efforts—for instance, a major tenant in an office building may have a significant rent increase become effective shortly after new management takes over.
>
> Management firms usually prefer a monthly fee based on whichever amount is greater, a percentage of the collected rental income or a set minimum monthly fee. For example, the management fee for a 50,000-square-foot office building might be four percent of the collected income versus a minimum fee of $2,000 per month. If the property experiences a significant period of high vacancy or a major tenant withholds rent, management would be guaranteed compensation for its services via the minimum fee. (The minimum fee is usually equivalent to the firm's cost to manage the property.)

Types of Fees. There are several services a real estate management company can offer. Each can be offered independently for a separate fee, or they can be bundled together and offered for a single fee. It is common for the base property management services to be bundled together for one fee (see accompanying box), with additional services provided for separate fees.

When establishing a *base management fee,* other potential fees that can be earned in conjunction with managing the property should also be considered. Leasing and brokerage commissions, rehab and major maintenance supervision fees, and tenant improvement supervision fees for commercial properties are examples. Because a fee based on the estimated cost to manage the property plus a profit factor may result in a proposed management fee above the market range, company executives must know the range of fees in the market and structure the company to operate efficiently and profitably so it can set its fees at the level necessary to obtain management accounts. Another possible approach to consider is inclusion of *incentive fees*—e.g., a predetermined dollar amount or a fractional added percentage as a bonus for the early or effective accomplishment of a specific objective—to help compensate for a more competitive base management fee.

For those properties that have on-site maintenance or management personnel, a separate *payroll administration fee* may be charged. Usually expressed as a percentage of the gross salaries paid to the on-site personnel, this fee is intended to reimburse the management firm for the additional time necessary for the accounting department to provide the payroll service and the added risk the firm carries in the form of possible claims against its workers' compensation account if any on-site personnel are injured on the job and against its unemployment insurance account if a site employee is terminated and files a grievance.

There are several opportunities to earn *construction and major maintenance supervision fees* on all types of properties because some kind of renovation, remodeling, or rehabilitation is likely to be done during their economic life. An opportunity often available in the management of commercial properties, especially office and medical buildings, is tenant improvement supervision. The manager of the property may be responsible for coordinating the design and construction of the improvements to a tenant's leased space, working with the property's architect or space planner and with the general contractor (and possibly subcontractors) and the tenant. The fee for construction supervision or coordination is usually a percentage of the cost of the job. Coordination and supervision of these construction activities is outside the scope of basic property management services. Planning and implementing major maintenance jobs such as replacing a roof or resurfacing a parking lot are likewise not considered normal duties under a management agreement. (Major maintenance is usually defined in the management agreement as a single job, the cost of which exceeds a predetermined amount—e.g., $10,000.)

A major source of revenue from commercial properties is *leasing commissions,* which can exceed the base management fee. For instance, the annual management fee for a 50,000-square-foot office building might be $38,000, while the commission for finding a tenant to lease 10,000 square feet at an annual rent of $20 per square foot for five years, based on five percent of the rent during the first five years of the lease, is $50,000. If the management company has the expertise and capability to provide marketing and leasing services for the property, an exclusive arrangement to lease the property can be sought. Even if the property owner selects another firm to lease the commercial property, management company executives may offer to supervise the leasing activity, negotiate the terms and lease provisions on behalf of the property owner, and prepare the lease documents. Since the real estate manager will have to administer the lease, this arrange-

> ### Income from Ancillary Services
>
> There are also countless sources of ancillary income for a real estate management company that has the capability to provide other services. These adjunct services can be offered individually or bundled together and offered to a property owner whose real estate investments are self-managed. Such services include:
>
> - Specific accounting and reporting services.
> - Specific maintenance or janitorial services.
> - Auditing a property's accounting or financial reporting to ensure that commercial tenants are billed correctly for their share of a building's operating or common area maintenance (CAM) expenses.
> - Providing consulting services for specific management, operations, or leasing assignments.
> - Serving as a court-appointed receiver.
> - Conducting a market survey to determine rental rates or a sale price.
> - Providing a broker's opinion of property value (this may require certification and licensing as an appraiser).
> - Performing due diligence for the acquisition or sale of a property.
> - Conducting regulatory compliance surveys regarding accessibility under the Americans with Disabilities Act (ADA), indoor air quality (IAQ), etc.
> - Giving expert witness testimony for a trial.
>
> It is also possible for a firm to unbundle its management services and offer them singly or in other combinations to address a property owner's specific needs. (More specific information on adjunct services can be found in Chapter 7.)

ment helps assure consistency of lease terms while averting problems that can arise if details related to operating expense pass-throughs (CAM costs) are not handled uniformly. The best way to avoid any misunderstandings among leasing agent, real estate manager, and prospective tenant in this type of situation is to document the arrangement—i.e., the leasing agent should keep the manager informed, in writing, of the progress of negotiations and any promises made to the tenant prospect. The fee for this service may be a percentage of the revenue generated (e.g., one percent of the rental income for each lease for the first five years of the lease term) or a rate per square foot (e.g., fifty cents or one dollar per square foot) for all spaces leased.

Another potential commission opportunity arising out of the management arrangement is the *sale of the property*. The management firm may attempt to obtain an exclusive to sell the property, but this is often very difficult to negotiate. If the "right to sell" cannot be secured, management company executives should ask for a *transaction fee* to compensate for the additional work required of the manager of the property and the firm's accounting and administrative staffs to provide the selling agent, prospective buyers, and lenders with the information they need to analyze the property, show the property, answer questions, and other activities (e.g., obtain estoppel certificates) required to complete the sale transaction. Any arrangements related to the sale of the property should be documented in a separate sales agreement and *not* part of the management agreement.

Still another possibility is a fee for *refinancing*. If someone other than the real estate manager refinances the property, management company executives may ask for a *loan coordination fee* for administrative and other services provided to assist in closing the loan. The justification of this fee is similar to that of the sales transaction fee.

Every year the manager should review the real estate tax assessment and recommend to the property owner whether to appeal the amount of the tax or the assessed valuation of the property. *Tax appeal* is another service that can be offered to the property owner for a fee (if the company has personnel qualified to do this).

Whose Management Agreement Will be Used?

Each management company may develop its own management agreement or use another firm's agreement (with permission) as the basis for developing its own form. The agreement should provide the management firm with the protections it believes are necessary for it to manage property for another party. At one time, real estate managers insisted on using their own agreement form, and this was not challenged because few property owners had access to an agreement form; nor did they want to incur the cost of having an attorney draft one for them.

However, as insurance companies, banks, and pension funds became owners of large portfolios of residential and commercial properties, they (or their advisors) developed management agreements of their own. Because of the size and complexity of their portfolios, these institutional owners needed a standard agreement form in order to administer all the properties in their portfolios and interface with several property management firms effectively. Another reason for developing their own agreements was to have a form that provided them with the protections they wanted.

Though either party's agreement is negotiable and changes are often made to whatever form is used, the party whose agreement is being used is usually in a better negotiating position. All their issues are presented in a format acceptable to them at the outset, and the other party must negotiate changes it wants made as well as put forward other issues that are not addressed in the agreement as presented. Seldom will an institution or its advisors agree to use the management firm's agreement form when it has its own. In these instances, management company executives must understand the provisions in the management agreement to be used and be skilled in negotiating so that each party's basic objectives will be met. In which case, it is simply good business practice to ask to review the property owner's agreement form in advance of final negotiations in order to better understand the issues and how they are addressed. A savvy management company executive might even offer to sign a *letter of intent* in order to impress upon the property owner that execution of the management agreement document will merely formalize the previously agreed-upon terms.

The property and its management requirements as well as the property owner's desires or level of sophistication should be considered in preparing the agreement documentation. Aspects of the management services to be provided often dictate the amount of detail necessary. A brief agreement is usually easier to understand because there are fewer issues. Its advantage is that an owner of a small property, for example, may find such brevity less imposing and be more willing to sign it. A more-extensive management agreement is needed to address issues in depth, especially complex issues that can lead to disputes between the management firm and the property owner. The goal is to enable each party to better understand what is expected from and by the other. Often the services of an attorney may be needed to provide guidance in addressing specific issues; legal counsel for both parties (owner and management) should review the negotiated document before it is signed. *This is very important.* Regardless of whose form is used, the agreement should spell out both management's authority to take action independently and those actions that will require consultation with and/or written approval from the owner.

We believe a real estate management firm should have its own management agreement form. If the firm manages both residential and commercial properties, a separate agreement for each property type will be necessary. However, one should be willing to negotiate the prospective client's agreement form if an account is worthwhile financially. (The IREM general Management Agreement form can provide some of the boilerplate language for a start-up company's initial form, or it can be used as is or with only slight modification for straightforward management arrangements.)

Contents of the Management Agreement

A well-drafted management agreement is essential to establishing and maintaining a good relationship between the management firm and the property owner. The agreement will state each party's responsibilities and authority and guarantee certain protections to one party from the other. A well-crafted and well-negotiated agreement should minimize or eliminate most misunderstandings between the parties. A poorly drafted agreement, on the other hand, will not resolve misunderstandings and may lead to disputes between the management firm and the property owner, raising questions of trust, undermining the confidence of the parties in each other, and creating an uncomfortable relationship for both parties. This type of situation often results in early termination of a management agreement and, possibly, litigation between the parties. (The requirement for written documentation to comply with state real estate laws was pointed out at the beginning of this chapter.)

There is no industry standard property management agreement form useable for all types of properties. Each property type has unique issues that must be addressed. For instance, the number of homeowners' association meetings the property manager must attend—and how much time to be spent there—is an issue specific to managing condominiums and cooperatives. Another example is the differences between the real estate manager's responsibilities and compensation for marketing and leasing, which is part of the management of residential properties but a separate activity at commercial properties. A particular property owner may require additional services or negotiate to eliminate a basic property management responsibility, such as accounting, because the owner has this service available in house. Each property and the agreement for its management requires individual attention to the details of the management activity in fulfillment of the owner's investment goals. The language of the contract must be clear and correct to facilitate interpretation of intent—or serve as documented proof—if issues regarding the management arrangement need to be adjudicated in a court of law.

The provisions described in the following sections are found in most management agreements. They are presented here from a management perspective. Additional or different provisions may be necessary to tailor an agreement to the specific needs of a subject property or to fulfill the requirements of the property's owner.

Establishing the Management Relationship. The first part of the document names the parties to the management agreement and establishes the date they entered into it. (It must show the name of the *owner in title* of the property and not just the owner's representative.) This is followed by appointment of the management firm as the manager of the property. If the property is an office or medical building, shopping center or industrial property, the manager may also be the exclusive leasing agent for the property. The property itself is defined by a name, address, and descriptive information. Additional details regarding its location may be necessary or appropriate, particularly if only a portion of a larger complex is the subject of the agreement or if similarity of street names or building names might bring the location or identity into question.

If on-site management personnel are required, the owner may be expected to allow the management company to have *office space* at the property—rent free—and the cost of operating the site office (e.g., telephone, office equipment, and supplies necessary for such management personnel to perform their duties) would be an operating expense of the property. (The on-site costs of managing a commercial property are often included in the operating expenses passed through to the tenants.) For an apartment building that requires an on-site manager, the property owner may be expected to provide an *apartment,* rent free, for the site manager and, possibly, for one or more maintenance personnel. If the building does not require a full-time manager on site, the owner may be asked to discount the rent for a part-time site manager.

The agreement may include a declaration that the management firm will devote its reasonable best efforts to managing the property in a first-class professional manner and performing its duties in a diligent, careful, and vigilant manner. However, such subjective verbiage may be omitted—it is inherent in the appointment of the manager that he or she (or the management firm) is to provide "best" services as negotiated with the owner.

There may also be a blanket recital of management's responsibilities—i.e., that management will not knowingly allow the use of the property for any purpose that might void the owner's insurance coverages or violate governmental restrictions, statutes, ordinances, or regulations; that management will use its best effort to secure full compliance of lessees, concessionaires, and anyone else occupying space at the property; and that management is authorized to refund security deposits to residents or tenants as required under their respective lease agreements. However, many of the components of this recital are usually addressed in specific provisions, and this separate declaration is not necessary. On the other hand, a short-form agreement may utilize such a blanket recital when more detailed provisions are not specifically required. The typical contents to address specific issues follow.

Bank Accounts and Related Items. Space is usually provided to show the name to be used in establishing the *operating and/or reserve account* for the property and its owner. The property owner is required to provide funds in advance *(initial deposit)* so that management can pay the operating expenses of the property from the moment of take-over. A specific dollar amount, based on anticipated expenses for the first month and expected receipt of rent payments, is usually stated. The property owner is also required to maintain a minimum balance in the operating and/or reserve account; if the balance *(contingency reserve)* falls below the agreed-upon amount, the owner would be required to deposit funds to restore the account balance. It may be appropriate to identify a mechanism for addressing such financial shortfalls—e.g., via electronic transfer of funds. (This provision may also authorize management to collect rents and to disburse, handle, and hold the monies collected. However, such authorizations are usually addressed separately and in detail.)

Some states and some property owners require all security deposits to be held in a separate *security deposit account* although the law in some states may allow the commingling of security deposits and operating funds of commercial properties. These separate accounts may be interest-bearing (e.g., bank savings accounts) or non-interest-bearing trust or escrow accounts. (Chapter 4 provides a more-detailed discussion of trust accounts from an accounting perspective.)

Since most property owners (and many states) require management to obtain *fidelity bonds* on all personnel who handle their money, it is wise to include a provision stating that the management firm will obtain a fidelity bond and indicate the amount of the bond (this may be stated as a dollar figure or a multiple of the monthly rental income). If the firm's coverage is inadequate for the owner's requirements, provision should be made for additional coverage, which may be secured at the owner's expense. (Some agreements may provide for all such bonds to be obtained at the owner's expense or reimbursed to the management firm out of property funds.) Fidelity bonding of management personnel who handle company funds as well as client's funds is a wise investment regardless of management agreement stipulations. (More information on bonding of employees can be found in Chapter 11.)

Collections and Receipts. Usually, management is specifically authorized to *collect rents and other payments* from lessees, concessionaires, and other occupants of the property. Management may also be authorized to institute legal proceedings in the owner's name and at the owner's expense, with or without the owner's prior written permission, in order to effect such collections. In addition, it may be necessary or appropriate to include specific authorization for management to turn over past-due accounts to a collection agency, in which case a delinquency period or dollar amount should be stated.

In the management of any type of property, management's authority to evict tenants for nonpayment of rent or to hire legal counsel with respect to eviction proceedings may be a desirable inclusion. State and local jurisdictions often prescribe specific procedures to be followed for evictions, and all parties to the management agreement should be aware of those requirements and define the eviction authority accordingly.

Usually management is also authorized to collect fees or charges for late payment of rent, returned checks, and other administrative expenses. (The amounts of such fees or charges may be stated in residents' or commercial tenants' leases.) Sometimes these monies are retained by management as compensation for the additional collection efforts if allowed by law. The agreement should state this fact clearly as a disclosure.

Payments and Disbursements. Management should be authorized to pay all expenses for operating the property to the extent that funds are available from rent receipts and other collections or provided by the owner. The agreement may state that management is authorized to pay all *operating* *expenses* without specific owner approval if these expenses are included in the owner-approved operating budget or if an unbudgeted expense is below a stated dollar amount. After all authorized expenses have been paid, all *proceeds* (funds in excess of the established contingency reserve) are usually remitted to the owner at the end of the month.

If the agreement form does not address items usually considered outside the domain of strict operating expenses—e.g., mortgage, taxes, insurance—the property owner should be required to inform management in writing if it is to make *debt service* payments or handle other major expenditures out of the operating account. (The contingency reserve should be reviewed and adjusted when such a change is made.) Ideally, the agreement will include a provision that addresses this issue and its ramifications.

The agreement should make clear that *management is not obligated to advance funds* to the property owner, or to the property's operating or security deposit accounts, in order to pay any of the owner's expenses. However, if any such advance is made, it should be considered a loan subject to repayment at a standard rate of interest and so stated in the agreement. (Although it may be advisable to provide for extenuating circumstances, any such advance should be solely at the firm's discretion. In actual practice, this is almost never done.)

Financial and Other Reports. Typically, management is required to maintain such *records, books, and accounts* as are necessary to document the financial transactions of operating the property. However, all such records belong to the property owner. For owners who require use of their own accounting formats, the agreement should require an example to be included as an exhibit.

Typically, the property owner will be sent the management firm's standard *accounting and financial reports* on or before a set date each month. The agreement should list the monthly reports provided routinely within the management fee and those reports, such as depreciation or amortization of real assets or interest accruals, which will not be provided to the property owner. (It may be appropriate to indicate other types of reports the firm has the capability of generating but are not part of the "standard" monthly array. These might be available but require advance notice and an additional charge.)

Management is typically required to prepare and submit to the owner an *annual operating budget.* Usually this provision not only states when the owner is to receive this budget, but also addresses its approval. The provision may further state that the property owner has thirty days to approve (or reject) the budget; if there is no response within that time, the budget may be considered approved and management authorized to operate the property in accordance with it. This latter proviso is important for continued operation of the managed property. However, it is more typical for ownership and management to have one or more discussions of the budget, resulting in a mutually agreeable spending plan approved by the owner.

Management usually has no responsibility for the preparation or submission of any federal, state, or local *income tax reports* on the owner's behalf. However, *real estate taxes* may be expected to be paid out of the operating account, as may *employer taxes* required because of the employment of on-site staff. (When on-site personnel are employees of the property owner, a *power of attorney* authorizing management to pay such employer taxes may have to be executed separately. This particular arrangement should be scrutinized by legal counsel.)

The agreement should provide for the property owner to have the *right to audit* management's accounts and records regarding the property. It is expected that such audits would take place during normal business hours. Such owner-initiated audits should be at the owner's expense.

Marketing and Leasing. Management agreements typically include a provision authorizing management to advertise the property for rent. For a residential property (e.g., apartment complex, mobile home park, single-family home), the *advertising* is an owner expense paid out of the property's operating account. Advertising vehicles are usually management's choice, but discussion with the owner beforehand will ensure "no surprises." Since commercial tenants are usually acquired through means other than advertising, as such, who pays this expense for a commercial property is negotiable.

The leasing process and the lease document differ with the type of property to be managed. The first three provisions discussed below are generally applicable, in principle, to any type of property; however, they are most often seen in agreements covering residential properties. The last three provisions are exclusively applicable to commercial properties, especially those at which leasing is addressed as an entirely separate process from management of the property.

> *Authority to Lease:* Management should be authorized to execute, modify, and cancel leases on behalf of the property owner. However, management may be required to obtain written permission to execute leases that exceed a certain period. For example, if apartment rentals are typically for a lease term of one year, a two-year lease would be an exception requiring written approval. Office building leases are typically for three to five years, so a ten-year lease would be an exception. Although management typically signs residential leases as the owner's agent, the agreement may call for the owner to sign commercial leases. (A copy of the agreed-upon lease form—the firm's standard lease or the owner's preferred form—may be attached to the agreement as an exhibit.)
>
> *Rental Rates:* Management should be authorized to establish, change, and revise all rents and other charges for the property; however, prior

written approval from the property owner may be required before rental rates are lowered.

Lease Enforcement: Management should be authorized to enforce leases by means of notices, court orders, and legal action, including eviction. All costs for the enforcement of any lease that are not paid by the resident would be a property expense. Note that limitations on how eviction proceedings are conducted within the local jurisdiction may further define management's role in these actions.

Exclusive Leasing Agent: Management may be appointed as the exclusive leasing agent for a commercial property.

Leasing Commission: If an exclusive leasing arrangement is negotiated, a provision should be included that states how the commission is to be determined and when it is to be paid. The commission might be a percent of the rental income or a dollar amount per square foot, and payment might be divided—e.g., half when the lease is executed by the property owner and the tenant and half when the tenant opens for business or when rent payment commences.

Leasing Supervision Fee: Another firm may have the leasing exclusive for the property, but the owner may ask management to supervise the leasing firm or participate in the lease negotiations on the owner's behalf. In such situations, a separate fee might be paid to management for this service. Alternatively, a leasing provision might only spell out management's role in the leasing process, and the relevant commissions or fees would be listed separately in the compensation section of the agreement.

To facilitate leasing, the agreement might include some basic parameters that would apply—rental rates, duration of lease terms, types of concessions acceptable to the owner (e.g., free rent, tenant improvement and/or moving allowances), financial or credit rating requirements for tenant approval. These might be stated as minimums or maximums or as a range, depending on the parameter and the property type.

Employment of Personnel. In most situations, management will be given *authority to hire on-site employees* for the operation of the property, all of whose salaries, benefits, and expenses would be paid out of the operating account.

In its supervisory role, management would be responsible to comply with all applicable federal and state labor laws. However, the property owner should be required to *indemnify (hold harmless)* the management firm and pay all court costs in the event of any suit or claim arising out of a labor law violation. To compensate for its payroll administration costs, a separate *administrative fee* is often paid to the management firm. (As stated earlier, this constitutes a reimbursement rather than a "fee for services." In some states, the revenue from this practice might be taxed as corporate income.) The fee should be stated in the agreement, either in the personnel section or in the section where other compensation is itemized.

Maintenance and Repairs. One or more provisions of the management agreement usually address property maintenance and repairs. Management should be given the authority to make *ordinary repairs, replacements, and alterations* to the property and pay the costs out of the property's operating account. However, purchase and maintenance *contracts* for the property are usually made in the name of the property owner.

Management should also be authorized to perform *non-budgeted repairs and maintenance* on the property provided the expense does not exceed a predetermined dollar amount, otherwise the property owner's prior (usually written) approval would be required for such an expenditure. However, provision should be made for *emergency repairs* to be made without the property owner's approval—i.e., situations that threaten the lives or safety of people on the property or preservation of the premises. Repairs of damage caused by storms or accidents are examples.

Management should be able to purchase as a property expense *equipment and supplies* that are budgeted. Usually, non-budgeted items are allowed to be purchased and charged to the property without prior owner approval unless the cost exceeds a predetermined amount.

Authority of the Manager. When the management arrangement is between a management firm and the property owner, the individual who will be assigned to manage the property may be identified in the agreement along with a provision for authorizing all employees of the management firm to act as the owner's agent or contractor. The management firm would be authorized to execute contracts and other documents on the owner's behalf in order to perform its obligation to maintain the property. Often there are stipulations regarding the terms of such contracts (duration, dollar amounts)—i.e., setting limitations on what management is authorized to do without prior written approval from the owner. Contracting may be addressed separately or within the section defining management's duties and responsibilities, usually with regard to maintenance of the property.

Owner's Obligations. The property owner should be responsible for obtaining adequate *insurance* on the property and its systems and facilities against physical damage and against liability arising out of injuries to people or damage to others' property that occurs at or on the managed property. In addition, the owner should be asked to list the management firm as an additional named insured party on all of the liability policies held for the property. Usually a management agreement—most notably those originating with the prospective management—catalog some if not all of the coverages expected to be in place. It may also provide for management to obtain appropriate insurance coverages, at the owner's expense (charged against the operating account), in the event such insurance is not in place within so many days of execution of the agreement. It is also desirable to include a requirement for a written notice of default or cancellation of policies to be sent to the manager as well as the owner.

Preferably, management should have no responsibility for *building compliance* with applicable laws and regulations other than to notify ownership of any noncompliance discovered or to forward to the owner specific complaints or notices regarding dangerous situations, hazardous materials, or other such problems. These include local building codes, life safety and fire codes, occupancy standards, energy codes, the Americans with Disabilities Act, and various regulations administered by federal agencies such as the EPA, OSHA, and HUD. Furthermore, the property owner should be required to indemnify the management firm and its personnel from all costs of compliance or litigation expenses arising out of the owner's or a third party's action regarding hazardous substances on the property. (In particular, the owner should be responsible for any clean-up costs or civil or criminal fines related to such hazardous substances.) Desirable as these types of provisions may be to preclude management being liable for building compliance, state or local laws may prohibit such language in an agreement.

Other Elements of the Relationship Between the Parties. Traditionally, a management firm was contracted as the agent of the property owner. However, some property owners have been hiring management firms as independent contractors rather than as agents. (These are mostly institutions concerned that the management firm might have too much authority as their agent or that management's activities might subject the ownership to additional liability.) The management agreement should state the relationship between the parties and incorporate appropriate protections for both parties. Typical of the provisions relating to an *agency relationship* are the following:

> *Agency:* The agreement should state that the appointed manager (and the management company) is the agent of the owner and that establishment of the management arrangement does not constitute a partnership or joint venture agreement; nor does it make the manager (or the management company) a direct employee of the property owner.
>
> *Waivers:* The agreement should declare that management makes no representations or warranties regarding profitability of the property to be managed under the agreement.
>
> *Management Assumes No Liability:* The management firm should not be liable for acts of the property owner, or any previous ownership or management of the property, or for the acts of commercial tenants and/or residents of the property.

Owner Representations: The owner should warrant that he or she is, in fact, authorized to enter into a management agreement, that there are no other agreements in force that affect the property to be managed, except leases, and that the property is in compliance with all applicable zoning ordinances, building codes, and such other laws, statutes, ordinances, and regulations as may apply to the property, including environmental regulations regarding hazardous materials.

Indemnification of Management: The agreement should require the owner to indemnify and hold the managing agent harmless from claims for personal injury and/or property damage occurring in connection with the property. It should further declare that this and other provisions regarding indemnification survive termination of the agreement in the event of any subsequent litigation arising out of the management company's role as agent under the agreement.

Management's status as an *independent contractor* may require modification of other provisions of a management agreement. (The distinctions between independent contractors and employees are explored in Chapter 5, and legalities of agency status are addressed in Chapter 12.)

Management Fees and Other Compensation. There are, as noted earlier in this chapter, a variety of fees that can accrue to a management company in addition to the base management fee. Leasing commissions and leasing supervision fees were addressed in the preceding discussion of marketing and leasing as management activities. Similarly, a payroll administration fee was discussed in regard to on-site personnel. In general, however, it is prudent to itemize all fees and commissions in a single section of the agreement to avoid misunderstandings about compensation issues. If statements about fees are included in provisions that address what those fees compensate, it may be appropriate to include a cross reference to the general compensation section, and vice versa, so a particular fee is addressed only once. Following are some of the types of fees that may be cataloged in a management agreement.

Management: The management fee should compensate the management company for its services in managing the day-to-day operations of the property. It is prudent to document exactly what management services will be compensated by this fee or, conversely, what services will *not* be included in the fee. This type of declaration—it may be a list attached to the agreement as an exhibit—defines the basic fee beyond which separate, additional compensation would be required. The agreement should include a specific statement addressing *how* the fee is to be determined—e.g., a flat fee (required in condominium or cooperative property management) or a percentage of the gross receipts versus a minimum monthly fee—and *when* it is to be paid, authorizing management to pay the fee as an operating expense. (When a percentage fee is negotiated, a definition of *gross receipts* should be included, along with a listing of specific inclusions and exclusions for purposes of computing the management fee.) Also, some states may charge occupation or "sales" taxes on professional services such as property management; the agreement should provide that any such taxes are to be paid by the property owner.

Residential Lease-Up Fee: For a new or rehabbed apartment property, the management firm might contract to achieve a successful lease-up—i.e., to a certain percentage occupancy—which would be compensated by a flat fee or a percentage fee. This might also apply in a "troubled" property with an extremely high vacancy rate in order to create rental income on which to base an adequate management fee.

Additional Services: Sometimes during the course of a management arrangement, a property owner may request services that are not customary management services or are not required under the management agreement. The agreement should require payment of a separate fee for any "additional" services that are not defined in the agreement.

Capital Improvements Supervision: Supervision of remodeling or rehabilitation of the property or major maintenance work whose cost exceeds a predetermined amount is not generally part of professional property management and should be separately compensated.

Tenant Improvement Construction Supervision: If management is to be responsible for supervising substantial tenant improvement construction at a commercial property, such supervision should be compensated by a separate fee charged to the property owner. (Typically, this fee is a percentage of the cost of the improvements.)

Additional Lessee Services: If a commercial tenant (or an apartment resident) requests or receives additional services that are not customarily provided under the management agreement, management should be allowed to charge the tenant (or resident) a fee for such services. (Such a fee would be paid direct to the management firm and not considered part of the property's income.)

Loan Coordination: If management's duties include assisting ownership in obtaining a new loan or restructuring the property's current loan (refinancing). such assistance should be compensated by an additional fee.

Money Management: Investment by management of property funds or other monies belonging to the property owner, at the owner's request, should be compensated by an administrative fee (often stated as a percentage of the interest earned).

Participation of management in the sale of the property, whether as exclusive sales agent under a separate sales agreement compensated by a brokerage commission or in a less direct role compensated by a transaction fee, is addressed earlier in this chapter and in Chapters 3 and 7 as well.

Duration and Termination. The *duration* or term of the agreement and its commencement and expiration dates are usually stated within the recitals at the beginning of the agreement form where the parties are named and management is appointed. It is often desirable to provide for continuity via automatic renewal from year to year unless the agreement is specifically terminated by mutual agreement of the parties or because of a specific breach. (This is sometimes referred to as an "evergreen" clause.)

The agreement should provide for *termination* by either party at the end of any term of the agreement (the initial period or subsequent renewal periods) upon written notice to the other party in advance. Usually a notice period of 10–30 days is provided. (Some property owners will insist on having the right to terminate the agreement *without cause* with a 30- or 60-day written notice.) It should also be possible for either party to terminate the agreement for a *breach of contract* that has not been corrected within a specified period—typically 30 days after receipt of notice—or upon transfer of ownership in the event the *property is sold*.

The owner's failure to act, inadequate liability insurance coverage, and excessive damage or condemnation (or taking under eminent domain) should also be addressed. The management company should be able to terminate the agreement if the owner permits insurance coverage to lapse or if, through other failure of the owner to take action, the property fails to comply with any applicable law or regulation. In these instances, termination should be effective upon service of written notice to the owner by the management company. In the event the property is destroyed or if it is taken by a governmental agency under eminent domain, either of which would preclude continued operation, the agreement should terminate automatically. If liability insurance coverage obtained by the owner is considered by management to be inadequate, and the parties cannot agree on an acceptable coverage amount, the agreement should be cancelable upon notice to the owner.

Termination compensation is a sensitive issue but one that needs consideration. The agreement should provide for management to be compensated if the agreement is terminated early, except when termination is for cause. Usually there is considerable expense incurred in the startup of management (physical take-over of management, verification of records, copying of documents, etc.)—a cost borne by the management company. The expectation is that the management fees earned over the term of the agreement will adequately compensate for the expense involved. Since early termination precludes recouping these costs normally, termination compensation of some kind is appropriate. The agreement may provide for the management fee to be prorated over the remainder of the term, although other approaches may work equally well.

After a management agreement is terminated or canceled, the management firm is obligated to return to the property owner (or his or her designated representative) copies of all documents and records pertaining to the management of the property; these belong to the owner. Likewise, all service contracts and personal property of the owner are transferred or assigned to the owner (or his or her designated representative). However, before these transfers can be made, operational details need to be addressed. Usually there is provision in the agreement for management to pay bills and close outstanding accounts before preparing a final accounting of the balance of income and expenses. This minimizes the hassle for both parties in "closing the books" on the management arrangement. (Specific termination procedures are outlined in Chapter 14.)

The obligations of the parties cease when the agreement is terminated, and the management company is entitled to receive whatever compensation is due it at the time. However, there is usually provision for a period of time to complete deals in progress when the agreement is terminated (typically 90–180 days). During this time, management can register with the owner a list of prospective tenants (or buyers) to whom overtures had been made regarding leasing (or sale) of the property. This also includes a proviso that if the property is leased (or sold) to any of those prospects within a predetermined time period (e.g., six months after termination of management), the management firm would be entitled to compensation for these types of activities (a fee or commission) as spelled out in the agreement.

Other Typical Contents. Management agreements also typically include clauses or provisions that address a variety of legal details. Following are examples:

Notices: Space is provided for the names and addresses of the individuals who are to receive notices on behalf of the parties, and usually there is a stipulation regarding the manner of delivery and what comprises receipt of notice.

Force Majeure: The management firm is excused for a delay in performance of its duties resulting from an event beyond its control (e.g., a strike or a natural disaster).

Applicable Law: Management agreements usually are governed by the laws of the state in which the property is located.

Entire Agreement: The agreement is declared to represent the full and complete agreement between the parties, that there are no other agreements or understandings between them regarding the particular property.

Agreement Binding The agreement is stated to be binding, not only on the parties, but on their heirs, successors, and assigns as well.

Tax Identification Numbers (TINs): Both parties' TINs are listed to facilitate their respective filing of federal information Form 1099 each year, if appropriate. (This allows the Internal Revenue Service to verify that the taxpayers reported earned income.)

Signatures: Space is provided for signatures of the authorized representatives of both parties; the authority of the signers should also be stated, and it may be appropriate to have the signatures witnessed or notarized.

Condominium Management Exceptions. In an agreement to manage a property where the residential units are individually owned—e.g., a condominium or homeowners' association—there should be provisions that address certain specific issues.

The management firm should be prohibited from providing maintenance services for individual units under the management agreement although the firm and the homeowner's association board may establish a separate written agreement that states how management may provide service to individual units and the manner in which such service will be compensated.

Usually there is a requirement for the manager of the property to attend meetings of the association board. A provision should be included that states the number of board meetings the manager must attend and the maximum time to be spent attending each meeting, with additional meetings and extra time being compensated on an hourly basis (at an agreed-upon rate). There should also be a provision that defines the common areas of the property and, thereby, delineates the maintenance responsibilities of the management firm.

Exhibits. An exhibit that itemizes the array of books, records, contracts, and plans, as well as an inventory of the owner's personal property, is often attached to and becomes a part of the management agreement. When that is the case, the agreement should include an acknowledgment of receipt of these items, usually under management services. (Transfer of records and other items usually takes place during official management takeover activities [see Chapter 10]; it may be acceptable or appropriate to catalog those items separately during take-over and have both parties acknowledge the exchange by their signatures. That document could be attached to the management agreement at a later time as an appendix.) Management agreements may also include as exhibits a legal description of the property, service contracts, and (possibly) a leasing commission schedule for commercial properties.

A Perspective on Management Agreements

Management agreements are the primary source of a management company's income and profits. Because the amount of income and the quality of the income stream are essential elements in determining the value of a management firm, management agreements and the relationships they establish are its life blood and vital to its continuing operation.

The Institute of Real Estate Management has published a general Management Agreement form and a Condominium and Homeowners' Association Management Agreement form, both of which provide serviceable boilerplate language for addressing most of the issues related to managing real estate. For a particular management arrangement, it is likely that some provisions in these generic forms may be modified or deleted, while others regarding details of the property's operations or the owner's requirements would have to be added. The respective Explanations provide supplementary information on negotiability of some issues, points that have specific implications or limitations, and provisions that may require amplification in a particular situation. The Explanations also include information on various laws that affect the management of real estate and should be taken into consideration in developing a management agreement. (While not necessarily requisite components of a specific agreement, the laws can affect how a property is managed and the cost of providing management services.) The Explanations further recommend seeking advice of legal counsel *before* using or modifying these generic management agreement forms, and we would underscore that recommendation.

10

Strategizing Management Take-Over

One of the most exciting activities in real estate management is assuming a new account. The prospect of additional income and profit for the management company brings with it the anticipation of taking on a new challenge. Each new account adds to the company's pool of experience and expertise, providing yet another selling point for your management services.

Take-over of a new account also includes considerable risk. Management is often assumed with little advance notice and little opportunity to prepare for the new account. The former management may have been relieved of the account—is also unhappy about losing it—and the property may have suffered from poor management. Sometimes there is no overlap in management that would allow you to obtain the records, review them, and have all of your systems in place on the day you take over. In addition to the possibility of making an incorrect decision while trying to effect a speedy transition, there is the danger of losing money for the property owner.

From the moment the new account is assumed, you will be expected to respond to requests from residents or commercial tenants, as well as the owner-client, and deal with contractors' questions, public officials' requests and demands, and assorted other problems and situations, even though you may not be adequately prepared. This obviously increases the potential for errors and may lead to problems in the future.

Take-over is a time for special care and caution. Before taking any action or answering any questions, it may be wise to do some research—better a correct response a bit late than a costly mistake that needs further correction. (In a perfect world, the management company would submit its bid for the management account, be awarded the contract, and have 30–60 days to perform its *due diligence* and prepare to take over.) This chapter will outline the procedure for assuming a new account, including use of a take-over checklist.

Planning the Take-Over

In planning the take-over of management, there are some basic questions that should be asked before you actually assume the new account. Answers to these questions will help you tailor a basic take-over checklist and establish time frames for completion of each step.

- What specific information do you need to have in order to do the job properly? As you contemplate this question, so many things will come to mind that you will quickly understand the need for a comprehensive checklist.
- When do you need the information? If the property will be taken over in January and the next real estate tax installment is not due till April, tax information will not be a high priority item initially. However, you must have it before the tax deadline. On the other hand, something that could shut down the building would be a very high priority—e.g., if the deadline for correcting a violation of the municipal fire code is imminent as you take over management. This kind of priority can be very intimidating since a new manager has enough to do immediately upon take-over without having to deal with emergencies. Putting off such items can only lead to more severe management problems in the future.
- Who will be responsible for gathering the information? While it is likely that more than one person will have some responsibility for collecting different types of information, especially in a large management company, only one individual should be in charge of overseeing the take-over procedures. Generally, the manager responsible for the property will be in charge, with assignments for collecting and analyzing specific information being given to accounting, maintenance, and other personnel. Regardless of how many people become involved in the process, the overall responsibility and authority should be vested in one person who is aware of the "big picture" and making sure that all the necessary information is collected and all the appropriate actions are taken in a timely fashion.
- Who will be using the information that is gathered? Different departments or functions within the management company will need specific information. For example, in taking over management of a shopping center, accounting will need sales reports from the retail tenants, but this information is also helpful to the manager in evaluating how successful individual merchants are. The maintenance staff will need

information about the work order system in place, but this information is also needed by accounting personnel because they will need to bill tenants for specific services. Emergency telephone number lists are of greatest importance to the manager of the property, but the accounting, leasing, and construction departments should also have copies in case they need to contact tenants or contractors directly when the manager is not available.

- Are there specific issues or considerations regarding the property that will require special attention, either by the manager or by outside experts? If such is the case, do these require priority upon take-over?

Other considerations in planning a take-over might include compatibility of the owner's and the management firm's accounting systems and adjustments that may be needed, the location of needed documents (they may be in the owner's hands, at the property, or with the current or prior management—or lost), and how the property is or was being managed (things you will have to change in order to manage the property effectively).

Typically, when one assumes the management of a smaller commercial property, there are few if any on-site employees to help a new manager find needed information or to maintain the relationship with the tenants during the transition period. At larger commercial properties with continuing on-site management, the third-party manager has more time and more flexibility. However, the new manager would still be well-advised to expedite the take-over process and minimize the need to rely on other people's word.

Conversely, most residential properties—with the exception of the smallest ones—have on-site employees who can assist in the transition. However, the sooner new management completes its due diligence, the sooner the manager assigned to the property will be working with facts rather than hearsay. Also, there is always a possibility that existing on-site employees may be sympathetic to the former management, in which case they may not be the most reliable source of information. (Strategies for acquiring different types of information are addressed later in this chapter.)

Creating a Take-Over Checklist

Because each property is a little different from every other property of its type, a checklist will ensure that all the necessary actions will be taken and that all records, plans, and other documents needed for management to run smoothly are acquired. While there may be valid reasons for having a separate checklist for every type of property managed by the firm, most take-over activities can be addressed by differentiating between commercial and residential properties and having one basic list for each.

A manager who has sole responsibility for take-over may create a simple numbered list of information items to be collected and actions to be taken, in the order of their general priority. Noting in the margin the date each item is completed may be an adequate record, especially if the property is small and take-over is straightforward. For most situations, however, it is necessary to anticipate a wide array of documents and issues. The larger the property and the more complex its operations, the more detailed the information needed.

It is generally a good idea to organize the take-over checklist items into larger categories (e.g., accounting, maintenance). This will make it easier to assign responsibilities to others and facilitate the transfer of information to other departments within the management company. While individual items can be numbered and the sequence within categories may be alphabetical, basing the order on relative importance may be more useful. On a pre-printed form, some blank spaces are usually included in each category so that unique features of a property or a particular management arrangement can be added. Creation of a master document as a computer file and having a separate library of optional items that can be incorporated to tailor the form for a particular residential or commercial property allows for flexibility while ensuring that basic points are always covered.

Regardless of how the checklist is prepared, it is fairly common to list the items to be checked in the left-hand column with spaces or columns at the right for making notes. Minimally there should be columns for indicating a due date and a completion date. Another column may be added to track assignments to other people. If some aspect is expected to require a period of time for completion, a column for listing a commencement date may be added.

Before you create a checklist form, there are some points to consider regarding your information needs, issues that may arise and ought to be anticipated, and some of the negatives that may be encountered if prior management was terminated for a reason other than expiration of their agreement.

Areas Needing Special Attention. Although real estate managers always try to be accurate and efficient, assuming a new account is inherently confusing. An unfamiliar office layout, a different approach to filing, duplication of information, and having to work against time limitations can make this activity extremely stressful for the manager. These conditions also represent potential for the situation to become chaotic. A generally cautious approach and careful attention to details are necessary to ensure that all the needed data are collected in a timely fashion. Because the information acquired during take-over will be the foundation of all your management activities throughout the term of your management agreement, the importance of such an approach cannot be overemphasized.

Since much of real estate management is paper-driven, all information should be carefully reviewed for accuracy before it is used as a basis for

> **Typical Categories for a Take-Over Checklist**
>
> - Accounting and administration—bank accounts, files, accounting records, collection procedures, payroll, budgets, etc.
> - Building and property—architectural drawings, plot plans, utility layouts, building systems (e.g., plumbing, HVAC), etc.
> - Compliance status—civil rights laws (fair housing, Americans with Disabilities Act, equal employment opportunity), labor laws (wages and hours), local building codes, etc.
> - Contracts/vendors—preventive maintenance and other services, leased equipment, etc.
> - Fire/life safety—fire extinguishing equipment, emergency procedures, applicable codes, etc.
> - Inspections—building exterior and interior, leased spaces, grounds, etc.
> - Insurance—types of policies, insurers, agents, etc.
> - Leases and leasing—application forms, lease forms, rent schedules, and other related information.
> - Legal issues—lawsuits and other claims.
> - Maintenance—equipment inventory, warranties, permits, etc.
> - Management office—employee benefits, personnel records, keys and key control, office procedures, equipment and supplies, etc.
> - Notice of new management—who needs to be notified, when, and how.
> - Occupants—current leases, security and other deposits, payment status, etc.
>
> This list is intended to be representative of a basic checklist. Unique aspects of different property types would also have to be documented. For example, commercial properties are likely to have tenant construction issues to be addressed as well as things like lease escalators, common area maintenance, and operating expense pass-throughs. Shopping centers typically have a merchants' association or marketing fund and sales reports for verifying percentage rents. Industrial sites and medical office buildings often have special waste-disposal considerations. At residential properties, there may be special features or amenities (e.g., coin-operated laundry facilities). For rental apartments, information on marketing strategies and rental traffic will be needed. Condominiums have the unique characteristics of monthly assessments to track, specialized documents and rules, and meetings of the board of directors and the homeowners. A manufactured housing community bills separately for utilities. Also, where large numbers of on-site employees are involved, a separate category for personnel may be appropriate; conversely, it may be useful to combine the legal and compliance categories. Things like building security, access controls, and accommodations for new technology are other likely checklist items for both commercial and residential properties.

decision making. Some areas to be concerned about in particular include the following:

- Commercial property lease summaries; residential property rent rolls—New *lease summaries* should be prepared for all office building, shopping center, and industrial leases and then compared to the summaries received from prior management. Where the two agree, you can assume they are accurate; where they differ, the information should be rechecked and finalized in correct form. The *rent roll* for a residential property should be checked against both rental agreements (leases) and actual units, not only to verify rent amounts, but also to ensure that any unit shown as vacant is actually not occupied. (Including the file data—unit number or leased space, occupants, rent, and required deposits—in the letter introducing new management to residents and commercial tenants and asking them to verify the particulars will provide additional validation of rent roll or lease summary information.)

- Delinquencies—When there is a change of management, some building occupants may attempt to challenge amounts they owe, trying to take advantage of the unsettled situation during the transition. This can happen at both commercial and residential properties. Delinquencies should be carefully checked and an audit (paper) trail created if and when these balances are disputed. Delinquent amounts should be reconciled as soon as possible. However, if some remain questionable despite your efforts at verification, it may be advisable to consider a write-off. It is very difficult to defend an old receivable in court if you were not part of the transaction unless the paper trail is quite clear.

- Unpaid bills—This is another area where disputes may arise, and it can be difficult to verify amounts and time frames if bills have remained unpaid for some time. If unpaid bills are presented during take-over, the client must be informed immediately of how much and to whom monies are owed. This situation is difficult for both parties as the supplier must prove that invoices were not paid while the new manager must verify that the materials or services were received but payment was *not* made. Because availability of specific services may be limited in some communities, it may be necessary to continue working with a particular contractor to ensure continued availability of that firm's services. In these situations, it may be desirable to negotiate a settlement of any payment disputes rather than dismiss (or be dismissed by) the contractor. Regardless of the particular situation, it is important to be prudent in handling any such late payments. If it becomes known locally that the new management will pay any amount submitted as a past-due bill, an unscrupulous contractor may try to take advantage of this.

- Condition of the property—It is important for the new manager to do a physical inspection of the property and inventory all items on hand so there is a clear record of so-called personal property (nonstructural items belonging to the building owner) and the overall condition of the property when new management took over. A residential property generally has a larger inventory of parts, tools, and equipment than does the typical commercial property. However, establishing exactly what is on hand at take-over is critical for both types of properties. The purpose of the inspection is primarily to protect the new manager and let the owner know the condition of the property at the time of the transition. Copies of these reports should be provided to the client as soon as they are complete. Additionally, it is a good idea to take photographs of critical areas of the property or record your inspection of the building on videotape, or both. Copies of the visual records can be sent to the client along with the written report. (The originals should be retained as a basis for measuring improvement and tracking the outcome of your actions over time.)

- Incomplete records—One of the most difficult areas for the new manager to cope with is incomplete records. It is not unusual to find that lease amendments, rental agreements, or subleases are missing; letters of agreement are no longer in the files; accounting records do not provide a complete audit trail, or contractors are working under oral rather than written agreements. The incoming manager should advise the client when the facts and the documents do not agree or when documents are obviously missing. Possibly the owner will have the necessary information and the gaps can be filled in easily. If the client does not have certain information, perhaps he or she can prevail on the former manager to track down what is missing.

- Unresolved problems—The former manager may have been dismissed because of an inability or unwillingness to deal with problems effectively. Once the new manager is known, commercial tenants or residents, contractors, and others will see hope of getting their problems resolved. This is not only an excellent opportunity for new management to demonstrate its ability to clear up situations and provide reassurance, but also an area which can be particularly problematic if decisions are based on incorrect or incomplete information. Everyone who has an unresolved dispute with the former management should be given a quick, attentive hearing so they can explain their side of the problem. The new manager should then research the situation, ascertain the facts, and resolve the problem as quickly as possible. Not only will this get the problem off the manager's desk, but everyone—clients, tenants or residents, contractors—will be impressed with new management's ability to get the job done.

- Differences in policies and procedures—The records maintained by the former management may not be entirely consistent with the policies and practices of the incoming management company. During the take-over process, it is incumbent on new management to be sure not only that they are receiving all the necessary information, but that it is also being made consistent with their company's policies and procedures. Working with someone else's data, without evaluating the information or making it conform to your current company standards, can build in problems that may be costly, both financially and in making decisions.

A Suggested Checklist Strategy. A good take-over checklist will identify the types of documents and activities necessary to ensure that the management company has all of the relevant information to undertake an orderly transition. Obviously a single take-over list will not fit all properties. We suggest creating a general list for each major property category (e.g., commercial properties) and including subcategories or modules for specific property types within that category—shopping centers, office buildings, and industrial space (warehouses or self-storage facilities). This approach helps standardize the take-over process while allowing you to address the different needs of individual properties. As an extension of this notion, it would be fairly easy to take a standard office module and add property-specific information to convert that subcategory checklist to office condominiums. Within the category of residential properties, there are important differences between conventional rentals and government-assisted or subsidized apartments, all of which differ from planed unit developments (PUDs), condominiums, and cooperatives where occupants are owners. These differences need to be checklist considerations.

One major objective of a checklist is to ensure collection of the information needed to meet the client's reporting requirements. It is not unusual for the records and reports created for day-to-day operations to be quite different from those needed by the client, especially if that owner is an institution. Managers have to be sure they have the required information and that it is in a format consistent with the client's requirements. Starting off a new account with improper, inaccurate, or late reporting is going to create a bad impression from the start—one that may never be overcome.

Another important consideration for an effective checklist is the proper grouping of required items. Logically, the first entries should include those items likely to be needed immediately or which may affect future decisions and current reporting needs. All items within this category can be grouped together for ease of collection as well as for tracking results. Accounting items should be grouped together. Payroll may be included here rather than as a separate item since it is an accounting function. However, it should not be included with other records of employees and their employment. (It might be a module that can be added where employees are a consideration.) Exhibit 10.1 presents many of the actions and documents that are components of management take-over. Exhibits 10.2 and 10.3 (pp. 262 and 263) list some of the checklist items peculiar to residential and commercial properties, respectively.

Although it is not unusual for all of the information to come from the former manager, one of the better sources of information in the take-over of an account will be the property owner. Most managers who are losing an account will be courteous and not give misinformation or try to mislead the new manager. However, a former manager who is bitter about losing the account could create problems if he or she were so inclined. The best approach is to assume the former manager is cooperating fully but verify all information (e.g., with the client) as soon as possible.

[NOTE: The IREM publication, *Transition: Taking Over a Management Account,* is an excellent resource on planning the take-over of new accounts. It includes basic checklist forms that address the major considerations for residential and commercial properties, respectively, and explains many of the points to be considered for different types of properties within these larger property classes.]

Information Acquisition Strategies

Whenever possible, the new manager should have 30–60 days in advance of an account take-over in which to collect all the records and documents needed and have them evaluated and entered into the new system before the actual transition takes place. The checklist, modified for the specific property, facilitates the tracking of what documents have been received, what actions have been taken, and what remains to be done. (The completed checklist should be retained as a record of take-over and to allow a smooth transition in the event the management arrangement is discontinued.) As the checklist is reviewed periodically for completion, a number of problem areas and missing items may be discovered. The following strategies can help expedite acquisition of needed documents and overcome certain types of problems.

Property Plans. Plans for the building may be difficult to locate, especially if the property has been under third-party management for some years or its ownership has changed several times. There are several places where one might obtain property plans (architectural blueprints, plot plans, engineering drawings). The first source to check is the outgoing manager. However, he or she may never have seen any plans and may have no idea whether they even exist. The owner should have a set of plans which can be copied for new management. If neither of these sources has copies of the plans, the original architect or general contractor may have retained a set that can be copied. (We found the only set of plans for one property in

Exhibit 10.1
Suggested Contents of a Management Take-Over Checklist

Physical Plant Data
1. As-built drawings and specifications (including utility controls)
2. Inventory of leased space*
3. Air-conditioning units inventory (number of units, size, location)
4. Inventory of operating equipment (elevators, escalators, major pumps, electrical panels, alarm panels and systems, etc.)
5. Inventory of all personal property (tools, ladders, supplies, etc.)
6. Warranties, operations manuals, technical information on all equipment
7. Certificates of occupancy for all buildings on the property
8. Prior physical inspections (where available)
9. Phase I or phase II environmental audits (if available)
10. ADA compliance information

Management Office Administration
1. Signed management contract
2. Insurance certificates received from clients
3. Insurance certificates sent to clients
4. Accounting notified of new account; account number requested

Project Files and Information
1. Copies of current year's budget
2. Copies of past years' budgets (where available)
3. Copies of operating statements (current and past years)
4. Original and copies of all leases and related documents*
5. Copies of latest estoppel certificates (if any)
6. Real estate tax files for current and past years*
7. Correspondence files, past and present
8. Rent roll*
9. Tenant invoices*
10. Delinquency list (current as well as historical)
11. Contractor files (contract, correspondence, and insurance certificates)
12. Service records on all operating equipment
13. Copies of all current and past available invoices
14. Contractor lists with emergency telephone numbers and contact names
15. Tenant or building occupant lists*
16. Client insurance policies (or summaries of policies, along with incident reporting requirements)

---

the hands of an appraiser who had "borrowed" them for an appraisal and never returned them.) The most recent prior owner may have held onto a set of plans, and it may be possible to obtain them (since they are no longer owners, they should have no further need of the plans) or borrow them to make copies. As a last resort, you might try local governmental agencies. Most municipalities require copies of building plans before issuing permits for development and rehabilitation construction. Usually they retain copies of old plans (e.g., on microfiche), and copies can be purchased. (Whatever

Exhibit 10.1 *(continued)*

Manager's "To Do" List
1. Change building signage
2. Visit all building occupants; verify occupant list information*
3. Meet with all contractors; verify contracts and duties
4. Obtain new insurance certificates from contractors, naming management company and client as additional named insured parties
5. Set up new lease and project files*
6. Conduct physical inspection of the property; convey result to client
7. Review litigation file; advise attorneys of change in management
8. Interview all employees (consider job descriptions, property needs, competency, etc.)
9. Evaluate existing emergency procedures (update plan if necessary; write new plan if needed)
10. Conduct market survey*
11. To extent qualified, evaluate insurance coverages including amounts
12. Gather insurance reporting requirements
13. Inspect property from a risk management point of view
14. Prepare management plan for operation of the property

Accounting "To Do" List
1. Assign new project number; advise manager assigned to property
2. Establish bank account; obtain necessary signature
3. Notify utility companies of new address for billing
4. Notify building occupants of new mailing address for payments*
5. Notify contractors of new billing address
6. Notify lender of new management company and contact name (if appropriate)
7. Notify taxing authority of new address for billings
8. Incorporate new project into computer system
9. Verify security deposits; establish special account if appropriate
10. Obtain payroll records
11. Verify business license needs; make application where necessary
12. Obtain checks, deposit slips, approval stamps, endorsement stamps, etc.
13. Set up automatic payments (via electronic bank transfer) for mortgages, time payments, monthly contracts, etc.
14. Establish on-site petty cash fund and controls
15. Obtain owner's taxpayer identification number for all tax matters
16. Establish accounting contact for all approvals
17. Establish tickler file for property (for rent increases, options, insurance expirations, etc.)

---

the cost, it will be worth every penny, especially if the building needs remodeling or you have to trace old utility lines, load-bearing walls, or other features.) Once you have copies of the plans, it is a good idea to verify that they represent the current components of the property (and consider having updated drawings prepared if they do not). Because these plans are a necessary and valuable resource for managing the property, it may be worthwhile to have new as-is plans drawn by an architect if you cannot obtain copies of current plans otherwise.

Exhibit 10.1 *(concluded)*
Establish Payroll (when appropriate)†
1. Verify information for all employees on site (rate of pay, vacation due, union status, etc.)
2. Set up employees on in-house payroll system
3. Set up employees on hospitalization plan
4. Prepare employee files
5. Review job descriptions (verify with property manager)
6. Set up procedures for time cards/time sheets, etc., for timely payment
7. Evaluate hiring plan for compliance with equal employment opportunity laws

*Indicates item may be identified more specifically for a residential or commercial property.
†If the management agreement requires continuation of existing employee benefits, prior payroll (and benefits) records will have to be obtained.

The listing here is not all-inclusive; it identifies most of the types of activities that are part of management take-over. However, a checklist form may be prepared in much greater detail, itemizing individual documents or records to be acquired or created, as may be appropriate for a management firm's or its client's needs.

For use as a form, we would set the checklist items in a narrower column at the left and include blank spaces in two columns (to the right) headed "date obtained" and "person responsible" (for initials on completion). Additional or different column headings may be necessary or appropriate for a particular usage.

For some types of properties, it may be appropriate to account for ground leases and/or master leases; any ongoing construction (completion of new development or rehabilitation) should be an added inspection item. It may be desirable, in general, to include resident or commercial tenant retention issues as a category to ensure that outstanding correspondence, pending maintenance requests, and other points of building occupants' satisfaction with management are identified and addressed.

Historical Records. One of the most difficult tasks for new management is locating records from past years that may be needed to recalculate monies due, facilitate return of long-standing security deposits, or help settle a dispute. Prior ownership and management may not have recognized the importance of these records to current and future day-to-day operations, and consequently the documents and files were stored away and forgotten. Finding and accessing historical records for a property can be a real challenge. For example, when taking over management of a small office building, the manager had to trace seven years of historical base-year information. The owner had just purchased the building and thought all the records had been transferred. The seller also thought this was so. The manager started searching and was able to obtain some billing records from the tenants involved. While this allowed the manager to compile some of the needed information, tenant records are not the best source. Once that resource was exhausted, the manager approached the seller and asked if any old records had been stored for safekeeping. The seller acknowledged that there were records in storage, but he did not think any of them pertained to

Exhibit 10.2
Some Adjunct Items for Differentiating a Residential Take-Over Checklist

Physical Plant Data
- Unit inventory by unit types
- Common facilities (laundry rooms, club rooms, office, health clubs, etc.)
- CC&R and PUD documents relevant to the property
- Property lines, common fences, etc., defined
- CFC and HCFC programs in place or required

Project Files
- Original and copies of all rental agreements or leases (including assignments, sublets, etc.)
- Laundry equipment contracts, ownership, etc.
- Tax files for current and past years (tax map)
- Utility, parking, and miscellaneous billings for past years
- Rent roll (start/end dates, options, increase dates)
- Resident invoices (rents, utilities, parking, etc.)
- Resident lists with home and business telephone numbers
- Individual resident files (rental application, resident screening/selection documents, security deposit agreement, unit inspection reports)

Manager's "To Do" List
- Provide verified resident information to accounting
- Inspect every unit; verify occupancy or vacant condition
- Inventory and verify "rentals in progress"
- Conduct market survey of competing projects in market area (recommend rental rates and lease—or renewal—incentives if appropriate)
- Evaluate marketing efforts and promotional materials
- Evaluate resident retention programs
- Evaluate social programs (appropriateness to property; cost effectiveness)

Accounting "To Do" List
- Notify residents of new mailing address for payments and payee information
- Verify laundry income and collection (payment) procedures
- Verify submeter billing procedures (are they accurate? up to date?)

Key to Acronyms
CC&R = covenants, conditions, and restrictions; PUD = planned unit development; CFC = chlorofluorocarbon; HCFC = hydrogenated chlorofluorocarbon.

Residential leases typically point out that the renter's personal property is not covered by the building owner's insurance policies and may require residents to insure their belongings. If documentation of renters' insurance coverages is requested or required as company policy (or by state law), this should be a checklist item. Residents may also be asked to have the management company and the property owner listed as additional named insured parties on their policies and provide proof of this (in the form of certificates of insurance).

If arrangements for parking are not included in the apartment lease or if parking is available for nonresidents, acquisition of relevant documents (space assignments, rental rates or fees, leases) should be a checklist item.

Exhibit 10.3
Some Adjunct Items for Differentiating a Commercial Take-Over Checklist

Physical Plant Data
- Space inventory (gross and net)
- Stacking plans/building layouts showing individual tenants and vacancies
- REA, CC&R, and PUD documents relevant to the property
- Ground leases where appropriate
- Verify boundaries, common fences, easements, etc.
- CFC and HCFC evaluations for programs in place
- Tenant environmental audits (where appropriate)

Project Files
- Original and copies of all leases (with any amendments, assignments, sublets, etc.)
- Copies of existing lease summaries for all tenants
- Tax files for current and past years (tax map, allocation basis)
- Insurance expense pass-through files for current and past years (allocation basis)
- Common area maintenance files (allocation basis, past billings)
- Base year information for taxes, escalations, etc. (where appropriate)
- Rent roll (start/end dates, options, increase dates, square footage)
- Tenant invoices (rents, CAM charges, utilities, merchants association, etc.)
- Tenant lists (including business owner and/or manager name, business and home office—company headquarters—telephone numbers and addresses)

Manager's "To Do" List
- Prepare new lease summaries; verify against old summaries and provide to accounting
- Inventory and verify "deals in progress"
- Inspect and evaluate tenant construction in progress
- Evaluate tenant insurance certificates; obtain new certificates for those out of date or missing
- Conduct market survey of competitive properties in the trade area
- Evaluate marketing materials (quantities and quality)
- Evaluate leasing efforts and leasing team

Accounting "To Do" List
- Notify tenants of new mailing address and payee information (major tenants may require a letter from the property owner to effect change)

Key to Acronyms
REA = reciprocal easement agreement; CC&R = covenants, conditions, and restrictions; PUD = planned unit development; CFC = chlorofluorocarbon; HCFC = hydrogenated chlorofluorocarbon.

Lease options and escalations are examples of additional items to include in a tickler file for a commercial property. If the lease allows it, tenants should be asked to include the management company as well as the property owner as additional named insured parties on their insurance policies.

For a shopping center checklist, common area agreements should be included as an item under physical plant data, and the manager's "to do" list should include a note to obtain retail tenants' sales reports and merchants' association or marketing fund information.

this property. When the manager asked for permission to go through the old files, the seller agreed, and the search yielded all of the needed historical base-year information.

Sometimes managers have been successful in obtaining historical information from former tenants. In the case of one shopping center, the property taxes had not been billed back to the tenants for six years. The taxing authority was helpful in providing the records for the preceding six years. Then, based on language in current and former tenants' leases, the manager was able to recapture a large percentage of those "lost" taxes.

Unsettled Disputes. One of the most difficult areas for new management is that of unsettled disputes of employees, contractors, and others with its predecessor. It generally comes down to the individual's word; no one knows exactly what happened anymore, and there are no records to substantiate either party's position. Rather than go back and forth between the parties, it may be more productive for the new manager to get both of them together, indicating up front that the purpose of the meeting is not to fix blame but to resolve the dispute between them. It is much more difficult to exaggerate or embellish their positions when the parties are face to face. The final decision should be based on what is necessary and appropriate to resolve the dispute rather than the believability of one person over another—unless the solution has become clear to everyone involved.

It may be possible (or desirable) to negotiate acceptable agreements among the parties. If services were provided, the property owner remains responsible for paying vendors under arrangements authorized by the former manager acting as the owner's agent. Disputed contractual terms may require the services of an attorney to establish an acceptable arrangement or cancel the agreement. Some disputes may require arbitration. Regardless of how a settlement is achieved, the results should be properly documented. The manager's goal should be to eliminate or minimize any outstanding disputes carried over from the prior management arrangement. If such disputes are not settled early in the new management term, they can be a source of continuing dissention, making the manager's job more difficult.

Issues of Noncompliance. It is not unusual for a property that is undergoing a change in management to experience problems with local authorities. There may be items that were supposed to be taken care of at an earlier date but were not done, and the deadline has passed. Upon discovery of such examples of noncompliance, it is very important for the new manager to establish communication with the agencies involved as soon as possible and explain that there has been a change in management. Often the fact of new management will buy some time to get things done. An honest and sincere attempt to resolve any problems will generally receive cooperation from public agencies.

The Manager's Priorities

One of the most difficult tasks facing the manager of a property during take-over is setting priorities, especially if the property has many problems. Many things have to be done either immediately or very soon after take-over. A thorough inspection of the property is one of the manager's first and most important take-over activities. It will reveal the extent of deferred maintenance as well as major and minor structural problems. Obviously, life safety is a primary concern, and anything posing immediate danger to building occupants or visitors should have the highest priority. The next priority is preservation of the physical asset—if any part of the property is in danger of collapse or deterioration that can be prevented, this should be addressed as soon as possible.

While the results of a physical inspection of the property and other data collection and evaluation activities will help determine some specific priorities for the particular property, a number of items that are general in nature are typical priorities for new management of any property. These include development of a residents' or commercial tenants' handbook and an emergency procedures manual, re-evaluation of the operating budget, preparation of an overall management plan for the property, and a thorough review of the terms of the contract (management agreement) under which the manager will be operating the property. Differences among property types commend a review of certain property-specific issues as well.

Residents' or Tenants' Handbook. This handbook should be designed as a resource and reference for the building's occupants. As such, it should contain important information on their relationship with the landlord—where to pay rent, when late fees apply, whom to contact for maintenance services, and how to contact security (if the property has a security force or a contracted service). It should also cover things like parking requirements, trash removal (separation of recyclables if applicable), periods when building access is limited or controlled, locations of common-use facilities and amenities, and the names and telephone numbers of personnel who are to be contacted for services or in emergencies. (Although emergency procedures may be included in a residents' or tenants' handbook, there may be advantages to having a separate emergency procedures manual. This is discussed in the next section.)

For a residential property, the handbook might include social activities at the property, as well as "house rules"—the rules and regulations under the lease that govern things like pets, care of appliances, smoke alarms, etc., that apply to all residents. At government-assisted or subsidized housing, social service programs and eligibility for assistance (certification requirements) would also be covered. Information about neighborhood facilities and services (schools, shopping, public transportation, libraries, etc.) may also be included to help residents make the transition to their new home.

A commercial property handbook would address things like building hours, CAM expense billings, and how to operate the air conditioners and trash compactors. Deliveries and shipments should be addressed, especially if there are time limitations on access or if the loading docks must be approached in a particular way. Signage and construction within the tenants' leased spaces are also likely topics, along with general cautions for the businesses and their employees. A handbook for an office building might include information on access controls and personal security in the workplace. One for a shopping center would likely include things like sales reporting, uniform store hours, and suggested approaches to dealing with shoplifting and providing shopper security. The function of the merchants' association or marketing fund for the center would also be addressed, including meeting dates, a calendar of scheduled activities, and funding requirements (i.e., payment of "dues").

Emergency Procedures Manual. An emergency procedures manual should provide building occupants with information about emergencies that are likely to occur and what to do if such situations arise. It may be worthwhile to consult with local emergency personnel—fire and police departments, hospitals, and social service agencies—regarding the specific course of action to be suggested in the manual. An emergency procedures manual should deal with natural disasters as appropriate. Fire, flood, weather-specific calamities (cyclones, tornados, hurricanes), mudslides, earthquakes, and even volcanos may be included, depending on location. It should also cover such man-made disasters as arson and explosions, as well as bomb threats and other criminal activities—e.g., prowlers, break-ins, and personal assault. Emergency telephone numbers for the police, emergency medical teams, and fire department should be included in the book along with instructions for orderly evacuation of the building. Locations of fire extinguishers, fire alarms, and other fire-fighting equipment may be provided on a building "map" along with locations of stairwells and building exits. Use instructions for the equipment may also be included as appropriate.

While the initial preparation of an emergency procedures manual is time consuming, once the information is stored in a computer, it can be modified and updated as necessary and new copies circulated to building occupants. (The IREM publication, *Before Disaster Strikes: Developing an Emergency Procedures Manual,* is a useful resource for this purpose.)

Operating Budget. In conjunction with the management agreement, the management firm and the property owner should have agreed on an operating budget for the first year of the contract term (or the calendar year). In the context of management take-over, the manager should review this budget and the assumptions on which it was based. If he or she was not involved in development of the budget, it is important for the manager to determine how every line item relates to the course of action being planned for the property and whether he or she agrees with the underlying assumptions. In developing a specific management plan, the manager may want to change the course of action for the coming year (with the owner's approval), and those changes will have an impact on the budget that has already been adopted. It is equally likely that the manager will agree with the prepared budget. Needless to say, the review process will provide an opportunity to become more familiar with the components of the financial plan for the coming year.

It is also possible that the new manager may be asked to develop an operating budget (new or revised) based on the financial data acquired during preparation for take-over. Review of the former manager's budget, if available, can be useful in this regard. It will help ensure that all sources of income and likely expenditures are identified. However, financial goals agreed between the owner and new management may necessitate consolidation of some budget line items into a single class or category, subdivision of others, and creation or elimination of line items or categories in order to be consistent with management's and ownership's reporting requirements and the planned course of action.

Management Plan. Most institutional owners require new third-party management to establish a management plan for the property. This can be fairly simple—a budget accompanied by an in-depth discussion with the asset manager—or a comprehensive multi-page document setting forth objectives and a plan of action for achieving them, specifically for the coming year and to a lesser extent for the next five years. Whether required by ownership or not, a management plan that sets financial and other goals for a property's operations serves as a yardstick for measuring management's success in meeting those goals. (See Chapter 3 for a detailed discussion of management plan components.)

In proceeding without a management plan or following someone else's (i.e., because ownership requested continuation of a plan implemented by prior management), you may soon discover that the actions being taken are not in the long-term best interests of the property. For instance, the former management may have concluded that the proper direction for what was clearly a distressed shopping center was to convert it to an off-price center, but they failed to establish any leases with that type of retailer. In taking over management, suppose you assume they were correct and proceed to "buy" a lead tenant, only to discover as you talk to other prospective tenants that the location of the property is not really appropriate for an off-price shopping center. In other words, following an unsupported assumption, you would have spent time and money heading in the wrong direction, and the focus of the property would have to be changed again. Had you done some homework and reviewed the basic assumptions and implementation strategies of the prior plan, you might have come to the same conclusion without the attendant expense. If you had done your own analysis of the property and its market, you might have proposed a different work-out plan for the property, one with an appropriate market-oriented focus and realistic, achievable goals.

A management plan should be written with little concern for what has happened in the past. Instead, it should be an objective look at the property as it stands in its current market and an evaluation of its potential to be successful. Once you have drawn your conclusions, you can review the history to see if you need to change the direction or modify the approach you would like to take.

Management planning includes realistic budgeting for day-to-day operations as well as possible capital expenditures (rehabilitation, change of tenancy, change of use) to achieve the desired results. The manager's recommendations to the owner should be grounded in a comparison of alternative approaches and a cost-benefit analysis of each of them. Proceeding without a management plan can result in wasted time and money and may prove to be totally contradictory to what the market is demanding.

Management Agreement. It is not unusual for one person to negotiate the management contract and another to be responsible for the day-to-day management of the property. Before getting started, the manager assigned to the property should review the management contract to find out what he or she is authorized to do and what is supposed to be done by others. For example, someone else may be responsible for leasing (typical for commercial properties), or the owner may already have legal counsel (preferred over management's attorneys). The owner may even have its own personnel who must be consulted on all construction matters. It is possible the owner may handle some payments directly—e.g., mortgage or insurance premiums. The incoming manager must know about these kinds of arrangements in advance because they will have an impact on his or her management decisions and actions.

Property-Specific Considerations. If the managed property is a shopping center, the manager should find out if there is a merchants' association or marketing fund in place. At shopping centers where there have been problems with prior management, these entities may become stronger as the merchants work together toward common goals. The incoming manager can create serious problems if he or she tries to launch new programs and activities without first talking with the merchants about difficulties they encountered in the past and the extent to which they were involved in trying to resolve the situations.

Among residential properties, condominiums and cooperatives present unique challenges because of their multiple ownership structures. It is most important for the new manager to meet with the board of directors of the homeowners' association. Management company executives may have already met with them during negotiations, but once the account is taken over, the manager assigned to the property should sit down with the board members and discuss specific goals and problems before he or she begins taking action. Preventing problems is preferable to trying to resolve them after the fact. Other considerations are the manager's responsibilities to attend board (and perhaps association) meetings and the established chain of communications. The one person to whom the manager will report and the preferred sequence of contacts if that individual is not available should be clear from the beginning.

A Perspective on Management Take-Over

Taking over a new account is one of the most hectic and potentially difficult situations real estate managers encounter. One cannot let the excitement of a new management opportunity override the need to exercise special care and diligence. Faced with all the things that must be done and heavy competition for the little time available to accomplish them, a real estate manager can easily convince himself or herself that cutting a few corners will get things done faster without causing any problems. The danger is that taking shortcuts at the start can have repercussions in the future—if the data are incomplete, you may make poor decisions or fail to act in a critical situation. The more hectic and demanding the assignment, the more the astute manager must be methodical and cautious. Everything the real estate manager does during management take-over has the potential to make the future of that account pleasant and profitable or a nightmare of regrets. The strategies outlined in this chapter should help prepare real estate managers and management companies to achieve the former.

Special Challenges
to Business

11

Strategies for Managing Risk

Risk management is one of the most critical areas of operating a business. Damage to or destruction of equipment owned by the company and liability for the consequences of actions taken by the firm's ownership or employees are risks inherent in any business. Loss of income, destruction of records, and damage to the firm's office—regardless of whether the space is owned or leased—are other examples of business risks. There are also risks involved in employing others to work for you. Some of these are legal liabilities (e.g., discriminatory personnel practices, payroll withholding requirements) while others have to do with the people who are hired (e.g., potential for criminal acts or workplace violence). For a real estate management company, marketing and leasing activities carry risks related to discriminatory practices that are prohibited by law. (These risks and the specific laws are discussed in the next chapter.)

Because of the many relationships involved in the management of real estate and because so many managed properties are accessible around the clock, there is potential for injury to building occupants, management employees, and visitors to a property as well as physical damage to buildings and equipment. For these reasons, it is necessary to do everything possible to minimize the risks while also carrying adequate levels of insurance in case a situation does arise.

Although some risks can be avoided and others can be controlled (see box on next page), businesses are more likely to choose between retaining a risk (self-insurance) and transferring it to a third party (an insurance company). Damage to an automobile can be used as an example. One can avoid this risk by not driving a car or, better, not owning one, but that is not very practical. This risk can be controlled to some extent by using great care

> **Risk Management Strategies**
>
> **Avoidance** One can choose to exclude certain services from one's offerings (e.g., certain grounds-keeping activities) or some features from a property (e.g., swimming pools) because of their inherent risks. For example, services like tree-trimming and application of lawn-care chemicals are inherently dangerous. Both require specialized equipment (high-speed saws and a means of reaching tall branches in the first instance, spraying devices and protective clothing in the second), and pesticide applicators have to be specially licensed. Similarly, potential risks of slip-and-fall injuries on a wet deck or death by drowning make a swimming pool a potentially dangerous amenity.
>
> **Control** One can take extra precautions to minimize the risks that attend certain aspects of operations. If every property in a large portfolio under management has large expanses of lawn and numerous shrubs that require attention on a continuing basis, it may be more cost-effective to employ qualified maintenance personnel as grounds keepers than to contract with a landscaping service, especially if those personnel can perform other related maintenance tasks. Likewise, not having a diving board, installing signage cautioning about the dangers of wet surfaces, and limiting the hours of access to a swimming pool can help reduce the risk inherent in this most desirable of residential amenities. Regular inspections of managed properties and periodic reviews of financial matters are extensions of this principle. By ensuring that potential problems can be identified early and dealt with before they become major concerns, real estate managers can limit (i.e., control) certain types of risks.
>
> **Retention** Careful weighing of the pros and cons of different risks can lead to a decision to accept the potential dangers and attendant liabilities when the likelihood of specific loss is low. This is intentional or active retention. (It is also possible to retain risk unintentionally or passively through ignorance of a particular risk.)
>
> **Transfer** Insurance is the most common example of risk transfer. In return for the premium paid by the insured party, the insurer assumes the burden of financial loss resulting from injuries to people or damage to property. Fidelity bonding of employees is another example. In the latter instance, the employer is protected against financial losses resulting from dishonest acts of employees.

when driving and not letting unqualified drivers behind the wheel, but this does not address the dangers posed by other drivers. Like the operation of a business, the risk management choices regarding automobile damage are more often going to be between retaining or self-insuring for the risk and transferring the risk by purchasing adequate insurance. Most people will accept the expense of repairing scrapes and dents on their cars because the cost to insure against these kinds of minor damage is very high while the actual loss (repair cost) is minimal. However, most car owners do carry insurance for replacement of the vehicle in the event it is destroyed in an accident. The cost of such coverage is fairly reasonable, and most individuals could not afford to replace their automobiles outright.

Real estate managers and owners use the same logic, accepting the responsibility and cost of minor repairs to buildings while insuring against complete loss of the asset. In transferring risk in this way, the insurance company agrees to assume the loss in return for payment of a specified premium, which makes the whole transaction acceptable to the insured. In reality, the risk is shared with the insurance company via deductibles. The larger the deductible the insured party is willing to accept, the lower the premium paid for the type of coverage. Each person has a different level of risk tolerance. Although the examples indicated in the discussion thus far have been specific to physical damage to property, the principles of self-insurance and transfer of risk apply as well in the more costly area of liability.

With regard to managed real estate, the types of insurance carried by the management company and the property owner are quite different. Some of the coverages are meant to include the other parties to a particular management agreement while other coverages are meant to protect the buyer of the policy exclusively. In years past it was assumed, for the most part correctly, that the interests of the property owner and the third-party manager were the same. If there was a loss or a lawsuit, the owner would protect the manager. This is no longer the case. For the most part today, the property owner and the third-party manager have distinctly separate areas of responsibility and liability. For this reason, it is critical for the management agreement to spell out clearly, not only the responsibilities of each of the parties, but also the necessary insurance coverages.

Insuring the Management Company

A management business will need a variety of insurance coverages in order to protect the interests of the business and its principals or owners. Life insurance should be carried on the business ownership *(key person coverage)*, whether a sole proprietor, several partners, or a corporation. This should benefit the management company financially, providing funds to operate during a transition period until new ownership can be installed or while the business is dissolved. Specific provisions may include naming of beneficiaries and providing direction for disposition of the business. (Other contingency planning strategies can be found in Chapter 3.)

Employment "benefits" to staff members typically include an insurance package. Major medical (hospitalization) and accidental death and dismemberment (AD&D) are fairly common coverages, and dental insurance is widely available. Premiums for medical and dental coverages increasingly are shared between employer and employee, and there is often provision for dependents to be covered as well. The package may or may not include life insurance that benefits the employee's family (typical policies are based on individuals' salaries). Long-term disability insurance is another possible offering. An insurance carrier may be able to put together a favorable package that includes all of these types of coverages. (Workers' compensation and unemployment insurance coverages, which are prescribed by law, are discussed in detail in Chapter 12.)

Business interruption insurance is another type of policy to consider. Just as property owners are encouraged to carry rent loss insurance in case some disaster interrupts the rental income stream, the management company should be insured in case activities at the management office are disrupted because of physical damage or other problems. (The usual casualty coverages replace physical losses only.) Other specific coverages real estate management companies should carry for the business are described in the following sections.

Errors and Omissions (E&O) Insurance. This type of professional liability insurance protects the management company against financial losses incurred by clients or others as a result of the firm's or its employees' mistakes or failure to act. It covers unintentional administrative and other specified errors as delineated in the policy, but it does not cover gross negligence or fraud.

While such insurance is clearly advisable, it may be difficult to obtain (applicants' loss history will be a consideration); and when it is available, it can be comparatively expensive due to the large dollar amounts that may be paid out in claims. However, the cost is manageable through high deductibles and having a capacity to absorb some measure of loss. E&O insurance is written on a "claims made" basis, which means claims are only covered during the time the current policy is in effect, regardless of when the incident took place.

Although the NATIONAL ASSOCIATION OF REALTORS (NAR) has an E&O insurance program for its REALTOR members, that offering does not apply to real estate management companies. The Institute of Real Estate Management is another organization that has arranged for E&O policies to be available to its membership.

Fidelity Bond. This is purchased to protect the company against losses due to dishonest acts, such as theft or misappropriation of money or property, by its employees. Such coverage is generally demanded by property owner-clients, especially large financial institutions or pension funds. Specific requirements would be stated in the management agreement as discussed later in this chapter.

General Liability Insurance. Liability insurance protects the management company from losses due to injury to persons or damage to other people's property occurring at its business premises or resulting from its

> **Fidelity Bond**
>
> Fidelity bonds are not strictly insurance because three parties are involved: A *surety* or guarantor, which may be an insurance company, agrees to answer for the *principal* (the covered party—i.e., the employee) if he or she does not perform as required by the *obligee* (the party likely to be harmed by a loss—i.e., the employer). A fidelity bond covers an employer or business for losses due to embezzlement, larceny, or gross negligence committed by employees. On the other hand, a *fiduciary bond* may be sought from a manager or a management company as an assurance of performance of the duties required under the management agreement.

employees' negligence. Such liability insurance may be written so that it also protects the firm's clients.

Institutional owners often require higher limits of liability coverage than may be carried by a small management company. However, it has been our experience that these owners may pay for the additional coverage if their requirements exceed the coverage limits normally carried by the management company.

Umbrella Liability Insurance. Typically, management companies will purchase basic liability coverage in amounts of $500,000 to $1,000,000, which make them eligible to buy additional multiples of coverages at fairly reasonable rates. The "umbrella" becomes available when a claim or claims exceeds the initial coverage amount.

Fire and Casualty Insurance. This type of coverage generally applies to the furniture and improvements in leased offices. If the management company operates out of a building owned by the firm, the coverage would also apply to the owned premises. In years past, management companies often chose to retain this risk (i.e., they self-insured in this area). The rationale for this was the assumption that there was little to be stolen from the office or damaged by fire, so a loss would likely have less economic impact than would the periodic insurance premiums. However, with the introduction of high-technology tools, management offices often have a substantial investment in computers, calculators, facsimile machines, photocopiers, and other devices, and the risk of loss from any source is too great to not carry this type of insurance. In fact, it may be advisable to carry additional insurance, as an endorsement, for damage to or loss of these types of personal property and such things as backup files (computer data) and records or files maintained off site, including archives where important information is stored for a required number of years.

Automobile Insurance. The automobile is an important component of real estate management activities. Managers must visit their assigned prop-

> **Typical Management Company Insurance Coverages**
>
> - Professional liability or errors and omissions (E&O) insurance
> - Fidelity bond
> - Comprehensive general liability insurance with umbrella coverage
> - Fire and casualty insurance
> - Automobile insurance
>
> Other coverages that may be considered include business interruption insurance, automobile non-ownership or hired car coverage, employment practices liability insurance, and crime insurance.

erties on a regular basis. If automobiles are owned by the management company, they must be insured by the company. (Many states also require that proof of insurance be carried in vehicles at all times.) Collision, medical payments, and liability are specific components of this type of policy. Often there is some protection in the event the other party in an accident is uninsured. It is usually possible to carry higher deductibles (for collision and medical coverage) and thereby lower the premiums.

The management company's insurer must be fully aware of how automobiles are used in conducting the firm's business. It is not unusual for accounting staff to take a deposit to the bank, a maintenance technician to go to the hardware store to purchase needed parts, or a security guard to transport an injured person to a medical care facility using their personal vehicles. All of these activities could put the company at risk if proper insurance has not been provided. (Even though the driver may carry automobile insurance, an accident occurring while the vehicle is used on company business can result in liability being shifted to the employer.) Minimal use of employees' vehicles may be covered under the company's liability insurance policy. However, if the use of employees' cars or leased vehicles is substantial, separate automobile liability coverage (automobile non-ownership or hired car insurance) should be carried. This can often be obtained as an endorsement to the firm's general liability policy.

Other Specific Coverages. Depending on the types of properties being managed and other business activities of the firm, other coverages may be of interest. Insurance can be obtained to cover the cost of defending claims of discriminatory rental practices. There is also employment practices liability insurance that covers both defense costs and potential awards from lawsuits claiming discrimination in promotion or hiring, sexual harassment, or wrongful termination. Crime insurance may be worth considering to cover losses due to employee fraud or theft. (This type of insurance is required of firms that seek the AMO® designation [see Appendix A]; strategies for preventing employee fraud are discussed in Chapter 4.)

A qualified insurance broker should be consulted regarding specific insurance coverages a management firm may need. While it is important to have sufficient coverage to protect the parties involved, cost is also a consideration. At some point, management companies self-insure for some of the risks they are less likely to face. They also implement strategies that will reduce risk and liability. (More information on specific risks and risk-reduction strategies can be found in the IREM Hot Topics publication, *Reducing Your Risks*.)

Management Agreement Considerations

As mentioned earlier in this chapter, institutions and other sophisticated owner-clients often require management agreements with them to include provisions for minimum insurance coverages. Most managers will also insist that the property owner provide minimum liability coverage as well. Although the contents of the management agreement are discussed in detail elsewhere (Chapter 9), the following sections look more closely at insurance and liability issues and ways to address these risks in management agreements for specific properties.

Hold Harmless Provisions. The owner and the third-party manager should agree to indemnify each other or hold each other harmless from their own criminal and negligent acts. The manager, as agent, will also want the agreement to include protection against problems and liabilities related to the property over which the manager has no control (e.g., an unknown construction defect, the presence of a harmful substance in the soil, or underground water contamination).

Liability Coverage and "Insured" Parties. The agreement should require the property owner to carry a minimum liability insurance policy and show the third-party manager as an "additional named insured party" on that policy. A copy of the endorsement should be provided to the manager as proof that this is in place. Owners will require the same thing of the manager and insist on receiving a copy of the endorsement as verification. In most cases, the owner is likely to carry much higher liability limits than the manager will need to protect his or her interests.

Fidelity Bond. Because the manager will be handling funds on the owner's behalf, the owner-client will want protection from employee theft, embezzlement, etc., in the form of a fidelity bond. Generally the amount of the bond should be sufficient to cover the largest amount of owner-clients' money likely to be in the management company's custody at any one time or, alternatively, the amount of money the management company collects during the month. (Having an operating policy that payment by check or money order is preferred over cash and issuing receipts for all payments received are internal controls that help reduce this risk.)

Since fidelity bonding can be expensive, it may suit both parties to the

> **Insurance and Liability Issues in the Management Agreement**
> - Hold harmless provisions
> - Owner's liability insurance coverage
> - Naming of insured parties
> - Fidelity bonding
> - Lease and contract requirements
> - Owner's insurance on the property
> - Manager's role as insurance administrator

agreement to work out a program that would reduce the maximum dollar amount of the client's funds that the manager will have on hand at any one time. This can be accomplished in a number of ways. One of the easiest is to have an automatic "sweep" of the account when the balance reaches a certain level. The amount over the agreed-upon maximum is deducted by the bank and forwarded to the client electronically (via wire transfer). In most states, a manager must obtain a "hard copy" record of such a transaction as an audit requirement. Another way is for the manager to send the owner a check for the excess funds. In some limited cases and generally with smaller properties, the rents may be sent direct to the owner for deposit, and the owner then provides funds to the manager to pay the bills or, alternatively, pays the bills when they are presented by the manager.

Lease and Contract Requirements. In addition to having their own specific insurance coverages, the property owner and the third-party manager should be afforded similar types of protections by commercial tenants who lease space at the property and contractors who provide services to the property.

Lease Protections. Today's commercial leases require tenants to carry specific insurance coverages via policies written by a reputable company. (Increasingly, residential leases are including a similar requirement.) The landlord must be listed as an additional named insured party on these policies, and a certificate of insurance must be provided as proof of coverage. In most cases, the third-party manager is responsible for collecting the certificates and making sure the coverages are current. Specific requirements vary somewhat according to property type.

Shopping Center Leases. Most shopping center leases require the tenant to have liability insurance in an amount of at least one million dollars. The tenant must also carry fire and extended coverage insurance on its inventory, fixtures, and improvements (not less than 80 percent up to 100 percent of the value) and boiler and machinery insurance to cover the air-conditioning compressor and motors and switch boxes. In the case of independent retailers, plate glass insurance is required; major and national tenants most often self-insure or have a right under their leases to self-insure for this risk.

Some third-party managers will ask to be listed as an additional named insured party on the tenants' insurance policies along with the property owner, but the tenants often refuse to do this because it is not required by the lease. We also know of instances where insurance agents refused to list the landlord as an additional named insured party on the tenant's fire and extended coverage policy claiming the landlord has no interest in that portion of the policy.

More and more, shopping center leases are requiring the tenant to carry business interruption insurance. If the business is forced to shut down temporarily (e.g., because of fire or other damage), the lease requirement to pay rent remains in place. Adequate insurance will ensure continued payment of the rent until the store can be re-opened.

Office Building Leases. In the past, office tenants were only required to carry liability insurance and to list the building owner as an additional named insured party on the policy. Managers have come to realize, however, that many small office tenants would not be able to re-open after a serious fire or other disaster if they were not insured. As a consequence, many office building owners now also require tenants to obtain fire and extended coverage insurance on fixtures and improvements to their leased space.

Industrial Leases. The insurance coverage requirements are much the same as those for office tenants, except that industrial tenants may be required to carry higher limits on their liability insurance, depending on how they are using the leased space.

Residential Leases. In the past, residential leases included a clause stating that the landlord was not responsible for loss of or damage to personal property belonging to residents, and that was considered adequate. More recently, however, landlords increasingly are requesting (or requiring) residents to carry renter's insurance, and the landlord may ask to be listed as an additional named insured party and to receive a certificate of insurance verifying this.

Contract Requirements. In most states, the building owner is ultimately liable for anything that takes place on the property. A small contractor or independent tradesperson who comes on site to do a small repair job and, while there, causes substantial damage, would be liable for the damage caused. However, if the contractor or tradesperson was uninsured or underinsured, the property owner would likely be called upon to cover the loss. For this reason, all contractors who work on managed properties should be required to have liability insurance (usually at least one million dollars' worth), automobile liability coverage, and workers' compensation insurance. If they are working in tenants' spaces, they may be required to have a fidelity bond as well. In this case, both the building owner and the third-party manager should be listed as additional named insured parties on the contractor's or tradesperson's insurance policies.

It is the manager's responsibility to obtain certificates of insurance and to be sure they are updated regularly for vendors who provide services on an ongoing basis. Except for emergency situations, there should be no exceptions to the requirement for contractors to provide proof of adequate insurance coverage *prior to* beginning work at the site.

For major repairs or construction, it is advisable to ask contractors to provide performance and payment bonds. A *performance bond* is an assurance that the contractor will perform the work as required under the contract. A *payment bond* protects the property owner against claims and liens brought after the project has been completed and final payment to the contractor has been made by assuring that the contractor will pay for all material, supplies, equipment, labor, and subcontractors used on the project.

Owners' Insurance Requirements. The agreement should state who will be responsible for specifying, bidding, and purchasing insurance coverages for the managed property. Although purchasing insurance for a client's property requires more knowledge of insurance coverages than most real estate managers have, the manager may be asked to handle it. When that is the case, the manager should only agree to purchase insurance if the owner has indicated the specific coverages wanted (based on consultation with a qualified insurance broker).

There are two serious dangers in recommending or acquiring insurance coverage for property owners. The first is not having all the coverage needed, as indicated by future events, or not having high enough limits to cover a problem. The second is that the policy might lapse for some reason, leaving the property uninsured, and the manager may be responsible and, therefore, liable.

Apart from the more common casualty and liability insurance policies, a number of adjunct coverages are also available. However, only the property owner can decide whether to pay for such additional insurance or carry the risk (self-insure). For example, we know of a shopping center owned free-and-clear by an individual. Although the property is very close to a major earthquake fault, the owner elects to self-insure for earthquake loss. However, the owner would still have a secure lifestyle, even if the center were to be completely destroyed by an earthquake, because the property is part of a much larger portfolio of investment real estate.

Apart from the coverages the owner may want, the mortgage holder may impose minimum insurance requirements to protect its interests. In California, for instance, it is more common for lenders to require earthquake coverage today than in the past. It is obvious that lenders do not want to take the chance that a property might be badly damaged in an earthquake and there would not be funds available to repair or replace the building. In other parts of the United States, flood insurance might be a lender requirement.

Insurance coverages carried by property owners may include most or all of the following:

Fire and extended coverage

Comprehensive general liability

Excess or umbrella liability

Rental income

Boiler and machinery

Workers' compensation and unemployment

Fidelity bond

Owners of multiple sites may be able to have a type of *blanket policy* written that provides the same coverages at all locations (this is sometimes called a *master policy*). A blanket policy offers the advantage of greater flexibility and reduces any limitations of value at any one location. It can also lower premium costs, depending on property type, age, and condition, deductibles that apply, coinsurance, and other factors.

Fire and Extended Coverage. This policy, which covers the basic building, is generally written on an "all risk" basis. Most of the risks that are not covered under such a policy (these may include earthquake, plate glass, and flood) generally can be covered at an additional cost as an endorsement to the basic policy. The policy should be written to include coverage of management company personal property (i.e., business equipment and records) maintained at the managed property.

Building ordinance coverage is especially desirable because rebuilding or repairs may have to conform with current building codes, and that can increase the cost of the work. The main concern is adequacy of the policy so that it will cover replacement cost of the building and meet any mortgage requirements that are in place.

Boiler and Machinery Insurance. This type of policy specifically covers the heating and air-conditioning equipment in the building as well as the major electrical panels, motors, and other components, for losses due to breakdowns, explosions, etc. It may also be extended to cover resulting loss of use or income.

> **Other Insurance Considerations**
>
> Insurance for property damage is written to address restoration of the loss. Policies may be written on an *actual cash value (ACV)* basis, meaning the insurer will reimburse the current value of an item adjusted for *depreciation*. If a piece of equipment with an expected use life of five years is destroyed after two years of use, ACV coverage would likely reimburse only 60% of the cost of new equipment. *Replacement cost coverage*, on the other hand, would reimburse the loss at the current cost of a comparable item—there is no depreciation deduction. Obviously, the difference in reimbursement affects the premiums—ACV coverage generally costs less because it reimburses less—but replacement cost coverage is preferable to expedite restoration.
>
> *Coinsurance* is also an option for insuring buildings. When this approach is chosen, a special clause is added to the policy providing that the property owner will pay a lower rate per $100 of coverage in exchange for agreeing to maintain coverage limits that equal a certain minimum percentage of the actual cash value of the insured property. (Typically these clauses are written at 80% or more of ACV.) In return, the insurer will pay 100% of the loss *up to but no more than the limits of the policy*. However, if the property is underinsured at the time of a covered loss, the owner becomes a *coinsurer*. (In other words, if the insurance has not been maintained at the prescribed level based on current replacement costs, the owner will be responsible for the difference.) An example would be a building valued at $1,000,000 (ACV)—replacement value less depreciation deductions. An 80% coinsurance clause would require the owner to maintain $800,000 worth of insurance coverage. If the insurance level is maintained, a loss would be reimbursed up to 100% of the $800,000 coverage limit of the policy. However, if the cost of restoring the building had increased (e.g., to $1,200,000) but the insurance coverage was not increased accordingly (i.e., it remained at $800,000), the amount the insurer would reimburse on the loss would be only 83%. (The policy would reimburse up to $800,000, but that would no longer be 80% of the ACV; the policy value should have been increased to $960,000.)

Comprehensive General Liability. This type of policy protects the building owner financially against third-party claims for property damage or bodily injury due to negligence on the part of the owner and/or employees of the building, often including medical payments. This broad form of coverage is meant to protect the insured in the areas of premises and operations, elevators and escalators, products, completed operations, and contractual and outside contractors' liability.

A more limited version of this coverage is *Owners, Landlords, and Tenants Liability (OLT) Insurance,* which is limited to premises and operations, including elevators if they exist. While it may be tempting to save a few dollars by carrying the more limited coverage, it is generally a good idea for owners to carefully evaluate the potential risks and make sure the policy that is chosen will cover the likely exposures.

> **Other Insurance Considerations *(continued)***
> The following formulas demonstrate the difference:
>
> **Basic Formula:**
>
> $$\frac{\text{Amount Carried}}{\text{Amount to be Carried}} = \text{Percentage of loss to be paid by the insurer up to the limits of the policy}$$
>
> **Full Insurance Coverage:**
>
> $$\frac{\$800{,}000}{\$800{,}000} = \text{100\% of loss to be paid by the insurer (up to the limits of the policy—\$800,000)}$$
>
> **Underinsurance:**
>
> $$\frac{\$800{,}000}{\$960{,}000} = \text{83\% of loss would be paid by the insurer (up to the limits of the policy—in this example, only the \$800,000 value maintained)}$$
>
> In other words, by not maintaining the full insurance coverage at 80% of ACV, the owner becomes a coinsurer in the amount of the $160,000 difference.
>
> Insurance premiums can be moderated in a number of ways. Sometimes it is preferable and possibly more cost-effective to insure some items via specific *endorsements* to a general fire and extended coverage policy. Higher *deductibles* generally mean lower premiums, although there will be a larger out-of-pocket expense before insurance reimburses specific losses. (Deductibles apply to all types of insurance, not just property damage.)

Excess Liability or Umbrella Coverage. Generally, property owners will have a basic liability policy (up to one million dollars) and then carry additional liability coverage to provide the level of protection they consider warranted. The likelihood of a large claim is remote, and the premiums are fairly low compared to the amount of coverage. This type of policy generally carries a fairly high deductible—in the range of $10,000–$20,000.

Rental Income Insurance. Since rental income provides the funds to pay the mortgage and operate the property, an owner can be in a very difficult position if the building is damaged and the loss prevents tenants from paying their rents. The need to make mortgage payments continues regardless, and often exterior maintenance of the building is needed even while the interior is being repaired. Rental income insurance provides replacement income, and the premium is based on the amount of rental income being insured. However, the coverage provided under this type of policy needs to be scrutinized because it is often subject to a deductible or a time limitation.

Workers' Compensation and Unemployment Insurance. Building owners who have employees will also have to carry workers' compensation and unemployment insurance. Even if there are no direct employees, it may be desirable to carry this type of coverage. While not a common occurrence, it is possible that in using outside contractors and subcontractors, a building owner may be held liable for workers' compensation claims if the direct employers' insurance coverage is inadequate or nonexistent. Because of this potential liability risk, it is a good idea always to have contractors provide evidence that they have workers' compensation coverage in force at the time they are doing work at a property. (This is in addition to proof of general liability coverage.)

Typically, workers' compensation insurance will provide benefits in the case of a worker's death on the job, medical costs and lost wages resulting from a work-related injury, and disability benefits ranging from temporary to total and permanent disability.

Fidelity Bond. A property owner who is also handling monies belonging to others (e.g., an outside client or joint-venture partner) is likely to carry a fidelity bond, or money and securities coverage, which protects third parties from losses due to misappropriation or embezzlement.

Administration of Insurance Coverages. While the third-party manager may not place the insurance, he or she is generally required to administer any losses (i.e., file claims) and work with the insurance company in regard to permits, inspections, corrections, and any paperwork involved. The management agreement should provide for the manager to have a copy of the actual insurance policies or, at least, a summary of the policy indicating the specific coverages in place and any deductibles or limitations in effect.

In addition, the manager should be provided a "report policy statement" by the insurance company. This indicates how and when loss reports are to be made and is a critical part of insurance administration. Most insurance carriers want to be notified of any incident that may result in an economic loss, no matter how small.

If the requisite policy documents are not provided to the manager, the property owner should be asked to request them from the insurance carrier. At the very least, the manager must have a contact for purposes of reporting potential insurance claims and to answer questions that may arise regarding potential losses at or on the property.

Minimizing Management Company Exposure. As noted earlier in this chapter in regard to liability claims, the interests of the property owner and the third-party manager are not the same. It is important to keep this in mind, as the following example illustrates.

> A shopping center owner, who was a new client, contacted the third-party manager who was taking over the new account. The

owner was refinancing the property and wanted the trees trimmed immediately because the lender was going to inspect the property. The take-over process was in the early stages, and the manager had not completed all of the due diligence. However, in an effort to please the new client, the manager immediately ordered all of the trees in the center trimmed.

As it turned out, a fast food restaurant on a corner parcel (outlot) was responsible for its own maintenance and took exception to the trimming of its trees. The restaurant filed a lawsuit against the third-party manager *and* the center owner. However, the center owner claimed to have no liability because he had not ordered the manager to trim the trees on the corner parcel. Ultimately, the manager's insurance carrier paid the restaurant owner for the alleged damage to its trees. If the owner had told the manager to trim all trees in the center, *including those on the corner parcel,* he would have been responsible for the damage.

Obviously difficulties can arise over subtleties. Had the take-over due diligence been completed, the manager would have known about the ownership of the corner parcel and thus avoided creating a problem. Asking for more specific instructions might also have helped the manager, but the owner's "request" seemed clear at the time.

There is no way for third-party managers to avoid liability completely. However, there are some precautions that can be taken to minimize risk exposure. The first is a properly written and negotiated management contract. Every effort should be made to limit the manager's liability to his or her own negligent acts. The manager should not be held liable for defects that exist in the building or for a contractor's negligent acts or for the property owner's failure to act. A well-drafted and negotiated management agreement will address these points and make clear which party is responsible for specific acts and conditions.

In contracting on the owner's behalf for maintenance or other services, the contract should be in the name of the owner of the property or of the building itself, with the manager (or the management company) acting as the owner's agent. (Likewise, related billing should be addressed to the owner or the property.) If such contracts are drafted in the name of the manager, he or she is likely to be held responsible for any problems arising out of that contract. One management company discovered it could be held liable for several thousand dollars in services (including carpeting, painting, and utilities) contracted for a residential property whose owner filed for bankruptcy because the services had been contracted in the management company's name—i.e., the contracts read ABC Management Company when they should have read XYZ Property care of ABC Management Company.

All contracts for maintenance and other services should be carefully drawn and include language requiring the contractor to have adequate liability insurance and to list the manager as well as the property owner and/or the building as additional named insured parties. (Contractors should also be required to provide proof of adequate workers' compensation coverage as noted previously.) Furthermore, the manager should make certain that the contractors are licensed and insured—i.e., request submission of certificates of insurance and other proofs *before* work is begun. Not doing so may save money on the work but cost the manager in the long run. For example:

> An uninsured "handyman" was hired to change lightbulbs in a commercial building. In order to reach the light fixture in one space, he stood on a tenant's copy machine instead of using a ladder. This caved in the top of the copier and damaged its internal mechanism. When the tenant asked the manager of the property to pay for the damage, the manager denied responsibility, indicating that she was just acting on behalf of the owner. However, the management agreement stated that the manager would hire only licensed and insured contractors. Because the agreement was specific, the manager had to pay for the copier damage.

Third-party managers should avoid making decisions or taking action beyond what is specified in the management agreement unless they obtain the client's approval beforehand. However, there are situations in which the manager may have to take the initiative in order to obtain that approval. Case in point: A prudent manager will advise property owners that a solid hiring practice would include a thorough screening—background check and aptitude test—for all apartment property staff. The costs of such steps are worthwhile when one considers the possible consequences (i.e., financial damages) of hiring someone without such care, as indicated by the following example:

> A manager hired a maintenance man who had a record of two convictions as a pedophile in another state. The manager's employment application did not even ask if applicants had ever been convicted of a felony. This became an important legal point in a third-party liability lawsuit. The man had been hired. He worked at the property for more than a year. Eventually, he was accused of abusing a resident's child. Upon his arrest, it became apparent that he had a criminal record. The parents of the abused child sued the property owner and the manager. The owner claimed that responsibility for such discoveries lay within the standard of care exercised by the manager in hiring personnel. The manager claimed the owner had granted her broad authority as agent but did not specifically allow expenditure of funds on criminal background checks or behavioral characteristic testing. In the court case, they both lost.

Some Residential Management Risks

The risks in residential management are often different in nature. As society becomes more litigious, there is increasing likelihood of lawsuits being filed by prospective residents for discrimination in marketing or leasing. For example, in discussing leasing strategies, an apartment owner might say to the manager, "You will rent *only* to the *right* people," or specify "no children *or* single-parent families" as residents. However, following this type of request would make both the management firm and the property owner liable in a discrimination lawsuit. The management company must establish marketing and leasing policies and procedures that are nondiscriminatory and train its leasing and management personnel to comply with fair housing laws. It must also let owner-clients know that such requests or requirements constitute illegal discrimination and that the management company will not follow them. The proper place to make the management company's policy clear to the owner is in the written management agreement. (Fair housing laws and sexual harrassment are discussed in detail in the next chapter.)

The management company may be held liable for illegal acts committed by unsupervised employees—for example, if a maintenance worker enters an apartment to perform repairs while the resident is at work but burglarizes the apartment instead. Other behaviors may be more difficult to substantiate—e.g., a painter may be accused of making racial remarks to children on the premises.

Another high-risk issue is the use of "master" keys. The management firm may be very careful in its hiring practices, conducting criminal record checks as well as scrutinizing other background information on all job applicants. However, the firm cannot restrict its employees' personal relationships. So, in spite of employment pre-screening, there is nothing to prevent a manager or other staff member responsible for master keys from "dating" an individual who, because of the personal relationship, is able to access the master keys and subsequently commits a criminal act on the managed property.

The various types of risks noted in this brief discussion are part of a larger picture of specific risks that need to be considered in establishing management policies and procedures and seeking insurance to cover specific liabilities.

It is also important for third-party managers to abide by all the laws that impact the property and its management. For example, if an owner-client should decide not to pay the real estate taxes on time and directs the manager to delay payment, thus incurring a penalty, the manager should insist on having those instructions in writing so his or her actions will not be questioned at a later date. Having only oral instructions in such circumstances can leave the manager open to future criticism. This is particularly problematic in instances where an asset manager gave such directions acting as the owner, and that person has since left the owner-company so there is no one available to verify the manager's statements.

The manager's behavior and actions are scrutinized by others as well as the property owner. For this reason, managers should avoid making any threats to tenants, contractors, or customers regarding collections, payments, violations of rules, or other matters. Rather, they should conduct the business of the property in a calm and professional manner, following the management agreement to the letter and observing good business practice at all times. As an example in the realm of commercial property management, if the agreement requires a credit check on all prospective tenants, this is exactly what should be done unless the owner gives written instructions that such is not necessary for a particular prospect.

As part of good risk management practice, the manager should inspect the property regularly for hazards and, if they exist, report them immediately to the owner along with recommendations for their abatement. If the hazard poses immediate danger in terms of health or safety or property condition, the manager has the right to correct the problem (within reasonable limits of expense) and inform the building owner of the action taken after the fact.

A Perspective on Risk Management

There are numerous risks inherent in operating any business. These include damage to company property and liability for the actions of its personnel, including discriminatory practices. Identifying potential risk exposures and implementing strategies to reduce them are important considerations along with specific insurance coverages as measures to protect the real estate management company.

Because buildings are open to the public, in some cases 24 hours a day, and have large numbers of occupants (residents, commercial tenants' employees) and visitors, the potential for liability exposure is very great. In addition to the potential financial implications, real estate managers are concerned about someone being injured or worse because they did not take action as they were supposed to or because they may have done something wrong. For these reasons, great care must be taken to ensure that managed properties are and remain in good condition and that the manager is not through direct action—or inaction—allowing a condition to exist that represents a potential danger to a building or the people in it. Managers and management firms must also have sufficient insurance coverage to protect themselves and others from financial losses that may occur in spite of their best efforts.

In addition to personal care and attention, it is important to seek advice and counsel from a qualified insurance broker and an attorney before taking any actions. This will help ensure you are doing all that is reasonable to protect everyone involved in the operation of buildings you manage.

[NOTE: This chapter provides a snapshot overview of management company risks and insurance needs. The type of services provided by a firm and the scope of its business operations will be important factors in determining specific insurance requirements, which should be evaluated in consultation with a qualified insurance broker. (Often it is possible for one's insurer to arrange for an audit to determine types and levels of risks.) More detailed discussion of these issues is beyond the scope of the book.]

12

Strategies for Avoiding Legal Problems

Well-intended laws and regulations create potential liabilities for property owners and real estate management firms. Penalties for violations can be costly and embarrassing and may even threaten a company's existence. In today's litigious and heavily regulated business environment, it is important to ensure that the company and the properties it manages are in full compliance with applicable laws. This requires management company executives to monitor legislative and administrative activities at all levels of government (federal, state, and local) and develop and implement operating procedures that minimize exposure to lawsuits. This chapter will discuss some of the laws that impact the real estate management business directly and then look at some of the regulations that affect the management of real estate. Receivership and other issues with legal implications are also addressed. (Legal requirements regarding business ownership and licensing are addressed in Chapter 2.)

[NOTE: The information provided here is intended to heighten the reader's awareness. Advice of legal counsel should be sought in regard to particular laws and their impact on an individual manager or management company.]

Laws Affecting the Real Estate Management Business

As indicated in Chapter 2, the practice of real estate management is affected by real estate licensing laws. The role of the management company and the real estate manager in representing the owner's interests requires an understanding of agency law. (The firm's management agreements, leases, and

> ### Real Estate Broker and Salesperson Defined
>
> **Broker** shall mean any person who, for a fee, a commission, or any other valuable consideration or with the intent or expectation of receiving the same from another, negotiates or attempts to negotiate the listing, sale, purchase, exchange, rent, lease, or option for any real estate or improvements thereon, or assists in procuring prospects or holding himself or herself out as a referral agent for the purpose of securing prospects for the listing, sale, purchase, exchange, renting, leasing, or optioning of any real estate or collects rents or attempts to collect rents, or holds himself or herself out as engaged in any of the foregoing.
>
> **Salespersons** are those individuals, other than brokers, who are employed by a broker and participate in the above activities under the auspices of a broker.

other contractual arrangements entered into on its own behalf or as the agent of a client are subject to requirements of contract law, which is beyond the scope of this text.)

Real Estate Licensing Requirements. The primary purpose of real estate licensing laws is to protect the public from harm from such things as real estate agents' misuse of accounts, commingling of funds, failure to maintain proper trust and escrow accounts, and other illegal activities.

Although management is not specifically addressed as a real estate function, a few states have included property management as a specific activity requiring a separate license. In most states, however, property managers are regulated under existing real estate broker-agent laws because real estate management traditionally involves renting, leasing, and rent collection activities performed on behalf of another for a fee or commission—activities that are generally covered under the broker-agent laws (see accompanying box). On-site managers may or may not be exempt from such licensing, depending on the specific wording of state statutes or interpretation of those statutes.

Many states require a real estate management firm to have a designated broker, and each real estate manager must have a real estate license. Some states require a written and executed contract to manage a property—i.e., a management agreement. Most states require an executed leasing or sales agreement for the real estate agent to be paid a commission.

It is important to ensure that the management firm complies with real estate licensing laws of each state in which the company manages or leases properties. Violations can result in the forfeiture of fees and commissions, penalties, and an order to cease and desist.

The Institute of Real Estate Management (IREM) has taken the following position in regard to licensing of property managers:

While the Institute of Real Estate Management acknowledges that the issue of separate property management licensing is a states' rights issue and should be left to the discretion of each individual state, IREM, as a national organization, believes that management of residential apartments; condominiums, cooperative and homeowner's associations; office buildings; shopping centers; and all other commercial property by independent contractors involves real estate activities and should require a license. IREM National is opposed to separate licensing for these property management activities and urges all forms of property management, including community association management, to be under the jurisdiction of existing state real estate broker and agent (salesman) licensing laws.

Further, the Institute encourages state real estate commissions, or appropriate governmental agencies, to take a stronger interest in professional property management as a real estate function in order to protect the public. This should be accomplished by adding property management curriculum to the broker and sales courses and property management questions to the testing process.

Specifically exempted from this are on-site residential managers and other on-site personnel. (This policy statement may be modified in the future.)

Agency Law. *Agency* is the legal relationship between two parties in which one party represents the interest of the other in transactions with a third party. In real estate, when one person or entity (the agent) represents the interest of another person—a seller, lessor, or property owner (the principal)—in financial dealings with others, the agent is also called a *fiduciary*. In a real estate lease transaction, an agency relationship is formed between the management company and the property owner. Agency is a consensual relationship and may be established by acts, deeds, or words of the parties. Although a written contract is not necessary to create an agency relationship, only a written management agreement or leasing agreement can be effectively adjudicated in a court of law. The agent is liable to the principal for any wrongful conduct committed by a subagent (licensed property manager); the principal may also be liable for wrongful conduct of its agent and subagents.

Although real estate managers represent the lessor (landlord) in a leasing transaction, they must be aware that lessees (tenants) may have a real estate agent represent their best interests. In a full-service real estate firm that handles sales transactions, a buyer may be represented by an agent. A buyer's or lessee's agent owes all fiduciary duties to the buyer or lessee. However, it is possible for a single agent to represent both parties to a transaction, a situation called *dual agency*.

There are two types of dual agency—disclosed and undisclosed. The

> **Duties of a Fiduciary**
>
> - Loyalty—Unswerving allegiance to the client, always acting in the client's best interest.
> - Obedience—The duty to follow directions of the principal.
> - Confidentiality—Maintaining the confidence of the principal.
> - Reasonable care and diligence—Using reasonable effort in the performance of the duties of the agent.
> - Accounting—Account for all of the client's funds the agent controls.

latter is also known as divided agency. Undisclosed dual agency is a dual relationship without the knowledge and informed consent of both parties; it is illegal. In a disclosed dual agency relationship, the brokerage firm discloses to and receives informed consent from both parties—the seller or lessor and the buyer or lessee—to act as agent for both. Informed consent is the central concept of dual agency disclosure. The courts have awarded substantial damages to principals who have been harmed by the actions of an agent that did not disclose its dual agency status. It is therefore important to be familiar with the laws of agency in each state in which the firm operates and to develop a company policy that requires compliance with all regulations regarding disclosure.

Laws Affecting the Management Company as Employer

The employer-employee relationship is one of the most regulated aspects of business. As an employer, the management firm must comply with labor laws, avoid discriminatory employment practices, and provide a safe working environment. The body of law regarding employment includes (1) federal laws passed by the U.S. Congress, (2) administrative regulations promulgated by state and federal agencies to enforce those laws, and (3) court decisions that arise out of employee lawsuits against employers.

One of the key components of a plan to avoid liability in the areas of employment law is training of supervisors, managers, and executives. Behaviors that may have been acceptable in the past may now be considered a violation of an employee's rights. (To ensure compliance, it is advisable to work with an attorney who specializes in employment and labor law. This individual should be available to consult with managers on specific employee problems, assist in developing an employee handbook, and conduct seminars on laws regulating the employer-employee relationship and "acceptable" workplace behaviors.) Many problems and potential liabilities can be avoided by careful attention to hiring practices.

Hiring Practices. A management firm's primary asset is the knowledge, experience and capability of its staff. It is critical to hire employees who

> **Some Federal Laws That Affect Employers**
>
> - Age Discrimination in Employment Act (ADEA) of 1967
> - Americans with Disabilities Act (ADA) of 1990
> - Consolidated Omnibus Reconciliation Act (COBRA) of 1985—group insurance continuation
> - Drug-Free Workplace Act of 1988
> - Employee Polygraph Protection Act (EPPA)
> - Employee Retirement Income Security Act (ERISA)
> - Fair Labor Standards Act (FLSA)—also called wage and hour law
> - Family and Medical Leave Act (FMLA) of 1993
> - Federal Insurance Contributions Act (FICA)—social security
> - Federal Unemployment Tax Act (FUTA)
> - Immigration Reform and Control Act of 1986
> - Occupational Safety and Health Act (OSHA) of 1970
> - Rehabilitation Act of 1973
> - Title VII of the Civil Rights Act of 1964
> - Veterans Re-employment Rights Act
>
> Several other laws address veterans' employment and re-employment, and other acts related to immigration may apply. Garnishment of wages, protections for employees who complain about employers (i.e., whistle-blowers, as under EPA and OSHA), equal pay for equal work, and health insurance portability are other issues addressed in federal laws. Compliance requirements change as new laws are passed and existing laws are modified or interpreted via court cases, so employers should review their employment practices periodically and seek advice of legal counsel to ensure their personnel policies and procedures are up-to-date.

have the ability and the proper attitude to perform particular jobs. Employers may select whomever they want, provided their decisions do not discriminate against potential candidates because of their membership in certain "protected classes" (i.e., based on race, color, religion, sex, national origin, age, disability). Some state and local laws prohibit discrimination on the basis of sexual orientation or other criteria. Nondiscrimination means that candidates for a job are considered on the basis of their capabilities and not on the basis of any characteristics that may be attributed to a group.

Discrimination in employment is prohibited under federal civil rights laws—e.g., Title VII of the *Civil Rights Act of 1964*—enforced by the Equal Employment Opportunity Commission (EEOC) as well as under state and local laws that may be more stringent in their requirements. Furthermore, Title I of the *Americans with Disabilities Act (ADA),* which prohibits discrimination in recruiting, hiring, promotions, compensation, training, and termination because of an applicant's disability, has set forth hiring guidelines for employers. (The substance of those guidelines is outlined in Exhibit 12.1). Specifically, the employment application should ask questions that are job-related. Information requests that can be construed as discrimi-

Exhibit 12.1
Employer Guidelines for Compliance with Title I of the Americans with Disabilities Act (ADA)

- An employer must provide an equal opportunity for an individual with a disability to participate in the job application process and to be considered for a job.
- An employer may not make any pre-employment inquiries regarding a disability, but may ask questions about the ability to perform specific job functions and may, with certain limitations, ask an individual with a disability to describe or demonstrate how he or she would perform these functions.
- An employer may not require pre-employment medical examinations or medical histories, but may condition a job offer on the results of a post-offer medical examination, if all entering employees in the same job category are required to take this examination.
- Tests for illegal drugs are not medical examinations under the ADA and may be given at any time.
- A test that screens out or tends to screen out a person with a disability on the basis of disability must be job-related and consistent with business necessity.
- Tests must reflect the skills and aptitudes of an individual rather than any impaired sensory, manual, or speaking skills, unless those are job-related skills the test is designed to measure.

---

natory include age, date of birth, year of graduation, race, religion, national origin, disabilities, physical characteristics, sex, marital status, and family status. (Some but not all of these items are necessary for participation in employee benefit programs, and those specifics should be acquired once an individual's employment begins.) Any tests used to assess ability or to measure expertise or motivation must be used within legal guidelines.

Another area of potential liability in hiring employees is negligence in verifying their qualifications. Background checks are a good business practice in general. For sensitive positions such as security guards, such checks are essential. In addition to business and personal references, employment history should be verified for all applicants; if allowed by state law, an applicant's criminal arrest and conviction records should be checked as well, although this practice may only be implemented for selected positions. (Strategies for managing employment liability risks are discussed in the box on page 298. See also Chapter 11.)

Employers must also verify employment eligibility. The *Immigration Reform and Control Act* requires employees to complete Immigration and Naturalization Service (INS) Form 9 and provide proof of their identity and eligibility to work.

Wages, Taxes, and Related Issues. Several federal laws affect both employers and employees. Some of these laws impose taxes on the employer and require submission of periodic reports and payments.

> **Other Employer Liability Issues**
>
> Hiring procedures should include a check of the selected candidate's references. The goal is to find out more than the fact that someone worked for a particular company for a specified period and how much he or she was being paid. Prior employers are rightfully reluctant to disclose more than rudimentary facts because a decision based on a negative reference may lead to claims of defamation against the former employer. However, if an individual whose references were not checked has a history of undesirable workplace behaviors (sexual harassment, verbal or physical violence) and subsequently displays those behavior patterns as your employee, you may be sued for your negligence in hiring that person. (Failure to remove the person who repeats the offenses may lead to claims of negligent retention.)
>
> One way to facilitate the acquisition of background information on prospective employees is to ask job applicants to sign a release form that can be sent to former employers. Minimally, this will state that the applicant grants permission for the former employer to release information without reprisal. Such a form should be developed in consultation with an attorney. Beyond this, you should know the law in your state—more than twenty-five states have passed laws that grant statutory immunity to employers. Some limit the immunity to select fields (e.g., health care); others apply it across the board. Several more states are considering this type of legislation as this book goes to press.
>
> The firm should also have a written policy stating causes for termination of employment. This may include a list of particular behaviors that are subject to immediate dismissal—e.g., not being truthful on application for employment, insubordination, falsifying of company records, discrimination in leasing or hiring, sexual harassment, and theft. Some actions or activities may be subject to progressive discipline, perhaps including a period of probation to allow for improvement but ending in dismissal if improvement is not forthcoming. The policy needs to be supported with specific procedures for notifying the employee and documenting the supervisor's and the employee's actions. This policy and procedure must conform to legal guidelines, or the firm could be subject to a claim of wrongful termination. Careful hiring, including background and reference checks, is a component strategy for minimizing these types of problems.

The *Fair Labor Standards Act (FLSA),* also known as the Wage and Hour Law, establishes minimum wage rates and requirements for overtime pay. Employees who work more than 40 hours per week must be compensated for the extra time at one and one-half times their regular hourly rate. However, salaried employees whose pay rates and job descriptions meet certain guidelines are exempted from the overtime requirement. States may set and enforce their own laws regarding minimum wages, overtime payments, and work schedules, and the state laws may be more stringent than the federal law. It is important to understand all the labor laws that apply in your area so that you can comply fully with them.

Federal income taxes must be withheld from employees' wages, and this necessitates keeping accurate records of time worked, wages paid, and taxes and other withholdings. Many states and some municipalities require payment of income taxes and withholding of these taxes from employees' wages. Employees are required to complete Internal Revenue Service (IRS) Form W-4, Employer's Withholding Allowance Certificate. A separate form may be required for state and local tax withholdings. (Individuals who are exempt from withholding requirements—e.g., independent contractors—should complete Form W-9, Request for Taxpayer Identification Number and Certification.)

Social security taxes must be collected in compliance with the *Federal Insurance Contributions Act (FICA)*. This law requires withholding of a set percentage from each employee's pay. An equal amount must be paid by the employer for each employee. Current requirements allocate separate portions to social security and Medicare.

Unemployment compensation is generally administered by the states, which establish eligibility requirements and payment amounts. Some states require regular payment of a percentage of each employees' wages which is held in an account for the employer. The amount is determined by the state and may be adjusted from time to time based on claims against the employer's account. The *Federal Unemployment Tax Act (FUTA)* is a separate federally mandated unemployment insurance program in which the tax is computed for individual employees' wages up to a certain dollar level. However, amounts paid to state unemployment programs can be credited toward the FUTA totals. (Income tax, FICA, and FUTA payment and reporting requirements are outlined in *Circular E, Employer's Tax Guide,* published by the Internal Revenue Service and revised annually.)

Employment Practices. Issues regarding employees' wages and hours that can become bases for lawsuits are overtime pay, compensatory time off, exempt and non-exempt status, and minimum wage. Employers must comply with both federal and state regulations regarding wages, hours, and other employment issues. Where state laws are more stringent than federal laws, the state laws will prevail. Management company executives can avoid violations by understanding the law, applying the law to all employees, and maintaining accurate and complete records. This is best accomplished by establishing employee and employment policies and procedures and making sure they are followed. (More information on personnel policies and practices can be found in Chapter 5.) To assure compliance with applicable laws, it is important to review and update your personnel policies and procedures periodically and communicate to your employees any changes made to them.

The company's employment policies and procedures can be summarized for distribution to all staff members in an *employee handbook* (see Exhibit 5.2). It is advisable for such a handbook to include a notice that it

> **Employment at Will**
>
> Under the doctrine of "employment at will," personnel may leave a company or their employment may be terminated by the employer at any time, without any reason, unless there is an express agreement to the contrary. Note, however, that if an at-will employee is discharged by the employer, he or she may bring suit claiming *wrongful discharge,* alleging that the termination was in violation of federal or state anti-discrimination laws, an implied employment contract, or other covenants.

does not constitute a set of promises or an employment contract. Depending on state law, this might include a statement that employment is at the will of the company, and that the company or the employee may terminate the employment at any time for any reason. It is more than just advisable to have the contents of your employee handbook reviewed by an attorney; not having it reviewed may be considered evidence of ineptitude.

Typically, such a handbook is given to new employees when they start work, and they should be required to sign a form acknowledging that they received and read the handbook and understand its application to their employment role and status. If the firm employs anyone who does not read or understand English, it is obligated to provide the information in the employee handbook to such individuals in a suitable translation. The translation can be in writing, and the employee can sign a translated version of the usual acknowledgment form. Alternatively, arrangements may be made for a translator to read the information to the employee and attest to the fact of the presentation and the employee's understanding. (The signed acknowledgment form or attestation should be retained in the employee's personnel file.)

Periodic formal *performance evaluation* interviews are an excellent opportunity for the supervisor to review an employee's performance, establish goals and time lines, praise good performance, and discuss areas of weakness and poor performance—also agreeing on ways to overcome the latter. A performance review should be a dialogue between supervisor and employee regarding responsibilities and performance and, for the participants to come to an understanding, it must be objective and fair. Too often, a supervisor rates an employee's performance as good—or acceptable—in several areas and thus avoids discussing areas of weakness. Such an incomplete evaluation is not only unfair to the employee, but can undermine the defense of a lawsuit if the employee challenges a termination. The most useful evaluations are documented—this is recommended practice—and both supervisor and employee keep copies for reference. If a management company uses a written performance evaluation, the form and format should first be reviewed by an attorney.

Termination of employment is one of the most difficult tasks a supervisor faces. In addition to the unpleasantness inherent in this action, the supervisor must be concerned with the manner in which the situation is handled. It is important to ensure that the steps taken prior to and during the termination process comply with applicable laws so the employee will not prevail in a lawsuit claiming *wrongful discharge*. Statements that are made regarding a terminated employee in responding to prospective employers or others can create liability for the company and the person making the statement.

Some companies have adopted a policy of not providing specific references or letters of recommendation. Instead, they will only provide a former employee's dates of employment and position title. This is a common practice regardless of why an employee has left a company (i.e., voluntarily or involuntarily). Usually the human resources manager or other individual responsible for maintaining personnel records is uniquely and exclusively charged with responding to requests for personal information. Many businesses make available a standard "consent for release of employment information" form for employees to sign. This allows the human resources manager to respond more specifically, especially if an employee needs a credit reference. The form can provide space to stipulate what information the employee wishes released.

It is important to establish a policy on providing references for former employees, and all supervisory personnel should be informed of what the policy is and reminded periodically of the implications of not following it. This is another area where the advice of legal counsel is warranted. At issue is the possibility of personnel outside the human resources arena making statements that could have a negative impact for the former employee seeking the reference and, consequently, for the individual who gave the reference and for the company. On the other hand, former employers may be sued for not providing information that would have prevented the hiring—and attendant problems resulting from the employment—of an individual whose behavior was unacceptable (e.g., sexual harassment) or who had been involved in workplace violence or other criminal acts during prior employment. Legal counsel can help you shape policies and practices to meet the specific needs of the management company. (This discussion has only highlighted some of the specific legal issues regarding employment practices. Information on the mechanics of hiring, training, and employee relations is presented in Chapter 5.)

Not all people working in real estate management are direct employees. A company may try to avoid placing someone on its payroll by calling the person an *independent contractor*. However, there are specific criteria that must be met to qualify for independent contractor status. Simply calling someone an independent contractor, and paying the person a fee, is not enough. In addition to the legal issues under the Fair Labor Standards Act (FLSA), the Federal Insurance Contributions Act (FICA), the Federal Unemployment Tax Act (FUTA), and the Internal Revenue Service (income tax) code, the distinction between employee and independent contractor has economic consequences for the company: If a worker who does not qualify for independent contractor status is injured on the job, he or she may file a claim or lawsuit against the company claiming employee status. However, the company may not have that worker covered on its workers' compensation policy because of the incorrect assignment of independent contractor status. (More information on the difference between employee and independent contractor status can be found in Chapter 5.)

The Work Environment. A number of issues related to the general workplace environment have specific legal implications. The subject of violence in the workplace has been addressed in numerous books and periodicals and is beyond the scope of this text. However, two topics that warrant an overview description because of their potential liability are sexual harassment and workplace safety.

An employee's rights may be violated during his or her employment because of the employer's action or inaction, and sexual harassment has become an issue of increasing concern. In this regard, the Equal Employment Opportunity Commission (EEOC) issued "Guidelines on Sexual Harassment in the Workplace," which describe *sexual harassment* as follows:

> Unwelcome sexual advances, requests for sexual favors, and other verbal or physical conduct of a sexual nature constitute sexual harassment when (1) submission to such conduct is made either explicitly or implicitly a term or condition of an individual's employment, (2) submission to or rejection of such conduct by an individual is used as the basis for employment decisions affecting such individual, or (3) such conduct has the purpose or effect of unreasonably interfering with an individual's work performance or creating an intimidating, hostile, or offensive working environment.

Three types of behavior are recognized as constituting categories of sexual harassment:

> *Verbal*—sexually oriented comments or suggestive compliments or remarks, pet names, threats, insults, jokes about gender-specific traits, sexual propositions.
>
> *Nonverbal*—flirting, leering, whistling, jeering, suggestive or insulting noises, obscene gestures.
>
> *Physical*—touching, pinching, restricting movement, coercing sexual intercourse, assault.

According to the EEOC guidelines, the best way for an employer to deal with sexual harassment is to:

- Take all necessary steps to prevent it (an explicit policy, communicated to employees and implemented).
- Raise the subject with employees and express strong disapproval.
- Develop appropriate sanctions and inform employees of their rights to raise the issue.
- Establish a procedure for resolving complaints.

Critical to achieving this goal is making sure *all* employees are sensitive to the issue, ensuring confidentiality, and protecting victims against retaliation. An individual who believes he or she has been the victim of sexual harassment can file a charge with the EEOC. Once a claim of sexual harassment is received, you should immediately contact your attorney and ask for guidance in handling the situation.

The workplace itself is subject to regulation. The *Occupational Safety and Health Act* of 1970 was intended to foster development and implementation of practices by both employers and employees that would reduce workplace hazards and improve existing safety programs. Its various regulations and standards affect all industries, including real estate management, and there are severe penalties for violations of this federal law. The Occupational Safety and Health Administration (OSHA) also approves workplace safety and health programs established by states, and these vary among the states. As with most regulations, the most stringent ones must be complied with, and state standards often exceed federal requirements.

An important component of OSHA compliance is worker training regarding known hazards, techniques for controlling such hazards, and emergency procedures for dealing with incidents—hazardous spills, injury to workers, damage to equipment or the workplace. Materials known to be even minimally dangerous require the manufacturer or distributor (or both) to provide a material safety data sheet (MSDS) for each material listing the type and degree of danger involved. Pesticides used for lawn care and extermination of vermin, chemicals used in systems maintenance and for cleaning metallic and other finishing materials, even the carbon ink (toner) used in photocopy machines, have listed hazards. Toxicity and flammability are common hazards to be communicated to workers, and they should receive training in how to handle hazardous materials to avoid accidents or injuries. Management of properties whose tenancies include health care providers and related testing facilities pose the additional risk of exposure to blood-borne pathogens—e.g., human immunovirus (HIV/AIDS), hepatitis B (HBV), and other transmissible viruses and bacteria—from handling medical wastes or cleaning up spills. While the degree to which particular types of hazards are regulated will vary, training employees to handle hazardous materials carefully, providing appropriate safety equipment and clothing, and establishing emergency procedures to address the types of

Twenty Ways to Minimize Liability for Sexual Harassment in the Workplace

1. Specifically state in your employment handbook that you are committed to creating and maintaining a workplace free of sexual harassment.
2. In your policy, define as "prohibited acts" such actions as improper suggestions, graphic comments or discussions about an individual's body or physical appearance, degrading verbal comments, and offensive flirtations.
3. Make sure all employees are fully aware of your company's policy and procedures on sexual harassment.
4. Establish a policy concerning disciplinary actions that may be taken against policy violators.
5. Develop a separate and specific grievance or complaint procedure for employees victimized by sexual harassment.
6. Ensure that someone other than an employee's supervisor is available to receive and investigate sexual harassment complaints.
7. Make sure your policy has been reviewed by legal counsel.
8. In your policy, specifically state that sexual harassment investigations will be conducted on a confidential basis.
9. Conduct routine training programs for all supervisors, managers, and employees on sexual harassment and your firm's policies.
10. Record the dates on which training sessions take place and keep attendance.
11. During the investigation process, make sure to interview the individual harassed, the alleged harasser, witnesses, and any other victims involved.
12. Before a charge is made, identify who would conduct the investigation.
13. Establish a procedure for communicating the results of the investigation.
14. Make an effort to act on complaints of harassment immediately and fully.
15. Discuss possible forms of discipline for violators of your policy (counseling, a job or department transfer, suspension, demotion, termination, no action).
16. Establish a list of factors that will influence the type of discipline that is administered (weight of evidence, nature of the harassment, position of the individual harassed, whether or not the complainant has an attorney, whether nor not the complainant has notified the EEOC or the press).
17. Calculate the cost to your organization of sexual harassment in terms of: awards and settlement fees, administrative costs, public relations costs, turnover, sick leave and personal time off, absenteeism, and lower productivity.
18. Do not allow employees to display lewd or indecent pictures or other materials depicting men or women as sex objects.
19. Do not allow sexually connotative remarks, sex-related jokes, or off-color stories routinely to be told in the workplace.
20. Make an effort to prevent a sexually charged atmosphere from permeating the workplace environment.

Source: *AMO® Perspectives*, Spring 1993, p.20. Copyright 1993 by the Institute of Real Estate Management. Reprinted with permission.

incidents that are likely to occur will ensure that your employees are properly protected.

Some states require that every business have a safety committee comprised of an equal number of management and non-management employees. This is a good business practice, regardless of state or other requirements. Investment in specific safety training and emergency preparedness —e.g., seminars, drills or mock incidents, cardiopulmonary resuscitation (CPR)—can pay huge dividends in lives saved, health preserved, property protected, and lawsuits avoided.

Other Legal Requirements. Under the *Family and Medical Leave Act (FMLA),* employers are required to grant employees time off without pay for medical conditions, child care, and other family situations. Employees' benefits must continue in effect for the duration of such unpaid leave, and returning employees must be restored to their original or an equivalent position. A variety of qualifications may apply, including a requirement for the employee to give advance notice and provide certification of a medical condition. Violations of this act can result in a civil lawsuit against the employer.

While it is important to check references and verify job applicants' experience, work history, and salary information, employers may also require candidates to undergo testing to verify skills (e.g., typing, accounting) or suitability to a particular position (e.g., attitudes). Psychological profile testing can yield invaluable information. However, such tests should be evaluated by a qualified professional to avoid biased interpretation and protect against potential claims of discrimination in hiring.

Except for certain types of positions and certain industries where polygraph testing is necessary, this type of test is rarely done. When it is used, there are rules that must be followed. Specifically, the *Employee Polygraph Protection Act (EPPA)* limits the employer's use of polygraph test results in making hiring decisions and provides safeguards for prospective employees who are asked to submit to such testing.

Employers are required to post notices regarding employment laws in a prominent place accessible by all employees. Federal regulations require the following to be posted:

- Minimum Wage (FLSA)
- Job Safety and Health Protection (OSHA)
- Equal Opportunity Is the Law (EEOC)
- Family and Medical Leave Act (FMLA)
- Employee Polygraph Protection Act (EPPA)

Where state or local laws or collective bargaining agreements impose a higher minimum wage or more stringent safety or other requirements, the latter prevail, and appropriate notices regarding them must be posted as well.

Workers' compensation insurance is required under separate laws in each state. The purpose is to provide compensation (replacement wages and costs of care) when employees become ill or are injured (or killed) on the job. Employers are required to obtain this type of insurance policy or to be self-insured. Usually a private insurance carrier is the source. However, some states (e.g., California) have their own workers' compensation insurance programs.

Employees who are terminated or voluntarily leave employment, or who would otherwise lose their benefits, must be offered an opportunity to continue their group health care (medical, dental, etc.) coverage for a period of time by paying the insurance premiums themselves. This is required under the *Consolidated Omnibus Budget Reconciliation Act (COBRA)*.

If the company establishes a pension plan of any kind, a promise has been made to employee-participants, and their rights are safeguarded under the *Employee Retirement Income Security Act (ERISA)*. Details of the requirements of this law can be found in the *Employer's Pension Guide,* a publication of the U.S. Department of Labor. Because having a pension program can impact the employer's tax status, it is important to be aware of the implications of different types of pension plans.

Laws Affecting the Management of Real Property

A variety of laws affect the management of all types of properties. These include landlord-tenant laws, environmental regulations, and the Americans with Disabilities Act. Residential properties are especially impacted by fair housing laws promulgated at federal, state, and local levels.

Landlord-Tenant Laws. Landlord-tenant laws vary in every state, and those regarding residential property often differ from the requirements for commercial properties. Generally, such laws spell out the respective rights and responsibilities of the landlord and tenant as well as the recourse available to each party in the event the other party defaults on its obligations. Requirements for serving of notice (timing and manner of delivery) are usually spelled out as well.

The most widely accepted source regarding the rights and responsibilities of landlords and residential tenants is the *Uniform Residential Landlord and Tenant Act* drafted by the National Conference of Commissioners on Uniform State Laws. Many states have adopted this law or some version of it. Local building codes regarding health and safety (i.e., issues of habitability) and ordinances that address tenants' rights (e.g., collection and disposition of security deposits) may also affect the landlord-tenant relationship and the lease document.

> **Some Other Legal Issues Encountered in Managing Real Estate**
> - Real estate managers who oversee tenant improvements at commercial properties or perform construction coordination need to be aware of local (and state) requirements under existing *building codes* and *zoning ordinances,* which are subject to change.
> - Managers of common interest realty associations (e.g., condominiums) will need an understanding of the state *condominium law* and how it relates to the various documents that create and govern the operation of the condominium owners' association.
> - The issue of residents' rights is one that confronts managers of apartments and other rental housing in many ways. Federal agencies that provide funding for government assisted housing encourage residents at these properties to form residents' organizations, and they provide guidelines for the role of the real estate manager. In conventional apartments, residents sometimes join together to take group action when the landlord (owner and/or manager of the property) is not responsive to their problems and concerns. In some locales, *tenants' rights ordinances* provide a legal basis for action to resolve problems with residential landlords.
> - Even though shopping centers are private property, they are often perceived as public venues because they invite the general population onto their premises. This perception can create problems when individuals or groups want to use the center property as a public forum to air their views —they may claim that not permitting such use violates their *first amendment* rights of free speech. Before any such use is permitted, local ordinances (and state and federal laws) should be reviewed and advice of legal counsel should be sought to determine what is legally required and establish a workable policy regarding dissemination of information at a managed shopping center.

If the residential tenant does not comply with the lease, the landlord may institute eviction proceedings. Depending on the jurisdiction, there may be requirements for serving one or more notices regarding the tenant's noncompliance, and such notices may have to be served by a court-appointed process server. In addition, the landlord may have to be represented by legal council in court proceedings or appear in person, or both. Those who manage residential properties should consult their attorneys regarding local requirements so that any necessary evictions are conducted according to the law. If they are not, the proceeding may have to be initiated again.

Similar issues are involved in commercial landlord-tenant relationships. In particular, local building codes may establish limitations on the size and placement of commercial signage in addition to occupancy requirements that include health and safety (habitability) standards.

Every real estate manager must know and understand the requirements of the landlord-tenant laws that apply in the jurisdiction where the property they manage is located. Violation of these laws robs residents or commer-

> **Environmental Laws That Impact Managed Real Estate**
> - Asbestos Hazard Emergency Response Act (AHERA)
> - Clean Air Act (CAA)
> - Clean Water Act (CWA)
> - Comprehensive Environmental Response, Compensation, and Liability Act (CERCLA)—also known as Superfund
> - Emergency Wetlands Resources Act (EWRA)
> - Endangered Species Act (ESA)
> - Resource Conservation and Recovery Act (RCRA)
> - Toxic Substances Control Act (TSCA)
>
> These federal laws and amendments to them are clarified on an ongoing basis via agency regulations and court rulings. In addition, laws mandating recycling of paper, plastics, and other materials have been passed in many states.

cial tenants of their rights and exposes the property owner and the management firm to potential liability that can lead to expensive lawsuits. (More information on landlord-tenant laws can be found in real estate management books that focus on specific property types, some of which are listed in Appendix C.)

Environmental Laws. Because environmental regulations are in a constant state of flux, real estate managers must understand current laws and be informed on the status of proposed regulations. Professional real estate associations, such as the Institute of Real Estate Management (IREM), the Building Owners and Managers Association (BOMA), the International Council of Shopping Centers (ICSC), and others, monitor proposed local and national regulations and lobby on behalf of the real estate industry. Though environmental violations by third parties cannot always be prevented, the potential for liability risk exposure on the part of the real estate management company can be reduced by being aware of and complying with environmental laws.

Everyone in the industry must have a basic understanding of the range of environmental problems that might be encountered on a property, the means of responding to such problems legally and ethically, and the prevailing laws that dictate specific actions. Under Superfund (the *Comprehensive Environmental Response, Compensation, and Liability Act*— CERCLA), liability and therefore responsibility for remediation or cleanup costs can be attributed to those who transported wastes to the site, those who arranged for wastes to be disposed of or treated at the site, and present and past owners or operators of the site. Thus a substantial amount of Superfund litigation has been devoted to attribution of liability, with many courts

> **Environmental Liability Protection**
>
> Under common law and civil law, a property manager may be liable for "toxic torts." A "tort" is generally defined as a wrongful act, not involving breach of contract, for which a civil suit can be brought. There are two types of torts—those that involve property damage (property torts) and those that involve personal injury or damages (personal torts). The only way the manager can distance himself or herself from any environmental liability that the owner incurs is to address the issue of tort liability in the management contract.
>
> Source: *Environmental Management for Real Estate Professionals* by David C. Parks, CPM®. Copyright 1992 by the Institute of Real Estate Management. Reprinted by permission of the publisher.

having ruled that there is "joint and several" liability under Superfund—i.e., the obligation may be enforced against all involved parties jointly or against any of them separately. The liability risks facing real estate managers are not clearly defined, although the agency role and the management function could be interpreted as bestowing "owner" or "operator" status on the manager. Some types of problems may be averted by seeking indemnification from environmental liability for the management company (and the individual manager) when negotiating management agreements. In addition, the language of the agreement should not refer to the fee manager as an "operator" or use the terms "operate," "operator," or "operations."

It is also appropriate to include environmental provisions in lease documents although these may not always be easily negotiated. Such provisions are especially desirable in commercial property leases, and they should include indemnification of the landlord *and its agents* from liability arising out of the tenant's activities.

Asbestos and asbestos-containing materials (ACMs) used as insulation and fire-retardant treatments, lead-based paint, polychlorinated biphenyl (PCB) heat-transfer agents used in electrical transformers, chlorofluorocarbon (CFC) refrigerants used in air-conditioning systems, and leaking underground storage tanks (LUSTs) no longer used to hold fuel oils are among the environmental issues likely to impact the management of real estate. All are addressed variously by federal, state, and local environmental regulations. Indoor air quality (IAQ), radon gas, and electromagnetic fields (EMFs) have also received a great deal of attention. These are all in addition to federal laws—and some state and local laws—regulating emissions *(Clean Air Act)*, toxic discharges *(Clean Water Act)*, and disposal of hazardous wastes in landfills *(Resource Conservation and Recovery Act)*. The *Endangered Species Act* and laws intended to preserve wetlands also may impact real estate transactions and operations.

Because state laws may be more stringent than federal laws (some counties and municipalities have also enacted environmental ordinances), consultation with an environmental attorney is recommended to ensure that management agreements and leases comply with applicable laws. An especially useful resource regarding all types of real estate activities is the IREM publication, *Environmental Management for Real Estate Professionals,* by David C. Parks, CPM®. In addition to summarizing the laws and their impact, the book includes examples of environmental lease and management agreement provisions.

Americans with Disabilities Act (ADA). In addition to its impact on employment practices (under Title I), one of the primary purposes of the ADA is to make all buildings that are open to public commerce accessible to disabled people to the maximum extent possible (Title III). Under this Act, all public areas of commercial properties are required to be accessible to persons with disabilities. Leasing offices and other areas of residential properties that are open to the public (swimming pools, clubhouses, etc.) fall within this domain. (The Fair Housing Amendments Act of 1988, discussed later in this chapter, prohibits discrimination against persons with disabilities in regard to housing and provides for reasonable modifications of rental units and *private* common areas at the resident's expense. The cost of mandatory removal of *barriers*—i.e., physical obstacles that inhibit movement and communication obstacles that inhibit personal interaction—as required under the ADA is a landlord's expense.)

The ADA attempts a tough balancing act between achieving accessibility for the disabled and providing enough flexibility to keep building owners from entering Chapter 11 (bankruptcy). Any private entity that owns, leases, or operates a place of public accommodation is responsible for implementing the requirements, which apply to existing public accommodations as well as new ones. Existing buildings that serve the public must be made accessible for people with disabilities whether or not the needed accommodations are readily achievable. New construction and renovations of commercial facilities must meet the accessibility standards described in the regulations. A *public accommodation* under the ADA is a facility operated by a private entity whose operations affect commerce and fall within at least one of twelve specified categories.

1. Places of lodging
2. Establishments serving food or drink
3. Places of exhibition or entertainment
4. Places of public gathering
5. Sales or rental establishments

6. Service establishments
7. Stations used for public transportation
8. Places of public display or collection
9. Places of recreation
10. Places of education
11. Social service centers
12. Places of exercise or recreation

In order to comply with the ADA's accessibility requirements, public accommodations must (1) modify discriminatory practices, policies, and procedures; (2) provide auxiliary aids and services to facilitate communication with disabled people; and (3) remove structural and communications barriers where removal is "readily achievable." (The law defines an array of twenty-one alterations that are considered readily achievable.)

The economic implications of Title III are wide-ranging, and a more detailed discussion of this law's implications is beyond the scope of this book. There are numerous publications on guidelines for complying with the Americans with Disabilities Act, including the IREM Hot Topics publication, *ADA Title III—Compliance Made Practical.* Several organizations (architectural firms, real estate management companies) offer ADA compliance assessment services.

Fair Housing Laws. The United States was founded on the belief that all men are created equal. Real estate managers have practical as well as moral reasons for following fair housing guidelines. Everyone is entitled to equal opportunities in choosing where to live. It is incumbent upon the managers and the on-site staff of residential properties to ensure that everyone with whom they come in contact, especially residents and prospective residents, is treated fairly, with objectivity, and in accordance with established fair housing laws. Violators of fair housing laws can be assessed substantial civil penalties, and victims of discrimination who successfully sue can receive actual and punitive damages.

The *Civil Rights Act of 1968* was the first federal law to devote an entire section (Title VIII) to fair housing. Title VIII prohibits housing discrimination, in both rental and sales practices, based on race, color, religion and/or national origin. In 1974, sex was added as a protected class by a provision in the *Housing and Community Development Act.* Title VIII applies to incidents that occurred before and after its enactment, and it makes several types of activities illegal, including refusal to rent, discriminatory language in advertising, and denying the availability of units. (Exhibit 12.2 lists more examples of discriminatory activities.)

Subsequently, the *Fair Housing Amendments Act* of 1988 added two

Exhibit 12.2
Examples of Discriminatory Activities

- Refusal to rent
- Refusal to negotiate rental
- Refusal to show available units
- Refusal to supply rental information, such as rental rates
- False representation of nonavailability
- Imposition of different rental charges, security deposits, or rental terms or conditions
- Discriminatory information requested on rental applications (e.g., asking about number of children or presence of handicap)
- Discriminatory qualification criteria, applications, or procedures
- Delay tactics to frustrate a person from pursuing rental
- Restrictions or different provisions in lease contracts
- Provision of different levels of services or facilities
- Sexual harassment
- Discriminatory notices or statements
- Eviction on the basis of a protected class
- Advertising indicating discriminatory preference or limitation through language or the use of locations, logos, or human models
- Selective use of media (e.g., advertising only in newspapers whose readership is predominantly one group)
- Steering (channeling minorities to certain parts of a community, building, or floor)
- Block busting or panic selling

more protected classes to Title VIII: handicap and familial status. It also made changes to the litigation process, enforcement provisions, and remedies available under Title VIII. The Fair Housing Amendments Act defines handicap as "a physical or mental impairment which substantially limits one or more of such person's major life activities, a record of having such an impairment, or being regarded as having such an impairment, but this does not include current, illegal use of or addiction to a controlled substance." Under the Act, housing providers are required to make *reasonable accommodations* in rules, policies, practices, or services and allow *reasonable modifications* of existing premises.

The Act defines familial status as "one or more individuals (who have not attained the age of 18) living with a parent or other person having legal custody of such individual or individuals, or the designee of such parent or other person having such custody, with the written permission of such parent or other person." This includes "any person who is pregnant or is in the process of securing legal custody of any individual who has not attained the age of 18." The Act does make provision for some exemptions. These include housing specifically designated for older persons and owner-occupied buildings.

Real estate management professionals must apply fair housing practices to almost every aspect of their jobs. The leasing process, from adver-

> **Some Tips for Avoiding Lawsuits**
> - Ensure that management's responsibilities and authority are clearly defined in a written management agreement.
> - Develop comprehensive knowledge of the property under management, from its ownership history to its physical condition and legal compliance status.
> - Understand the person (and the personality) of the owner-client.
> - Establish and maintain frequent communication between the manager and the owner-client.
> - Practice full disclosure of facts. By the same token, clearly differentiate opinion from fact.
> - Avoid conflicts of interest.
> - Maintain complete written records, including a chronological record of actions taken or not taken in a particular situation.

tising to qualifying residents, is where most managers are vulnerable to complaints of discrimination. The types of pictures and symbols used in advertising (e.g., showing only white people) may imply that those are the only type of people being sought as residents.

Each site office should establish policies and procedures for every aspect of leasing that encourage fair housing practices, and these should be followed to the letter for every phone call or visit from a prospective resident. Following the same procedure the same way every time is the only way to be sure that every prospect receives identical treatment, fills out the same forms, and is subject to the same objective selection criteria. Your commitment to fair housing practices can be demonstrated to the public by displaying the Fair Housing poster and using the Equal Housing Opportunity logo in printed advertising.

In addition, every employee should receive training on the intent of fair housing laws and possible repercussions for violating them. If a discrimination complaint is filed, the chain of liability extends all the way to the property owner. Under federal laws, not only is the person who discriminated liable under a complaint, but that person's supervisors and employers can also be liable, even if they were unaware of the discriminatory activity. Real estate management personnel also need to be aware of state and local fair housing laws and ordinances and their implications. In some jurisdictions, discrimination on the basis of lifestyle or sexual preference is specifically prohibited in addition to the protected classes under federal laws. In all situations, the laws that are most stringent prevail. It is therefore prudent to have residential lease forms, rental marketing and promotional copy, and leasing policies and procedures reviewed by legal counsel to assist in maintaining nondiscriminatory practices. (More information about the implications of fair housing laws can be found in the IREM publication, *Fair Housing Practices for Every Day: Treating People Right*.)

Other Considerations

Difficult economic times that increase the numbers of troubled properties and foreclosures create opportunities for real estate managers to serve as court-appointed receivers. This role has very specific legal requirements that must be met. In addition, many types of documents have specific legal implications. Not only management agreements, but maintenance contracts, leases, and promotional materials require periodic review by legal counsel to ensure that they provide adequate protections for the management firm within the current business environment.

Receivership. Lenders seek appointment of a receiver because a loan has been defaulted. The default can be monetary (e.g., nonpayment) or non-monetary (e.g., allowing the property to fall into disrepair). The lender's petition to the court to appoint a receiver may be concurrent with an action to foreclose—most receiverships end in foreclosure. In asking to have an independent party take possession of the property during foreclosure proceedings, the lender's objectives are to prevent the borrower from using the income from the asset for any purpose other than payment of the loan or lowering the value of the property in any way and to halt the deterioration of the property.

Appointment as a receiver requires an awareness of the responsibilities of the role and the attendant issues of liability. Because there is potential for conflict between the lender who is seeking to foreclose the property and the previous owner who has defaulted on the loan, the receiver has to be impartial and prevent the property from being used by either party against the other. The receiver's primary goal is to conserve the value of the real estate asset until the receivership is dissolved (usually at the culmination of the foreclosure).

The court order of appointment gives the receiver authority to monitor leases and sign new ones. However, written approval should be obtained from the court before any long-term leases are signed. In addition, a receiver should have the authority to collect all rental income, protect the property and maintain it (at least in its current condition), honor the rights of tenants on the property, and safeguard the health and welfare of occupants and guests. If the receiver is submitting monthly reports to everyone concerned (property owner, lender, the court) stating exactly what actions are being taken, how much money is being collected, and how much is being spent, it will be difficult to challenge the receiver's actions at a later time.

To protect the appointed receiver and the management company from liability, an attorney should be hired and the receiver should be named on all insurance policies covering the property in receivership. If the receiver's own company will provide management services, this action requires prior approval from the court. Court approval should also be sought for any extraordinary expenses to avoid liability in the event those expenses are contested. Use of a separate service corporation to hire existing on-site employees from the property in receivership is also recommended.

To avoid being held liable as an individual, the receiver should sign no documents pertaining to the receivership other than as the receiver (in all cases, the order of appointment issued by the court should be referenced). A final report should be completed at the end of the receivership period absolving the receiver of any liability pertaining to the property. While a bond protects the lender and the property owner from any inappropriate actions of the receiver, it does not protect the receiver; such protection requires indemnification from the lender. (More specific information on this subject can be found in the IREM Hot Topics publication, *A Guide to Managing REO and Receivership Properties*.)

Documents Requiring Legal Attention. There is an endless array of issues that have the potential of creating risks or liabilities for a real estate management company. The following are some areas that require particular attention and review by legal counsel.

> *Maintenance agreements*—Management companies should have their own maintenance agreements, and these should include necessary hold-harmless provisions to protect the firm and the property owner against negligent acts or inadequacies of work performed by vendors or contractors. The agreement should also require that the vendor or contractor carry specific types of insurance, with minimum limits of coverage, and list the management company as an additional named insured party. The contract should also state that the individual is not an employee of the management company or the property owner (i.e., an independent contractor).
>
> *Management agreements*—The insurance indemnification provision of management agreements must be carefully negotiated. The management firm and the property owner may have different positions in suits brought by third parties.
>
> *Leasing and sales agreements*—Leasing and sales agreements should include provisions that protect the agent from inaccurate information provided by the property owner and provide for payment of commissions after the expiration of the agreement for transactions initiated while the agreement was in effect.

In addition, brochures and site plans for commercial properties should include statements allowing the property owner to modify, change, or expand

---

Some Tips on Hiring an Attorney

- Anticipate the need for an attorney's services, and have counsel in place as early as possible, preferably before a problem becomes a lawsuit.
- Identify prospects by asking for recommendations from other real estate management professionals you know.
- Prepare yourself. Collect all the facts of the situation (favorable and unfavorable) and develop specific questions to ask.
- Interview prospective attorneys. Ask about their prior experience with your particular type of problem and the results they achieved. Other points to ask about include how they will approach your case, who will actually do the work, how long the process may take, and how much it is likely to cost (also the basis for billing).
- Ask for references—current and former clients—and follow up with them.
- Evaluate the prospects' competence, the cost information provided, and the person's "fit" with you and your needs. You need to choose an attorney who will work with you, as well as for you, at a cost you can afford.
- Have the representation arrangement documented in writing. The agreement should identify participants (attorneys, other staff), the roles they will play, and the charges for each one (including whether the fee is hourly, fixed, or contingency based); specify what you have hired the attorney to do for you and whether the relationship is to be ongoing; state the expected time frame for completion of the specific case, including interim deadlines as appropriate; and spell out the types of other expenses that may be charged to you, when you will be billed (preferably billing should be at least monthly), and what the bill will show (how much detail will be itemized).

---

the property and to change or eliminate any tenants to ensure the success of other tenants. Commercial leases need to be carefully summarized—including lease restrictions, such as exclusives, first right of refusal provisions, etc.—and the summaries should become part of the management and leasing plan for the property.

A Perspective on Legal Issues

The variety of laws and regulations impacting business in general and real estate management in particular make it imperative to have access to qualified legal counsel. Furthermore, issues related to the management company and the conduct of its business often require expertise in areas outside the realm of real estate law. Like the real estate profession, the legal profession has multiple disciplines. An attorney with expertise in landlord-tenant law may have only limited understanding of employment laws. Contract law differs from environmental regulations.

A management company will need different attorneys to represent its

> **Some Tips on Hiring an Attorney *(continued)***
>
> Because many attorneys do not charge for an initial consultation (ask if they do), you should interview several before making a hiring decision. You are likely to have need of different types of legal expertise in different situations and may have more than one attorney on retainer at a time. Once an attorney has been hired, you should receive periodic reports on his or her progress with the case and itemized billing statements showing the specific service performed along with the date and amount of time. If other people in the attorney's office provide services, these should be specified, and costs not specific to the lawyer's activities (outside expenses) should be clearly differentiated.
>
> As with other contractual arrangements, many terms are negotiable. Strive for an arrangement that best suits your needs. Make sure the written agreement includes all the points agreed to by you and the attorney (this is very important because anything omitted could have repercussions later). Be sure you understand the terms of the agreement; if you have questions, ask them.

interests and provide guidance on handling different issues. In choosing among law firms and individual attorneys, one needs to consider many factors, among them expertise in a particular area, availability for consultation on relevant questions, ability to handle legal matters in a timely manner, and a fair fee.

13

Strategies for Maintaining Ethical Practices

Virtually every business organization and professional group has a code of professional ethics. Ethical practices are a critical part of the business and social fabric of the United States. The presumption of a strong ethical approach is the basis of all management agreements as well as real estate managers' actions on a day-to-day basis. Often they are acting in situations that cannot be completely defined by a specific set of policies and procedures, and they must rely on the good judgment of those acting on their behalf to do so honestly, legally, and ethically.

Obviously one's actions can be legal and still not be ethical. It may be perfectly legal to accept a $1,000 stereo from someone who secured a maintenance contract on a large property you manage, but is it ethical? Sometimes the management agreement or employment agreement will be very specific on the acceptance of gifts (perhaps indicating a dollar value, a type of item, or particular circumstances as *exceptions*)—and sometimes it will be silent; however, the ethical response is to refuse gifts under these circumstances.

The Certified Property Manager® (CPM®) Code of Ethics

The Institute of Real Estate Management requires that all CPM members agree to abide by a Code of Professional Ethics (Exhibit 13.1). The Code includes a statement about the consequences of violations of the Code by CPM members (article 13, Enforcement) and provides for disciplinary action to be taken in accordance with IREM bylaws and rules and regulations. Complaints regarding potential ethical violations are investigated; there

Exhibit 13.1
Code of Professional Ethics of the
CERTIFIED PROPERTY MANAGER® (CPM®)

Introduction
To establish and maintain public confidence in the honesty, integrity, professionalism, and ability of the professional property manager is fundamental to the future success of the Institute of Real Estate Management and its members. This Code and performance pursuant to its provisions will be beneficial to the general public and contribute to the continued development of a mutually beneficial relationship among CERTIFIED PROPERTY MANAGER members, candidates for membership, REALTORS, clients, employers, and the public.

The Institute of Real Estate Management, as the professional society of property management, seeks to work closely with all other segments of the real estate industry to protect and enhance the interests of the public. To this end, members of the Institute have adopted and, as a condition of membership, subscribe to this Code of Professional Ethics. By doing so, they give notice that they clearly recognize the vital need to preserve and encourage fair and equitable practices and competition among all who are engaged in the profession of property management.

Those who are members of the Institute are dedicated individuals who are sincerely concerned with the protection and interest of those who come in contact with the industry. To this end, members of the Institute have subscribed to this professional pledge:

I pledge myself to the advancement of professional property management through the mutual efforts of members of the Institute of Real Estate Management and by any other proper means available to me.

I pledge myself to seek and maintain an equitable, honorable, and cooperative association with fellow members of the Institute and with all others who may become a part of my business and professional life.

I pledge myself to place honesty, integrity and industriousness above all else; to pursue my gainful efforts with diligent study and education to the end that service to my clients shall always be maintained at the highest possible level.

I pledge myself to comply with the principles and declarations of the Institute of Real Estate Management as set forth in its Bylaws, Regulations, and this Code of Professional Ethics.

---

may be a hearing before the Ethics Hearing and Discipline Board which, by secret vote, can discipline a violator via a letter of censure, suspension, or termination. There is also an Ethics Appeal Board which may affirm, modify, or reverse the prior determination.

It is instructive to include the CPM Code of Ethics at this point as a reminder of the issues that are involved from the real estate manager's point of view. The following discussions address each of the articles and their practical implications. Some anecdotal examples are included to show how real estate managers encounter ethical issues in their daily activities.

Fiduciary Obligation to Clients. It is fairly clear that the client is putting a great deal of trust in the real estate manager and has every right to

Exhibit 13.1 *(continued)*

1. **Fiduciary Obligation to Clients** A CERTIFIED PROPERTY MANAGER shall at all times exercise loyalty to the interests of the client and shall not engage in any activity which could be reasonably construed as contrary to the best interests of the client. A CERTIFIED PROPERTY MANAGER shall not represent personal or business interests divergent or conflicting with those of the client, unless the client is first notified in writing of the activity or potential conflict of interest, and consents in writing to such representation. A CERTIFIED PROPERTY MANAGER, as a fiduciary for the client, shall not accept, directly or indirectly, any rebate, fee, commission, discount, or other benefit, monetary or otherwise, which has not been fully disclosed to and approved by the client.

2. **Disclosure** A CERTIFIED PROPERTY MANAGER shall not disclose to a third party any confidential or proprietary information which would be injurious or damaging to a client concerning the client's business or personal affairs without the client's prior written consent, unless such disclosure is required or compelled by law or regulations.

3. **Accounting and Reporting** A CERTIFIED PROPERTY MANAGER shall at all times keep and maintain accurate financial and business records concerning each property managed for the client, which records shall be available for inspection at all reasonable times by the client. A CERTIFIED PROPERTY MANAGER shall furnish to the client, at mutually agreed upon intervals, regular reports concerning the client's properties.

4. **Protection of Funds** A CERTIFIED PROPERTY MANAGER shall not commingle personal or company funds with the funds of a client or use one client's funds for the benefit of another client, but shall keep the client's funds in a fiduciary account in an insured financial institution or as otherwise directed in writing by the client. A CERTIFIED PROPERTY MANAGER shall at all times exert due diligence for the maintenance and protection of the client's funds against all reasonably foreseeable contingencies and losses.

5. **Relations with other Members of the Profession** A CERTIFIED PROPERTY MANAGER shall not make, authorize or otherwise encourage any unfounded derogatory or disparaging comments concerning the practices of another CERTIFIED PROPERTY MANAGER. A CERTIFIED PROPERTY MANAGER shall not exaggerate or misrepresent the services offered as compared with the services offered by other property managers. Nothing in this Code, however, shall restrict legal and reasonable business competition by and among property managers.

6. **Contract** Any written contract between a CERTIFIED PROPERTY MANAGER and a client shall be in clear and understandable terms, and shall set forth the specific terms agreed upon between the parties, including a general description of the services to be provided by and the responsibilities of the CERTIFIED PROPERTY MANAGER.

7. **Duty to Firm or Employer** A CERTIFIED PROPERTY MANAGER shall at all times exercise loyalty to the interests of the employer or firm with whom the CPM is affiliated and shall be diligent in the maintenance and protection of the interests and property of the employer or firm. A CERTIFIED PROPERTY MANAGER shall not engage in any activity which could be reasonably construed as contrary to this obligation of loyalty and diligence and shall not accept, directly or indirectly, any rebate, fee, commission, discount, or other benefit, monetary or otherwise, which could reasonably be seen as a conflict with the interests of the employer or firm. A CERTIFIED PROPERTY MANAGER shall at all times exercise due diligence for the protection of the funds of the employer or firm against all reasonably foreseeable contingencies and losses.

8. **Managing the Property of the Client** A CERTIFIED PROPERTY MANAGER shall not exaggerate, misrepresent or conceal material facts concerning the client's property or any related transaction. A CERTIFIED PROPERTY MANAGER shall exercise due diligence in the maintenance and management of the client's property and shall make all reasonable efforts to protect it against all reasonably foreseeable contingencies and losses.

Exhibit 13.1 *(concluded)*

9. **Duty to Former Clients and Former Firms or Employers** All obligations and duties of a CERTIFIED PROPERTY MANAGER to clients, firms and employers as specified in this Code shall also apply to relationships with former clients and former firms and employers. A CERTIFIED PROPERTY MANAGER shall act in a professional manner when, for whatever reason, relationships are terminated between a CERTIFIED PROPERTY MANAGER and clients and firm or employer. Nothing in this section, however, shall be construed to cause a CERTIFIED PROPERTY MANAGER to breach obligations and duties to current clients and firm or employer.

10. **Compliance with Laws and Regulations** A CERTIFIED PROPERTY MANAGER shall at all times conduct business and personal activities with knowledge of and in compliance with applicable federal, state, and local laws and regulations, and shall maintain the highest moral and ethical standards consistent with the membership in and the purposes of the Institute of Real Estate Management.

11. **Equal Opportunity** A CERTIFIED PROPERTY MANAGER shall not deny equal employment opportunity or equal professional services to any person for reasons of race, color, religion, sex, familial status, national origin, age, or handicap.

12. **Duty to Tenants and Others** A CERTIFIED PROPERTY MANAGER shall competently manage the property of the client with due regard for the rights, responsibilities, and benefits of the tenant and others lawfully on the property. A CERTIFIED PROPERTY MANAGER shall not engage in any conduct which is in conscious disregard for the safety and health of those persons lawfully on the premises of the client's property.

13. **Enforcement** Any violation by a CERTIFIED PROPERTY MANAGER of the obligations of this Code shall be determined in accordance with and pursuant to the terms of the bylaws and rules and regulations of the Institute of Real Estate Management. Disciplinary action for violation of any portion of this Code shall be carried out by the Institute of Real Estate Management in accordance with the bylaws and rules and regulations established by the Governing Council of the Institute. The result of such disciplinary action shall be final and binding upon the affected CERTIFIED PROPERTY MANAGER, and without recourse to the Institute, its officers, councillors, members, employees, or agents.

© 1997 by the Institute of Real Estate Management; reprinted by permission of the copyright holder.

expect that his or her interests will be first and foremost in the mind and activities of the manager. The real estate manager's role as a fiduciary affects how all of his or her responsibilities are undertaken. For instance, suppose the client wished to dispose of a piece of equipment—e.g., a parking lot sweeper—and set a price of $5,000 for it. If, in the course of his or her activities, the manager found a buyer for the sweeper and that buyer was willing to pay $7,000 for the sweeper, the full amount of the payment should be credited to the account of the client and not result in a secret profit for the manager. It could be argued that if the client asked for and received $5,000, no one would be injured by the higher dollar transaction, but the manager keeping the $2,000 difference would clearly be unethical. It is the responsibility of the real estate manager to act in the best interest of the client despite the client being satisfied with the price of $5,000. On the other hand, if the client indicated a net price of $5,000 for the machine and stated that the manager was welcome to any additional monies made from the sale, the manager would be entitled to keep the added profits unless the client was clearly misinformed about the value of the machine. In order to avoid any misunderstandings, the safest and best approach would be to see that the client received any and all funds from the sale of the equipment.

A similar situation arises in the area of commission splits. The client may agree to pay a commission of five percent of the gross rent on an office lease. Suppose an outside broker brings in a lease and is therefore entitled to the full commission. Suppose further, however, that in the process of making the deal, the broker offers the manager $1,000 of the commission for "helping" make the deal. This agreement must be disclosed to the client. The client may agree that this is a reasonable compensation to the manager, but it should be the client's decision. It is not the manager's place to decide that the client would not have a problem with such a transaction and, therefore, not disclose the fact of it to the client.

Sometimes personal relationships create potential for unacceptable behaviors. For example, a supervising manager of a large institutionally owned apartment community learned that a trusted and effective subcontractor who provided carpet-cleaning services at the property was the brother-in-law of the on-site manager and they were splitting the profits of the carpet-cleaning service. The site manager did not disclose this; the supervising manager learned of the arrangement from another source. When told by the supervising manager that this matter had to be fully disclosed, the site manager was able to demonstrate that the carpet-cleaning service was superior in terms of response, effectiveness, price, courtesy to residents, and innovative problem-solving. The site manager even offered to split her share of the carpet-cleaning profits with the supervising manager or the property owner. The supervising manager dismissed the site manager and the vendor for cause and sent the owner a written anthology of the events leading up to this action. The site manager had acted unethically, and the supervising manager responded appropriately.

Disclosure. Disclosure of confidential client information is a very difficult area within the business of real estate management. Real estate managers pride themselves on being willing to share information and being helpful to other managers, but great care must be taken to be sure proprietary information is not being given out without the client's approval. In all cases where we have indicated that client approval should be obtained, such approval should be in writing so that one has evidence of approval at a later date in case a question arises and the original parties are no longer available.

Because of the willingness of real estate managers to share information, it is likely that less information is considered truly proprietary than is the case in some other fields. However, if something is generated by the client or has come to use from the client—and is not common to the industry—

you should seek approval from the client before giving it to anyone else. For example, a management firm was presented with an operations manual from one of its clients that was very well done, and the firm's management personnel wanted to share it with others in the industry. The client contact was approached, and the firm was given permission to pass the information along—with some minor modifications. As it turned out, the client firm had also acquired some of the information components and presentation formats of its operations manual from others within the industry and, thinking that they had gained by sharing, the client was quite willing to do the same. It is easy to see, however, that a client may invest considerable time and money in developing a unique operations manual and, as a result, be unwilling to share it with others, which is the client's right. When in doubt, ask permission. (This should be obtained from the owner of the client firm, in writing.)

Accounting and Reporting. The accounting and reporting function is very specific, and there should be no misunderstandings regarding what is right and what is wrong. Accounting for clients' funds must be timely, complete, and accurate. While some clients may be willing to have all accounting records rounded to the nearest dollar, others will want the records accurate to the penny. That is a client decision.

The accounts handled for the client should be able to pass inspection at any time without prior notice. We know of a management firm that managed an account for a large pension fund. The client maintained a set of duplicate books at the home office, and their books and the management company's were expected to agree at all times. In spite of this dual activity, the client's auditor would show up at the management office about once a year—early in the morning, unannounced—and ask to see the books. He would conduct a test audit to see if everything was in order, in which case he would be on his way to the next audit. Although the management firm did not experience any problems, the auditor confided that he had performed audits where funds were obviously missing, and he had been able to protect his employer (the pension fund) at an early stage before the amount of money had become very large.

The manager is obligated to report all financial transactions made on behalf of the client and to ensure that those reports are completely accurate. A manager does not have the right to "borrow" funds from the client and alter the reports to cover up the loan because he or she knows the amount can be made up next month. Nor does the manager have the right to take discounts on goods and services, then pocket the discount and report the face amount of the invoice to the client.

A manager also may not "profit" from the clients' funds. Suppose a management firm were to "sweep" all its property accounts daily, depositing the funds into an interest-bearing account in the name of the manager.

Suppose further that the funds are kept until the last day of the month when bills are paid so the manager profits from daily accrued interest on the funds. This is clearly unethical because any interest earned on a client's monies belongs to the client.

Protection of Funds. Real estate managers are typically required to keep clients' funds in a financial institution of the client's choice. However, if the manager is given the choice of institutions, he or she must ensure that those funds are protected. Typically, this means that the financial institution used must be fully insured for the amount deposited in case there is a failure of the institution—for example, banks are so insured through the Federal Deposit Insurance Corporation (FDIC). If the funds of the client exceed the maximum insured amount, the total may have to be divided among several accounts or otherwise apportioned so that the level of funds kept in any one institution remains below the insurable maximum amount.

Protection of clients' funds includes being certain there is no commingling of funds with those of either the manager or other clients. In years past, it was not unusual for a real estate manager to have a master account and keep all client funds in that account, regardless of the number of clients. The manager would then keep separate ledgers on each client's funds. However, there is potential for accidental commingling in this situation: If one client has a tenant whose check bounces, that portion of the account could become overdrawn; but the bank has no way of separating those funds. Today almost all real estate managers deposit funds into an interest-bearing account dedicated to one client only. This eliminates any chance for accidental commingling of funds.

Deliberate commingling of accounts is specifically prohibited. At one time, there was a very small management company that would pay its client's bills out of the company's funds, and vice versa, settling or reconciling the accounts on a monthly basis. It is easy to see how this practice could get out of hand and become confusing. It is in all parties' best interests to keep all funds separate and fully accounted at all times.

Relations with Other Members of the Profession. The purpose of this article of the Code is to foster good relations between real estate managers by setting a standard for conduct. It is not meant to limit activities that are construed to be healthy competition. Rather, the intent is to preclude a manager from using disparaging information or unfounded rumors about another manager or management firm in the hopes of gaining a competitive advantage. It is easy to see how such practices could have a negative effect on the entire industry. Real estate managers are similarly discouraged from "puffing up" their own services when competing for business. All are encouraged to present their accomplishments and abilities in the best light possible. However, to imply that the lease-up of a building was accomplished in record time when that is clearly not the case or suggest that a company has in-house construction supervision capability when it has never done that type of work before is clearly unethical.

Contract. While many contracts for property management services are dictated by the client, the manager has an obligation, especially under this article of the CPM Code of Ethics, to be sure that the language is clear as to what the obligations and terms are for both parties and that there are no areas of misunderstanding. All contracts between a client and a real estate manager should be carefully considered and crafted to eliminate any areas of confusion. It is much easier to resolve problems while you are negotiating a management agreement initially; conversely, it is often difficult to sort out who should have done what when something goes wrong. Often the reason for not wanting to clarify a situation at the time of negotiation has to do with the possibility that one will not get the account if the item becomes an issue.

Such concerns can take many forms. Several years ago, a manager starting a new company was unable to obtain a bond because she was operating as an individual. The insurance company said she could not insure herself. The issue came up in the negotiation of her first management agreement, and the potential client indicated that a bond was a must. When the insurance company's position was communicated, there was some fear that the account might be lost because this was an important issue for the potential client. However, in this case, the client called his insurance agent and learned that he could place the required bond, get a separate quote for the premium, and be reimbursed by the manager for the cost of the bond. The problem was put on the table and, with the help of the client, resolved. Imagine the possible damage to the relationship—or worse, the loss of funds—if the manager had said she could get the bond, then stalled while trying to figure out how to handle the problem, and a loss had occurred. The contract between the client and the real estate manager must be based on the true facts, and it must be clear as to responsibilities and terms.

Duty to Firm or Employer. The requirement to be loyal to one's current employer or firm is absolute. If a management company, as employer, asks an employee to do something illegal or unethical, that employee has a right—and an obligation—to let the employer know he or she thinks what is being asked is not right and that, therefore, he or she should not be obligated to carry out the request or order. If such a declaration does not solve the problem, the employee clearly has the right to refuse to act.

However, barring something illegal or unethical, a real estate manager has an obligation to look out for the well-being of his or her employer. For example, if the manager has been thinking of moving to another management company while negotiations are underway with a potential client, it is clearly unethical to try to put that potential client on hold so the management account can be delivered to the new company. As another example, suppose a management company has a bonus program under which real estate managers will be given 20 percent of any commissions earned on properties managed by the firm, and along comes an outside broker who, knowing the arrangement, offers to take the deal and give the manager 40 percent under the table. It is clearly unethical for the employee to be involved in such a deal. It is also clearly unethical for the outside broker to make such an offer.

Gifts from third parties that will have a negative impact on the employer must be turned down; this applies even if there is only the potential for a negative impact on the employer. For example: A commercial tenant offered a manager a pair of men's dress suits, free of charge, with a comment relating to the fashion items—i.e., "because they are you." While there may have been no "quid pro quo" mentioned at the time of the offer, the acceptance of such a gift would have put the manager in a difficult position if any problem arose with that tenant in the future. Even though the management company did not have a policy against such things, the manager refused the offer saying that company policy did not allow acceptance of such gifts. This approach was tactful (there was no need to hurt the tenant's feelings if the gift was really offered in good faith), and using "company policy" allowed the manager to distance himself from the action and avoid the potential for personal ill will that could have resulted from the turndown.

Managing the Property of the Client. This article requires complete honesty in the management of the client's property. If the manager is or becomes aware of material facts that would have an impact on the property, he or she must be honest about them. This pertains to what information may or may not be revealed to the client, tenants, potential tenants, and even the public as it relates to the client and the property.

We know of a situation in which a manager was in the process of leasing a space in an office building. This lease would have produced a substantial commission for the manager, and all current *written* information regarding the prospective tenant (e.g., the credit report and financial statements) was positive. However, telephone follow-up with the credit information source revealed the likelihood that the tenant was in default of its current lease and could be facing imminent eviction. Although it meant the loss of a nice commission, the manager revealed the additional information to the client; it was checked out and confirmed, and the lease was not processed further. The ethical dilemma here is obvious.

In a similar situation, a manager working on a lease for a vacant space in a shopping center had spent considerable time working with a prospective tenant for the space who was "marginal" at best. About the time the manager thought he was close to receiving a commitment, an outside broker came to him representing another merchant who would be a better prospective tenant for the property. However, if the new prospect was accepted instead of the one the manager had been working with all this time, the commission he would receive would have to be split with the other broker. Even though it meant a lesser commission, the manager was obligated to tell the owner about the new prospect; he did, and the property was better off in the long run.

Duty to Former Clients and Former Firms or Employers. A manager working with or for a given company or client often sets in motion situations that will not appear as problems until much later. Sometimes situations arise long after the individual has been gone from the company, yet because he or she negotiated the item or oversaw the activity, that person is in the best position to indicate the intent of the original agreement or deal. The manager has a duty to former clients and/or employers to be helpful in resolving previously established situations about which he or she has specialized knowledge. Professional managers are also obligated to be honest about former employers, clients, and others and not give out incorrect or misleading information just because they may think their employment was terminated without reason or an account was lost for reasons other than the ones stated at the time.

One of the most difficult situations for a real estate manager is to have been responsible for a specific property, which was then sold, and subsequently to be appointed as manager by the new owner. This creates all sorts of obligations, some of which could be in conflict in regard to what information is revealed, to whom, and when. Because the potential for future misunderstandings is tremendous, it is essential to be certain that all parties understand the various relationships and that anything which might be considered questionable is brought out in the open and resolved among the parties.

Compliance with Laws and Regulations. It is incumbent upon real estate managers to be aware of and ensure compliance with all laws, regulations, and ordinances that pertain to the property and its operations. These may include requirements to obtain building permits, certificates of occupancy, and a business license; civil rights laws related to employment practices and apartment leasing procedures; environmental regulations; and ordinances regarding such things as fire safety, elevator inspections, and signage. As an employer, there are also wage and hour laws, income taxes, and relevant reporting requirements to be addressed. It is not sufficient as a defense to say, "I didn't know about the law," and expect to be excused because of one's ignorance.

The real estate management environment is very complex, and managers must be informed as to what is required under the law and then be sure that they and the property are in full compliance. The sheer number of federal regulations, state laws, and local ordinances that impact real estate today is truly awesome, and compliance with all that are applicable is imperative. (Specific laws that impact real estate management are discussed in Chapter 12.)

Equal Opportunity. This is straightforward: The manager agrees to be an equal opportunity employer, not only as regards his or her own employees, but for any employees hired on behalf of the client's property as well.

Duty to Tenants and Others. Although the real estate manager may work for the client or the management company, he or she also has an obligation to act legally and ethically with regard to the tenants on the property. For example, an inexperienced tenant moved into a store space after signing a lease that said the tenant would accept the premises "as is." The tenant, having heard the term before, thought it was an industry standard and accepted the lease as written. Upon move-in, the tenant found that the water heater did not work and had to be replaced, so he replaced it. Later, when the manager visited his store, the tenant mentioned the problem and asked if the property owner might pay for it, but he was not particularly demanding. The manager also thought that, in spite of the lease, it was not right for this expense to be the tenant's responsibility. After some discussion, the property owner was convinced that he should pay for the new water heater. The effective manager is often an "ombudsman" for the tenant in interpreting the lease on behalf of the owner. This also relates to a resident's expectation of a "habitable" apartment and the right to "quiet enjoyment" of the leased premises.

In negotiating an office or store lease with a commercial tenant or an apartment lease with a resident, the expectation is that the benefits of the agreements will be realized on behalf of the owner-clients. However, real estate managers also have an obligation to be fair and reasonable and to keep the welfare of the tenant in mind, even while they are serving the best interests of the client. Although some owners may believe one should never give the tenant anything that is not specifically required under the lease, it sometimes happens that the written document does not represent a fair or reasonable resolution of a particular matter. In such situations, it is usually in everyone's best interests to go beyond the lease terms and strive for a compromise that is acceptable to everyone involved.

The Accredited Management Organization® (AMO®) Code of Ethics

The Accredited Management Organization (AMO) designation is one of the most respected certifications in the field of real estate management. As part of its overall activity, an AMO firm must be engaged in third-party management for a fee. AMO companies are considered highly qualified management firms with substantial third-party management experience. They, too, have a specific code of ethics (Exhibit 13.2).

It is easy to see that the ethical requirements for those who hold the

Exhibit 13.2
Code of Ethics for the
ACCREDITED MANAGEMENT ORGANIZATION®

Relations with Clients

An ACCREDITED MANAGEMENT ORGANIZATION must engage in property management on a fee basis.

An ACCREDITED MANAGEMENT ORGANIZATION shall be capable of performing duties for clients including but not limited to:
 Collection of rents and assessments,
 Supervision of employees at the properties,
 Tenant and owner contact in regard to complaints,
 Purchase of minor operating supplies and repairs,
 Hiring and dismissal of employees at the properties,
 Purchase of major repairs (e.g., roofs, exterior paint, masonry),
 Purchase of major supplies (e.g. fuel),
 Preparation of specifications covering major expenditures,
 Consultation on major replacements, additions, or remodeling,
 Negotiation of leases,
 Ordering and supervision of tenant decorating,
 Obtaining competitive bids on major repairs and alterations,
 Preparation of payroll deductions, social security taxes, etc.,
 Payment of real estate and personal property taxes,
 Recommendations about rental rates,
 Preparation of operating budgets, or
 Other management activities.

An ACCREDITED MANAGEMENT ORGANIZATION shall exert due diligence for the protection of clients' funds against all foreseeable contingencies. The deposit of such funds in an escrow, trust, or agency account with an FDIC or equivalently insured financial institution, or as otherwise required by the management agreement, shall constitute due diligence.

An ACCREDITED MANAGEMENT ORGANIZATION shall not permit any of its employees to make any misleading or inaccurate representations to the public.

An ACCREDITED MANAGEMENT ORGANIZATION shall have at least one (1) CERTIFIED PROPERTY MANAGER (CPM) in an executive position who directs and supervises the property management activity of the firm.

An ACCREDITED MANAGEMENT ORGANIZATION shall conduct its operation in such a manner so as to comply with the Code of Professional Ethics as prescribed for a CERTIFIED PROPERTY MANAGER and shall be responsible for the conduct of its employees and others over whom it has supervision or control.

Any actions by an ACCREDITED MANAGEMENT ORGANIZATION emanating from its headquarters office or any of its branch offices or occurring at any of the properties it manages shall be subject to . . . [this] Code of Ethics.

An ACCREDITED MANAGEMENT ORGANIZATION shall constantly strive to achieve and maintain a sound business reputation in the community, and shall encourage its employees and associates to take leadership roles in local, civic, and governmental organizations.

Each ACCREDITED MANAGEMENT ORGANIZATION shall, whenever possible, have a written management agreement with each of its clients.

Exhibit 13.2 *(continued)*

Operating Practices

An ACCREDITED MANAGEMENT ORGANIZATION shall use due diligence in selecting and placing tenants for its clients so as to ensure stability of the properties in compliance with all federal, state, and local laws and regulations.

An ACCREDITED MANAGEMENT ORGANIZATION shall not deny nor permit any of its employees to deny equal employment opportunity or equal professional services to any person for reasons of race, gender, religion, familial status, national origin, age, or handicap.

An ACCREDITED MANAGEMENT ORGANIZATION shall vigorously and legally pursue the collection of any rental accounts to insure prompt payment of rents and revenues when due.

In accordance with the management agreement, an ACCREDITED MANAGEMENT ORGANIZATION shall, on behalf of the client, demonstrate its experience, with diligence and imagination, in the marketing and merchandising of rental space.

In accordance with the management agreement, an ACCREDITED MANAGEMENT ORGANIZATION shall disburse the funds of the client in such a manner so as to make prompt payment of all obligations as they become due or as requested by the client.

In accordance with the management agreement, an ACCREDITED MANAGEMENT ORGANIZATION shall make reasonable efforts to conserve the resources of the client and shall take full advantage of discounts, purchasing opportunities, and other ethical means at its disposal when purchasing or contracting for supplies, services, or material on behalf of the client.

An ACCREDITED MANAGEMENT ORGANIZATION shall at all times keep and maintain accurate financial records properly marked for identification concerning the properties managed for its client and shall render a statement of receipts and disbursements in accordance with the management agreement in sufficient detail to reflect an account for the funds of the client and the status of the property. Such records shall be available for inspection at all reasonable times by each respective client.

In accordance with the management agreement, an ACCREDITED MANAGEMENT ORGANIZATION shall make or cause to be made regular physical inspections of the property of its clients and shall not neglect to keep its clients informed as to the condition of their properties. The frequency of regular inspections shall be as mutually agreed upon with the client.

An ACCREDITED MANAGEMENT ORGANIZATION shall endeavor to expend funds of its clients with wisdom and integrity so as to achieve the greatest benefit for its clients.

Certified Property Manager and the Accredited Management Organization designations are quite similar in many respects. However, the Accredited Management Organization designees have to meet additional requirements related to the capabilities of the management company in carrying out the responsibilities they may assume.

Because the AMO firm is thought of as a very sophisticated, experienced real estate management company, it could easily be assumed that every company with an AMO designation can meet the specialized needs of all potential clients. The AMO Code of Ethics requires that AMO companies actually be able to provide the services required by the client, rather than take on an assignment and then "go to school" at the client's expense. (The requirements for a real estate management company to be accredited as an AMO firm are outlined in Appendix A.)

Exhibit 13.2 *(concluded)*

An ACCREDITED MANAGEMENT ORGANIZATION shall not commingle its funds with any of the funds of its management clients but shall deposit all such funds in an FDIC or equivalently insured financial institution or as otherwise may be directed in writing by the client, and all such receipts and revenues shall be deemed to be trust funds held in trust for clients or clients' accounts or as otherwise provided in the management agreement.

An ACCREDITED MANAGEMENT ORGANIZATION shall have sufficient staff and administration to ensure the capable handling of the client's property during any absence of the executive CERTIFIED PROPERTY MANAGER from the office.

Neither an ACCREDITED MANAGEMENT ORGANIZATION nor any person connected with it shall receive from third parties or suppliers rebates, gifts with a value of more than fifty dollars ($50), or other consideration in connection with the management or property which is not disclosed to the client.

Neither an ACCREDITED MANAGEMENT ORGANIZATION nor others of the organization engaged in property management shall hold themselves out to anyone as being an ACCREDITED MANAGEMENT ORGANIZATION at any time before it is accredited or after the expiration or revocation of any accreditation.

An ACCREDITED MANAGEMENT ORGANIZATION shall advise the client of the need to obtain proper insurance.

An ACCREDITED MANAGEMENT ORGANIZATION shall assist in the negotiation of union contracts when called upon to do so.

Relations with the Institute of Real Estate Management
An ACCREDITED MANAGEMENT ORGANIZATION shall remain in full compliance with all rules and regulations governing the ACCREDITED MANAGEMENT ORGANIZATION program and shall report to the Institute of Real Estate Management in a timely fashion any changes within the firm that may affect its status as an ACCREDITED MANAGEMENT ORGANIZATION.

NOTE: The AMO Code as presented here is intended to show how it parallels the CPM Code of Ethics. The complete Code includes an introductory declaration regarding compliance.

© 1997 by the Institute of Real Estate Management; reprinted by permission of the copyright holder.

State Commissioner's Code of Ethics

In most states, if you are doing third-party fee management, you are required to have a real estate license. At least one member of the firm's management must be a licensed real estate broker and is therefore subject to the Commissioner's Code of Ethics for that state. The areas of representation, disclosure, and other relations with clients covered under the commissioners' regulations are similar in intent to the requirements outlined by the Institute of Real Estate Management in its codes of ethics, except that the latter are tailored for the field of real estate management.

Because we are most familiar with the State of California and because California has generally had one of the more stringent real estate license programs in the United States, the California Commissioner's Code of Ethics will be used to make the case. It addresses three types of professional conduct:

1. Unlawful conduct
2. Unethical practices
3. Beneficial conduct

Unlawful conduct, as such, will not be addressed here; it is beyond the scope of this text. However, the items outlined in beneficial conduct point out some areas that are helpful in considering ethical behavior. Before doing that, we will review the Unethical Practices portion of the Code of Ethics which, even though written primarily to apply to real estate agents and brokers who deal in single-family home sales, can be related to real estate managers as well.

Unethical Conduct. The California Commissioner's Code of Ethics defines unethical conduct as those activities that are not necessarily violations of the law, but which could result in disciplinary action.

Puffing Representing, without a reasonable basis, the nature and/or condition of the interior or exterior features of a property when soliciting an offer.

> In a leasing situation, this would apply if the leasing agent or the property manager told a prospective commercial tenant that the sign on the front of the building is included in the lease, when, in fact, the previous tenant owns the sign and is likely to return to claim it. Another example would be if the leasing agent stated that all parts of the building are in "good condition," despite the fact that they have not been tested and no one really knows whether or not the equipment works.

Responding to Principal Failing to respond to reasonable inquiries of a principal as to the status or extent of efforts to market property listed exclusively with the licensee.

> This would apply more to leasing, although it could apply to management as well. It consists of failure to answer the legitimate requests of the client for information about any part of the agreement which is covered by the need to have a real estate license.

Misrepresenting Compensation Representing as an agent that any specific service is free when, in fact, it is covered by a fee to be charged as part of the transaction.

> In real estate management, accounting services for the property operations are almost always included in the overall management fees. It would be unethical to indicate to a prospective client that you would include the accounting services at no additional charge if you are given their management business. By

the same token, a leasing agent would be in violation of this section if he or she indicated that the advertising for prospective tenants would be free if he or she was given the contract. Generally, advertising costs for commercial properties are included in the commission structure. Rental advertising for residential properties is usually considered an operating expense of the property.

Beneficial Interests Failing to disclose to a person, when first discussing the purchase of real property, the existence of any direct or indirect ownership interest of the licensee in the property.

This regulation applies almost exclusively to property sales but could have implications in a leasing situation as well. When one is acting both as a principal and an agent, that fact must be disclosed.

Escrow Referrals Recommending by a salesperson to a party to a real estate transaction that a particular lender or escrow service be used when the salesperson believes his or her broker has a significant beneficial interest in such entity, without disclosing this information at the time the recommendation is made.

While the language indicates escrow services and lenders, it applies equally well to any contract for services in which the agent or broker may have a less-than-obvious interest in the company being employed. For example, suppose the broker-owner of a management company also has a half-interest in a landscape maintenance company. If the real estate manager, knowing this information, recommends the landscape maintenance company to the client without disclosing the nature of its ownership, the manager has acted unethically.

Expertise Claiming to be an expert in an area of specialization in real estate brokerage (e.g., appraisal, property management, industrial siting) if, in fact, the licensee has had no special training, preparation, or experience in such area.

One of the most tempting areas for real estate practitioners is that of appraisal. Most agents and brokers understand how a property is appraised, and most have given their opinion as to value at one time or another, so it seems an innocent step to indicate that one is an "appraiser." Unless you have the education and experience, such claims would be unethical.

Appraisal Using the term "appraisal" in any advertising of offering for promoting real estate brokerage business to describe a real property evaluation service to be provided by the licensee, unless the evaluation process will involve a written estimate of value based upon the assembling, analyzing, and reconciling of facts and value indicators for the real property in question.

> This could apply to a leasing service, and possibly to a management company, which might offer such a service as a way of introducing themselves to potential clients. If either were to do so, it would be an ethical violation.

Reporting Redlining Failing to disclose to the appropriate regulatory agency any conduct on the part of a financial institution which reasonably could be construed as [redlining].

> Although this section would not generally apply to commercial transactions, the leasing agent or real estate manager must not discriminate in leasing under any circumstances. (Fair housing laws are very explicit about what constitute discriminatory practices in leasing—and marketing—as well as home sales.) Although for purposes of tenant mix in shopping centers, uses can be denied in the lease, one cannot decide to lease a store space to a Caucasian business owner and deny a similar lease to someone who is a member of a protected class solely on the basis of race or other such classification.

Franchise Affiliation Representing to a customer or prospective customer that, because a licensee or his or her broker is a member of or affiliated with a franchised real estate brokerage entity, such entity shares substantial responsibility with the licensee or his or her broker for the proper handling of transactions if such is not the case.

> This has little application in real estate management because there are no nationally recognized franchise operations for either leasing or management. However, if a manager or leasing agent were to indicate that any affiliation provided levels of protection which were, in fact, not available, such claims would constitute unethical conduct.

Beneficial Conduct. This section of the California Commissioner's Code of Ethics opens with the following statement: "In the best interest of all licensees and the public they serve, brokers and salespersons are encouraged to pursue the following beneficial business practices."

Measuring Success Measuring success by the quality and benefits rendered to the buyers and sellers in real estate transactions, rather than by the amount of compensation realized as a broker or salesperson.

> This is directly applicable to real estate management because profitability cannot be ignored. However, management firms that focus on profits to the exclusion of the people involved

(clients, residents, commercial tenants) are not likely to be in business for long. A firm that is so poorly capitalized that its executives believe it cannot afford to do the "right thing" probably should not be in the business of real estate management. All a firm has to sell in this business is reputation, and reputation is easily tarnished and very difficult to restore.

Honesty Treating all parties to a transaction honestly.

This, too, applies directly to real estate management practices. While absolute honesty may not be a legal obligation for managers, the attitude that "honesty is the best policy" is likely to foster much better long-term relationships.

Reporting Violations Promptly reporting to the California Department of Real Estate any apparent violations of the real estate law.

Violations of real estate law are much more visible in the area of home sales where there is often multiple-listing activity and more people are involved in the transaction. In the area of real estate management, it is not very likely that one managing agent would be aware of another's violations of state law. However, to the extent that a licensed real estate manager is aware of the illegal activities of another manager, he or she has a duty to report that activity.

Care in Advertising Using care in the preparation of any advertisement to present an accurate picture or message to the reader, viewer, or listener.

This has direct bearing on real estate management. While management firms may not do a lot of advertising for property management business, what advertising they do must be accurate and not misleading. It would be improper for individuals who have managed one or two rental houses to represent themselves as having been managers of apartment complexes.

Submitting Offers Submitting all written offers as a matter of top priority.

This would apply more to leasing activities than to real estate management. Holding back an offer because one would have to split a commission or waiting for an offer from someone else so the agent would be paid a full commission constitutes improper activity. Once a lease offer is prepared, it must be conveyed to the building owner as quickly as possible.

Complete Records Maintaining adequate and complete records of all one's real estate dealings.

This is particularly germane to real estate management, especially in the area of accounting for clients' funds.

> **Strategies for Maintaining Ethical Practices**
>
> Ethics in business is the practice of good will in both intent and actions. Ethical behavior is a long-term business strategy and deserving of special attention.
>
> - Develop a code of ethics for your company and enforce it.
> - Involve your employees in the development process.
> - Publish the code of ethics in your employee handbook.
> - Demonstrate ethical behavior by example, from ownership and senior management through all the ranks.
> - Make sure your training includes acceptable (and unacceptable) practices and behaviors.
> - Reinforce the training through meetings where ethical (and unethical) practices are discussed and clarified.
>
> Honesty in one's dealings is a prerequisite to establishing trust, for without trust there can be no cooperation. Negotiate in good faith and keep the promises you make. Corollary to this is the need to avoid exaggeration (inflated capabilities) and not make promises you cannot keep. Whenever possible or practical, incorporate the firm's code of ethics into marketing and proposal/presentation materials.

Keeping Current Keeping oneself current on factors affecting the real estate market in which the licensee operates as an agent.

> Real estate management is an area in which information and requirements change at a rapid pace. If managers do not keep up on the latest information, they are not likely to do the best possible job of managing their clients' properties.

Cooperation Making a full, open, and sincere effort to cooperate with other licensees, unless the principal has instructed the licensee to the contrary.

> This applies to real estate management in the area of sharing market information. Cooperation and information-sharing create a stronger management presence in a given market, benefiting clients, tenants, and the general public.

Settling Disputes Attempting to settle disputes with other licensees through mediation or arbitration.

> In real estate management, there are few disputes between licensees. However, many client contracts now call for arbitration rather than legal action to resolve differences, and to that extent it is still beneficial conduct.

Codes of Ethics Complying with these standards of professional conduct, and the Code of Ethics of any organized real estate industry group of which the licensee is a member.

This, of course, has direct application to real estate management. If an individual has achieved the Certified Property Manager® (CPM®) designation or a firm holds the Accredited Management Organization® (AMO®) designation, they are obligated to abide by the respective Codes of Ethics discussed earlier in this chapter (see Exhibits 13.1 and 13.2). Through the direct affiliation of the Institute of Real Estate Management, both groups of designees are also subject to the Code of Ethics of the NATIONAL ASSOCIATION OF REALTORS.

A Perspective on Professional Ethics

In the distant past, the unorganized real estate industry suffered from a poor reputation because of the free-wheeling activities of unethical practitioners. More recently, however, real estate practitioners have come to realize that they will only survive by building relationships and not taking advantage of a client's funds without providing the agreed-upon services in exchange. They have become professionals who want to render quality service and garner repeat business. Real estate managers will only be able to accomplish this end if they treat each customer and client in the manner in which they would like to be treated themselves in the same situation.

Most of them know what is and is not legal because such activities are defined in the law. The area of ethics, however, is more complicated and has many gray areas. Typically, in real estate management, if there is any doubt about a transaction—if you have to ask yourself, "should I or shouldn't I?"—it is very likely that the answer is you should not. If you have questions about a transaction involving a client, you cannot go wrong if you make the decision to disclose. The real estate manager and the client can agree to anything that is legal so long as both parties are fully aware of the facts surrounding the transaction, and the manager can take the requested action if proper (preferably written) approval has been granted by the client.

Managing Change

14

Management Termination Strategies

A variety of circumstances can lead to termination of a management arrangement. Management agreements are contracts for a fixed period and subject to nonrenewal when the term expires. The owner may sell the property, and the agreement with one owner generally cannot provide for a management arrangement to continue under new ownership. Although nonrenewal of the agreement and sale of the property are most likely reasons for termination, default of the contractual arrangement by management or ownership, foreclosure by a mortgage lender, and death of the property owner are other possible grounds. Sometimes incompatibility of the parties—i.e., philosophical or personality differences—may prevent management from operating a property effectively, or despite management's efforts, the operation may not be profitable. When such situations arise, termination of the agreement may be preferable to trying to manage in adverse circumstances. Ideally, the parties to a management arrangement will anticipate the possibilities and address termination specifically in the management agreement.

Because a professional, organized approach to this activity is critical, the firm's standard operating procedures should include a checklist and guideline for handling termination of management. A checklist tailored to the specific property and management arrangement will facilitate the tracking of documents and other items returned to the owner, record actions that have been taken to date, and identify those things that remain to be done, including the person or persons responsible for different steps.

Management Agreement Considerations

A properly written management agreement will provide for termination of management by either the property owner or the management company.

> **Benefits of Using a Termination Checklist**
>
> - Ensures that information and records returned to the owner (or forwarded to new management) are up-to-date, accurate, and complete and that all funds are properly accounted.
> - Documents that management personnel have followed appropriate closing procedures and that all materials transferred have been distributed to the appropriate parties.
> - Fosters attention to details, assures that nothing important is overlooked, and minimizes potential problems or questions arising during the transition or afterward.
> - Assures careful, efficient, speedy handling of the transition activities.
> - Documents that information is current, that management's obligation to the owner has been fulfilled, and that the account has been closed effectively.

Although the duration of the contract term is finite, it is customary to include a provision for the agreement to continue on a month-to-month basis if it is not officially renewed (or cancelled) on the anniversary of the management term. Usually, the agreement also includes provision for *nonrenewal* by either party upon appropriate notice, in advance. Regardless of the circumstances of a termination, a management agreement should include the following provisions which protect the management company:

- The owner's indemnification of the agent under the agreement is to survive termination.
- All representations and warranties of both parties are to survive termination.
- An agreement by the owner not to hire any of the management firm's employees for a stated period following termination.

The latter usually requires reimbursement to the management company for the costs of training its employees if they are hired by the owner within that period.

Because it takes time to update records, prepare a final accounting, and transmit information to the owner, the management agreement should allow for a transition period in which management can perform these tasks. It should also provide for ownership to assume responsibility for any contracts executed on its behalf by the managing agent, as authorized under the agreement, and require the owner to provide the funds for management to discharge any obligations it incurred on the owner's behalf. Because negotiations of one or more commercial leases may be in progress at the time an agreement is terminated, there should also be provision for compensation to the management company if those negotiations lead to subsequent acceptance of the tenant. Usually this requires registering a list of prospective tenants with the owner as part of the termination transition.

Termination for Cause. Several other conditions and circumstances should also be addressed within the agreement. For example, it is appropriate to provide for termination by either party in case of a material breach of the contract—i.e., for cause (generally defined as "a legally enforceable" reason)—and usually there is provision for curing the breach within a specified time period. Monies owed to management not being paid promptly or the owner failing to advance the funds necessary to operate the property are examples of cause for termination by management. Not keeping within agreed-upon spending limits, failing to disclose information about relationships that might comprise conflicts of interest, and commingling of funds are some issues that might be cause for termination by ownership.

Issues of Management Liability. It is desirable to include a provision allowing management to terminate the agreement immediately by notifying the owner if the insurance coverages on the property are allowed to lapse or become inadequate or if the property fails to comply with applicable laws and regulations. At issue is the likelihood of the managing agent being uninsured or liable because of conditions arising out of the owner's actions or failure to act, although the management company may be protected in such a situation under its own general liability insurance.

Furthermore, management should be able to terminate the agreement if, after having signaled that its interests are not adequately protected under the owner's current liability policies, the parties are unable to agree on adequate liability insurance coverage.

Other Reasons for Terminating Management. The time to consider possibilities is during negotiation of the agreement and subsequent preparation for taking over the management account. Because destruction of the property as a result of a calamity or taking by a governmental agency under eminent domain can make it impractical if not impossible to continue operations, there should be provision for termination if either of these situations arise.

If the owner's personal financial position becomes precarious, a mortgage may be foreclosed by the lender. This event may make continuation of management impossible or inadvisable. Appointment of a receiver to safeguard the asset during foreclosure proceedings almost always leads to a change of management. Therefore, it may be prudent to include in the management agreement a provision for termination in the event of foreclosure.

A property owner who is a sole proprietor may face advancing age or ill health, in which case it may be advisable to stipulate terms and conditions under which management is to be continued or to provide for termination of management in the event of the owner's death. This may be more appropriately handled as an addendum or rider to the agreement rather than in the document itself. Also, the manner in which this provision is addressed may be subject to regulation under state laws regarding wills and probate as they affect the transfer of ownership of real estate.

Sale of the premises may be addressed by providing for advance notice to management and allowing management to continue during the transition and transfer of records so these activities can be handled appropriately. Depending on the complexity of the property and its operations, termination because the property is sold may warrant additional compensation to the manager.

Other Considerations. Not all events that might warrant termination of management can be anticipated, and a management agreement can become unwieldy if too much detail is included regarding this negative prospect. Provision for amendment by adding addendums or riders and language that allows some flexibility in interpretation can serve both ownership and management needs in this regard.

Profitability is not guaranteed, and changing market conditions can create financial havoc for a managed property and its ownership. If a property cannot generate sufficient income to cover its operating expenses, which include at least a minimum management fee, management or ownership may want to consider terminating the arrangement immediately or at the end of the current term of the agreement. Depending on the circumstances —an owner with deep pockets may prefer to continue operations "out of pocket" to see if the problem can be turned around—financial insolvency might constitute "cause" for termination or be addressed as a simple nonrenewal of the contract.

Because owners and managers may have different ideas about the best approaches to managing a particular property, they may find themselves in conflict over policies, procedures, and management goals. Sometimes people's personalities or viewpoints get in the way of effectively operating a property. These types of situations may warrant consideration of not renewing an agreement at the end of the term, although either party may be so uncomfortable that they mutually agree to terminate the management arrangement with proper notice.

Best practice is to anticipate reasonably likely eventualities and include language that will allow both parties to exit an arrangement gracefully. Legal counsel can best advise what may be warranted in a given situation and ensure that termination provisions in a management agreement comply with applicable laws. (Management termination issues and negotiation of indemnification clauses are discussed in Chapter 9 as specific contents of the management agreement.)

Developing a Checklist for Terminating Management

Termination of management requires the management firm to curtail its activities at the managed property, close the books on the account, and transfer records, property funds, and other things to the property owner or the owner's designated agent. The best way to ensure that all the details of this transition are accomplished properly and in a timely fashion is to use a termination checklist. (Contents of a checklist are discussed later in this chapter.)

More than a list of documents and other items to be returned to the property owner, a good checklist will document when various items were completed and by whom. Although most of the transition activities may be accomplished within a matter of days, some of the fiscal details may necessitate waiting to receive bank statements or outstanding invoices. If it is important to accomplish the transition in the least possible time, you may have to make arrangements for reimbursement or proration of payments so the books can be closed.

There should be specific directions from the owner—preferably in writing—for disposition of documents and funds. Although it is likely that everything will be returned to the owner, you may be asked to transfer some documents, in particular, to new management. This requires consideration of what new management needs to know in order to take over the account. Records may only need to be transferred as paper originals or copies, but more likely some or all of the operating records will be computer files. In that case, transfer via floppy disks may be warranted; however, this assumes the owner's or new management's computer system is compatible with that of exiting management. On the other hand, computer hardware and software purchased for use on site (if it was an owner expense) would be left in place for turnover to new management.

Use of a comprehensive termination checklist will expedite the transition process. This is to the firm's advantage because a terminated account is no longer generating income from management fees. Furthermore, attention to conducting an orderly transition will enhance the firm's reputation and minimize the likelihood of liability or other claims resulting from termination of the management account.

Issues of Timing. In creating a checklist procedure, one should anticipate how much time will be needed to perform various tasks, such as:

- Organize and update specific records of property operations through the effective date of termination.
- Prepare and distribute appropriate notices to residents or commercial tenants, vendors, contractors, or others with whom the management company is doing business on behalf of the property and its ownership.
- Arrange for the physical transfer of records and funds.

The various time requirements form the basis for scheduling individual tasks and setting priorities. For example, the management agreement or tenants' leases may require a specific period of notice. If the period allowed for a transition is 90 days, notices may have to be sent out 45 days prior to the effective date of termination. On the other hand, if a transition has to be accomplished very quickly (i.e., in 30 days or less), notices will have to be sent out immediately by the most rapid delivery method. Bank accounts can be closed at any time, but it may be advisable to follow the normal banking cycle to facilitate reconciliation of the checking account. Bank charges may be an added consideration—the bank may assess a fee for closing in mid-cycle or for handling checks that have not cleared as of the closing date. (The time frames suggested here are guidelines from our experience. If events beyond the control of the manager or the owner dictate otherwise, a specific deadline might not be met. It is important to ensure that any time requirements stated in the management agreement include provision for contingencies that would preclude or minimize adverse consequences of not meeting a deadline—e.g., financial penalties or a lawsuit).

It may be worthwhile to include in the checklist guideline some specifications for completing some tasks *before* the effective termination date (e.g., 30 days, 15 days, 5 days) and others within a brief period *afterward* (e.g., 24 hours, 72 hours, 7 days). It is important to consider the individual account. It may require six weeks or longer after the termination date to take care of all the details. This is especially likely in the event termination is a consequence of a court-appointed receivership.

It may be useful or desirable to relate completion dates to the effective termination date. However, for purposes of a checklist, it may be best to set deadlines based on individual tasks, differentiating which ones can be completed immediately and which ones require extensive preparation or have to follow other items or actions. This approach allows for setting priorities and ensures that everything can and will be completed on time. It also allows sufficient time for completion of individual tasks so they can be performed correctly and information will be entered accurately.

Information Needed. Before termination proceedings can begin, some specific information is needed so the checklist can be tailored to the property and the account. This includes:

> The reason for terminating management and its effect on the transition.
> The effective date of termination.
> The period allowed for the transition.
> What documents, records, etc., are to be returned to the owner.
> Any specific accounting or legal requirements that must be met.
> If new management has been appointed, the name, address, and telephone number of that entity.
> Any additional persons or entities to be notified of the termination.

The reason management is being terminated may affect the time allowed for the transition. It can also determine the disposition of documents and what the management company should retain to protect itself in the event of future questions, challenges, or litigation.

If anything is to be transferred to someone other than the owner, you will need to know the names of individual recipients and dates the transfers are to be effected. In a case of foreclosure, copies (or original documents) may need to be sent to a lawyer or trustee, the lender, or a governmental agency.

Specific written directions regarding disposition of records and monies can be very important. If the property has been sold, some documents may need to be transferred to new ownership. To expedite take-over, the owner may ask to have certain documents or monies or both transferred to new management. It may even occur in some instances that all of these entities require copies of the property documents and account records, which will necessitate preparation of multiple copies. Ordinarily, "originals" (e.g., of contracts or other signed documents) would be returned to the property owner, with exiting management retaining photocopies of such documents as it deemed necessary. If multiple copies are to be distributed, it will be important to determine who is to receive "originals." (As a protection for the management company, itemized receipts should be obtained for all items returned to the owner or transferred to others.)

Notice of termination should be sent to building occupants (residents, commercial tenants), site staff, contractors, and vendors—those who have any business connection with the property should receive a formal notification, properly delivered. Other entities that may have to be notified include mortgage lenders and financial institutions where property funds are held in accounts. If there is pending or ongoing litigation, legal counsel and interested parties may have to be notified of this change. Others who have to receive specific notification will depend on the individual situation.

It is also important to determine, beforehand, what documents (copies, permanent records) are to be retained by the exiting management company. Likewise, you will need to know what can be destroyed or otherwise disposed. Different types of business documents have to be retained for various periods because of their nature or their implications. Retention of some types of business records is prescribed by law. Questions regarding specifics should be directed to an accountant or attorney or the appropriate local, state, or federal governmental agencies because the requirements are subject to change. The property owner, especially an institutional owner, may have specific policies in place regarding retention of records, in which case this issue should be addressed in the management agreement. It may also be advisable for exiting management to plan on retaining copies of some documents as a protection in case of future litigation. (Requirements under federal laws and regulations are listed in *Guide to Record Retention Requirements* published annually by the U.S. Government Printing Office.)

Another consideration is who will be responsible for the transition. It is likely that more than one person will have some responsibility for assembling different types of information for return to the owner. This is especially so in a large management company. However, only one individual should be in charge of overseeing the termination activities, and this assignment is usually given to the manager of the property, although accounting, maintenance, and other personnel may be asked to collect specific information and update certain records. Regardless of who will be involved in the transition process, having overall responsibility and authority vested in one person helps ensure that all the necessary information is collected and updated so that the account will be closed in a timely fashion.

Contents of a Termination Checklist Form

Although the approach to documenting the mechanics of management termination is similar, it is not simply a reversal of the management take-over process. During the period of management, a wealth of data will have been collected and analyzed, and some of this cumulative information—e.g., market demographic data, rent comparisons, statistics on the local economy—is likely to be retained for future reference by management company personnel. Decisions will have to be made about what data can be retained and what rightly belongs to the property owner.

The specific contents of a termination checklist will depend on the type of property—residential or commercial. Within those larger classifications, there will be other differentiating factors related to property type (rental apartments versus condominiums; office buildings versus shopping centers), the period of management and the challenges encountered, and the specific responsibilities authorized under the management agreement. Management agreements with institutional owners (e.g., insurance companies, pension funds, nonprofit organizations) and arrangements with governmental financing agencies (HUD, FHA, etc.) and similar entities usually establish specific operational and reporting requirements which can have profound effects on the management of a property and the development of a checklist for terminating the account. Because of their variability, these types of considerations are beyond the scope of this text.

Grouping together related tasks and documents will help ensure accuracy and completeness. It is likely that separate sections of the checklist form will be created to address:

General administrative issues (notices, inventories, etc.)

Leases and resident or tenant files (rent roll, lease summaries, etc.)

Accounting and financial issues (receivables, payables, etc.)

Building maintenance and operations (service contracts, schedules, etc.)

It is also appropriate to include separate sections for the steps in the final disposition of documents and other transmittals (transfer of funds, copies of receipts, etc.) and return of miscellaneous items to the owner (architectural drawings, documentation of pending insurance claims and lawsuits, etc.). If there is site management in place, administrative and personnel issues should be components of the checklist. (The list in Exhibit 14.1 indicates types of information that must be returned to the property owner or transferred to new management—or a new owner.)

Organizing checklist items into larger categories (e.g., accounting, leasing, maintenance) will make it easier to assign responsibilities to specific individuals and expedite the transfer of documents and other items to the property owner or others designated by the owner. Individual items can be numbered or the contents of specific categories may be listed in alphabetical order. If a termination checklist is to be created as a preprinted form that will be copied when needed, it is advisable to start each category with the items that apply (or are expected to apply) to every managed property. These can be followed by items that are common to most residential or commercial properties. (As in management take-over, it is most useful to differentiate termination checklists for the larger categories of residential and commercial properties.) This approach will ensure that the basics are always covered. Including some blank spaces at the end of each category will permit you to tailor the form to an account by adding unique features of the property or the management arrangement. Creating a master document in a computer, with separate lists of optional items that can be incorporated into different sections, allows for the greatest flexibility in tailoring a termination checklist form for a particular residential or commercial property.

There is a variety of checklist formats that work equally well. A simple listing of items at the left with space at the right for noting when a task was completed and the initials of the person responsible may be adequate for a termination that is uncomplicated. A more sophisticated approach might employ a grid format that encloses each line item in a box, with columns at the right for indicating a due date and the name of the person assigned to each task, as well as the completion date and the responsible person's initials. When many people are involved and the transition will take several weeks to complete, such details help the person supervising the termination keep track of what has been completed and what remains to be accomplished—a quick glance across the columns will tell where gaps exist.

It may be advisable to create a cover sheet for the checklist form. Here you might provide space to identify the property and its ownership (names, addresses, telephone numbers) and list the name of the manager and the account number. Inclusion of spaces to identify the management personnel responsible for completing the form and approving the completed checklist and for indicating approval by the owner (signatures or initials and dates)

Exhibit 14.1
Management Termination Checklist Information

Property and Ownership Information
- Legal description of the property
- Architectural drawings and plot plans (as-built drawings or other representations showing measurements and indicating locations of utility controls, plumbing and wiring layouts, HVAC systems, etc.)
- Total number of units plus numbers of different unit types and their sizes
- Specific features and amenities on the property
- Contractors and vendors who provide products or services to the property on a contractual or open purchase order basis; copies of notices sent to them
- Insurance policies and related information—agent or broker (contact name); premiums (amounts, payment schedule); coverages (including any pending claims)
- Real estate tax information (assessed valuation; reassessment schedule; amount and payment schedule; any pending appeals)
- Personal property tax information, if applicable
- Inventory of equipment and tools belonging to the property
- Inventory of furniture and fixtures belonging to the property
- Form of ownership (impact on the transition process)

Legal Information
- Business licenses and permits, as applicable to the property
- Business licenses and permits (and occupancy permits) required for individual tenants, file copies
- Any pending litigation (eviction proceedings, discrimination suits, liability claims, contested real estate tax assessments, etc.)
- Applicable landlord-tenant law
- Other applicable laws and their impact on the property (zoning ordinances, environmental regulations, etc.)
- Name(s) of property owner's attorney(s)

---

is also appropriate. Because the termination checklist is a record of the transition activities, it is advisable to provide space on the cover sheet for listing those individuals or entities who are to receive copies of the completed, approved form. (The IREM publication, *Transition 2: Terminating a Management Account,* provides a guideline for developing a termination procedure and sample residential and commercial checklist forms that can be modified as needed.)

In developing a termination checklist, a good place to start is the take-over checklist prepared when the account was acquired. As a standard operating procedure, completed take-over checklists should be retained as a record of the documents received and the actions taken for each new property brought under management. If management is terminated, the take-over checklist can be a useful resource in identifying documents and other items that should be returned to the owner. When the account is closed, a copy of the termination checklist should be retained as a record of the transition along with receipts acquired as items were transferred. If questions

Exhibit 14.1 *(continued)*

Financial and Accounting Information
- Mortgage payment data (institution, contact name, payment amounts and schedule)
- Current and prior operating statements (income/expense balance sheet, cash flow)
- Operating budgets (current, prior year)
- Purchasing records (including copies of contracts), as appropriate
- Accounts receivable status—rents due, delinquencies, other income and receipts
- Prepayments, prorated portions for transfer
- Security deposits, accounting and disposition
- Accounts payable status—outstanding invoices, open accounts, contracts, and other expenses and disbursements
- Operating funds
- Capital reserve funds
- Any additional funds accounted separately (concession revenues, merchants' association dues)

Tenant/Leasing Information
- Tenants' names and addresses (including contact names, if different)
- Copies of all leases and rental documents, any applicable easements or operating agreements, certificates of insurance, estoppel certificates, etc.
- Detailed rent roll or tenant roster, including current rental rates, rentable versus usable square footage (if applicable), and other relevant data
- Tenant lease files, ledger cards, etc.
- Status of existing leases (expiration dates, rent increases, special terms)
- Listings of vacancies and delinquencies (including status of leasing and collection efforts)
- Brokerage arrangements, outstanding commissions, etc.
- House "Rules and Regulations" (currently in effect)
- Copies of notices sent to tenants

Personnel Information
- List of site employees, their positions or titles, and their duties
- Personnel files (individuals' employment applications, performance reviews)
- Payroll data (wage rates, withholding amounts)
- Employment or union contracts, if applicable
- Employee bonds, if applicable
- Employee benefits programs currently in effect and whether payroll withholdings apply
- Compliance status, equal employment opportunity laws

or problems arise after the account is closed, these documents should help clarify the procedure that was followed and the disposition of particular items.

Facilitating the Transition

Assuming an amicable parting, early appointment of new management may afford an opportunity for face-to-face or telephone conversations that facilitate handling of details that are not expected to change. For example, there may be contractual arrangements or other activities that will continue beyond the current management arrangement, or the monthly management reports may have to be prepared in a format mandated by the owner that ne-

Exhibit 14.1 *(concluded)*

Maintenance and Operations Information
- Inventories of maintenance equipment, supplies, tools, etc.
- Warranty records (in particular, which ones remain in effect)
- Service contracts exclusive to the property (e.g., landscaping, snow removal, trash removal, recycling, pest control, elevators, escalators, window washing, metal cleaning/polishing, floor cleaning/waxing/polishing, security, coin laundry facilities)
- Maintenance records (maintenance log, work schedules, work orders)
- Janitorial procedures and schedule
- Inspection reports, current and prior, including information about deferred maintenance and compliance with the Americans with Disabilities Act (ADA)
- Emergency procedures currently in effect (including emergency contacts)
- Keys (identified in a list; request a receipt)
- Parking (information about access, controls, fees, etc.)
- Fire extinguishers, sprinkler systems, smoke alarms—records of inspections and maintenance
- Other safety features/equipment (OSHA compliance, as appropriate)
- Security features and systems currently in place
- Information about the status of any ongoing construction or rehabilitation, including work that has been planned and approved but not started
- Environmental compliance status, including permits if applicable

Marketing/Promotional Information
- List of lease negotiations in progress
- Marketing support materials that are still usable (photographs, testimonials, etc.)

Notification
- Names and addresses of everyone notified of the termination of management (tenants, employees, utilities, vendors, insurers, lenders, tax authorities, etc.)
- Press release/announcement (public notice of change)

Additional Information, as Applicable
- Building code compliance status
- Zoning variance status (obtained, applied for, etc.)
- Compliance with environmental regulations
- Insurance certificates from contractors and others working on the property
- Compliance with Americans with Disabilities Act (ADA) in employment
- Compliance status, fair housing laws
- Compliance with rent control laws
- Government housing subsidy program participation

Reprinted with permission from *Transition 2: Terminating a Management Account* (Chicago: Institute of Real Estate Management, 1994).

---

cessitates handling of accounting data in a special way. Among the types of issues that might be addressed between departing and new management are:

- How operating funds, capital reserves, and security deposits are handled.
- When and how management reports are to be submitted.
- Details of making mortgage payments (e.g., when payments are made and whether coupons are required).

- Current real estate taxes (payments, due dates) and anticipated assessment changes, if any appeals are in process, and whether taxes are accrued in an escrow account.
- Insurance coverages, premium payment schedules, and related information.
- Collections problems such as delinquencies, outstanding late fees, evictions in progress.
- Upcoming lease expirations, rent increases, and related information.
- Preventive maintenance schedules and contracts.
- Maintenance procedures (i.e., how service requests and work orders have been handled).

Employees who are to remain at the property, enforcement of "house rules," and who is to be notified of the change in management are also likely items for such a discussion.

This type of professional courtesy ensures that new management understands the obligations they are assuming while allowing an opportunity to ask questions. However, it does not preclude the need to transfer information in writing.

A Perspective on Management Termination

Not only must the transition be effected quickly and correctly, but careful attention must be paid to the management firm's relationships with the property owner and others. Improper handling of a termination can have negative consequences beyond the transition itself. It could preclude an amicable parting with the property owner and raise ethical questions or lead to a lawsuit. Furthermore, the management company or the individual manager may be subjected to criticism that can hurt both of their reputations.

Consider, too, the human consequences: In addition to the financial impact of losing a management account, which is always substantial, there will be an emotional impact on the management company's personnel. The manager of the property and others who were directly involved in the termination may experience a sense of loss or failure. If a lost account represents a major portion of the firm's income or if more than one account is lost in quick succession, some staff positions may be in jeopardy. (The possibility of layoffs or terminations may need to be considered to maintain solvency of the company, especially if such losses cannot be replaced quickly with new accounts.) To foster continued goodwill among your staff members and as part of your internal evaluation of the transition process, the reason for a particular termination should be explored together so that future problems can be minimized or averted.

While simple nonrenewal of a management agreement is usually a benign event, a default of the contract requires review of the circumstances to prevent a similar occurrence. Errors or omissions on the part of management mean company policies and procedures may need an overhaul. (If you are not carrying professional liability insurance, such a termination would warrant your discussing errors and omissions coverage with your insurance agent.) Any allegations of wrongdoing should be addressed with legal counsel.

Because termination of management is inevitable, each such event should be regarded as an opportunity to learn. Your goals should be to determine better ways of expediting the transition and to fine-tune your procedures and checklist for future use. Beyond the mechanics of the change, it is important to explore the manner in which termination procedures are handled. In spite of the loss, it is desirable to foster courtesy and graciousness among all the people involved. Efforts to facilitate take-over by new management or by the owner will generate immeasurable goodwill and enhance the firm's professional reputation.

15

Strategies for Valuing a Management Company

Whether in anticipation of selling the business or merging it with another company, or as a basic requirement for some type of financial transaction (e.g., to obtain a line of credit or borrow operating capital), at some time it will be important to know what your real estate management company is worth. This chapter will discuss strategies for determining the value of a management company.

Selling a management company, which is primarily a service business, is very different from selling a company that is built around a product. Once a product is established in the market and the business has earned a reputation for quality and good service, its customers are generally more attuned to the product than to the company's ownership. Because of such brand name recognition, it is much easier for an owner to sell a product-oriented business without being overly concerned that such a change will be detrimental. However, in real estate management, especially in smaller firms, the owner is the heart and soul of the company. Quite often its management contracts are very personal in nature—there is a bond between the company's owners and the clients it serves, a trust related more to the people than to the company. Furthermore, the real value of the management business is its management contracts. Yet most management agreements can be cancelled with thirty days' notice at the client's request, and many longer-established contracts may be continuing on a month-to-month basis, making it a challenge to transfer contracts to a buyer.

In spite of these circumstances, management companies are bought and sold on a regular basis, and within the industry, some guidelines have been established over the years to help potential buyers and sellers establish a reasonable basis for the price and terms of a management business sale. An ac-

> Exhibit 15.1
> ## Case Study—Sale of a Small Real Estate Management Company
>
> The proprietor of a small commercial property management company in the Midwest was experiencing some health problems and this, coupled with the desire to "back off," led to his decision to see if it made sense to sell the business. At the time the sale was being considered, the company had eighteen commercial properties under management and was recognized locally as a specialist in the field. Consequently, the seller was concerned about the quality of management services that would be provided by the buyer and the philosophy that would back up the management activities.
>
> In earlier attempts to sell the company, the buyers had been rejected, primarily because of the seller's belief that the potential buyers—most of them developers—were not really attuned to providing third-party management services. At that time, the seller had had two specific concerns: The first was for his company's clients and the relationships that had been established with them. The second, on a more pragmatic basis, was that clients might become dissatisfied and terminate the accounts, thereby reducing the value of the business. For these reasons the right combination of company and management approaches was a must.
>
> **The Issues** All of the management contracts at the time of the proposed sale had one-year terms with a clause providing for cancellation upon 30 days' notice from the clients. The client base included large national institutions, regional developers, and two smaller local owners. The properties had been in the management company's portfolio for different periods ranging from two to eight years.
>
> In addition to the income generated from property management fees, there was income from leasing that was sufficient to be taken into consideration in pricing the business for sale. While the company also offered other services (consulting, etc.) that contributed to the income stream, these services were not likely to be offered by the buyer and, therefore, were not to be considered in the negotiations.
>
> The potential buyer, a company very active in residential management with some commercial properties in its portfolio, believed that acquisition of another commercial portfolio would strengthen its position in that area and establish a greater presence in the marketplace. However, the office furniture, computers, calculators, telephone system, and other equipment were of little interest since the buyer already had these items in place. With the exception of some files and specific pieces of furniture, the buyer preferred that the seller dispose of the remainder as he saw fit. It was therefore agreed that the physical inventory of furnishings would be handled outside of the buy-sell contract.

tual case study of the sale of a small commercial property management business can be used to point out the methods of valuation and the considerations of the buyer and the seller in the transaction (see Exhibit 15.1).

Major Considerations in Valuation

One of the most important considerations in the purchase or sale of a real estate management business is profitability, and the percentage of profits for management businesses has varied sharply over the years. The average

Exhibit 15.1 *(continued)*

The overriding issue for the seller was how to approach the sale of the business without disturbing the existing clients. The proposed buyer was a well-established management company with a good reputation for service, so whether it could do the job well was not a consideration. The seller was concerned, however, that the clients might not give the buyer a chance to prove its ability to do the job because their relationships with the current owner were of long standing and a close personal nature.

The Deal With all of these considerations in mind and following guidelines in the IREM Foundation report, *Valuing a Property Management Company* by Shannon P. Pratt, the following deal was negotiated between the parties.

The seller, as most sellers will, valued the company at a higher level than the market would suggest. The buyer, on the other hand, wanted to be fair in the purchase price but did not want to overpay. After reasonable negotiations, the parties agreed to value the company at one year's net income (for the twelve months preceding the sale transaction), and the furniture, fixtures, etc., would *not* be included in that price. (Disposition of the office furnishings had been decided earlier.)

At first they decided to structure the transaction with 20% down and a 3-year payout with interest. Because of the seller's expressed concerns about clients terminating accounts, there would be a reduction in the purchase price for any management account lost during the payout period, with an adjustment for when the loss occurred—i.e., how far into the purchase contract period. After some deliberation, the seller decided that the down payment would not be advantageous to him because of the income tax implications. He was also concerned that the buyer might have to be reimbursed if the loss of an account resulted in an overpayment at any point.

For these reasons, the transaction was restructured so that the sale price of one year's net income would be paid out over a 3-year period in monthly installments equivalent to 25% of the buyer's gross management fees. Obviously, a lost account would result in a reduction of those fees, but no monies would have to be returned to the buyer at any time. This approach did not entail any down payment; nor did it involve payments of any interest.

After much consideration and calculation, the buyer concluded that 25% of the management fee income was too much to sustain on an ongoing basis, and a counter offer of 20% of the management fees earned over a period of 42 months instead of 36 months was made. While this would result in approximately the same total payout, it also allowed the buyer a better margin of profit during the payout period. However, this approach did not recognize any of the income from leasing, so it was determined that any income above the base management fees derived from the purchase would result in a separate payment to the seller of 10% of those additional monies. The buyout payments were to be calculated at the end of each month, after the total fees had been determined, and paid to the seller within 10 days thereafter. A full accounting of fees earned and monies due was to accompany payment.

---

profit for real estate management firms has been reported between less than one-half percent and greater than eight percent, depending on economic conditions in the market. (These results were recorded over a period of thirteen years in a research study titled *The Real Estate Management Office: Income, Expenses, and Profits,* which is published periodically by the Institute of Real Estate Management. See Appendix C.) Such a range of variability suggests that the value of real estate management companies will also vary over time.

Exhibit 15.1 *(concluded)*

The only other issue for consideration by the parties at the time of the sale was the seller's employees. Two who had been contemplating retirement with the sale of the company chose to retire. The secretary/administrative assistant who was a fairly new employee was thought by the buyer to be lacking in experience, and this person was laid off at the time of the sale. A bookkeeper who had been with the firm a long time and was considered a valuable employee was offered, and accepted, a job with the buyer.

In many instances, a seller may want to continue working with the new owner, and negotiation of a salary and employment conditions would be necessary. Although the seller in this case wanted to step back, both parties thought some level of continued involvement by the seller was desirable. For this reason, and to foster the perception among the clients that the change was not a major one, *the transaction was treated as a merger of the two companies*, with the business continuing under the buyer's name. The seller was retained as a consultant, and an office was maintained for him at the buyer's main office. As part of the consulting arrangement, the seller would not engage in any day-to-day management operations, but he could actively consult with the clients, work on some of the more complicated tenant issues (negotiations, billings), and generally stay in touch with his former clients while they adapted to the new arrangements.

By using the approach described here, the final outcome of the transaction was that (1) the seller was paid more for the company than he would have received if there had been a fixed price with offsets for lost accounts and a 3-year payout with interest, and (2) the buyer retained a very high percentage of the accounts over the buyout period. After the buyout was completed, with all payouts having been made and no additional monies being due, the parties were able to continue their relationship and sustain a mutual feeling that they both benefited by continuing to work together.

Obviously, this type of arrangement would not be appropriate for selling a larger, more-complicated management business; however, it was a unique approach that addressed the conditions and concerns of both parties at the time of the sale.

It is possible that a company may show only a very small profit margin yet yield a substantial return on the owner's investment or provide a very nice lifestyle in terms of salary and benefits or both. The owner may travel at company expense to acquire new management accounts and attend professional association meetings and seminars, meanwhile enjoying the travel itself. Perhaps the owner has a country club membership or credit card account that is paid by the company. Even if such perquisites are used primarily or exclusively to entertain clients, there is some personal benefit to the owner. However, while these kinds of things make the company valuable to its current ownership, they are of no consideration to a prospective buyer unless an equivalent amount would fall to the bottom line of profitability if a change were made. The company must be valued on the basis of its ability to generate income or attain and maintain a market niche that is advantageous to the buyer's future plans.

In determining potential profitability of a company for sale, a buyer should want to look at both income and expenses, including the current owner's compensation. Omitting the latter from total expenses will increase

> **Considerations in Valuing a Management Company**
>
> - Profitability of the business—overall and adjusted for the current owner's compensation.
> - The marketplace in which it operates—the market segment it serves and the strength of that segment.
> - The portfolio under management—the specific properties being managed and their relationship to the buying company's portfolio.
> - The company's relationships with clients—long-term established relationships versus a new or changing clientele.
> - The existing management accounts—specific terms of written agreements.
> - A history of account acquisition—how the company was marketed; who was assigned the responsibility for acquisition; how successfully the property is being managed.
> - A history of account turnover—type of property; type of client; reason for loss of the contract; who was assigned to the account.
> - The ownership structure—sole proprietorship versus partnership; S corporation versus C corporation.
> - The company's size and geographic location—large versus small; age and quality of office equipment; existing lease for office space.
> - Management and support personnel—professional qualifications and skills; duration with the company; loyalty to the current owner.
> - Goodwill—the intangible component that is difficult to measure but adds immeasurably to a deal.
>
> Also an important consideration is whether the transaction being contemplated is an asset sale, a stock sale, or sale of (management) contracts.

the percentage profit and improve the overall picture. Regardless of specific calculations, however, it is imperative to disclose to the buyer the amount of the owner's total compensation and how it is accounted—as a line expense or as a share of the profits.

More than one owner has decided not to sell a management company when the likely selling price that could be achieved (market value) was compared to the overall personal benefits that the business generated for the owner.

The Basis for Valuing a Management Business

No single item sets the value of a management company in the marketplace. Several factors need to be examined, and then the entire company and its operations must be evaluated to determine the value of the company for a particular transaction. In particular, seller and buyer will have very different perspectives on what comprises the "value" of a particular management operation. The following discussions address some of the characteristics a *buyer* is likely to consider.

Market Factors. The strength of the local market in which the company for sale is operating is a major consideration in a purchase decision. One should look at the market niche that the company serves and evaluate its current strength and how it is likely to change in the future, for better or worse. If the company specializes in managing mid-sized apartment complexes, and that segment of the market is currently saturated, the potential for future growth is likely to be limited. Future growth potential may also be reduced if the population base in the market area is declining. If the company specializes in shopping center management and the market is currently overbuilt, one would look at competing shopping centers to see how they are managed and determine whether they are likely to represent additional management opportunities.

One would also want to examine the management company's competitors and assess their strength in the marketplace compared to that of the company being considered for purchase. If the competitors are comparatively stronger and have a larger share of the market, the target company may have been built on personal contacts, and there is little likelihood of it being able to expand beyond its current size. However, it is also possible that the firm is very good at managing properties but not very good at marketing its services. In that case, it may be possible under new ownership to improve the marketing efforts and results or that the combination of talents—i.e., via a merger—could create a very strong presence in the marketplace.

In truth, much depends on the reason the buyer is seeking a company to purchase and what the buyer's goals and objectives are. One small management company was purchased simply to acquire the services of its owner, an individual who had excellent skills in the area of marketing management services. The company's management portfolio was not a consideration.

Management Portfolio Considerations. There are several likely reasons why an individual or company might want to buy an established real estate management business. One is to facilitate taking management in house—for example, a real estate developer who has previously contracted management of the company's properties to others. In recent years, developers have been taking management of their properties back in house for a variety of reasons.

1. A desire to retain the management fees and, hopefully, contribute to offsetting the company's overhead.
2. The perception that they would have better control if they did the management themselves.
3. Having good institutional contacts and believing they could acquire additional management business if they can demonstrate capabilities in this area.

> **Reasons for Buying a Management Business**
> - To enhance in-house capabilities—e.g., a developer planning to retain management or eliminate existing third-party management services.
> - To augment an established portfolio—e.g., a desire to add residential management expertise to a commercial management-focused business, or vice versa.
> - To eliminate a competitor—i.e., to increase the company's share of the market.
> - To facilitate expansion outside one's primary market—i.e., to avoid starting over in a new geographic area.
> - To acquire specialized expertise—e.g., the negotiating skills of a sole proprietor.
> - To access a different client base—e.g., a desire to manage government-assisted housing or to work for institutional owners.
> - To increase the marketability of the buying company—e.g., to enhance its reputation (quality of portfolio, duration of client relationships).
> - To position a company for further acquisition—i.e., as a buyer or as a seller.

There is no quicker way to become a known quantity in the field than to buy out an existing, well-thought-of management operation.

Another reason to buy an existing management company is to compliment an in-house portfolio. As in the case study described previously (Exhibit 15.1), when the buyer company is very strong in residential management but not so strong in commercial management, acquiring a company whose strength is a commercial management portfolio can give the buyer instant credibility in the commercial arena.

One company buying another to eliminate competition is also a possible reason. An aggressive small company may be gaining market share rapidly, and a long-established company may decide to acquire the newcomer rather than compete against it head-to-head.

It is also possible that an established company wants to expand into surrounding areas. Rather than set up a company or branch office in that area, it may be easier to go into that market and find an existing company to purchase.

There is also the example of a management company that was sought out by a large single-family home brokerage operation so property management services could be added to its offerings. The potential buyer was of the opinion that the company's own strong client base would prove a good source of potential management accounts. Acquiring the management capability is a sound business decision. Many real estate companies that handle home sales have started their own management operations thinking their contacts and client base would easily transfer to the field of property management. What they discovered was that their clients may have been very happy with their brokerage services, but those same clients were unwilling to transfer that relationship and confidence to their property management services unless the firm had a demonstrated capability in that area. This is not surprising since most real estate management companies could not easily transfer their client base into home sales either.

Another possibility is that an existing management firm has had little success in accessing the institutional market. Institutional clients seeking management services generally look for a company with a proven history of managing a specific type of property and experience in working with institutions. The purchase of a company with established contacts would make it easier to enter the institutional market.

Many of the reasons one company will want to buy another have to do with the specific properties under management. The target company might specialize in federally subsidized housing, and the potential buyer wants to enter that field. The properties may be exactly the same types managed by the potential buyer, and an acquisition will allow the buyer to expand into another geographic area or increase its market share.

In addition to property type, the potential buyer is likely to look at the quality of the managed properties. If a company's entire portfolio consists of older, hard-to-manage, troubled properties, it is not as likely to be a candidate for purchase as would one whose portfolio comprises newer, institutional-grade properties.

A major consideration is the duration of the relationships with its clients. Obviously, the longer the company for sale has had its management contracts in place, the more likely it is that those clients are satisfied and not interested in changing management companies. The existence of long-term contracts also speaks well of the management company: It must be doing a good job and exhibiting sensitivity to the needs of its clients, otherwise there would probably not be any long-term relationships.

Fiscal Considerations. Ownership structure would also be an important consideration. Successful sole proprietorships usually have satisfied clients. However, there is a real concern in taking over a solo operation if the intent is to keep that person involved in the business: If something happens to that individual, will the accounts disappear? On the other hand it can be very difficult to buy out a partnership. Partners often have individual goals, disparate needs, and different ways of valuing the business they own. Before much time and money is spent working out a deal that will satisfy all the partners, it is prudent to ascertain that the partners are in agreement about their goals and that their agreed-upon price range or value of the company is acceptable to the buyer. While sole proprietors and partnerships may seem the most likely candidates for sale or purchase, one corporation buying out or merging with another corporation is a commonplace in every industry, including real estate management.

The financial health of the company being purchased is of interest to potential buyers, especially if there is long-term debt (e.g., bank loans) or a long-term lease on office space that would no longer be needed in a combined operation. A buyer may only want to acquire the management contracts, leaving disposition of the company's physical assets and debt to the seller. However, one would have to be certain that there were no actual or potential liens against the contracts once they were assigned. A buyer who is taking over all the assets and liabilities of the company for sale would have to look carefully at individual items. For instance, much of the outstanding debt might be on a computer system purchased two or three years ago and financed over a period of five to seven years. That computer system may already be obsolete or its intended use may not have been well-conceived at the time of purchase, making it a liability rather than an asset.

One should have access to and carefully examine the annual operating statements for at least the past three years. Operating statements can indicate the profitability of the company, the direction in which it is heading, and the level and types of expenses being incurred. In addition to the operating statements, it is always a good idea to look at the income tax returns for the same period. While sellers might enhance the figures on operating statements, it is not likely they would willingly pay taxes on the inflated figures. If a buyer is not particularly adept at reading and understanding operating statements, the cost of having a good accountant interpret these documents would be money well spent. Data on the firm's credit rating should also be obtained and reviewed.

Numbers do not always tell the whole story: Owners of a start-up management company thought the proper image to present to potential clients was one of success. To have an impressive address, they leased office space in one of the premier buildings in town. They installed the best-quality carpeting and paneling, and they bought expensive furniture. All their business cards, brochures, and announcements were printed on the highest-quality paper. They also leased impressive automobiles. Unfortunately, their business started very slowly, and eventually they had to declare bankruptcy. They made several attempts to sell the company, but the amount of debt compared to the accounts in hand made no financial sense.

On the other hand, some level of debt is prudent—i.e., making sure the company has the required tools (computers, fax machines, photocopiers, file cabinets, work stations, telephones, pagers, and cellular phones) at the level of sophistication needed to conduct its business efficiently and effectively. Potential buyers look more for sound financial health than for a debt-free company. Some commonly used financial tests include the following:

Current ratio (current assets ÷ current liabilities)

Quick ratio (cash *plus* accounts receivable ÷ current liabilities)

Return on assets (net operating income [NOI] ÷ total assets)

Debt/liquidity ratio (borrowed funds ÷ cash and cash equivalents)

Debt coverage ratio (net operating income [NOI] ÷ annual debt service)

Debt equity ratio (borrowed funds ÷ equity funds)

Management contracts are the basis for the management company's financial soundness. They are its primary if not sole source of revenue and, therefore, a component of the business's assets. In most states, one must have a written contract in order to manage real estate for others. Without a contract, almost everything that is done—or not done—is subject to disagreement. One of the main purposes of a contract is to be sure that the parties understand what is expected of them. Without a written contract, there is tremendous potential for misunderstanding and greater likelihood that accounts will not be held for long. The importance of having written management agreements is not that the owner of the selling company is a tough negotiator and has the tightest contracts in the business, but rather that the company has accounts where the contracts were carefully negotiated and the parties understand the terms of the relationship. It would be helpful if some of the contracts were long-term. However, in most cases, clients have the option to cancel on as little as 30 days' advance notice, so having a requirement for long-term contracts would just about eliminate the chances of finding a company to buy.

On the other hand, a buyer can be expected to hesitate about purchasing another management company, even one with a substantial portfolio, if there are no written management agreements in place. It is very difficult to value a management company without written contracts. Obviously, each of the firm's clients could be interviewed, but most business owners would agree that they really would not want anyone talking with their accounts at a preliminary stage. Such contacts are only likely to raise doubts in the clients' minds. Once a buyer has been identified and a deal has been made, introductions to clients are a must, but until the arrangements are finalized, it is not a good idea.

Other Characteristics of the Company. The location of the company for sale may be a major factor in an acquisition decision. The company may dominate its local market, providing a buyer with instant access to that market. Even if both companies serve the same geographic area, the selling company may fill a void in the buying company's current overall market. For example, if a company were very strong in northern California and wanted to expand into southern California, it might be much easier to acquire a management company that is already established in and knowledgeable about the desired market than to open a new office and try to penetrate that market on its own. On the other hand, we know of two situations in which the office of the selling company was of no interest at all to

> **Some Other Considerations That Affect Value to a Buyer**
> - Age and reputation of the company for sale.
> - The firm's ability to sustain profits over the preceding 3–5 years.
> - Whether any single client represents more than 10% of the firm's income.
> - Turnover of management contracts—high turnover signals a problem.
> - Turnover of personnel—high turnover signals a problem.

the buyers: In one instance, the buyer wanted the management portfolio and was in a position to service the properties from its existing facilities. In the other, the buyer wanted the expertise of the selling company's owner, and the office location was not a consideration. If the buyer has no interest in the seller's physical location, the existence of a long-term lease for office space would be a likely concern in a sale.

The size of the company for sale is another important consideration. When two large firms are merged, there is almost always substantial duplication of personnel and facilities, and decisions regarding individual staff members, offices, and business equipment add to the complexity of the merger negotiations. On the other hand, acquisition of a very small company may mean there are not enough people available to get the job done. Small management companies are often very lean, operating with only a minimum of personnel. The owners compensate for this by working longer hours themselves. While such a strategy may work well for a sole proprietor because more of the business's income goes into the owner's pocket, there is often little capacity to handle emergencies or explore unforeseen opportunities. Generally, company size will also determine the sophistication of its equipment and the management policies and procedures that are in place at the time of the sale.

Personnel. The seller's personnel can be a major benefit to the buying company if they are experienced, have recognized credentials or expertise within the industry, know their market, and are dedicated to the business. A buyer would want to know how long each one has been with the company and in the field of real estate management, and how many of them hold professional designations (e.g., ARM, CPM, CSM, RPA). The latter indicates people's willingness to improve themselves within the industry on their own time, as well as the willingness of the company owner to invest in them.

A buyer would also want to know about the experience levels of the heads of the various operating departments. For example, is the accounting department headed by a neophyte or a CPA? (The salary requirements of a certified public accountant are substantially higher.) Another point a buyer would consider is whether the staff members' workloads appear to be reasonable by industry standards. If the selling company is "running lean," its personnel may be spread too thin. The company may be showing a bigger profit, but the properties may not be getting the attention they should—a situation that could eventually become a liability. On the other hand, if the company is successful but overstaffed, careful evaluation and application of sound management principles could make it even more profitable.

The area of personnel is one of the more difficult ones to evaluate when considering the purchase of a company because people's behavior will be quite different in different circumstances. An employee who appears to be a lackluster performer may become a star performer for a new owner. Perhaps the individual believed there were no opportunities to move up in the company as it was originally structured, and new ownership has offered not only possibilities but probabilities. On the other hand, there may be tremendous loyalty to the original owner and resentment of the change in ownership, making management of the selling company's employees difficult at best and potentially problematic in the future. What the prospective buyer should ascertain up front is:

1. Will the existing staff be needed after the sale? If so, are they likely to remain with the company after it is sold?
2. Are there employment contracts in place and do they include non-compete clauses that will survive the sale? Or are the personnel "employees at will"?
3. If some of the people decided to leave the company after the sale, how likely would they be to take management accounts with them? If they did so, what impact would it have on the new combined company?

A company's personnel are not only a critical component of its financial picture, they are also its goodwill ambassadors.

Goodwill. Goodwill is intangible. Yet, it is the one asset of a business that most sellers point to when it is suggested that the prices of their companies are too high. Most real estate managers believe they do a good job and that the effort earns them goodwill that can be clearly defined. If the seller is personally involved with client relationships and is recognized as "the company," his or her goodwill would be more valuable if an ongoing relationship or continued employment with the new owner could be arranged.

While goodwill has a value in the sale of a business, it is more likely to be accounted in the overall formula used to determine the value of the company than defined as a separate item. There are those in the industry who think the goodwill of an established management company may be worth up to an additional ten percent if that company enjoys an especially good reputation. On the other hand, common sense should dictate a cautious approach. A buyer could be acquiring goodwill and nothing else. The economics of the transaction must make sense overall, in spite of—not because of—the goodwill.

Structuring a Purchase

The final purchase price will be subject to considerable negotiation and the terms of payment will be as important as the price itself. As noted previously, because management companies often do not generate high profits, they are not likely to sell for the price the original owner expected. This is because the value perceived by the owner of a small real estate management company cannot always be realized by a buyer of that company.

However, one cannot look at the profit margin exclusively in deciding on a price, a point that is equally important for both buyer and seller. The owner of a small management company may have many things going on that will impact the firm's bottom line. For example, the owner of one small company was always complaining that his company was not profitable even though the portfolio under management seemed fairly substantial. The company's operations appeared to be fairly well structured, with a minimum number of employees, and the offices were not opulent. However, during an informal chat, this owner let it be known that his country club dues were charged to the company as a business development expense. He also believed a luxury automobile was necessary for the company's image, and the lease payments were charged to the company. He belonged to two trade organizations and attended many of their meetings, charging the expenses to the company. Additionally, his salary was substantial in relation to the company's size. In trying to establish the profitability of the company, these expenses left little "profit" to consider. However, if adjustments were made for all these expenses in consideration of a potential sale, the company would be doing fairly well overall.

Although profits and profitability are vital considerations, a selling price is more realistically determined applying a mathematical formula to the income stream. Two formulas are frequently used to value a management company: The first is a gross multiplier formula that values the business based on its gross revenue. This is probably the least-effective (and least popular) approach because gross income has little to do with profitability. The second approach, the one most commonly used in the industry, applies a multiplier or a capitalization rate to the company's net income. Either of these may yield a similar end result. The important consideration is to be sure the net income is properly calculated and evaluated. Net income for this calculation would be the amount before depreciation, interest, or taxes have been deducted. The discussions that follow reflect past practices; specific multipliers will vary with market conditions and the intended transaction.

Gross Revenue Multiplier Approach. The most likely range of gross multipliers is between 50 percent and 85 percent (and occasionally up to 100 percent) of gross revenue, depending on the terms of the sale and the quality of the income stream. The formula used in the buying and selling of real estate management companies is 50–60 percent of the gross income for the most recent year of operation (or, sometimes, the average for the three most recent years). For example, if the management company's gross income for the current year is $2,400,000, the selling price would likely be between $1,200,000 and $1,440,000. If the company is growing, the seller may argue that the price should be based on the coming year's gross, rather than this year's, but that is a decision to be made by the prospective buyer. If there is provision in the purchase contract for loss of accounts, the seller's argument may have some merit. On the other hand, if the seller has only one management account—a developer for whom five properties are being managed—but the client is considering managing those properties in house, the value of the current gross income stream would be very much in doubt. Anyone purchasing that company based on its gross revenue would definitely want to have some built-in price reduction based on the direct loss of business. Obviously the gross income of $2,400,000 does not in any way indicate profitability. If the potential buyer wants to use the value indicated by the gross multiplier method, there should be no problem because additional research and due diligence will establish the profitability before the transaction is finalized. It is generally believed, however, that the gross multiplier approach will overvalue such a management business at the outset and only complicate the decision-making process.

Net Income Multiplier Approach. The more-accepted approach is to base the value on a multiple (or capitalization) of the company's net income. That multiple can be as low as three and as high as five times the amount of net income. (This translates into capitalization rates of 33 percent to 20 percent.) An example can be shown using the company in the preceding discussion, which may have gross revenue of $2,400,000 but *net income* of only $100,000. Using the net income multiplier approach and the high multiple, the sale price would be $500,000 ($100,000 ÷ .20). This is in sharp contrast to the selling price of $1,200,000–$1,440,000 calculated with the gross revenue multiplier. The true value of this company would likely be somewhere in between these figures.

Net income multipliers are likely to drop when competition is fierce. Buyers become reluctant to offer a higher price for a company when the industry is seeing developers entering the management business, institutional owners setting up their own management companies, and other types of real estate operations trying to expand into management because their primary businesses are not generating the profits they desire.

The multipliers also move up: Buyers are usually willing to pay higher prices when taking over another company offers a better way of expanding one's market than starting a new business or branch office or when there are likely to be fewer potential competitors. Other real estate businesses may tend to be less interested in adding real estate management activities or taking management in house when their primary operations are profitable.

Strategizing a Hypothetical Sale

Various pricing (valuation) approaches can be demonstrated using a hypothetical real estate management company as an example. We will assume the company is owner-operated and manages a variety of properties. We will further assume it has been established for eight years and has a history of good operations and internal stability. Income and expenses for the current year are shown in Exhibit 15.2.

Determining a Price. Depending on the approach taken by the buyer, this company could be valued very differently. Using the *gross revenue multiplier* formula, its value would be between $553,000 (50 percent) and $663,600 (60 percent) of the gross income ($1,106,000). In this example, one consideration would be whether the intent was for the current owner to remain with the firm under new ownership. In that case, the executive compensation would have to be evaluated in the context of the new entity. The owner may have taken a lesser salary so that the daily cash flow needs of the business could be met. On the other hand, if the owner's compensation has been inflated beyond what might be paid in the open market for the same type of job, the value of the company—the purchase price—would have to be adjusted for the salary difference. This should also increase the net profit.

The various sources of income also warrant specific consideration. If a change in ownership means the current owner is *not* going to remain in place and most of the company's personnel would be terminated, how likely is it that income from the existing brokerage, consulting, and construction supervision activities will continue to be generated? These income sources may have more to do with the company and its employees than with the owner specifically. However, the individual contacts of the current owner may be directly responsible for this extra income. If it were determined that these sources of extra income are likely to be lost to a new owner, it may make sense to apply the gross multiplier after deducting these extras. In that case, the gross income of $1,106,000 would be reduced by $132,000, yielding an adjusted gross income of $974,000 and a potential sale value in the range of $487,000 (50 percent) to $584,400 (60 percent).

Because the $132,000 represents nearly 12 percent of the gross revenue ($132,000 ÷ $1,106,000 = 11.9%), an analysis of the effect this loss would

Exhibit 15.2
CASE STUDY—Income and Expenses

INCOME

Residential Management Fees		$580,000
Non Residential Management Fees		240,000
Leasing Commissions		64,000
Miscellaneous Management Income		90,000
Brokerage Fees		76,000
Construction Supervision		36,000
Consulting		20,000
Total Income:		**$1,106,000**

EXPENSES

Payroll		$780,000
Executive	$163,000	
Property Managers	196,000	
Secretarial	106,000	
Bookkeeping	145,000	
Profit Sharing	44,000	
Payroll Taxes	66,000	
Other Payroll	60,000	
Facilities		$106,800
Rent	$64,000	
Furniture	28,000	
Utilities	8,800	
Other Facilities	6,000	
Office Expenses		$82,400
Telephone	$22,000	
Printing/Copying	8,000	
Supplies/Postage	17,400	
Computer Operations	14,000	
Computer Development	10,000	
Other Office	11,000	
Operating Expenses		$86,000
Legal/Audit	$14,000	
Insurance	16,600	
Taxes/License	6,000	
Advertising	8,000	
Travel	6,600	
Dues/Meetings	6,000	
Auto Expense	18,000	
Misc Expenses	10,800	
Total Expenses:		**$1,055,200**
Net Income (Profit)/Before Taxes:		$50,800
Percent Profit:		4.59%
Expense as a Percent of Income:		95.41%

have on net income is also in order. Often such income is generated without additional personnel or facilities so it is said to flow directly to the bottom line. The question is, would there be a corresponding reduction in expenses if this income were eliminated? It is not likely that a smaller office, less office equipment, or fewer staff members would be needed if these income items were eliminated. However, if the business were to be absorbed into the buying company such that the new owner's facilities and personnel would be able to handle the added management accounts, the economics could be very favorable for the buyer, even without the additional income from brokerage, construction supervision, or consulting.

On the other hand, if the potential buyer elected to base the purchase price on a multiple of the firm's net income, the price would be dramatically reduced. Using the highest *net income multiplier* noted earlier—i.e., five times net—the company would be valued at only $254,000 ($50,800 × 5). Assuming the net income could be sustained or, at the very least, that protection would be built into the purchase contract to reduce the price if business is lost, most real estate management companies would probably pay such a price for another business with little hesitation.

The more likely outcome, however, is that a potential buyer would perform the necessary due diligence, adjust the expenses, possibly eliminate some of the income (which may be left with the seller), and then make an offer somewhat lower than five times the net. The ultimate price is likely to be closer to 50 percent of the adjusted gross income, but the numbers will have been analyzed to see that the projections result in a profitable operation.

Using a net income of $50,800 and the gross multiplier-calculated price of $553,000, the buyer would have a return on investment of slightly more than nine percent ($50,800 ÷ $553,000 = 9.2%). Management companies are often not very profitable on a percentage basis. More than likely, the seller might believe the buyer should receive approximately the same return as the seller has been receiving and base the selling price on a return of about five percent. This would set the price at approximately $1,000,000 or nearly equivalent to one year's gross income. However, it is not likely that such a price would be acceptable to the buyer. The seller's return is based on the company's income, while the buyer's return is based on its investment.

If the owner of the company for sale is going to have an ongoing position with the new entity, and the owner's current salary and benefits are commensurate with what that individual could obtain in the open market, it is possible that he or she might accept less than the market indicates in a new position because there is a future attached to the sale. Personal compensation is a sensitive issue, however, and it should be approached with caution. Some owners of small real estate management businesses are fiercely independent, and these individuals might not perform as successfully under the supervision of others. There may be some feelings of resentment because the new owners are not doing things the "right" way—i.e., the original owner's way. An owner usually has a very close personal feeling about a company he or she has built from nothing, and it is not easy to turn this over to others. Both seller and buyer should be aware of these possibilities and prepared to deal with them.

Structuring the Deal. Once a price has been established, the terms of the deal are critical. Ideally, the seller would be able to agree on a price, receive a check, and depart from the business. However, that is not the way the sale of a real estate management company takes place. The typical sale involves a down payment in the area of one third to one half of the agreed purchase price, and the balance is generally paid out over a period of time—usually between three and five years, subject to a negotiated interest rate.

Along with these terms, the contract will include some formula whereby the overall price of the company will be reduced if or when an account is lost. Usually, that formula will be closely tied to the formula used to set the price in the first place. As the payment period progresses, the amount of such a price reduction is generally smaller because all the parties to the transaction understand that the buyer will have had the benefits of the individual accounts for some of the time. There is always a degree of concern about this type of clause in the sales contract because of the possibility that the buyer will not be sensitive to some needs of a management client, and as a result, the seller will suffer for the loss of the account. Unfortunately, that is a risk that has to be borne by the seller—it is not likely that a buyer will pay for the income stream and *intentionally* risk such a loss. However, the possibility of losing accounts is lessened when the seller remains involved in the business after the sale, and that is often a consideration in the economics of the transaction.

Even when the seller is not going to stay with the purchasing company, there is generally a brief period—e.g., two to three months—in which the seller agrees to work with the new ownership to facilitate handling of negotiations in progress or unusual situations. Depending on the price and terms of the sale, this time may be compensated or computed as part of the purchase price.

Non-Compete Clause. While price and payout terms are critical, other components of the transaction will also need to be documented. One of the more important clauses in the sale agreement is a non-compete clause. Usually, it requires the seller to not compete in the property management business for an agreed-upon period. Most often, that period will be the same as the payout period. However, it is possible for that time to be longer, and there can be circumstances under which it might be shorter. A non-compete clause is fully negotiable. For example, we know of one agreement that had a non-compete clause effective for the period of the payout, but with a twist: It was limited to the geographic area that was served by the selling company at the time of the sale. This not only gave the buyer protection against the seller competing in the immediate area, but also afforded the seller an opportunity to start up again in another geographic area if so desired.

We are also aware of a non-compete clause whereby the seller agreed not to compete as long as the payout exceeded an agreed-upon amount. The rationale behind this arrangement was that the seller would stay out of the business as long as the buyer was doing a good job of retaining the established accounts and maintaining the seller's income level. However, if at some point the income to the seller were to be dramatically reduced because of accounts being lost, the seller could go back into the same business. One can only hope that the parties in this situation would be continually talking, trying to resolve any difficulties before the seller would simply decide to go back into business. There are a number of ways to structure a non-compete agreement so that both buyer and seller can be comfortable with its terms.

Notification. While it may not be written into the purchase agreement, both parties must agree on how and when the clients will be notified of the sale. In the case study presented in Exhibit 15.1, for example, the buyers, upon advice of counsel, wanted to send a notice to all the seller's clients before the sale was consummated so they could obtain the clients' approval to assign the accounts to the buying company. However, the seller was fearful that this might trigger concern among the clients and possibly even lead one or two of them to go elsewhere for management services, without giving the new ownership entity a chance. After much additional negotiation, it was decided that the transaction would be treated as a merger, with the seller becoming involved in the new ownership and the clients being notified accordingly. In addition, the president of the buying company and the seller visited all the clients personally to assure them that their accounts were still in good hands.

Other Considerations. It appears that the most valid approach to determining a fair purchase price is either a gross multiplier with proper due diligence, or a multiple of the net income, again with a close look at the figures. Each of the parties to the transaction has to understand the position being taken by the other, and both must be very comfortable with each other, or the sale is not likely to work. If the seller were to be cashed out at the start of the transaction, there would be no need for concern with the relationship. However, most sales of real estate management companies

> **Some Reasons for Selling a Management Business**
> - The owner's desire to retire or leave the field of real estate management.
> - An opportunity to merge with a larger company in order to benefit from its size (expanded market opportunities, potential clients, types of properties).
> - The owner's heirs are not interested in continuing the business.
> - Family illness or disability, divorce, or other lifestyle change creates a need to liquidate the business.
>
> A "sale" may also be structured as a means of raising capital or inviting equity participation via a partnership arrangement, or it may be necessary or desirable to restructure ownership for income tax purposes. These considerations may impact how the business is valued. For example, adding business partners may justify a higher value than sale to a third party. (Using the net income multiplier approach, a lower cap rate—in the range of 15%—may be warranted for a "sale" that brings in new partners or is highly leveraged.)

have an extended payout period and some continued involvement of the prior owner after the sale.

While it is instructive to look at other sales of real estate management companies, each company operates in a unique set of circumstances that will have an impact on the likely sale or purchase price of that company. A number of additional factors can be important considerations in determining "value" to a potential buyer, even though they are not directly related to the selling firm's income stream. Employment contracts may include financial or other terms that would have to be honored in the event the company is sold. There may be pending litigation against the management company, or brought by the company against others, and the outcome may have an impact on the firm's operations and financial condition or its reputation. Past claims against insurance policies, particularly liability policies, may yield additional information to be taken into account.

In the negotiation and finalizing of the sale of a management business, it is critical for the seller, especially, to have good advice from an income tax consultant and an attorney to be sure the deal is structured to his or her best advantage. It is also wise to provide for a letter of credit or some other form of collateral in the event of default of the purchase contract by the buyer (i.e., nonpayment).

Finally, no matter how friendly the buyer and seller may be, the final contract should be reviewed by legal counsel to be sure that both parties are protected and that the contract will actually accomplish what they intended. The language of a contract usually means little until there is a dispute, and then each word becomes critical. A well-crafted buy/sell agreement can minimize the danger of serious misunderstandings and possible litigation.

Employees as Potential Purchasers

The discussion to this point has assumed an outside third party as the buyer of the real estate management business. However, that is not the only option available. How the management company is owned and the reason for the sale may weigh against a third-party buyer. A sole proprietorship may involve other family members in the business. A partnership arrangement may provide for partners to have an opportunity to buy out a participating partner who wants to leave the business. If none of the family members or partners has any interest in taking over a management business, one possibility that can be considered is a sale to the firm's employees. There are really two logical ways to accomplish this: The first would structure the sale with the same kinds of terms and conditions as were discussed in regard to selling to an outside party—i.e., a direct buyout. The alternative is an employee stock ownership plan (ESOP).

Direct Buyout. The main drawbacks of a direct buyout are the questions of (1) how shares will be allocated to the parties and (2) who will be in charge of the company when the sale has been accomplished. Perhaps the organizational structure of the company is sufficiently clear that a natural line of succession is obvious. However, if there are concerns about how a new structure might work, the buyout can be set up so that the original owner would remain at the helm for a period of time to help with the transition and provide continuing guidance while new leadership is being prepared to take over. A series of meetings with the employees to discuss all the issues may be the most productive approach. If the company is large, there may be two or three people in line for the top spot, in which case a buyout by the employees might cause dissention, even to the detriment of the existing operation. This does not mean that selling to the employees is a bad idea. If the business is doing well and the employees have been involved in building the company, the people would seem to have the talent and an interest in helping to continue the success of the business. Here again, meetings to air problems and deal with difficult situations will likely improve the chances of the employee buyout being successful.

Employee Stock Ownership Plan (ESOP). An ESOP is a defined contribution plan that invests in the stock of the corporation in which the employees work. As such, it is especially appealing for real estate management companies because their operations are labor-intensive. As an alternative to a direct buyout, an ESOP has advantages to the owner and ultimately to the employees, including deferment of income taxes. It also has disadvantages: There is a substantial cost to set up and administer an ESOP. There are rules and regulations regarding reporting—an ESOP is regulated as a pension program under the Employee Retirement Income

Security Act (ERISA) of 1974. Also, while the company owners can retain control, some autonomy is lost due to the employees owning some of the stock.

If a management company owner wants to explore the possibilities afforded by an ESOP, it is wise to contact an ESOP management organization or an experienced CPA and an attorney to determine whether the company qualifies for such a plan and the proper structure to be set up for the particular situation. Because creation of an ESOP has income tax implications for a company and its ownership, and tax rules are subject to change, a detailed discussion is beyond the scope of this book. However, we can outline, in very general terms, the basic workings of an ESOP and indicate what we think are some of the advantages and disadvantages of such a plan.

ESOPs are often leveraged at the start. Money is borrowed from a lender by an Employee Stock Ownership Trust set up for the purpose of overseeing the plan and purchasing stock on behalf of the employees. Depending on the situation, the shares can be existing stock or newly issued. Funds are generally borrowed for a five- to ten-year term, and tax credits are available for the corporation because the stock is being purchased for the benefit of the employees. This results in a lower-than-market interest rate on the loan.

Once the ESOP is created, the corporation may contribute an amount equal to 25 percent of its payroll to the ESOP. That money is used to pay off the stock purchase loan. Dividends from the stock are also used to pay off the loan, thereby reducing the payback period. As the loan is paid back, the stock becomes free of debt. It can then be assigned to employees' individual investment accounts based on a predetermined formula.

If the owner elects to sell more than 30 percent of the business to the ESOP, income from that sale can be sheltered, provided those funds are invested in either bonds or stocks of another United States corporation within a specified time frame. If the owner holds onto those securities for the rest of his or her life, the securities will be valued in the owner's estate at their worth at the time of his or her death.

Although one may be concerned that control must be surrendered when setting up such a plan, that is not necessarily so. As mentioned earlier, the shares of stock in the ESOP are under the control of a trustee, and the owner can vote himself or herself as the trustee, thereby assuring control over the voting rights of the stock. Under this arrangement, more than 50 percent of the company stock can be sold to the ESOP, and the owner can still retain control of the company.

As is the case with most retirement plans that shelter income from taxes as one of their benefits, there are specific rules that must be followed. All employees of the company must be qualified to participate in the plan. In the past, this particular rule has raised questions in the real estate management business over the issue of site employees. Because property owners either cannot or do not want to have employees of the property on their corporate payrolls, site personnel are often carried on the management firm's payroll. However, owners of management companies have not found this to be a problem, as many of the "qualified" employees do not stay with the company long enough to become vested, and those who do are the ones the company wants to reward with the additional benefits.

There are two ways employees may become vested in the plan. One allows for vesting at the end of five years (but not before); the other allows for gradual vesting over a seven-year period, increasing the employees' percentage of vesting each year of the plan until they reach 100 percent at the end of the seventh year. (Often this is structured in twenty-percent increments beginning in year three.)

The main advantage of an ESOP to a company owner is that there is no requirement for the company to meet a minimum level of profitability or provide a fair return on investment in the stock. Additionally, the company owner can defer taxes on the sale of the stock indefinitely, if that is desired, by reinvesting in other stock as mentioned earlier. The owner can buy back the stock of the company if that becomes desirable. There is also the option of contributing stock directly to the ESOP in lieu of cash.

Before you become lulled into thinking that an ESOP is a be-all and end-all approach to selling the business to your employees and minimizing income taxes, there are some negative aspects to be considered. An ESOP is fairly expensive to set up, and you must determine if the company is qualified to enter into an ESOP. This would include review of ERISA requirements as they apply to the company, feasibility of financing (creation of a leveraged ESOP can have a negative impact on the value of the company), a cost-benefit comparison against other exit strategies, and an annual appraisal of the company's worth (fair market value of its stock). Also, a trust has to be created and the lender must be identified.

Once the program is established, you will be required to communicate with the employee participants to keep them aware of what is going on, although the company does not have to open the books of the ESOP to the employees. There is also the matter of keeping track of who is vested and the status of individual employees in the vesting process, as well as the need to establish a mechanism for buying out vested employees who leave the company and can no longer be ESOP participants. Finally, it may not be possible to sell all of the owner's stock to the ESOP at once—a purchase or payment schedule may have to be worked out.

While an ESOP may not be the answer for everyone in the real estate management business, there are many advantages to having such a plan. At best, an ESOP would be one of many considerations in the long-range planning for a company.

> **Getting Ready to Sell**
> - Analyze the business objectively. Consider its assets (and liabilities) and how it compares to other small businesses.
> - Establish your stability and profitability. Take time to tie up loose ends and create a record of consistent earnings.
> - Have a professional accountant review your financial records and certify them.
> - Plan how you would structure the sale, including negotiating points.
> - Establish the credentials (credit history, net worth, management reputation) of potential buyers before a deal is consummated.
> - Consider payment/compensation alternatives. Sometimes a deferred compensation plan has advantages at a personal level. (This might be a workable option for a seller who continues with the buying company in some role.) The same can be said for stock and stock options in the successor company.
> - Understand the tax effects of a sale. (This relates to the form of business. For example, the benefits of an S corporation often outweigh the benefits of a C corporation when one considers the level of taxation involved in a sale—C corporation "profits" are taxed twice.)
> - Make sure you are selling for the right reasons (get the emotion out of it).

A Perspective on Valuing the Management Company

Valuing a real estate management business is both an art and a science. There are many factors that can impact the value of a management company, and one cannot take a single approach and be comfortable that this will set the value for all companies. The valuation process is further complicated by the fact that most management contracts can be cancelled on fairly short notice, so the basis of the purchase of the business can be quickly lost to the buyer.

Often the strength of the selling company is its owner, and if that person is not going to stay with the business after the sale, there is immediately some question as to the number of existing accounts that will be retained. Both buyer and seller have to be concerned about the ability of the seller to work well within the buying company if that individual is coming on board as the result of the sale. Because real estate management is a very personal business, and the relationships with clients often have a social component in addition to their business basis, there is a closeness to the clients that is hard to sever just because the business has been sold. Obviously, that relationship can continue, but the business side of the relationship now rests with the buying company and not with the seller.

The final value for any real estate management company will be the result of very careful evaluation by seller and buyer on both a personal and financial level. The agreed-upon price must represent a fair and equitable "deal" for both parties in order for the transaction to work at all.

In order to have the best possible outcome, sale of the business should be part of the long-range strategic plan for the company. The owner's personal goals may need to include retirement or succession planning. Other exit strategies should be explored with one's accountant, legal counsel, and financial advisor.

16

Strategies for Adapting to Change

The Boy Scout motto, "Be Prepared," is also a good watchword for the real estate management industry. In order to survive—and thrive—management firms need to be able to adapt to change. The decade of the 1990s has been a period of rapid and diverse change, and it is not likely that the pace will lessen. The decade began with a diminishing confidence in real estate as an investment. New construction took a back seat as lenders favored rehabbing projects for development loans. Where there was new development, regional malls were favored over smaller scale shopping centers; suburban office properties were favored over city locations (most urban markets were overbuilt), and condominiums began making a comeback. Pension funds had become the primary source of real estate capital. Repercussions from the S&L debacle at the end of the 1980s were still being felt. (The Resolution Trust Corporation created by the U.S. Congress in 1989 to liquidate the affected real estate assets by December 31, 1996, was shut down at the end of 1995, a year ahead of schedule.)

Past the middle of the decade, some of these activities were being reversed. There was renewed enthusiasm for real estate as an investment, but efforts to support higher rents included controlling the supply of rental space. Although funding for retail development was difficult to obtain, small shopping centers were still being built. On the tenants' side, retailers were seeing their sales eroded by electronic shopping vehicles (computer programs, cable television). Office space demand was being impacted by new technologies and corporate downsizing. Many overbuilt office markets were making a comeback as central business districts in major cities became

24-hour environments. This was partly a result of construction of new residential properties or conversion of commercial space to condominiums or rental apartments, changing the in-city mix of uses. In addition, as the excess of office space from the overbuilding of the 1980s was absorbed or converted to other uses, there were, once again, opportunities for development of new office buildings. Although pension funds were still the dominant source of capital, commercial mortgage-backed securities offerings and REITs had allowed Wall Street investment bankers to become major players.

The expectation that technological developments would reduce demand for office space has not materialized as anticipated. As we write this book, the adoption of home officing, hoteling, and other strategies that allow more people to do their jobs outside company offices has not yet affected huge numbers of workers. Interestingly enough, the growth of the Internet and its World Wide Web, one of the technological advances expected to erode demand for office space, is actually generating space demand because of the increasing numbers of service firms needed to support it. We have also noted that major cities (e.g., Boston, Chicago, Seattle) are experiencing a resurgence of urban retailing as specialty retailers are opening downtown stores. As for the economy, throughout this decade there has been much tinkering and micro-management of interest rates and the money supply, which have tended to hold down inflation. In the area of financing, it appears that insurance companies and banks are divesting real estate holdings while REITs and pension funds are being joined by opportunity funds as real estate investors and sources of capital. The close of the decade—and the twentieth century—is likely to see a different mix of investors and investment opportunities along with changes in the ranks of residents and commercial tenants and their needs and expectations.

This brief overview of roughly three quarters of the decade of the 1990s only touches on some of the particular changes that have occurred within the real estate industry. Along the way, real estate investors and the professionals who manage their properties have come to realize that they have to look at a more distant horizon when they are planning. Strategic planning that looks down the road three years or five years or longer is vital to the management of real estate and to the businesses of those who provide this service.

Changes Brought by Technology

Technology impacts everything real estate managers do. It has expanded the array of tools managers can utilize to work more efficiently and cost-effectively. It has also had a tremendous impact on the lifestyles of consum-

> ### A Perspective on Change
>
> Every business is constantly undergoing change; real estate management companies are no exception to this. New employees join the management team, and others move on to pursue career opportunities with different firms. The market changes and you modify your operations to adapt to it. New technologies offer better ways to do things, and new equipment brought into the company changes how tasks are performed and, perhaps, the tasks themselves. As staff members gain new skills, they work differently; shifts in personnel assignments redefine your relationships with your clients. These are just some of the ways businesses change internally.
>
> Change in and of itself is neither good nor bad. However, the attitudes people develop toward change have long-term consequences. Embracing change without considering why and how and how much it will cost can have a negative impact on both operations and profits. Avoiding change can mean missed opportunities—to provide better services to clients, to allow staff more flexibility in handling assignments, to increase efficiency and profitability. Successful companies accept change and manage its consequences.
>
> Change can be most beneficial when it is planned in advance, implemented in stages, and monitored continually. Often change is viewed as an end in itself. Company A is made over into company B and that is that. However, true change in a business environment is an ongoing evolutionary process. New information or equipment or strategies are introduced, tested, and adopted, modified, or discarded. Those that survive and are accepted become part of the company and its culture, preparing the business and the staff for the next round of "new" or different information, equipment, or strategies. A business is not likely to survive if change is a one-time event. Companies compete most effectively by evolving new strategies for serving their clients' needs. They never fully arrive because they are in a constant state of becoming. Success in any business and especially in real estate management requires a continuing adaptation to external changes in the marketplace and internal changes in its culture and its personnel.

ers and the commercial enterprises that serve them. These effects, in turn, have implications for managed real estate.

Impact on Real Estate Management Companies. Computers allow management companies to work with a variety of different accounting and management software programs so clients' reporting needs and requirements can be met. Unfortunately, the purchase of computer hardware and software is not a one-time investment. Within a very short time span (less than a decade), computers have become smaller, faster, and cheaper. The dream of portability has been fulfilled in the form of laptop computers, and newer models are increasingly smaller in size and lighter in weight (notebook computers, personal digital assistants). They also operate at faster speeds and have more operational and memory capacity. Storage media have evolved from magnetic tape to various smaller sizes of "floppy" diskettes and compact disks.

Computers have also made possible internal and external communications via electronic mail—e-mail, for short—which allows transfer of written messages over telephone lines almost instantaneously. The advent of the Internet and its graphics supporting component, the World Wide Web, has created a new medium for advertising products and services and transmitting purchase orders. As this book is being written, several real estate companies and professional organizations have already established "home pages" on the World Wide Web, and their numbers can be expected to increase. However, the Internet and the World Wide Web do have their downsides. Among them are the lack of confidentiality and the potential to access your files. (If future efforts at encryption are successful, payments and other transactions requiring confidentiality could be made electronically via the Internet.) Software enhancements that can prevent unauthorized access to internal data already exist, but information imported from web sites—including software programs available for free on the Internet—can carry with it a data- or program-destroying virus. Software that scans for viruses and disinfects files and programs is a must for any computer user who incorporates information into an existing system off the World Wide Web or via floppy disks from an external source.

Another downside to the Internet is that it is not always easy to access specific information. So-called web browsers—special software that facilitates accessing web sites and searching for data—make the process easier, and enhancements to these programs continue to appear on the market. Having a home page on the web and posting e-mail addresses there introduces still another potential problem—unsolicited information and promotions. Even e-mail has a "junk mail" component.

Other high-technology tools have also been evolving toward smaller size and lower cost. Voice communication is another area where portability was desirable, and the wish was fulfilled via cellular telephones and hand-held radio-controlled models. Deregulation of the telecommunications industry has opened the door to competition, and the mix of media that can transmit voice and written messages already includes cable television and computers in addition to telephone service companies. Though somewhat bulky when first offered, there are now portable telephones that fit into a pocket. Answering machines were and are a wonderful adjunct to the telephone. Nowadays, however, you can purchase telephones with the answering machine built-in. As an alternative, many businesses have embraced voice mail. In general, as innovations have been introduced, demand for the product has escalated so that selling prices could be lowered.

High-technology tools give you a competitive edge. The key is to select the right ones and use them properly. It is not necessary to embrace every new bell and whistle that comes along, but real estate management companies need to stay aware of the changes in computers and their adjuncts and upgrade their hardware and software as necessary to serve their clients' needs *and* their internal need for information, documentation, and analysis of their operations and profits. They also need to provide communications devices that will allow real estate managers and other personnel to perform their jobs more effectively. Things like pagers and portable telephones have become necessities because they allow people to be reached directly while they are away from their offices or workstations. Conference calls and videoconferencing permit individuals at remote locations to participate in group discussions without leaving their offices. In addition to saving time, they also eliminate the costs and the hassles of travel.

Clients increasingly expect providers of management services to have sophisticated computers and communications tools. Direct access to management data on their properties is required by many owners, institutions in particular. As clients become more reliant on these types of tools, the companies that provide services to them—including real estate management and adjunct services—can expect to be required to have compatible hardware and programs to facilitate such interfaces.

Indirect Effects. As costs have come down, more individuals have become inclined to install computers and other high-tech devices in their private residences. Consequently, consumers are using many of the same kinds of tools as are available to businesses. Telephones with built-in message capabilities or separate answering machines are increasingly popular. Modems have made the Internet and its World Wide Web available to anyone with a computer, and on-line services have made access economical. With these tools in place and addition of a fax machine, technologically sophisticated households are in a position to operate a business, and many of them do.

Regardless of whether individual employees have their own equipment, many employers are making it possible for portions of their staff to work at home. While this may have been desirable for external sales personnel initially, job functions that rely on computers and related equipment can easily make the same type of transition. People who only need to be in the office occasionally can be accommodated by setting aside an area for their use on an as-needed basis. Called hoteling, this strategy allows people who work outside the main office to book space to work "inside" when they need it. A desk, a telephone, and a computer—or access to support personnel who can provide "typing" services—can serve many employees while helping cut down the need for leased space. Regular staff members may be able to work at home several days a week if they have e-mail and fax capabilities that link them directly to the main office. These telecommuters may share a work area at the office, or they may work inside on projects that require more sophisticated graphics or printing capabilities than they have in their equipment at home. They may simply schedule their inside time to attend meetings, give reports, or otherwise interact with other staff members.

In many businesses, technology has supplanted people. Digitized voice messaging and computer-generated invoices based on computerization of telephone services and their attendant records has meant large numbers of telephone operators and billing clerks were no longer needed by telephone companies, so they have begun systematically downsizing. Other types of businesses have adopted the same approach. While voice mail has helped capture opportunities for small businesses, it has obviated the need for receptionists at some larger ones. The capability of retrieving and revising data and forms stored in computers has diminished the need for administrative positions whose primary function was typing letters, documents, etc. One person can do the work formerly done by several staff members. Looked at another way, technology has provided a means of reducing or eliminating some repetitive and often boring tasks while also allowing workers to be more creative. Having a "leaner" staff may actually mean that more work is being done more efficiently by fewer people. Where office space is expensive, some of the work-at-home strategies may be perceived as opportunities to reduce a company's space requirements.

The impact on the business arena is ongoing. Downsizing and allowing personnel to work at home can mean that many companies need less space to conduct their business. Although downsizing has gotten a lot of media attention, the move toward working at home has been reported mostly in business publications and has not been as obvious. To the extent they are being encountered in some office markets, these types of changes pose challenges to real estate managers and management companies. Will existing leases have to be amended in order to retain a tenant? Will the property owner consider allowing a tenant to relinquish a portion of its leased space or relocate to a smaller space in the building before the lease term expires? Will leases in the future need to include provisions that will accommodate the possibilities of downsizing and other types of changes in tenants' businesses?

On the other hand, big companies may continue to offer the same goods and services as when they had larger staffs. Most of these goods and services are likely to be acquired for repackaging and resale from small- to mid-sized specialty companies. In fact, some of their downsized employees may be doing the same work, but as independent contractors. As the numbers of these intermediates increase, the need for office and store space may actually remain stable or grow as multiple small space users replace some of the large space users. In other words, occupancies may change as an office building houses more tenants in smaller spaces. The real estate manager's administrative responsibilities may well become more complicated for having to deal with larger numbers of tenants and smaller proportionate shares of the common area maintenance expenses to be allocated among them. This may encourage automation of more of management's operations and accounting services in order to hold down costs.

Consumers' adaptation to new technologies has challenged traditional retailers as well. Home shopping programs on cable television channels make it possible for products to be demonstrated and sold directly to anyone who can order by telephone and pay by credit card. Special software programs permit direct communication with supermarkets so that groceries can be ordered via computer and paid for by check, credit card, or electronic transfer. The process includes delivery to one's door and a money-back guarantee of satisfaction. There is a monthly membership fee and a service charge for each order, but they can be a small cost when compared with the value of people's time.

The range of merchandise offered means that home shopping programs compete with local merchants and chain store outlets. The success of such ventures is likely to mean fewer customers and sales for traditional retailers who have to carry the overhead costs of inventory, service personnel, and leased space. Those retailers who can embrace the shop-from-home merchandising strategies may need less store space—e.g., grocers can select and pack foodstuffs in a warehouse, reducing or eliminating the need for in-store displays and restocking. Those who cannot eventually may be bankrupted for lack of sales revenues.

Managers of shopping centers will be challenged to entice consumers via aggressive marketing strategies that promote the shopping experience —the tempting aromas from a food court, the opportunity to try on clothes and select accessories (one-stop shopping), and the ability to make hands-on physical comparisons of things like tools, televisions, and housewares. Entertainment venues such as multiplex cinemas and related merchandisers (Disney, Warner Bros., and similar stores) and eating places other than self-service vendors (i.e., food courts) add to the perception of a center as a destination beyond the shopping experience. In the past, shopping centers have changed their business hours to make shopping more convenient for working people. Shopping hours may need to be adjusted further so centers can compete effectively with television shopping programs that can be transmitted via cable any time of the day or night.

Automated teller machines (ATMs) dispense cash when you insert a bank card and input a set of numbers. They also accept deposits to existing bank accounts. While some services allow the size of a single withdrawal to vary, it usually has to be a multiple of a set amount—e.g., $50, $100, $150, $200. Other services may require separate transactions to obtain the maximum allowable withdrawal amount. Use of ATMs directly linked to the bank where one has an account may be free of charge while use of other facilities may incur a fee. The popularity of ATMs has encouraged banks to re-evaluate their internal teller services, and some have taken steps to reduce them.

The move toward debit cards that deduct payments directly from one's checking account is a counterpoint to the co-called credit card. Cards used at ATMs actually function as debit cards. More importantly, some supermarket chains are partnering with ATM-type services to facilitate direct payment for grocery purchases via these cards. Electronic transfer of funds by pre-arrangement with a bank has been in place for many years. Payroll direct deposits and payouts to utility and mortgage companies are used by many consumers. Bank-by-phone services similarly allow consumers to make direct payments to creditors. Their checking accounts are debited without any checks being written. Those who use the full array of services from a single bank may receive a single monthly statement itemizing all the different kinds of transactions they have made.

Among the expenses that can be paid via electronic transfer is apartment rent. If residents are willing to make the arrangements for automatic payment of their rent, apartment managers can collect rents on time and reduce the need for late fees. The difficulty with this means of payment is that it is not likely to become universal. While some portion of an apartment building's population may leap at the opportunity to forego writing a check each month, others may balk at the idea of not having control over when the payout is made. (Electronic transfer is instantaneous; it eliminates the need to allow time for delivery by mail and processing by the recipient's and the sender's banks.) Electronic rent payment is an option that can be offered for those who want it. It may be easier to sell electronic transfer as a means of paying rent for commercial space, particularly if a business uses or would like to use this means of paying other expenses as well. (Rent may be the largest single expense of a business entity other than its payroll.)

Perhaps electronic transfer of funds offers the greatest opportunity to real estate managers in their role as the property owner's agent. As noted in the example checklists for management account take-over, it can be desirable to arrange for electronic transfer payment of utilities and, if appropriate, for the mortgage on the building. Electronic transfer is also the means of "sweeping" excess funds from the property operating account to the owner's designated depository. Technology can be expected to change the way consumers and businesses deal with banks in the future, and real estate managers need to be aware of the opportunities for cost savings and income enhancement afforded by strategies that utilize newer banking technologies.

Competition Is as Competition Does

Consider what factors give your management firm a competitive edge. You cannot know this without first knowing what your competition is doing. What services do they offer? What properties do they manage? Who are the owners of those properties? How well are they managed? Also, the software they use and their reporting capabilities define an important area of competition—can they serve your clients as well as or better than you do?

Clip and read your competitors' advertisements. Obtain copies of their marketing materials and annual reports (if available). You can focus your information search if you know you want particular types of information. Also, as more and more businesses create home pages on the World Wide Web, it becomes easier to learn about competitors. Real estate management companies advertise their client services as well as leasable spaces on the Internet. Subscribing to—and reading—trade magazines, professional journals, local and national newspapers, and other business publications (e.g., *Business Week* and *The Wall Street Journal*) provides a big-picture perspective on the business environment. Customer surveys of owner-clients and tenants will tell you how well you are (or are not) doing, and properly structured, they can yield insights about your competition.

Talk to their people. In real estate management, it is extremely likely that your managers know one or more of your competitors' managers through affiliations with local business and real estate organizations. Local and national meetings of professional organizations provide excellent opportunities for networking, not only to acquire business, but to evaluate your competitors.

Obviously, technology can give a company a competitive edge. Computers and allied equipment allow access to external marketing databases. Increasingly, they provide the capability of running different kinds of software. A company that keeps up with technology has the tools and the information to better serve its real estate owner-clients. The technology also affords opportunities for greater creativity in finding solutions to problems, especially those relating to numbers (financial and statistical analyses). Financial modeling, including projections based on varying assumptions, is only one example. Cost-benefit analyses and other numerical components of budgeting and management planning exercises are others. An added advantage is access to more information by more people. In theory, any employee could access needed information to answer questions from clients or tenants. To safeguard client confidentiality and protect proprietary information, you can institute a system of passwords that allow you to limit access.

Maintaining a Competitive Edge

Within the area of real estate management, the 1990s saw many entrepreneurs and small companies being absorbed into other, sometimes larger, companies or going out of business. Often the merger or sale was sought because of the need to invest major capital in technology, which is only one component of a competitive edge. Another one is people.

When a merger or buyout takes place, facilities, equipment, and staff that have become redundant are frequently dealt with by downsizing. Because real estate management is a people business, downsizing of personnel can have a lingering impact. Personnel turnover may be viewed by clients as a lack of stability. However, the personnel issue demands attention for other reasons. Because real estate investors' and owners' motivations have changed, firms that manage the real estate for them have to change as well. When contemplating a purchase or sale or merger of real estate management businesses, it is important to analyze the move from the perspective of the clients and the employees as well as the companies. Especially in a merger, retaining the key employees (company leadership, property management personnel) is often critical to retaining the existing management accounts.

Hire People Who Like People. Research on the subject has indicated that a company's employees are the largest contributor to its reputation. (Substantially more respondents indicated that they learned about a company from one of its current or former employees, compared to seeing their names on buildings or vehicles, hearing or reading news stories about them, or seeing their advertising.) Consider your employees as company ambassadors. Provide them with proper tools, including information, and treat them well. In return, they are more likely to say complimentary things about you, and positive word-of-mouth is known to be the single best means of advertising any product or service.

One of the major movements in people management in the 1990s has been a decentralization of authority, moving decision-making and authority to act down the chain of command. Those who embrace this type of management philosophy need to consider how they approach its implementation. Empowering people to make decisions and act on them can backfire if personnel are not properly prepared for the change. In the absence of a higher authority to make or approve a decision, some may make bad decisions or choose not to act at all. Regardless of the management philosophies a company embraces, there is a fundamental set of real estate management skills that is both effective and efficient. Perfected by practice, they represent experience—i.e., knowing how to do things right—and in most situations real estate managers encounter that require decisions, there is no substitute for experience.

In order for employees who are not managers to become effective decision-makers within their area of assigned responsibility, they may need specific training in how to make good decisions. They are also likely to need continuing support and encouragement from those who delegated this new authority to them. In particular, communication of management's expectations and defined parameters of the delegated authority are critical to making this type of change successfully.

Have Enough Staff to Do the Job Right. For many businesses in the waning 1990s, running a "lean" operation may be desirable or necessary to maintain profitability. Sometimes a staff is reduced by attrition. A person leaves and the vacant position is not filled immediately. Other staff members fill in, and the work continues to be done. If the position remains vacant long enough, it may never be filled. However, this type of unintentional downsizing can lead to staff overload as work is redistributed among the remaining personnel, and that can lead to resentment and reduced productivity.

It is a far healthier approach to periodically assess your personnel needs and implement strategies that will maintain high levels of productivity without creating ill-feelings. If possible, when people terminate employment by their choice, rather than automatically replace them, try to examine the duties and responsibilities of the position being vacated and where it fits into the overall organization. Is it now a full-time position? Is it likely to become or remain a full-time position? Can any other person or position in the organization assume any or all of the duties and responsibilities of the vacated position? Could the company be as well or better served with a part-time person? The same questions should be asked if intentional downsizing was not the immediate reason for a company to terminate an individual's employment.

As typically happens when a person is in a position for a long time, the person and the job may become one. Someone with a "take charge" personality may have grown in the job or extended the range of activities performed within the position by willingly taking on additional assignments. At the other end of the spectrum, you might find an individual who was perceived to work hard and do a good job but, in fact, did not perform some small or large percentage of the tasks assigned to the position. Any personnel change warrants an evaluation of the job description. How much of the function or role of the position was attributable to the person filling it?

When downsizing is an option being considered, the question may be where to apply it. Does the company need the role performed by the person or position? What are the unique characteristics of the position—or the person—that should commend its retention? How can (how will) the company get the job done without this person or position? One way to ensure the company's capability of providing the quality and level of service expected by clients is to cross-train staff members whenever possible. Administrative personnel can be trained as assistant property managers so they can handle such tasks as scheduling maintenance requests. Similarly, managers can perform administrative duties on an as-needed basis if they receive proper cross-training. Not only does this enhance service capabilities without expanding staff, but the people involved feel they have a greater stake in the organization.

Perhaps it is more an issue of personnel administration than staff size. If that is the case, there are companies that can fill the personnel role for a business. Using your existing staff or providing qualified personnel for the jobs you need to fill, these types of personnel agencies recruit, hire, and train employees for you and administer the payroll function—income tax and social security withholdings, etc.—including benefits such as medical insurance coverage. You obviate the need for a personnel or human resources department by leasing the entire staff. This may be worth exploring as a way to control personnel costs while allowing your small business to compete more effectively for qualified employees by offering benefits comparable to those offered by larger firms.

Embrace Technology to Perform Better. Advances in technology make it possible for tasks to be performed more rapidly and more cheaply. Computer processing speeds increase with each new generation of hardware, and software advances include more ways to evaluate and display information. As sophisticated owners perceive advantages for analyzing their real estate investments and monitoring their properties' operations, they will seek management services from companies that can provide the information they need in the form they want it. Some of the capabilities that already exist include:

- Specific accounting formats
- Spreadsheet analyses (budgets; "what-if" projections)
- Maintenance monitoring (work orders, log records)
- Inventory records and controls
- Intranet transmission of computer files (documents and data)
- Internet transfer of information as e-mail attachments
- Tickler file reminders
- Time management (planning)

These and other types of software are directly related to real estate management and your business. As for the hardware, having computers on site allows input of "live data" for remote monitoring and decision-making at the supervisory and ownership levels.

Computers also serve as marketing tools. Word-processing, desktop publishing, and a variety of graphics programs permit in-house generation of complex documents, newsletters and marketing brochures, and proposal materials that include photographs and drawings. These types of programs provide greater control over the content and quality of a firm's documents and presentations, which are important components of its marketing efforts to acquire clients and to attract prospective residents and commercial tenants to properties they manage. They also offer the added advantage of flexibility and cost savings. Retention of "boilerplate" language facilitates tailoring of agreements, leases, and accounting forms to the particular requirements of a management arrangement or client account. Being able to retain promotional and proposal "art" as computer files expedites updating and revision of individual documents and allows recycling of images and blocks of copy.

Many computers—including portable models—can accept and project images stored on compact disks (CD-ROM), giving users the ability to make multimedia presentations. Flow charts, bar graphs, before-and-after images, and other visuals are effective adjuncts in demonstrating the benefits of your firm's services and showing the expected outcome of changes you are recommending in a proposal or management plan. The same technology can be used to "show" rental spaces—especially apartments—to prospects. Such demonstrations are especially effective when the photography gives an all-around view of unit interiors.

A home page on the World Wide Web can be an effective adjunct marketing and leasing tool. This medium already permits display of color images (photographs, drawings), frequent updating to keep marketing information current, and inclusion of rental applications and other types of forms that can be downloaded, filled out, and returned via e-mail (or printed and sent by fax or U.S. mail). An especially nice feature of the Web is the ability to monitor the number of "hits" a site receives. E-mail can also expedite placement of purchase orders with vendors.

Because most business telephone services are computerized, the capability to accept messages in voice-mail can also be used to deliver messages to callers. By following a series of prompts—e.g., to learn more about XYZ Management Company, press "1"—callers can access specific prerecorded messages and leave requests for information to be sent to them. This feature can also be used to play music or deliver promotional messages while callers are on "hold."

Fax machines and e-mail programs that support fax transmissions make it possible to send broadcast faxes (or e-mail messages) to numbers of recipients. Such instantaneous communication can be advantageous for disseminating important announcements to clients and others. Fax machines and e-mail transfer of attached files mean important documents can be delivered directly to meet tight deadlines. These may even be acceptable means of transmitting legal documents when appropriate signatures are shown on faxes or embedded in electronic files.

Apply "Customer Service" Strategies. A host of customer service strategies have been described in countless books on the subject. There are even texts devoted to implementing these types of approaches in resident and tenant retention programs (see Appendix C). Many ideas that are the underpinnings of customer service in retailing can be applied effectively in the operation of a real estate management business.

Every contact between an employee of the management company and a client's personnel or a resident or commercial tenant has the potential for a positive or negative outcome. Everyone on your staff should be trained in ways to make these encounters into positive experiences for your clients or tenants. This can be demonstrated in terms of communications. Use of pagers and cellular telephones to maintain contact with managers and other staff members when they are away from their offices or the property allows management personnel to be reached at any time. Giving their telephone numbers to clients and tenants permits direct contact and facilitates an immediate response or affords additional response time when information must be obtained elsewhere. (Personnel "in the field" can immediately contact other staff members to initiate an information search or request copies of documents, making the whole response more efficient.) Portable computers and e-mail serve the same purpose when clients and tenants have the same capabilities.

Communications tools also encourage follow-up contacts, not only to ask if the requested information was received or the needed service was performed, but also to obtain feedback on the accuracy or completeness of the information transmitted or the quality of the service provided—i.e., how well the customer was served. The request for feedback is also an opportunity to ask if additional information or service is needed. The substantive perceptions of clients and tenants are primarily the one-on-one personal interactions that, over time, can make or break a relationship.

People who work in real estate management must have finely tuned "people skills" and project an attitude of wanting to provide the requested service or otherwise fulfill the client's or tenant's needs. These are attributes to be sought in the hiring of your personnel. Some job functions require greater skill or more complex knowledge, or both, but these requirements can usually be met by giving individuals additional or specialized training. On the other hand, you really cannot train someone to treat clients and tenants in ways that let them know they are valued customers of the management firm. These qualities are inherent in the individual, and your impressions acquired during applicant interviews should include a sense that the person not only can do the job, but will be a pleasure for clients, tenants, and other staff members to work with. In other words, in addition to objective measures of work skills, you need to take note of your subjective reactions to people and determine whether they will represent you and your company's interests in the way you want that done.

Imitate Others' Success. In analyzing your competition, you should want to look beyond the types of properties they manage and the clients they serve. Which of their managed properties have they had in their portfolio the longest? Which of their clients have renewed their management agreements year after year? Which have come to them for adjunct services? Which have added new properties to those already managed by the firm? If you can find out what they do to keep their clients happy, you can compare your company's management performance and client retention strategies against theirs. It may be the kinds of services they offer or the way they perform those services—or the people who work for them.

Your competitors may employ new technologies more effectively to meet their clients' information needs and reporting requirements. They may be able to create a perception of doing things better or more quickly or with fewer questions or hassles. Can you adopt or adapt their approaches to improve your own performance and increase your client retention rate?

This type of analysis, called benchmarking, can also be applied outside the realm of real estate and its management. Any marketing or customer retention strategy that works successfully for any other type of business—a retailer, a service provider, a hotel, a restaurant—can be adapted for use in acquiring management accounts, communicating with clients and tenants, and responding to requests for services and information. You might be impressed by a company's letterhead or the look of a magazine or newsletter. An advertisement for perfume or shoes or an appliance may strike you as particularly effective because of the placement of images or the use of type. A sales clerk or hotel employee or a server in a restaurant may make you feel especially well treated. These are among the kinds of things you can encourage your staff to incorporate into office forms, company newsletters and press releases, or their personal encounters with clients and tenants.

Measuring Your Company's Performance

One key strategy for adapting to change is developing tools to evaluate your company's performance. When clients' and tenants' expectations of service are not met, they will surely let you know it. However, this communication may only take the form of nonrenewal of a management agreement or a lease, and you could continue doing things the same way and never learn where problems exist. On the other hand, it is human nature to take for granted the companies and the people who fulfill one's expectations. A real estate management company needs to know not only whether but how well its clients and tenants are being served, and the only way to find out is to ask them—often and in different ways.

It is possible to work with outside consultants to develop evaluation tools and analyze the data that are collected. One innovative company has created a customer satisfaction measurement tool that surveys building occupants (residents or commercial tenants), the property owner, and the manager. They can analyze the data collected from these three sources and compare them to each other and to results from other real estate management companies in their national database. Alternatively, you can work with a market research firm to develop your own surveys. This can help you get started in the measurement process and ensure that the data you collect will be valid. Working with a third party also helps minimize potential for biased interpretation of results. The goal should be to learn what clients and tenants think of your company and its services and identify areas that need to be improved. While you want to believe you are doing well—survey results that say what you want them to say will confirm your belief—identifying problem areas and challenging yourselves to overcome them will be more fulfilling and provide a better measure of your performance overall.

Because there is also a human tendency to give up in the face of problems, even when they are not overwhelming, it is helpful to take the initiative where problems are likely to occur or are already known to exist. The client reports that were not mailed on time or were incomplete, the tenant who had to call three times to have a service request handled, and other similarly "small" events can add up to a poor or failing grade on management performance in clients' and tenants' minds. One way to overcome these types of problems and avoid bigger ones is to constantly and repeatedly ask your clients and tenants, "How are we doing?" The cover letter accompanying client report packages might include a request to call if there are any questions or concerns about the contents. If there is no cover letter, enclosure of a handwritten note with the same simple request will at least let clients know you want to "make good" on any problems that arise. Occasionally including a return postcard that asks whether the package arrived on time and if the client is satisfied with the reports will initiate some specific feedback. On the tenant side, follow-up on service requests by telephone or return card that asks whether the work was performed satisfactorily will identify areas of dissatisfaction. Questions such as, "How soon after your request did a maintenance worker arrive?" and "Was the work completed to your satisfaction?" invite the tenant to give quick yes-or-no answers. A rating scale (1 to 5; excellent to poor) provides a subjective mea-

> ### Opportunities Are Where You Find Them
>
> One strategy for adapting to the changing real estate management environment is to look for other sources of revenue. Among the services that firms provide under the umbrella of real estate management are several obvious potential sources of adjunct income. Development of comprehensive management plans suggests a number of examples. Market (regional, neighborhood) and property analyses and cost-benefit comparisons of several alternatives (e.g., rehabilitation versus change of use) are components of management plan preparation that might separately serve a particular real estate investor's needs. We discussed a wide array of other opportunities in Chapter 7.
>
> In many markets, there are nontraditional opportunities to apply some or all of a firm's management expertise.
>
> - Local school districts often have large real estate holdings and just as often are strapped for cash. Can you develop an expense management program that focuses on what is necessary to properly maintain school facilities and will save the district money? Are there revenue opportunities for the school district through "leasing" classroom space and other school facilities to other organizations—e.g., for evening adult education classes, summer educational and recreational programs?
> - Sometimes office buildings and shopping centers have space that is not easily leasable because of its size, location, or features. Could the space be outfitted as leasable spaces for short-term users or businesses whose space needs are small? Is it possible (and practical) to provide a conference area, business services, and access to high-technology equipment for use by several business entities? Use as business incubators or "executive suites" may fill a need and create a niche leasing opportunity.

sure of their satisfaction. Open-ended questions that ask for comments and opinions will yield more personalized responses, but these may be perceived as time-consuming and require additional follow-up just to collect the comments.

A Perspective on Adapting to Change

The thrust of this chapter has been to highlight some of the changes that have been taking place in the world of business and in the real estate management industry in the 1990s. The one thing real estate management professionals can anticipate for the future is more change. The message we would send is a recommendation to anticipate change and adapt to it. Embracing change is not without its downsides. Changing a company requires planning and, within the planning process, consideration of the consequences as well as the costs and benefits of individual strategies. The strategies themselves must also be looked at in the aggregate. Some approaches may work better than others for a particular company or situation. It is also

> **Opportunities *(continued)***
> - The U.S. Department of Defense has made it possible for the armed services to contract for development and management of military housing. Are there military bases in your area where you could offer housing management services?
> - Sometimes the most practical approach to staffing a new facility or an out-of-town branch office is to relocate some key personnel. Are there local companies providing relocation services in your area? If so, perhaps some type of strategic alliance could be arranged so apartments you manage are shown on priority or leased as furnished interim housing for relocating executives and managers. In a fast-growing market, helping businesses relocate to the right space—in a building you manage—might be another opportunity for adjunct income worth exploring.
>
> Other types of opportunities may become apparent as you explore your local market. For example, the issue of affordable housing is being addressed in some urban areas by developing (new or via rehab/conversion) single-room-occupancy (SRO) residences. While these are not comparable to multifamily apartments, they are facilities and they do need management, including rent collection and provision of maintenance services.

important to find out how the individual strategies impinge on each other so that efforts to make a company more successful are not counterproductive. Embracing change also requires a commitment from everyone within the organization and enough time to observe how the implementation of a strategy impacts your business and your clients.

Appendix A

The Accredited Management Organization® Designation

Since 1946, the Institute of Real Estate Management has awarded the Accredited Management Organization® (AMO®) designation to real estate management firms that achieve standards of excellence through education and experience. It is the first and most prestigious recognition given to real estate management firms.

In order to qualify for the AMO designation, a firm must have been engaged in real estate management activity for at least three years and have a Certified Property Manager® (CPM®) member of IREM directing and supervising the firm's real estate management activity. As part of the Institute's education requirements, the AMO firm's CPM executive must successfully complete IREM courses related to aspects of managing a management company. AMO firms must also abide by a formal code of ethics established by IREM. (The AMO Code of Ethics is discussed in Chapter 13; see especially Exhibit 13.2.)

Each applicant firm must receive approval from the local IREM chapter, a process which includes an interview of the firm's CPM executive and, sometimes, a visit to a property managed by the firm to confirm that its practices conform to the AMO Code of Ethics. In addition, six letters of reference must be submitted from individuals who have knowledge of the firm's operation and can attest to its integrity—three of these must be from clients.

Each applicant firm is subjected to an independent financial review and must demonstrate financial stability and integrity. IREM also requires AMO firms to obtain a fidelity bond covering all management employees and officers or owners of the firm and depositor's forgery and alterations insurance.

The primary benefit of AMO accreditation is increased opportunities for marketing and business development. AMO firms are promoted to financial institutions and other real estate-related organizations through a direct-mail marketing program. Brochures emphasizing the professional image of member firms are mailed each year to a variety of real estate executives, including builders, developers, investors, brokers, counselors, and appraisers. Image advertisements aimed at real estate owners and investors are published in various investment magazines with national audiences. AMO firms may also participate in the IREM professional Yellow Pages advertising program, a coordinated promotion through which listings appear under the heading Real Estate Management or Property Management in their local telephone directories.

As part of a specialized public relations program enhancing the national image of AMO firms, media personnel representing daily newspapers, television and radio stations, trade publications, and news services are sent press releases on a variety of AMO-related topics periodically. Many of the releases are also sent directly to AMO firms to be personalized and delivered to their local news media.

Each AMO headquarters and branch office is listed in the IREM *National AMO® Directory for Investors,* with its street address, telephone and fax numbers, Internet address (when available), and the names of CPM members employed there, as well as its management specialties. This directory is distributed annually to real estate investors and owners nationwide. It is also distributed upon request to those seeking to hire a real estate management firm, and a copy may be sent to a specific investor, courtesy of an AMO firm, upon request. In addition, AMO firms are listed in a special section of the *CPM®/AMO® Membership Directory,* which is distributed annually to IREM members.

Each AMO headquarters and branch office receives copies of *Inside IREM,* a newsletter focused on Institute members and activities, and the *Journal of Property Management,* which addresses the information needs of all real estate management professionals. Subscriptions to these periodicals are included in the annual AMO membership fee. Other perquisites of accreditation include a personalized AMO certificate and a copy of the AMO Code of Ethics which can be framed and displayed at the management company's office. Every AMO firm is entitled to a free copy of the AMO promotional video which portrays what a real estate owner or investor should look for when choosing a management company (a variety of owners and property types are included), and the ending of the video can be personalized for the AMO firm. Other items that can be used by AMO firms to promote themselves and their accreditation status are also available. These include announcement cards, property and office decals, personalized property certificates and frames, and AMO image ad "slicks" as well as professionally designed promotional brochures.

In order to guarantee the integrity of the accreditation program and ensure that all AMO firms remain in compliance with its requirements, each firm must apply to the Institute of Real Estate Management for reaccreditation every three years.

Appendix B

Professional Organizations and Designations

Real estate management can be characterized as a very competitive industry, yet one in which professionals share information, experiences and solutions to problems. The attitudes about and willingness to share experiences are based in the network of professional organizations and trade associations that serve the industry. Though each organization has a staff, the exchange of information comes primarily from the hundreds of volunteers who dedicate their time and share their expertise while serving on committees, as instructors, and in leadership positions.

A real estate manager's career will be enhanced by active participation in one or more of these organizations. Professional organizations and trade associations offer education, networking opportunities, and leadership experience. A study by one of the largest real estate executive search firms found that, when the qualifications of two individuals are similar, the candidate who has a professional designation will typically have a starting salary fifteen percent higher than the candidate who does not. The education and experience required to achieve a professional designation is rigorous and shows that the individual is dedicated to the real estate management profession and has initiative, perseverance, and commitment.

While there are dozens of professional organizations and trade associations that serve the real estate industry, only a few serve the real estate management industry exclusively or primarily; others serve all real estate practitioners within a segment of the industry or based on a specific property type. A few of the more prominent organizations are identified here. (A more complete listing can be found in the *Encyclopedia of Associations* published annually by Gale Research.)

Institute of Real Estate Management

The Institute of Real Estate Management (IREM), an affiliate of the NATIONAL ASSOCIATION OF REALTORS®, was founded in 1933. IREM awards the Certified Property Manager® (CPM®) designation to individuals who have distinguished themselves in experience, education, and ethical conduct. A candidate for the CPM designation must pass a certification examination, preparation for which may include attending a series of IREM courses, submit a comprehensive management plan, and have substantial experience managing real estate based on a minimum portfolio size and performance of specific property and asset management functions, with real estate management being the principal (i.e., greater than 50 percent) business activity. Related education and experience and achievement of other real estate-specific designations also contribute to a candidate's qualifications. CPM members must also abide by a code of ethics established by the Institute (see Exhibit 13.1), and those who violate the code are subject to revocation of their designation.

Similarly, the Accredited Residential Manager® (ARM®) service award, which is granted to residential site managers, has educational and experience requirements that include passing a certification examination and attendance at IREM courses. (The Accredited Management Organization® designation, which is conferred on real estate management companies, is described in detail in Appendix A.)

IREM offers one of the most extensive property management education programs in the industry. Intensive one- and two-day courses offered at the fundamental, intermediate, and advanced levels address the spectrum of skills and knowledge required to manage different types of real estate. Maintenance and operations, marketing and leasing, insurance and risk management, human resources, and ethics are some of the broader categories. Ownership issues, financial analysis, business development, and legal issues are a few of the more specific topics. In addition, a series of three courses—Introduction to Real Estate Management, Introduction to Apartment Management, Introduction to Commercial Property Management—is sponsored by local IREM chapters and offered at local colleges.

IREM publishes numerous professional books, monographs, audiocassettes, videotapes, and the leading property management periodical, the *Journal of Property Management*. It also issues annual *Income/Expense Analysis*® reports for conventional apartments, federally assisted apartments, office buildings, and shopping centers, and an *Expense Analysis*® for condominiums, cooperatives, and PUDs.

The IREM Mid-Year Conference held each year in June, and the Annual Convention held in November offer education sessions and networking opportunities, along with Institute business (committee) meetings, trade shows, and social activities over a period of five days. In late winter or early spring, IREM also brings together asset managers and property managers from across the United States for three days of education, networking, and socializing at its annual Asset Management Symposium.

There are approximately one hundred local IREM chapters in the United States and Canada that meet on a monthly basis. They provide one of the best opportunities for professional networking, in addition to educational offerings and social activities. There are also chapters in some other countries.

International Council of Shopping Centers

The International Council of Shopping Centers (ICSC), founded in 1957, offers extensive educational programs at the regional and national levels. The week-long annual school for professional development offers courses on development, design and construction, finance, leasing, management, and marketing. One-, two- and three-day seminars on specialized topics (called Idea Exchanges) are offered throughout the United States, featuring speakers, a trade show, exhibits, and a leasing mall. ICSC also offers several one-week courses on shopping center management, advanced shopping center management, marketing, and promotions. In addition to periodicals—*Shopping Centers Today, Journal of Shopping Center Research, Retail Challenge, ICSC Research Quarterly, Government Affairs Report, Legal Update*—ICSC publishes books, technical reports, and legal reports; other specialized bulletins; and checklists designed for use in the field. The ICSC annual spring convention features education sessions, nationally known speakers, and a trade show. The highlight of this event is the three-day leasing mall where retailers, developers, and brokerage firms have booths and make deals.

ICSC awards five designations: two for shopping center management—Certified Shopping Center Manager (CSM) and Senior Certified Shopping Center Manager (SCSM); two for marketing malls and strip centers—Certified Marketing Director (CMD), formerly Accredited Shopping Center Promotions Director (ASPD), and Senior Certified Marketing Director (SCMD); and one for leasing—Certified Leasing Specialist (CLS).

The objectives of the CSM program are to establish and advance high standards in shopping center management, recognize managers who meet these professional standards, encourage others to train for careers in shopping center management, and establish and maintain educational standards for the profession. The CSM examination, first administered in 1964, initially consisted of an eight-hour essay examination followed the next day by a testing interview before a committee. In the early 1980s, this was changed to a multiple-choice examination and an "in-box" test of specific management issues. The testing covers all areas of shopping center management, including operations, accounting, finance, leasing, construction, marketing and promotions, retailing and merchandising, community relations, insurance, and legal issues.

In 1971, ICSC developed the CMD program for professionals who are responsible for marketing, promoting, and advertising malls and shopping centers. The objectives of the CMD program are to establish high professional standards in the marketing activities of shopping centers, give industry-wide recognition to marketing/promotion directors who achieve professional standing, establish educational standards for the profession, and encourage others to train for careers in shopping center marketing. The multiple-choice CMD examination covers marketing plans, media planning, shopping center merchandising, retailing, product development, and store merchandising, public relations, and administration.

With the objective of encouraging continued education and professional development of recipients of the CSM and CMD designations, ICSC developed a Senior recognition program. The Senior designation is awarded for active participation in the areas of education and service, as well as professional recognition within the shopping center management industry.

The CLS designation, new in 1993, recognizes the experienced shopping center leasing specialist. To qualify, individuals must meet specific education and experience requirements.

Building Owners and Managers Association

The Building Owners and Managers Association International (BOMA) was founded in 1908 by a group of 75 office building managers as the National Association of Building Owners and Managers. (The name was changed in 1966). Their first convention, held in Chicago in 1908, included discussions of such topics as economy in electric lighting, ventilation, cleaning problems, varnishes, and division of costs of services in buildings—all of which continue to be discussed today.

The industry's first major research report on office building operating expenses was published by the association in 1920. Compiling and analyzing income and expense data from more than 3,000 office buildings across the United States and Canada, the annual *Experience Exchange Report for Downtown and Suburban Office Buildings* provides a standard of comparison for performance of all office buildings. The report is the leading reference guide for office building operations. *Skylines* is the only periodical devoted solely to the office building industry. BOMA also offers several publications on office building management and leasing—*Standard Method for Measuring Floor Area in Office Buildings,* in particular, is a handy leasing reference—and the annual volume *Trends.*

The Building Owners and Managers Institute (BOMI) provides college-level courses leading to the Real Property Administrator (RPA), Facilities Maintenance Administrator (FMA), and Systems Maintenance Administrator (SMA) certifications. The courses, taught locally in the United States and Canada, are also available through home study.

The RPA program comprises a number of advanced education courses that cover building design, operation, maintenance, administration, finance and investment, leasing, insurance, legal concepts, and environmental issues. The FMA and SMA programs are a separate curriculum covering building design, operation and maintenance of building systems, energy management, and employee supervision.

BOMA has chapters in every major metropolitan area and in many smaller cities. The chapters hold monthly meetings, conduct miniseminars, and lobby on behalf of the industry. The national organization also holds an annual convention and office building show.

National Apartment Association

The National Apartment Association (NAA), devoted solely to serving the needs of the multihousing industry, was founded in 1939 as the National Apartment Owners Association. It is a federation of 160 state and local associations of fee managers, owners, and others in the multifamily housing industry. NAA awards three professional designations—Certified Apartment Manager (CAM), Certified Apartment Maintenance Technician (CAMT), and Certified Apartment Property Supervisor (CAPS). Its publications include *UNITS* magazine, an annual *Survey of Income and Operation Expenses in Rental Apartment Communities,* and the annual *NAA Organizational Manual.* NAA conducts an annual convention and exposition, seminars, and an annual National Legislative Conference.

Community Associations Institute

The Community Association Institute (CAI) was formed in 1973 to meet the objective recommended in *The Home Association Handbook* (published by the Urban Land Institute in 1964)—i.e., creation of an organization that would provide education and information for members of homeowners' associations. CAI offers the Professional Community Associations Manager (PCAM) designation. The four courses in its professional management development program are designed to provide managers of condominiums, cooperatives, and homeowners' associations with the tools needed to effectively perform their responsibilities. CAI publishes several books, along with a number of periodicals—*Board Briefs, Common Ground, Community Association Law Reporter,* and *The Ledger Quarterly.*

International Facility Management Association

The International Facility Management Association (IFMA) was founded in 1980, and in 1992, it established the Certified Facility Manager (CFM) designation. IFMA has local chapters; and seminars, conferences, and expositions are held throughout the year. It also publishes *Facility Management Journal, IFMA News,* and an annual membership directory.

NACORE International

Originally established as the National Association of Location Analysts and Negotiators in 1969, it became the National Association of Corporate Real Estate Executives (NACORE) in 1973, changing the National to International in 1983, and then dropping all but the acronym in 1987. Its objective is to serve the education and information needs of corporate real estate professionals. NACORE publishes *Corporate Real Estate Executive* and the annual *Who's Who in Corporate Real Estate* along with several books and transcripts, and cassette tapes from their annual symposiums.

NACORE maintains the Institute for Corporate Real Estate as its educational arm and offers two professional designations—Master of Corporate Real Estate (MCR) and Associate of Corporate Real Estate (ACR).

Since corporate real estate encompasses many fields and descriptions, NACORE has developed the following nine councils, Associate Council, Commercial Council, Development and Investment Council, Economic Development Council, Financial Services Council, Industrial Council, International Council, Restaurant Council, and Retail Council. Each NACORE member is entitled to participate in one "primary" and one "secondary" council.

NACORE services include seminars, publications, conventions, a surplus property exhibit, job assistance, a compensation survey, real estate software directory, and an international corporate activity database.

National Association of Industrial and Office Properties

The National Association of Industrial and Office Properties (NAIOP) was founded in 1967 as the National Association of Industrial Parks to serve the industrial and office park developers, owners, brokers, and property managers. In 1992, it was renamed National Association of Industrial and Office Parks (NAIOP); and in 1994, the acronym was given precedence in the name NAIOP—The Association for Commercial Real Estate. The current name was adopted in 1996.

With local chapters throughout the United States, NAIOP conducts national and local seminars, holds an annual convention, and publishes several periodicals—*Development Magazine* and *NAIOP Update*—along with books and cassette tapes.

Counselors of Real Estate

The Counselors of Real Estate, formerly the American Society of Real Estate Counselors, was founded in 1953. Membership is selective, extended by invitation only on either a self-initiated or sponsored basis, and all members are entitled to use the professional designation Counselor of Real Estate (CRE). Applicants are interviewed and must submit counseling reports as part of their qualifications for membership. The Counselors of Real Estate offers *The Counselor* and *Real Estate Issues* periodicals along with numerous other publications, seminars, and an annual convention.

Commercial Investment Real Estate Institute

The Commercial Investment Real Estate Institute (CIREI) is an organization of brokers, developers, asset managers, and others involved in commercial investment real estate. Members who successfully complete 240 hours of graduate study in property analysis, valuation, and related courses; submit a resume of qualified transactions or consultations or both; and complete an 8-hour examination are awarded the Certified Commercial-Investment Member (CCIM) designation. CIREI publishes *Commercial Investment Real Estate Journal* and a *Roster of CCIM Designees*.

Appendix C

Resources

There is a wealth of resources available to assist real estate management companies in finding appropriate information for their various business activities. The information provided here is intentionally selective, providing only a sampling of sources we consider particularly relevant to the content of this book. It is focused primarily on the business aspect of real estate management and some of the adjunct tools to facilitate business development activities. Inclusion of particular organizations or publications does not constitute endorsement by the authors or the publisher.

Organizations

Professional organizations and trade associations are potential resources for information on real estate management activities, professional designations (see also Appendix B), and other relevant subjects. These comprise the first group of organizations listed here. The nature of their memberships and goals commend certain other associations as possible sources for specialized information and expertise on things like business management, accounting, insurance, legal issues, personnel, etc. Some might even be sources of potential business. These are the second group listed. The *Encyclopedia of Associations* published annually by Gale Research (835 Penobscot Building, Detroit, Michigan 48226-4094) can be consulted for additional organizations and more detailed descriptions of those listed here.

Associations of Real Estate Professionals

Apartment Owners and Managers Association of America, 65 Cherry Plaza, Watertown, CT 06795 (phone: 203-274-2589; fax: 203-274-2580).

Building Owners and Managers Association International, 1201 New York Avenue, N.W., Suite 300, Washington, DC 20005 (phone: 202-408-2662; fax: 202-371-0181).

Commercial Investment Real Estate Institute, 430 North Michigan Avenue, Chicago, IL 60611 (phone: 312-321-4460; fax: 312-321-4530).

Community Associations Institute, 1630 Duke Street, Alexandria, VA 22314 (phone: 703-548-8600; fax: 703-684-1581).

The Counselors of Real Estate, 430 North Michigan Avenue, Chicago, IL 60611 (phone: 312-329-8427; fax: 312-329-8881).

Institute of Real Estate Management, 430 North Michigan Avenue, Chicago, IL 60611 (phone: 312-329-6000; fax: 312-661-0217).

International Council of Shopping Centers, 665 Fifth Avenue, New York, NY 10022 (phone: 212-421-8181; fax: 212-486-0849).

International Facility Management Association, 1 East Greenway Plaza, Suite 1100, Houston, TX 77046 (phone: 713-623-4362; fax: 713-623-6124).

NACORE International, 440 Columbia Drive, Suite 100, West Palm Beach, FL 33409 (phone: 407-683-8111; fax: 407-697-4853).

National Apartment Association, 291 North Union Street, Suite 200, Alexandria, VA 22314 (phone: 703-513-6141; fax: 703-513-6191).

National Association of Industrial and Office Properties, Woodland Park, 2201 Cooperative Way, Herndon, VA 22071 (phone: 703-904-7100; fax: 703-904-7942).

National Association of Real Estate Investment Trusts, 1129 - 20th Street, N.W., Suite 305, Washington, DC 20036 (phone: 202-785-8717).

National Association of Realtors, 430 North Michigan Avenue, Chicago, IL 60611 (phone: 312-329-8200; fax: 312-329-8576).

National Multi Housing Council, 1850 M Street, N.W., Suite 540, Washington, DC 20036 (phone: 202-659-3381; fax: 202-775-0112).

National Property Management Association, 380 Main Street, Suite 290, Dunedin, FL 34698 (phone: 813-736-3788; fax: 813-736-6707).

Other Professional Associations

American Bar Association, 750 North Lake Shore Drive, Chicago, IL 60611 (phone: 312-988-5000; fax: 312-988-6281). Association of attorneys in good standing; state and local bar associations can be found in the Yellow Pages telephone directory.

American Industrial Real Estate Association, Sheraton Grande Office Center, 345 South Figueroa, Suite M-1, Los Angeles, CA 90071 (phone: 213-687-8777; fax: 213-687-8616). Southern California organization whose members comprise title companies, mortgage lenders, and others involved in industrial and commercial real estate activities.

American Institute of Architects, 1735 New York Avenue, N.W., Washington, DC 20006 (phone: 202-626-7300; fax: 202-626-7421). Association of professional architects; publishes books and materials on related subjects.

American Institute of Certified Public Accountants, 1211 Avenue of the Americas, New York, NY 10036 (phone: 212-596-6200; fax: 212-596-6213). Professional association of accountants; establishes auditing and reporting standards.

American Insurance Association, 1130 Connecticut Avenue, N.W., Suite 1000,

Washington, DC 20036 (phone: 202-828-7100; fax: 202-293-1219). Publishes books on insurance and liability laws and their implications.

American Land Title Association, 1828 L Street, N.W., Suite 705, Washington, DC 20036 (phone: 202-296-3671; fax: 202-223-5843). Members comprise attorneys, title insurance companies, and others specializing in real property law.

American Management Association, 135 West 50th Street, New York, NY 10020 (phone: 212-586-8100; fax: 212-903-8168). Provides training and publications on practical business skills.

Association of Real Estate License Law Officials, P.O. Box 129, Centerville, UT 84014 (phone: 801-298-5572; fax: 801-298-5576). Organization of state officials who administer real estate licensing laws.

Center for Creative Leadership, P.O. Box 26300, Greensboro, NC 27438 (phone: 910-288-7210; fax: 910-288-3999). Addresses information needs of upper and mid-level managers in business and other fields; sponsors management development programs.

Insurance Information Institute, 110 William Street, New York, NY 10038 (phone: 212-669-9200; fax: 212-732-1916). Association of property and casualty insurers; provides information and educational services to the general public.

International Association of Assessing Officers, 130 East Randolph Street, Suite 850, Chicago, IL 60601 (phone: 312-819-6100; fax: 312-819-6149). Member organization of state and local officials concerned with valuation of property for real estate tax purposes.

International Mass Retail Association, 1901 Pennsylvania Avenue, N.W., 10th Floor, Washington, DC 20006 (phone: 212-861-0774; fax: 202-785-4588). Conducts research and educational programs on mass retailing and studies industry practices.

National Association of Mutual Insurance Companies, 3601 Vincennes Road, P.O. Box 68700, Indianapolis, IN 46268 (phone: 317-875-5250; fax: 317-879-8408). Compiles and analyzes information on insurance and loss prevention and loss reduction.

National Association of Real Estate Companies, P.O. Box 958, Columbia, MD 21044 (phone: 410-821-1614; fax: 410-992-6363). Organization concerned with financial management of real estate companies, including accounting and financial reporting issues.

National Business Incubation Association, 20 East Circle Drive, Suite 190, Athens, OH 45701 (phone: 614-593-4331; fax: 614-593-1996). Members are entities that provide shared office space and other facilities for small companies to help newly formed businesses succeed.

National Society of Environmental Consultants, P.O. Box 12528, San Antonio, TX 78212 (phone: 210-271-0781; fax: 210-225-8450). Professional association that encourages awareness of environmental risks and regulations regarding their impact on real estate value; bestows Environmental Assessment Consultant (EAC) and Environmental Screening Consultant (ESC) designations.

Real Estate Educators Association, 11 South LaSalle Street, Suite 1400, Chicago, IL 60603 (phone: 312-201-0101; fax: 312-201-0214). Members comprise individuals involved in real estate education and training; offers Real Estate Instructor certification.

Risk and Insurance Management Society, 655 Third Avenue, New York, NY 10017 (phone: 212-286-9292; fax: 212-986-9716). Supplies information to assist in the purchase of insurance.

Society for Human Resource Management, 606 North Washington Street, Alexandria, VA 22314 (phone: 703-548-3440; fax: 703-836-0367). Association of human resource professionals; offers certification through its affiliation with the Human Resource Certification Institute.

ULI—The Urban Land Institute, 625 Indiana Avenue, N.W., Suite 400, Washington, DC 20004 (phone: 202-624-7000; fax: 202-624-7140). Association of financial institutions, planning commissions, developers, and others interested in urban planning and development.

Publications

There are countless publications that can be helpful in providing current information on business practices and the real estate industry, *Business Week* and *The Wall Street Journal* among them. The list that follows is not intended to be all-inclusive but rather to suggest possibilities. Other potentially useful books and periodicals can be found by consulting *Books in Print* and *Periodicals in Print,* both of which are commonly available in local public libraries. Many professional organizations maintain collections of relevant resources, and the business departments or schools at colleges and universities may permit use of their specialized libraries.

Books

ADA Title III—Compliance Made Practical (Chicago: Institute of Real Estate Management, 1992).

Alexander, Alan A., and Muhlebach, Richard F.: *Managing and Leasing Commercial Properties: Complex Issues* (New York: John Wiley & Sons, Inc., 1993).

Alexander, Alan A., and Muhlebach, Richard F.: *Managing and Leasing Commercial Properties: Practice, Strategies and Forms* (2d ed., 2 vols.; New York: John Wiley & Sons, Inc., 1996).

Alexander, Alan A., and Muhlebach, Richard F.: *Operating Small Shopping Centers* (New York: International Council of Shopping Centers, 1996).

Alexander, Alan A., and Muhlebach, Richard F.: *Shopping Center Management* (Chicago: Institute of Real Estate Management, 1992).

Alexander, Alan A., and Muhlebach, Richard F.: *Shopping Center Tenant Relations: A Manager's Guide to Tenant Retention* (New York: International Council of Shopping Centers, 1992).

American Society of Real Estate Counselors: *Real Estate Counseling* (Englewood Cliffs, N.J.: Prentice-Hall, 1984).

Barrett, G. Vincent, and Blair, John P.: *How to Conduct and Analyze Real Estate*

Market and Feasibility Studies (2d ed.; New York: Van Nostrand Reinhold Company, Inc., 1988).

Before Disaster Strikes: Developing an Emergency Procedures Manual (Chicago: Institute of Real Estate Management, 1996).

Black, Henry C., et al.: *Black's Law Dictionary* (abr. 6th ed.; St. Paul, Minn.: West Publishing Company, 1991).

Boe, Anne, and Youngs, Betty B.: *Is Your "Net" Working? A Complete Guide to Building Contacts and Career Visibility* (New York: John Wiley & Sons, Inc., 1989).

Bonner, John T., Jr.: *Human Resources Management in Real Estate* Scottsdale, Ariz.: Gorsuch Scarisbrick, Publishers, 1990).

Brown, Robert K., et al.: *Managing Corporate Real Estate* (New York: John Wiley & Sons, Inc., 1993).

Cagann, Robert A.: *Rehabilitating Apartments: A Recycling Process* (Chicago: Institute of Real Estate Management, 1994).

Collins, James C., and Lazier, William C.: *Beyond Entrepreneurship: Turning Your Business into an Enduring Great Company* (Englewood Cliffs, N.J.: Prentice-Hall, 1992).

Cook, Mary E.: *The Complete Do-It-Yourself Personnel Department* (Englewood Cliffs, N.J.: Prentice-Hall, 1991).

Cotts, David G., and Lee, Michael: *The Facility Management Handbook* (New York: AMACOM, Division of American Management Association, 1992).

Crego, Edwin T., Jr., et al.: *How to Write a Business Plan* (3d ed.; Watertown, Mass.: American Management Association, 1990).

Crispell, Diane: *The Insider's Guide to Demographic Know-How: Everything You Need to Find, Analyze, and Use Information About Your Customers* (3d ed.; Ithaca, N.Y.: American Demographics Books, Division of American Demographics, Inc., 1993).

Expense Analysis®: Condominiums, Cooperatives & PUDs (Chicago: Institute of Real Estate Management, annual).

Fair Housing Practices for Every Day: Treating People Right (Chicago: Institute of Real Estate Management, 1992).

A Guide to Managing REO and Receivership Properties (Chicago: Institute of Real Estate Management, 1992).

Harmon, Laurence C., and McKenna-Harmon, Kathleen M.: *The Resident Retention Revolution* (Chicago: Institute of Real Estate Management, 1994).

Income/Expense Analysis®: Conventional Apartments (Chicago: Institute of Real Estate Management, annual).

Income/Expense Analysis®: Federally Assisted Apartments (Chicago: Institute of Real Estate Management, annual).

Income/Expense Analysis®: Office Buildings (Chicago: Institute of Real Estate Management, annual).

Income/Expense Analysis®: Shopping Centers (Chicago: Institute of Real Estate Management, annual).

Institute of Real Estate Management Foundation: *Managing the Future: Real Estate in the 1990s* (Chicago: Institute of Real Estate Management Foundation and Arthur Andersen, 1991).

Kelley, Edward N.: *Practical Apartment Management* (3d ed.; (Chicago: Institute of Real Estate Management, 1990).

Leasing Retail Space (Chicago: Institute of Real Estate Management, 1990).

Levesque, Joseph D.: *Manual of Personnel Policies, Procedures and Operations* (2d ed.; Englewood Cliffs, N.J.: Prentice-Hall, 1993).

Levinson, Jay Conrad: *Guerrilla Marketing for the Nineties: The Newest Secrets for Making Big Profits from Your Small Business* (Boston: Houghton Mifflin Co., 1993).

London, Sheldon I.: *How to Comply with Federal Employee Laws* (Washington, D.C.: London Publishing Company, Inc., 1991).

Lundeen, Howard K.; Harmon, Laurence C., and McKenna-Harmon, Kathleen M.: *The Tenant Retention Solution: A Revolutionary Approach to Commercial Real Estate Management* (Chicago: Institute of Real Estate Management, 1995).

McKenna-Harmon, Kathleen M., and Harmon, Laurence C.: *Contemporary Apartment Marketing: Strategies and Applications* (Chicago: Institute of Real Estate Management, 1993).

Holland, Barbara K.: *Successful Residential Management: The Professional's Guide* (Chicago: Institute of Real Estate Management, 1995).

Minimum Standards for Property Management Accounting Software, 1995 Edition (Chicago: Institute of Real Estate Management Foundation, 1995).

Morey, Scott, and Giudice, Don: *A Survey of Property Management Accounting Software* (Chicago: Institute of Real Estate Management, 1995).

Occupational Outlook Handbook (Washington, D.C.: U.S. Department of Labor, Bureau of Labor Statistics, 1996).

Office Building Lease Manual (Washington, D.C.: Building Owners and Managers Association International, 1986).

Parks, David C.: *Environmental Management for Real Estate Professionals* (Chicago: Institute of Real Estate Management, 1992).

Perritt, Henry H., Jr.: *Americans with Disabilities Act Handbook* (2d ed.; New York: John Wiley & Sons, Inc., 1990, 1991).

Potential Unlimited, Inc.: *The Correlation of Behavioral Traits with Specific Property Management Tasks* (Chicago: Institute of Real Estate Management Foundation, 1986).

Pratt, Shannon P.: *Valuing a Property Management Company* (Chicago: Institute of Real Estate Management Foundation, 1988).

Principles of Real Estate Management (13th ed.; Chicago: Institute of Real Estate Management, 1991).

Randolph, Patrick A. (Ed.): *The Commercial Property Lease: Structuring Agreements, Assessing Expenses, and Preventing Liabilities for Landlords and Tenants* (Chicago: American Bar Association, 1993).

The Real Estate Management Office: Income, Expenses, and Profits (Chicago: Institute of Real Estate Management Foundation, 1983, 1987, 1991, 1996).

Real Estate Software Guidelines: Property Management (Chicago: Institute of Real Estate Management, 1984).

Reducing Your Risks (Chicago: Institute of Real Estate Management, 1994).

Roberts, Duane F.: *Marketing and Leasing of Office Space* (Rev. ed.; Chicago: Institute of Real Estate Management, 1986).

Senn, Mark A.: *Commercial Real Estate Leases: Forms* (2d ed; New York: John Wiley & Sons, Inc., 1990).

Senn, Mark A.: *Commercial Real Estate Leases: Preparation and Negotiation* (2d ed.; New York: John Wiley & Sons, Inc., 1990).

Senn, Mark A.: *Negotiating Real Estate Transactions* (New York: John Wiley & Sons, Inc., 1988).

Standard Method for Measuring Floor Area in Office Buildings (Washington, D.C.: Building Owners and Managers Association International, 1996).

Terry and Rue: *Principles of Management* (4th ed.; Burr Ridge, Ill.: Irwin Professional Publishing, 1982).

Transition: Taking Over a Management Account (Chicago: Institute of Real Estate Management, 1993).

Transition 2: Terminating a Management Account (Chicago: Institute of Real Estate Management, 1994).

Wiley, Robert J.: *Real Estate Accounting and Mathematics Handbook* (3d ed.; New York: John Wiley & Sons, Inc., 1993).

Forms

BOMA International Standard Agency Management Agreement (Washington, D.C.: Building Owners and Managers Association International, 1986), 5 pages.

Condominium and Homeowners' Association Management Agreement (Chicago: Institute of Real Estate Management, 1989), 16-page form accompanied by 12-page Explanation and 1995 addendum (4 pages).

Management Agreement (Chicago: Institute of Real Estate Management, 1988), 16-page form accompanied by 8-page Explanation and 1995 addendum (4 pages).

Periodicals

American Demographics (American Demographics, Inc., 127 West State Street, Ithaca, NY 14850).

Digest of Real Estate License Laws (Association of Real Estate License Law Officials, P.O. Box 129, Centerville, UT 84014).

Harvard Business Review (Harvard Business School Publishing Corporation, Boston, MA 02163).

HR Focus (American Management Association, 135 West 50th Street, New York, NY 10020).

HR Magazine (Society for Human Resource Management, 606 North Washington Street, Alexandria, VA 22314).

Journal of Property Management (Institute of Real Estate Management, 430 North Michigan Avenue, Chicago, IL 60611).

Nation's Business (U.S. Department of Commerce, 1615 Howard Street, N.W., Washington, DC 20062).

Personnel Journal (ACC Communications, Inc., 245 Fischer Avenue, B-2, Costa Mesa, CA 92626).

Quality Update (Philip Crosby Associates, Inc., 3260 University Boulevard, P.O. Box 6006, Winter Park, FL 32793).

Real Estate Accounting and Taxation (Warren, Gorham and Lamont, 31 St. James Avenue, Boston, MA 02116).

Real Estate Finance (Federal Research Press, 155 Federal Street, Boston, MA 02110).

Real Estate Finance Journal (Warren, Gorham and Lamont, 31 St. James Avenue, Boston, MA 02116).

Sloan Management Review (Massachusetts Institute of Technology, Sloan School of Management, 292 Main Street, E38-120, Cambridge, MA 02139).

Training (Lakewood Publications, Inc., Lakewood Building, 50 South Ninth Street, Minneapolis, MN 55402).

Newsletters

Assisted Housing Accounts and Audits Insider (Brownstone Publishers, Inc., 149 Fifth Avenue, 16th Floor, New York, NY 10010).

Assisted Housing Management Insider (Brownstone Publishers, Inc., 149 Fifth Avenue, 16th Floor, New York, NY 10010).

CarlsonReport for Shopping Center Management (Raven Communications, Inc., P.O. Box 502830, Indianapolis, IN 46250).

CB Commercial Market Watch (CB Commercial/Torto Wheaton Research, 200 High Street, Third Floor, Boston, MA 02110).

Commercial Lease Law Insider (Brownstone Publishers, Inc., 149 Fifth Avenue, 16th Floor, New York, NY 10010).

Commercial Leasing Law and Strategy (Leader Publications, Division of New York Law Publishing Company, 345 Park Avenue South, New York, NY 10010).

Crime Prevention News (CD Publications, 8204 Fenton Street, Silver Spring, MD 20910).

Housing Affairs Letter (CD Publications, 8204 Fenton Street, Silver Spring, MD 20910).

Landlord Law Report (CD Publications, 8204 Fenton Street, Silver Spring, MD 20910).

Landlord Tenant Law Bulletin (Quinlan Publishing Company, 23 Drydock Avenue, Boston, MA 02210).

Managing Housing Letter (CD Publications, 8204 Fenton Street, Silver Spring, MD 20910).

MarketSource (Appraisal Institute, 875 North Michigan Avenue, Chicago, IL 60611).

Mortgage and Real Estate Executive Report (Warren, Gorham and Lamont, 31 St. James Avenue, Boston, MA 02116).

National Property Law Digests (Stafford Publications, Inc., 590 Dutch Valley Road, N.E., Postal Drawer 13729, Atlanta, GA 30324).

Premises Liability Report (Stafford Publications, Inc., 590 Dutch Valley Road, N.E., Postal Drawer 13729, Atlanta, GA 30324).

Professional Apartment Management (Brownstone Publishers, Inc., 149 Fifth Avenue, 16th Floor, New York, NY 10010).

Real Estate Workouts and Asset Management (Warren, Gorham and Lamont, 31 St. James Avenue, Boston, MA 02116).

Shopping Center Management Insider (Brownstone Publishers, Inc., 149 Fifth Avenue, 16th Floor, New York, NY 10010).

Strategic Advantage (CEL and Associates, Inc., 12121 Wilshire Boulevard, Suite 505, Los Angeles, CA 90025).

Index

A

Accounting, 42, 44, 81–122, 205–206. *See also* Financial accounting; Managerial accounting
  bank accounts, 90–91, 100–103
  chart of accounts, 83–84, 96–97
  computer systems, 107–109
  financial reports, 239–240
  manual systems, 107
  on-site, 117–118
  personnel, 109–111
  real estate owners' requirements, 91–97
Accounting costs, 118–120
Accounting department operations, 97–117
  accounting systems, 106–109
  internal controls, 98–106
  personnel, 109–111
  records and reports, 111–116
Accounting methods, 88–89, 92–93
Accounts payable function, 110
Accounts receivable function, 110–111
Accredited Management Organization® (AMO®) designation, 12, 181, 182, 399–400, 402
  code of ethics, 329–331
Accredited Residential Manager® (ARM®) award, 8, 365, 402
Accrual-basis accounting, 88, 89, 93

Actual cash value (ACV) basis, 284–285
Adapting to change, 380–397
Adjunct services, 20, 47, 73–74, 192–193. *See also* Specific services
  contracting, 193
  ethical issues, 49
  fees, 73–74
  income source, 186–187
  marketing, 192
  reporting, 193
Advertising, 180, 181, 240
Agency bank accounts, 95–96
Agency law, 294–295
Agency relationship, 243
Americans with Disabilities Act (ADA), 194–195, 296–297, 310–311
Ancillary income, 186–195, 233
Annual budget meetings, 159–160
Annual property management plan, 55
  typical components, 58–60
Apartment buildings, 21–22
Association networking strategies, 180
Attorney, hiring tips, 316
Audits, performance, 100–101
Automated teller machines, 386–387
Automobile insurance, 273–275, 277–278
Avoidance, risk management strategy, 274

B

Balance sheet, 82–83, 112
Bank accounts
  clients' funds, 93–96
  management agreement, 237–238
  management company, 90
  reconciliation, 100–103
Base management fee, 231–232
Bidding contracts, 62–63
Bonds
  fidelity, 45, 99, 238, 276, 277, 279–280, 282, 283, 286, 325
  payment, 282
  performance, 282
Bookkeeper, full-charge, 110
Brochures, company, 186, 392
Broker, defined, 293
Budget meetings, 159–160
Budgets, 112–115, 206
  managed properties, 112–115
  management company, 91
  management proposal, 206
  operating, 239, 266–267
Building Owners and Managers Association (BOMA), 140, 141, 177, 195, 403–404
Business development, 169–195
  advertising, 180, 181
  ancillary sources of income, 186–195
  contact list, 184–186
  developing credibility, 173–177, 179–184
  establishing market niche, 170–173
  management opportunities, 172–173
  marketing strategies, 169–186
  networking, 176–177, 180
  newsletters, 183–184
  promoting expertise, 173–176
  public relations, 180–183
  public speaking, 175
  teaching, 176–177
  writing, 178–179
Business operations, 17–50, 51–80
  analyzing managers' portfolios, 75–80
  annual property management plan, 55, 58–60
  clients' ownership goals, 52–54
  clients' reporting requirements, 54–55
  communicating with clients, 61
  company policies and procedures, 64–71
  contracting on behalf of owners, 61–63
  economics, 71–74
  focus on management company, 64
  focusing on clients, 52–64
  monthly management report, 54–57
  operations manual, 68–69
  relations with tenants, 63–64
Business ownership, structure, 26–28
Business plan, 33–48
Buying a management company, 389. *See also* Valuing a management company

C

California State Commissioner's Code of Ethics, 331–337
Capital improvements supervision, 245
Capitalization, initial, 34–35, 47–48
Cash-basis accounting, 88, 89, 92–93
Certified Apartment Manager (CAM) designation, 8, 404
Certified Commercial-Investment Member (CCIM) designation, 189, 406
Certified Leasing Specialist (CLS) designation, 145, 403
Certified Marketing Director (CMD) designation, 145, 403
Certified Property Manager® (CPM®) designation, 9, 144–145, 182, 207, 365, 402
  code of ethics, 319–321
Certified Shopping Center Manager (CSM) designation, 9, 144, 145, 365, 403
Change, adaptive strategies, 380–397
Chart of accounts. *See also* Company chart of accounts
  commercial properties, 96, 97
  residential properties, 96
Circular E, Employer's Tax Guide, 299
Civil Rights Act (1964), 296
Civil Rights Act (1968), 311
Clean Air Act, 309
Clean Water Act, 309
Client relations, 152–166. *See also* Communications with clients
  adding personal touch, 165
  addressing hot buttons, 155–156

communicating with owners, 156–163
company service capabilities, 153–154
conflicts of interest, 154–155
dealing with difficult clients, 164
ownership goals, 153
understanding clients' concerns, 152–155
Client report package, components, 54, 56–57
Client retention strategies, 152, 164–166, 393–394
Client satisfaction surveys, 162–163
Clients. *See also* Client relations, Owner-clients
 accounting for funds, 92–93
 fiduciary obligation, 319, 321–322
 focus in business operations, 52–64
 measuring satisfaction, 162–163, 394–396
 separation of accounts, 91
Coinsurance, 284–285
Collections and receipts, 238
 accounting function, 111, 121
Commercial Investment Real Estate Institute (CIREI), 177, 406
Commercial property management, 20–21. *See also* Specific property types
 on-site accounting, 117–118
 pass-through expenses, 113–114
 sales reports, 115
Commercial proposal, 213–216. *See also* Management proposal
 exhibits, 215–216
 leasing, 216–217
 management plan, 214–215
 property analysis, 213–214
Commingling of funds, 91, 324
Commissions. *See also* Fees
 leasing, 232–233, 241
 sales, 74, 189, 230, 233–234, 246
Common interest realty associations, 22–23, 24–25
Communication basics, 158–159
Communications
 employees, 143, 145–147
 nondefensive, 147
 skills, tips for improving, 146
 technologies, 30–33, 383–384, 392–393

Communications with clients, 61, 156–163, 226
 direct personal contact, 161
 meetings, 157–160
 surveys, 162–163
 thank-you letters, 163
Community Associations Institute (CAI), 140, 177, 404–405
Company
 bank accounts, 90–91
 brochure, 186
 budgets, 91
 operations manual, 68–69
 vision, developing, 38–39
Company chart of accounts, 83–88
 income accounts, 84–85
 suggested components, 85
 expense accounts, 85–88
Compensation. *See also* Commissions, Fees
 employee package, components, 131
 management agreement concern, 223–224
 termination of management, 246
Competition, 36, 172, 229, 387–388
Competitive advantages, 171
Competitive edge, maintaining, 388–394
Compliance surveys, 194–195
Comprehensive Environmental Response, Compensation, and Liability Act (CERCLA), 308–309
Comprehensive general liability insurance, 284
Computers, 30–31, 391–393
 accounting systems, 107–109
 impact on management companies, 382–384
Condominiums, 7, 22
Conflict of interest, 154–155, 193
Consolidated Omnibus Budget Reconciliation Act (COBRA), 306
Construction supervision, 74, 190–191
Consulting, 187–188
Contact list, creating and using, 184–186
Contingency planning, 70–71
Contracted services, 41, 44
Contract maintenance, 154–155
Contractors, insurance coverages, 281–282, 285–286, 287–288, 315

Contract requirements, 281–282
Contracts
  bidding, 62–63
  employment, 141, 366
  long-term, 62
  specifications, 63
  utility, 61–62
Control, risk management strategy, 274
Cooperatives, 7, 23
Corporate downsizing, 380, 385
Cost accounting, 83–84, 121. *See also* Financial accounting
Cost of accounting functions, 118–120
  sample calculation, 119
Counselor of Real Estate (CRE) designation, 188, 405
Cross-training, 109, 390–391. *See also* Training
Customer service strategies, 393–394

D
Deductibles, insurance, 285
Deposit controls, 100
Designations. *See* Professional designations
Disbursement, 238–239
  net cash flow, 116–117
Disclosure
  confidential client information, 322–323
  conflicts of interest, 154–155
  dual agency, 294–295
  ethical requirement, 157, 331
  management proposal, 196
  retention of fees, 238
Discrimination in employment, 136, 296
Discrimination liability insurance, 278
Downsizing, 380, 385, 390. *See also* Outsourcing
Dual agency, 294–295
Due diligence, 251, 252, 287. *See also* Take-over of management

E
Economics of management companies, 71–74
Education, 46
  employee retention strategy, 144–145
Elderly housing, 21

Electronic home shopping, 380, 386
Electronic mail (e-mail), 161, 383, 392–393
Electronic "sweep" of bank accounts, 99, 116–117, 280, 387
Electronic transfer of funds, 116–117, 121, 386, 387
Emergency procedures manual, 266
Employee handbook, contents, 142
Employee Polygraph Protection Act (EPPA), 305
Employee Retirement Income Security Act (ERISA), 306, 375–376
Employees. *See also* Personnel, Personnel function
  cross-training, 109, 390–391
  education and retention, 144–145
  fostering loyalty, 124–125
  independent contractor status, 140
  insurance, 275–276
  leased, 391
  preventing fraud, 103–104
  productivity, 390
  purchase of management company, 375–377
Employee stock ownership plan (ESOP), 375–377
Employee turnover
  averting, 130–132
  contributing factors, 129
  hidden costs, 130
Employers, recordkeeping requirements, 138
Employer taxes, 240, 297–299
Employment at will, 300, 366
Employment contracts, 141, 366
Employment policies and procedures, 138–139
Employment practices, 132–150, 299–302
  checking references, 137–138
  hiring procedures, 134–139
  interviewing job applicants, 136–137
  legal issues, 299–302
  liability insurance, 278
  recruitment procedures, 134–136
Endangered Species Act, 309
Endorsements, insurance, 283, 285
Environmental laws, 308–310
Environmental liability protection, 309

Equal Employment Opportunity Commission (EEOC), 296
Errors and omissions (E&O) insurance, 45, 276
Ethical practices, 48–49, 318–337
   accounting and reporting, 323–324
   Accredited Management Organization® code of ethics, 328–331, 337
   beneficial conduct, 334–336
   Certified Property Manager® code of ethics, 318–328, 337
   compliance with laws and regulations, 327
   contractual obligations, 325
   disclosure, 322–323
   duty to firm or employer, 325–326
   duty to former employers, 327
   duty to tenants, 328
   equal employment opportunity, 328
   fiduciary obligation to clients, 319, 321–322
   maintaining, 318–337
   managing the client's property, 326–327
   professional relations, 324–325
   protection of clients' funds, 324
   state commissioner's code of ethics, 331–337
   unethical conduct, 332–334
Excess liability or umbrella coverage, 285
Exhibits
   commercial proposal, 215–216
   management agreement, 248
   management proposal, 209
   residential proposal, 211–213
Expert witness testimony, 191–194

F

Fair Housing Amendments Act, 310, 311–312
Fair housing laws, 311–313
Fair Labor Standards Act (FLSA), 298, 301
Family and Medical Leave Act (FMLA), 305
Federal Insurance Contributions Act (FICA), 299, 301
Federal Unemployment Tax Act (FUTA), 299, 302
Fee management, 5–7
Fees, 228–234. *See also* Adjunct services, Commissions
   administrative, 241, 245
   audit, 86
   base management, 231–232
   construction supervision, 232, 245
   factors determining, 230
   incentive, 232
   leasing, 73–74
   leasing supervision, 241
   lessee services, 245
   loan coordination, 234, 245
   major maintenance supervision, 232
   management, 72–73, 84, 223, 228–230, 244–245
   payroll administration, 232
   refinancing, 234
   residential lease-up, 245
   transaction, 233–234
Fidelity bond, 45, 99, 238, 276, 277, 279–280, 282–283, 286, 325
Fiduciary, 62, 92, 294
   duties, 295
   obligation to clients, 319, 321–322
Financial accounting, 82–83. *See also* Accounting
   balance sheet, 82–83
   profit and loss statement, 83
Financial reporting, 91–92
Financial tests, 363–364
Fire and casualty insurance, 277, 283
Fiscal year, 55
Forms of ownership, 20–26
Fraud, preventing, 103–104
Full-charge bookkeeper, 110

G

General liability insurance, 276–277
Generally accepted accounting procedures (GAAP), 82
Goodwill, 366–367
Government-assisted housing, 22
Gross revenue multiplier approach, 367, 368, 369, 371

H

Hiring, change strategy, 389–390
Hiring practices, 295–297
Hiring procedures, 134–139
   probationary status, 148
Historical records, 261, 264

Hold harmless provisions, 279. *See also* Indemnification of management
Housing and Community Development Act, 311
Housing for the elderly, 21

I

Image advertising, 180
Immigration Reform and Control Act, 297
Income, 42
  additional sources, 47
  ancillary services, 233
  developing ancillary sources, 186–195
  measuring net, 46–47
Indemnification of management
  environmental liability, 309
  management agreement, 224, 241, 243, 244, 279, 315
  receivership, 315
  termination of management, 342, 344
Independent contractor, 139, 244, 301–302, 385
  versus employee status, 140
Industrial buildings and parks, 21
Industrial leases, 281
Industry information, 139–140
Information acquisition strategies, 258–264
In-house management, department versus company, 28–30
In-house training, 141–143
Institute of Real Estate Management, 140, 141, 176, 177, 179, 195, 401–402
Institutional advertising, 180
Institutional owners, 25. *See also* Clients, Owner-clients
Insurance. *See also* Risk management
  actual cash value (ACV) coverage, 284–285
  automobile, 277–278
  boiler and machinery, 283
  building ordinance, 283
  business interruption, 71, 276, 281
  coinsurance, 284–285
  comprehensive general liability, 284
  crime, 278
  deductibles, 285
  errors and omissions (E&O), 45, 276
  fire and casualty, 277, 283
  general liability, 276–277
  rental income, 285
  replacement cost coverage, 284–285
  umbrella liability, 277, 285
  workers' compensation, 285–286, 306
Insuring the management company, 45, 71, 275–279
  key person coverage, 71, 275
Internal controls, 98–106
  approval of invoices, 103–106
  bank account reconciliation, 100–103
  deposit controls, 100
  payment approval stamp, 106
  payments received, 99
  preventing fraud, 103–104
Internal management, 5–7
International Council of Shopping Centers (ICSC), 140, 177, 402–403
Internet, 381, 383, 391
Interviewing job applicants, 136–137

J

Job description, sample, 133–134
Job function descriptions
  accounts payable, 110
  accounts receivable, 110–111
  full charge bookkeeper, 110
  portfolio supervisor, 8, 9–10
  regional property manager, 10, 133–134
  rent collections, 111
  site manager, 8–9
Journal of Property Management, 139, 178

L

Landlord-tenant laws, 306
Lawsuits, tips for avoiding, 315
Leases
  enforcement, 241
  industrial, 281
  office building, 281
  protections, 280
  residential, 281
  risk management issues, 280–282
  shopping center, 280–281
Lease summaries, 254–255
Leasing, 188–189, 205, 216–217, 226, 315
Leasing commissions, 73–74, 232–233, 241

Legal problems, avoiding, 292–317.
  See also Specific laws
  avoiding lawsuits, 313
  documents, 315–316
  employment laws, 295–306
  hiring an attorney, 316
  management of real property, 306–316
Liability coverage and "insured" parties, 279
License, real estate. *See* Real estate license
Loan coordination, 234, 245

M

Maintenance agreements, 315
Maintenance and repairs, 205, 242
Maintenance services, 189–190
Management agreement, 222–249, 268, 315, 392
  additional services, 227–228
  communications, 226–227
  computerization, 392
  conflict of interest, 228
  funding of operations, 224–225
  importance of legal review, 235
  indemnification of management, 224, 244
  letter of intent, 235
  management company concerns, 223–225
  need for written, 222
  negotiating positions, 228
  preparing for negotiations, 227
  property owners' concerns, 225–226
  risk management issues, 279–290
  take-over of management, 268
  termination of management, 341–344
  whose agreement will be used, 234–235
Management agreement contents, 235–248
  agency relationship, 243
  agreement binding, 248
  applicable law, 247
  authority of manager, 242
  bank accounts, 237–238
  collections and receipts, 238
  condominium exceptions, 248
  duration and termination, 246–247
  relationship of the parties, 243–244
  employment of personnel, 241–242
  entire agreement, 247
  establishing the relationship, 236–242
  exhibits, 248
  fees, 228–234, 244–246
  financial reports, 239–240
  force majeure, 247
  indemnification of management, 244
  maintenance and repairs, 242
  management accepts no liability, 243
  marketing and leasing, 240–241
  notices, 247
  office space, 236
  owner representations, 244
  owners' obligations, 242–243
  payments and disbursements, 238–239
  signatures, 248
  tax identification numbers, 248
  termination compensation, 247
  waivers, 243
Management contract. *See* Management agreement
Management fees, 72–73, 84, 223, 228–230, 244–245
Management firm characteristics, ranking, 11
Management liability issues, 343
Management opportunities, 2–5, 172–173
  nontraditional, 396–397
Management plan, 207–208
  annual property, 55, 58–60
  commercial proposal, 214–215
  residential proposal, 210–211
  take-over of management, 267–268
Management proposal, 196–221. *See also* Request for proposal
  client references, 203–204
  commercial leasing, 216–217
  commercial property, 213–216
  company personnel and operations, 201–203
  company portfolio, 203
  contents, 199–209
  contract terms, proposed, 208–209
  costs of developing, 196–197
  creating winning, 218–219
  disclosure in, 196
  exhibits, 209, 211–213, 215–216

Management proposal (*continued*)
  management company information, 201–204
  management plan, proposed, 207–208, 210–211, 214–215
  preliminary considerations, 197–199
  presenting, 216–217
  property analysis, 206–207, 209–210, 213–214
  residential property, 209–213
  services offered by company, 204–206
Management take-over. *See* Take-over of management
Management termination. *See* Termination of management
Managerial accounting, 83–91. *See also* Accounting
  accounting methods, 88–89
  company bank accounts, 90–91
  company budgets, 91
  company chart of accounts, 83–84
  expense accounts, 85–88
  income accounts, 84–85
Manual accounting systems, 107
Manufactured housing communities, 7, 22
Marketing, 169–186, 192, 205, 392
Marketing meetings, 160
Material safety data sheet, 303
Medical office building, 20–21. *See also* Office buildings
Mission statement, 38, 200
Mobile home communities, 7, 22
Modified accrual accounting, 88, 89, 93
Money management, 245
Monthly management reports, 54–55, 115–116
  commercial property-specific, 113–115
  components, 56–57, 91–92, 112

N

National Apartment Association (NAA), 141, 177, 404
Negligence in hiring, 297
Negotiation. *See* Management agreement
Net income, measuring, 46–47
Net income multiplier approach, 367, 368–369, 371–372

Networking, 176–177, 180
Newsletters, 163, 183–184, 392
News releases, 181–183
Non-compete clause, 372–373
Noncompliance, 243, 264

O

Occupational Safety and Health Act, 303
Office buildings, 20–21, 281
Office contents insurance, 45
Operating budget, 239, 266–267
Operating statement, 54, 83
Operational planning, 39, 41–42
Operations manual, 65–71
Orientation. *See* Training
Outsourcing, 172, 194
Owner-clients. *See also* Clients
  accounting requirements, 91–97
  insurance requirements, 282–286
  tax accounting, 74
  type to be served, 24–25
Owners, landlords, and tenants liability (OLT) insurance, 284
Ownership goals, 52–54

P

Payment approval stamp, sample, 106
Payroll, 85–86
  accounting function, 121
Pension funds, 380
Performance, measuring company, 394–396
Performance audits, 99, 100–101
Performance evaluation, 147–149, 300
Personnel. *See also* Employees
  accounting, 109–111
  management proposal information, 201–203
  management company value, 365–366
  needs, assessing, 390–391
Personnel function, 123–151. *See also* Employees, Employment practices
  averting employee turnover, 130–132
  components of compensation package, 131
  components of exit interview, 132
  determining individual workloads, 125–128

developing a training program, 128–130
education and employee retention, 144–145
employee handbook, contents, 142
employer recordkeeping requirements, 138
employment contracts, 141
employment market, 135
fostering employee loyalty, 124–125
general staffing considerations, 123–132
independent contractor status, 140
internal opportunities for promotion, 149–150
orientation and training, 139–143
professional and trade association meetings, 141
recruitment and hiring, 134, 136–139
salary increases, 149
sample job description, 133–134
setting goals and evaluating performance, 147–149
supervision and communication, 143, 145–147
work environment, 150
Planned unit development, 23
Plate glass insurance, 281
Portfolio analysis, 75–79
Portfolio supervisor, 9–10
Productivity of employees, 390
Professional Community Association Manager (PCAM) designation, 144, 145, 404
Professional designations, 46, 49–50, 401–406. *See also* Specific designations
Professional meetings, 141, 177, 179
Profitability, managers' portfolios, 80
Profit and loss statement, 83
Pro forma, 35–36, 42–47
Promotional advertising, 180
Property analysis, 206–207
  commercial proposal, 213–214
  residential proposal, 209–210
Property management tasks, ranking, 12
Property manager, 9
Property plans, 258–260
Property specialization, 7–8

Proposals, creating winning, 218–219. *See also* Management Proposal
Proprietary lease. *See* Cooperatives
Protection of clients' funds, 324
Public housing, 22
Publicity, 176, 180–183
Public liability insurance, 45
Public relations, 176, 180–183
Public speaking, business development strategy, 175
Purchase order, sample contents, 105

R
Real estate investment trusts (REITs), 2, 6, 25
Real estate licensing, 18, 29, 293–294
  IREM position statement, 294
Real estate management business, 1–17, 77–78
Real estate management industry, 2–3
Real estate managers' portfolios, analysis, 75–80
Real estate owned (REO) properties, 25
Real Property Administrator (RPA) designation, 9, 144, 145, 182, 365, 404
Receivership, 314–315
Recordkeeping, employer requirements, 138
Recruitment procedures, 134–136
Regional property manager, 10. *See also* Portfolio supervisor
  sample job description, 133–134
Rent, office, 44, 87
Rental apartments, 7
Rental income insurance, 285
Rental rates, 240–241
Rent collections function, 111
Renter's insurance, 281
Replacement cost coverage, 284–285
Reporting, 193, 239–240. *See also* Monthly management reports
Request for proposal (RFP), 185–186, 197–199, 219, 220, 221
Residential leases, 281
Residential lease-up fee, 245
Residential property management, 21–23. *See also* Specific property types
  on-site accounting, 117
  specific risks, 289

Residential proposal, 209–213. *See also* Management proposal
   exhibits, 211–213
   management plan, 210–211
   property analysis, 209–210
Residents. *See* Tenants
Resolution Trust Corporation, 380
Resource Conservation and Recovery Act, 309
Retention, risk management strategy, 274. *See also* Self-insurance
Risk management, 273–291. *See also* Indemnification of management, Insurance
   insurance administration, 286
   insuring the management company, 275–279
   lease and contract requirements, 280–282
   management agreement considerations, 279–290
   minimizing management company exposure, 286–290
   owners' insurance requirements, 282–286
   residential management risks, 289
   specific strategies, 274

S

Sales commissions, 74, 189, 230, 233–234, 246
Salespersons, defined, 293
Security deposit account, 237–238
Self-insurance, 273–275
Selling a management company, 389. *See also* Valuing a management company
Separation of clients' accounts, 91
Service bureau, 42, 44, 86, 98, 106, 120
Sexual harassment, 302–304
Shopping centers, 20, 280–281
Single-family homes, 7, 21
Single-room occupancy (SRO) residences, 21, 397
Site manager, 8–9
Site visits, 160–161
Special reports, 226–227
Staff size, 390–391
Starting a management business, 17–50. *See also* Start-up company
   analyzing your competition, 36–39
   assessing progress, 41
   business expertise, 17–18
   components of a business plan, 40
   developing a business plan, 33–48
   developing a company's vision, 38–39
   equipping the office, 30–33
   ethical issues, 48–49
   financial feasibility, 42–48
   in-house management, 28–30
   location, 23–24
   management specialization, 19–25
   owner-clients to be served, 24–25
   ownership considerations, 27
   ownership structure, 26–28
   personal satisfaction, 50
   professional designations, 49–50
   property market assessment, 18–19
   real estate licensing, 18, 29
   sample pro forma, 43
Start-up company
   accounting costs, 119–120
   accounting function, 97
   chart of accounts, 84
Strategic planning, 33–39
   plan components, 34–35
   planning process, 35–38
   questions to be answered, 37
Supervision of employees, 143, 145–147
Surveys, 162–163, 194–195

T

Take-over checklist
   commercial specifics, 263
   creation, 252–258
   residential specifics, 262
   suggested contents, 259–261
Take-over of management, 246–247, 248, 250–269. *See also* Take-over checklist
   acquiring information, 258–265
   emergency procedures manual, 266
   historical records, 261, 264
   issues of noncompliance, 264
   management agreement, 268
   management plan, 267–268
   manager's priorities, 265–269
   operating budget, 266–267
   planning, 251–252

property plans, 258–260
property-specific considerations, 268
residents' or tenants' handbook, 265–266
unsettled disputes, 264
Tax appeals, 74, 223, 234
Teaching, business development strategy, 176–177
Technology, instrument of change, 381–387
Tenant Rental Assistance Certification System (TRACS), 121
Tenant retention strategies, 63–64, 393–394
Tenants
 handbook, 265–266
 retention, 63–64, 393–394
 satisfaction, 394–396
Termination of employment, 300–301, 343
Termination of management, 246–247, 341–354
 benefits of using a checklist, 342
 for cause, 343
 checklist contents, 348–351
 compensation, 246
 developing a checklist, 344–348
 facilitating the transition, 351–353
 impact on the firm, 353–354
 information needed, 346–348
 issues of timing, 345–346
 management agreement considerations, 341–344
 management liability issues, 343
 reasons for termination, 343–344
Trade association meetings, 141, 177, 179
Training, 128–130, 139–143. *See also* Cross-training
 developing program, 128–130
 in-house, 141–143
 orientation, 139–143
 seminars and courses, 140–141
Transfer, risk management strategy, 274. *See also* Insurance
Trust accounts, 94–95

U
Unemployment insurance, 76, 283, 285–286

Uniform Residential Landlord and Tenant Act, 306
Utility contracts, 61–62

V
Valuing a management company, 355–379
 basis, 359–367
 buyer considerations of value, 365
 determining a price, 369, 371–372
 direct buyout by employees, 374
 employee stock ownership plan, 375–377
 fiscal considerations, 362–364
 getting ready to sell, 378
 goodwill, 366–367
 gross revenue multiplier approach, 368, 369–370, 373
 income and expenses, case study, 370
 major considerations, 356–359
 management portfolio considerations, 360
 market factors, 360
 net income multiplier approach, 368–369, 371–372, 373
 non-compete clause, 372–373
 notification of clients, 373
 other characteristics of company, 364–367
 other sale considerations, 373–374
 personnel, 365–366
 reasons for selling, 374
 sale, case study, 356–358
 structuring a purchase, 367–369
 structuring the deal, 372
Vision, developing a company's, 38–39
Voice communications, 383
Voice-mail, 33, 392

W
Wages, 297–299
Work environment, 150, 302–305
Workers' compensation insurance, 276, 282, 283, 285–286, 306
Workloads, determining individual, 125–128
World Wide Web, 381, 383, 392
Writing, business development strategy, 178–179
Wrongful discharge, 301

About the Publisher

The Institute of Real Estate Management (IREM) was founded in 1933 with the goals of establishing a Code of Ethics and standards of practice in real estate management as well as fostering knowledge, integrity, and efficiency among its practitioners. The Institute confers the CERTIFIED PROPERTY MANAGER® (CPM®) designation on individuals who meet specified criteria of education and experience in real estate management and subscribe to an established Code of Ethics. Real estate management firms that meet specific organizational and professional criteria are granted the status of ACCREDITED MANAGEMENT ORGANIZATION® (AMO®). Individuals who meet specified educational and professional requirements in residential site management and subscribe to a Code of Ethics are granted the status of ACCREDITED RESIDENTIAL MANAGER® (ARM®).

The Institute's membership includes more than 9,000 CPM members, more than 3,800 ARM participants, and some 640 AMO firms. Among CPM members in the United States, nearly 45% manage conventionally financed multifamily rental housing, 15% manage federally assisted housing, and 18% manage condominium and cooperative properties; approximately 54% manage office buildings, more than 39% manage shopping centers and retail strip stores, and roughly 28% manage industrial parks and warehouses.

For more than sixty years, IREM has been enhancing the prestige of real estate management through its activities and publications. The Institute offers a wide selection of courses and publications about real estate management and related topics. To obtain a current catalog, write to the Institute of Real Estate Management, 430 North Michigan Avenue, P.O. Box 109025, Chicago, Illinois 60610-9025, or telephone 1-800-837-0706. Also visit our home page on the World Wide Web: http://www.irem.org.